Strikes,
Dispute Procedures,
and Arbitration

Recent Titles in Contributions in American Studies
Series Editor: Robert H. Walker

Sons of Liberty: The Masculine Mind in Nineteenth-Century America
David G. Pugh

American Tough: The Tough-Guy Tradition and American Character
Rupert Wilkinson

Uncle Sam at Home: Civilian Mobilization, Wartime Federalism,
and the Council of National Defense, 1917-1919
William J. Breen

The Bang and the Whimper: Apocalypse and Entropy in American Literature
Zbigniew Lewicki

The Disreputable Profession: The Actor in Society
Mendel Kohansky

The Formative Essays of Justice Holmes: The Making of
an American Legal Philosophy
Frederic Rogers Kellogg

A "Capacity for Outrage": The Judicial Odyssey of J. Skelly Wright
Arthur Selwyn Miller

On Courts and Democracy: Selected Nonjudicial Writings
of J. Skelly Wright
Arthur Selwyn Miller, editor

A Campaign of Ideas: The 1980 Anderson/Lucey Platform
Clifford W. Brown, Jr., and Robert J. Walker, compilers

Dreams and Visions: A Study of American Utopias, 1865-1917
Charles J. Rooney, Jr.

Mechanical Metamorphosis: Technological Change in Revolutionary America
Neil Longley York

Prologue: The Novels of Black American Women, 1891-1965
Carole McAlpine Watson

Strikes,
Dispute Procedures,
and Arbitration

Essays on Labor Law

WILLIAM B. GOULD IV

Contributions in American Studies, Number 82

Greenwood Press
Westport, Connecticut • London, England

Library of Congress Cataloging in Publication Data

Gould, William B.
  Strikes, dispute procedures, and arbitration.

  (Contributions in American studies, ISSN 0084-9227 ;
no. 82)
  Bibliography: p.
  Includes index.
    1. Arbitration, Industrial—United States.   2. Strikes
and lockouts—Law and legislation—United States.
3. Trade-unions—Law and legislation—United States.
4. Labor laws and legislation—United States.   I. Title.
II. Series.
  KF3424.G68   1985   344.73'01   85-944
  ISBN 0-313-24468-5 (lib. bdg.) 347-3041

Library of Congress Catalog Card Number: 85-944
ISBN: 0-313-24468-5
ISSN: 0084-9227

First published in 1985

Greenwood Press
A division of Congressional Information Service, Inc.
88 Post Road West
Westport, Connecticut 06881

Printed in the United States of America

10 9 8 7 6 5 4 3 2 1

To the memory of my professor and friend,
the late Kurt Hanslowe.

Contents

Preface   ix

Introduction   3

1. Substitutes for the Strike Weapon   5

   Bibliographic Essay on Substitutes for the Strike Weapon   13

2. Managing Emergency Strikes   19

   Bibliographic Essay on Managing Emergency Strikes   23

3. Public Employment: Mediation, Fact Finding and Arbitration   29

   Bibliographic Essay on Public Sector Collective Bargaining   37

4. The Status of Unauthorized and ''Wildcat'' Strikes under the National Labor Relations Act   45

   Bibliographic Essay on '' 'Wildcat' Strikes''   75

5. On Labor Injunctions, Unions, and the Judges: The Boys Market Case   79

6. On Labor Injunctions Pending Arbitration: Recasting *Buffalo Forge*   129

7. Employer's Remedies: Arbitration and Section 301   159

8. Wildcat Striking Employees Are Not Liable in Damages for Breach of a No-Strike Clause   163

   Bibliogaphic Essay on Legal Constraints on Strikes During the Term of a Collective Bargaining Agreement   171

9. The Established Relationship Between Labor and Management   175

   Bibliographic Essay on the Established Relationship Between Labor and Management   195

10. Taft-Hartley Comes to Great Britain: Observations on the
    Industrial Relations Act of 1971   197
    Bibliogaphic Essay on Taft-Hartley Comes to Great Britain   263
11. Solidarity Forever—or Hardly Ever: Union Discipline,
    Taft-Hartley, and the Right of Union Members to Resign   267
    Bibliographic Essay on Solidarity Forever   309
    Index   311

Preface

The idea of this book is to present my thinking about the strike, its legal status, and the arbitration system. "Substitutes for the Strike Weapon: The Arbitration Process in the United States," 28 *Arbitration Journal* 111 (1973), describes arbitration as it has evolved in America. "Managing Emergency Strikes," *The New Leader*, March 14, 1966, and the *American Bar Association Journal* piece, "Public Employment: Mediation, Fact Finding and Arbitration," 55 *American Bar Association Journal* 835 (1969), address the strike issue particularly in the public sector—and the adaptation of arbitration to the public sector. The purpose of the latter is to provide workers with some vehicle for resolving issues that are not resolved through collective bargaining where the strike is not well tolerated.

The *Cornell Law Quarterly* article, "The Status of Unauthorized and 'Wildcat' Strikes Under the National Labor Relations Act," 52 *Cornell Law Quarterly* 672 (1967), describes the legal status of the strike in the private sector and some of the peculiar problems relating to "wildcat" or "unauthorized" strikes—"unofficial" as the British would call them—under the National Labor Relations Act. Here the focus is upon the extent to which workers, acting on their own without the union, engage in "protected activity" which immunizes them from discharge and discipline.

The focus shifts in my articles, "On Labor Injunctions, Unions, and the Judges: The Boys Market Case,"1970 *The Supreme Court Review* 215, "On Labor Injunctions Pending Arbitration: Recasting *Buffalo Forge*," 30 *Stanford Law Review* 533 (1978) and—with the exception of "Solidarity Forever—Or Hardly Ever: Union Discipline, Taft-Hartley, and the Right of Union Members to Resign," 66 *Cornell Law Review* 74 (1980)—all of those portions of articles which appear after these two. Again, the subject is whether the right to strike may be limited in the public interest. In *The new Leader* and *Cornell Law Quarterly* articles, the concern was with strikes in the public sector and private sector emergency, which, it is alleged, threaten the well being of society, as well as with "wildcats," which undermine the union's status as exclusive bargaining agent and make it difficult for the employer to bargain. In the next section of articles, I have dealt with limitations on the strike in the private sector on theories that have their roots in the existence of the labor contract, the availability of arbitration and the idea that arbitration contract procedures are the *quid pro quo* for the strike and forms of economic pressure during the term of the collective bargaining agreement.

Some of the articles have had sections removed from them altogether or the sections have been moved into other areas of the book. A portion of "On Labor Injunctions, Unions and the Judges: The Boys Market Case," 1970 *The Supreme Court Review* 215, was removed because, in retrospect, it did not seem to bear upon the basic theme. Moreover, the section from my *Cornell Law Quarterly* article, "The Status of Unauthorized and 'Wildcat' Strikes Under the National Labor Relations Act," dealing with employer remedies, which discusses employer remedies against unions in a "wildcat" strike situation where it is alleged that the union or employees are in breach of contract, was moved into the section following my *Supreme Court Review and Stanford Law Review* pieces. My thinking here was that this portion of my *Cornell Law Quarterly* article appeared more appropriately after a discussion of other issues involving a union's breach 'Wildcat' Strikes under the national Labor Relations Act," dealing with employer remedies for it in the *Supreme Court Review* and the *Stanford Law Review* pieces.

Again, only a portion of "The Supreme Court's Labor and Employment Docket in the October 1980 Term: Justice Brennan's Term," 53 *University of Colorado Law Review* (1981)—the paper that I delivered to the Labor and Employment Law Section of the American Bar Association in August of 1981—was included because a discussion of the Supreme Court's treatment of liability of employees for a breach of a no-strike clause was appropriate after the earlier discussion of union liability for a strike and breach of contract. The portion of the *Colorado* piece included attempts to deal with a wide variety of remedy problems relating to violations of the no-strike clause as well as providing an update of both *Boys Market* and *Buffalo Forge* issues discussed in the *Supreme Court Review* and the *Stanford Law Review*.

The same reasoning led me to include only a portion of my article, "Recent Developments Under the National Labor Relations Act: The Board and the Circuit Courts," 14 *U.C. Davis Law Review* 497 (1981). This portion of the article deals with union and employee liability in the unfair labor context where the no-strike obligation is undercut. Finally, the strike issue figures in my "Solidarity Forever" *Cornell* piece which appeared five years ago. However, this time the discussion is about union discipline in the strike context and its lawfulness under the National Labor Relations Act.

I wish to express my gratitude for research assistance provided by Joseph Costello, Ed Attanasio, and Roosevelt Cox, as well as the typing of the bibliographic essays which was done by Beth Sherman.

Strikes,
Dispute Procedures,
and Arbitration

Introduction

The articles appearing in this collection have emerged over nearly a 20 year period. In these articles I have attempted to address what were then, and continue to be now, abiding tensions and problems in industrial relations and labor law in this country and throughout the industrialized world. The focus has been upon strikes, dispute resolution procedures, and union sanctions imposed in connection with strikes.

I have begun with the assumption that the right of free men and women to withhold their labor and to engage in various forms of economic pressure is one of the most fundamental rights that can exist in a democratic society. That is one of the reasons why I have advocated a careful balance of competing interests in connection with union discipline relating to dissident members and strikebreakers.

But what is important here is that a balance is involved. In modern industrialized economies that are interdependent, we have recognized that other interests as well as the right to strike are at stake. I believe, therefore, that the emergence of peaceful procedures and alternatives to the strike are extremely important and deserving of support through our national labor policy.

The problems addressed here remain with us today. As one can see from the bibliographic essays, the difficulties in revitalizing the grievance-arbitration machinery, the complexity of the public sector and the question of the right to strike, as well as the general difficulty in utilizing law in connection with industrial action or economic pressure of any kind, with or without the existence of a collective bargaining agreement, in Great Britain as well as the United States, are issues that are particularly alive.

Indeed, the Supreme Court will undoubtedly soon address the issue of union discipline in the strike context—the issue which I have discussed in my *Cornell* piece, *Solidarity Forever.*

These then are essays written during what may be the halfway point in my professional career. One can see, again particularly in *Solidarity Forever*, issues about which I have had to rethink and modify my views. That process never ceases.

1
Substitutes for the Strike Weapon

The phenomenal rise in stoppages in Great Britain during the past four years (the increase in the number of days lost during this time having more than quadrupled) may tempt British labor, management and the public to think about more effective alternatives to the strike in certain circumstances. During the past two years the debate that has taken place in Great Britain over the Industrial Relations Act has focused upon the American answers to industrial strife. Yet the discussion has become stuck upon those aspects which are the least important, i.e., the provisions of the Taft-Hartley Act from which it is alleged the new British statute borrows.

Although the Code of Practice which accompanies the Act specifically encourages "rights arbitration" over disputes arising during the term of an agreement, the American experience in this area has not been looked at carefully—even though America has often been cited by both major political parties. This is particularly unfortunate since the reality is that most disputes between labor and management in the United States are resolved through private, voluntary arbitration machinery negotiated through the mutual consent of the parties—a pattern which contradicts the impression the British have that American industrial relations is law ridden.

Arbitration in the United States is encouraged by both the Taft-Hartley Act and Supreme Court decisions handed down during the past fifteen years. However, the practice developed prior to Taft-Hartley—and indeed in some circumstances *in spite of law itself,* since in some jurisdictions arbitration agreements were considered void as against public policy. Jealous courts did not wish to have their jurisdiction undermined.

Beginning in the United States before the turn of the century, appearing in the form of the so-called "umpire system" of the Anthracite Coal Commission in 1903, and accepted by the hosiery and clothing industries under the form of the "impartial chairman" system in the 1920's, arbitration was well on its way even prior to the Wagner Act, let alone the Taft-Hartley 1947 amendments. It gained greater impetus through the War Labor Board which, operating under the emergency conditions of World War II, encouraged, nurtured and in some instances imposed both no-strike obligations and arbitration machinery upon the parties. All of this was well in advance of Taft-Hartley. That law merely ratified a trend which the parties had evolved for themselves.

What do Americans mean when they talk about arbitration? It is, of course, something quite different from mediation and conciliation, which involve third party intervention. But here the third party's function is to clarify the issues, appeal to the parties' reasoning process by using arts of persuasion, sometimes merely carrying messages or coffee back and forth, making suggestions, and, where the parties wish one to do so, making recommendations.

Arbitration in the United States and in Great Britain means a decision making process, although many arbitrators rely upon mediatory skills as well. Indeed the use of mediation was a prominent characteristic of both the impartial chairman system and some of the permanent umpireships during the 1940's. In the final analysis, however, a decision or award can be issued by the third party.

Moreover, in the United States we have attempted to distinguish between so-called rights and interests arbitration. Interests arbitration is a fairly rare phenomenon although, as collective bargaining has extended into the public sector where the strike is considered more unacceptable, it has become more popular. However, it is grievance or rights arbitration involving disputes during the agreement which is the most important aspect of the American experience.

Ninety-four percent of collective agreements negotiated between labor and management in the United States contain arbitration clauses—and all but 1% permit one of the two sides to obtain arbitration during the term of the contract without obtaining an agreement from the other side to arbitrate the dispute in question. To be sure, there are exceptions to this pattern. In the national trucking agreement, there is no provision for arbitration. In the construction industry, only 70% of the agreements contain arbitration clauses—and it appears as though arbitration is used less than is the case in manufacturing even where it is provided for by contract.

Also, we must distinguish at the outset between different modes of arbitration. Most arbitration in the United States is *ad hoc*, i.e., the selection of an arbitrator to hear a particular dispute arising during the term of the contract. At one time it was thought that so-called permanent umpireships during which one individual (there can be a rotating list of individuals as well) is chosen for the term of the agreement were going to be the wave of the future. However, despite the fact that such an arbitrator is not a stranger to the industry or company and is therefore presumably more expert, only 12% of arbitration clauses provide for permanent umpireships.

Where there is *ad hoc* arbitration, the arbitrators are often chosen from lists prepared by the Federal Mediation and Conciliation Service or the American Arbitration Association, a non-profit organization which has its principal office in New York City and which provides arbitration services to private parties. No one really knows how much arbitration takes place in the United States since most arbitrations appear to arise out of private communication between the parties and the arbitrator, and not the official agencies such as FMCS and AAA which provide services and keep records about the number and kinds of arbitration going through their agency.

Generally, the more experienced arbitrators are in a professional association called the National Academy of Arbitrators, which has approximately 350 to 400 members, who are chosen on the basis of the number of cases they have heard and what the parties say about them.

Why have Americans used arbitration rather than the courts to resolve their disputes? In my judgment, there are five principal reasons. The first is that the system is voluntary, devised by the parties to deal with their problems. The American system is intended to fit the parties' own peculiar needs: this then is the reason for its rich diversity and the difficulties in making generalizations about it.

Secondly, grievance arbitration machinery, in most relationships, normally resolves problems at a lower level than arbitration itself, prior to the time at which arbitration is invoked as a court of last resort. Most contracts provide for between three to five "steps," in which discussions take place between labor and management representatives (the higher the step the more elevated or senior the participants) without the involvement of the outside impartial—and at these steps an attempt is made both to resolve differences on an informal basis (in the first instance, between employee and/or union steward and foreman), and clarify what is in fact in dispute.

The third reason for the acceptance of arbitration is its relative informality. Lawyers can be present and the parties are nearly always represented by someone. Examination and cross-examination of witnesses and the introduction of exhibits are involved. Yet witnesses are usually not sworn and arbitrators do not follow the court rules of evidence concerning testimony. My own judgment is that the more formal the proceeding the less mature is the relationship.

Fourth, the principal attraction of arbitration for both sides is that arbitration is relatively expeditious compared to litigation —although the American system has developed some recent deficiencies in this respect, many of which, in my judgment, are being attacked by both the parties and the AAA.

Finally, arbitration, to some extent, serves as a substitute for the right to strike for a period of time. While the American system by no means has eliminated "wildcat" or unauthorized stoppages in breach of contract, it has reduced an inclination to strike—particularly with regard to discipline and discharge disputes where workers know that an impartial, and not management, will determine their case on its own merits. Unions with negotiated peace machinery, even with no-strike clauses that permit them to strike after an exhaustion of procedures or over certain subject matter, rarely make the strike the weapon of first resort. It is generally the last tactic invoked.

What happens when an arbitration takes place? First of all, the hearing is usually held on the company's premises since that is where the parties are and where most of the witnesses will be. If the union wants "neutral" ground, usually that can be arranged. I sometimes hold hearings at my Law School and, if the parties are willing, I may invite students. This decision is for the parties alone, since it is their process.

The hearing usually begins with an opening statement by each side, summarizing their position—as well as a submission which should indicate what issue is in dispute. Sometimes the parties can take the better part of a day or more in that quest and it becomes necessary to move on to the evidence in the hope that the issue will become clearer as one learns more about the case.

As I have noted, there are exhibits, examination and cross-examination. Usually a transcript is not taken—the arbitrator attempts to write his own notes on the testimony as it is given. When a transcript is taken, it is easier for the arbitrator—but nothing can boost the cost of arbitration more quickly for the parties.

When the hearing is concluded, the parties will sometimes submit briefs and the arbitrator will then retire to write an opinion and award. Although an opinion is not required, the practice is to write one—in contrast to the British rules before the old Industrial Court, now called the Industrial Arbitration Board.

However, on the West Coast docks the parties follow the practice of relying upon bench awards in connection with walkouts over safety disputes. The arbitrator goes down to the docks, simply listens to the arguments and issues an award. While the parties are entitled to get an opinion in writing, they generally do not ask for one.

Indeed, perhaps the point to be made in connection with American arbitration is to stress the fact that many of the parties are so satisfied with it. Although appeals may be taken to court, generally the parties adhere to the arbitrator's award. (And the Supreme Court decisions have made it quite difficult as a practical matter to challenge the award in court.) In this atmosphere, it is not the least bit surprising that the parties pay the arbitrator themselves—the fee and costs are usually shared equally—although they need not be. Sometimes the loser pays all and sometimes the company pays all, regardless of the outcome. But these contractual obligations (the contract always governs) are the exception to the equal sharing rule.

The kinds of disputes which come before arbitrators involve a wide variety of matters—the most prominent being dismissals, discipline, and questions relating to seniority, i.e., who is to be promoted and who is to be laid off. Disputes over job classifications and what kind of work is to be performed and whether employers can contract out to other employers work which has been performed by bargaining unit employees are all grist for the arbitrator's mill.

Contrary to what I find to be very common British belief, this is not a legalistic process. To be sure, contract interpretation is usually involved—but there is much more than that. After all, great scope is left to the arbitrator who must determine whether a worker has been dismissed for "just cause" within the meaning of the collective agreement. A good deal of common sense—not a technical knowledge of labor law—is a prerequisite.

Moreover, the labor agreement in the United States has been analogized to a "shotgun marriage" which is dictated by economic force or law. When one has a shotgun marriage, there are many ambiguities and gaps remaining to be filled in. Sometimes the parties will be aware of a problem and yet also recognize that it makes more sense to submit it to an effective dispute resolution process because of the cost of disagreement at a particular point in time. One is dealing with a document which, while much more comprehensive in detail than its average British counterpart, is nevertheless a generalized code.

For the union, two of the main attractions are (1) the ability to have a built-in planned dismissal machinery, and (2) the removal of the union from the political crossfire that is inevitably involved in disputes over who should be promoted or transferred to a particular job. Since seniority is all-important, the union is removed from the political battle by defending a relatively objective standard before the employer and, if necessary, the arbitrator.

For the employer, what is particularly significant is the fact that industrial peace is usually guaranteed for an uninterrupted period of time. Moreover, although employers are required in many instances to consult with unions before engaging in unilateral changes in working conditions, the assumption behind the arbitration process is that management goes first and the union challenges employer authority through the grievance machinery.

There are, however, problems with grievance arbitration in the United States. William J. Usery, FMCS Director, has recently noted that one out of three strikes takes place during the term of the agreement—although it is not clear to what extent these stoppages are in fact in defiance of arbitration and no-strike machinery or to what extent the machinery—when it is applicable—is deficient. There are greater delays and increased costs today. Moreover, the arbitration process has had considerable difficulty in coping with the problems of employment discrimination in the United States. This, of course, is not altogether surprising since unions and employers control grievance arbitration—and they are the parties which are generally accused of discrimination.

CONCLUSION

It is difficult to determine whether grievance arbitration can take to the soil of Great Britain. The negotiation of more comprehensive collective bargaining agreements on the plant level may fix the wage aspect of the bargain with more preciseness than is the case in the current "two tier" system and therefore make more of what is in controversy so-called "rights disputes"—which seem to be more amenable to third party adjudication. The comprehensiveness of the agreement may supply an element which Donovan* regarded as critical and found missing, i.e., a document *susceptible* to third party interpretation. Nevertheless, there are, of course, continuing basic differences between the countries—a higher dues structure (arbitration is usually financed by local unions in the United States), more comprehensive agreements, and the exclusive bargaining representative—a principle which permits the union to act as a broker between competing interest groups. (Perhaps the Industrial Relations Act, through its espousal of the somewhat different "sole bargaining agent" principle, will diminish this difference.)

There are practical reasons for a more widespread acceptance of arbitration in Britain today. The first of these is the ideological confrontation taking place between the trade unions and the Government in the continuing dispute about the Industrial Relations Act. Those trade unionists who recognize that there is an industrial relations problem in Great Britain may be inclined, along with their employer counterparts, to look around for a more suitable forum.

Moreover, the dismissal machinery contained in the Industrial Relations Act both lacks the most effective remedy, i.e., reinstatement, and permits the parties to opt out by devising their machinery. Thus far, because the unions have refused to apply for so-called "designating orders," inasmuch as this would involve recognition on their part of the Act and its institutions, no one has taken advantage of this opportunity. But the way is open for them to devise their own machinery—unenforceable if they wish because of Section 36 of the Act which permits agreements to be unenforceable. Ironically, trade union refusal to apply for designating orders both ensnares the labor movement in the statute which they oppose and deprives their members of the more meaningful reinstatement remedy.

Finally, it is important to note that the National Industrial Relations Court has quietly gone about the business of attempting to conciliate disputes between unions and employers that have come before it. The Industrial Relations Act encourages this. The parties may soon get the idea that many of the matters that they now take to the Industrial Court could be just as effectively dealt with under the auspices of a private third party as a public one.

---

* Royal Commission on Trade Unions and Employers Associations Report CMND. No. 3623 (1968).

Perhaps most important, there are stirrings in Britain—albeit primarily on the employers' side—which reflect a basic belief that a better way must be found to resolve disputes than what exists at present. How soon this will all happen, of course, is a matter for great speculation.

Bibliographic Essay on Substitutes for the Strike Weapon

A vast literature has developed on the subject of grievance arbitration, encompassing a multitude of issues. Readers searching for other articles on the subject should begin with the *Arbitration Journal*, published by the American Arbitration Association, and the annual volumes of the National Academy of Arbitrators, published by the Bureau of National Affairs. Some of the standard texts are *The Labor Arbitration Process* by R. Fleming (University of Illinois Press, Urbana, Ill., 1965) and *How Arbitration Works* by F. Elkouri and E. Elkouri (BNA, Washington, D.C., 3rd ed., 1973). One of the more recent texts is *Labor Agreement in Negotiation and Arbitration* by Zack and R. Block (BNA, Washington, D.C., 1983). A comprehensive collection of materials is to be found in *Private Dispute Settlement* by Merton C. Bernstein (The Free Press, New York, 1968).

Some of the more interesting articles deal with five major issues: the relationship between arbitration and employment discrimination claims; grievance arbitration in the public sector; the National Labor Relations Board's policy of deferring to arbitration; expedited arbitration; and the role arbitration could play in the doctrine of wrongful discharge.

Anthony F. Bartlett explored the issue of the role of arbitration in the disposition of employment discrimination claims.[1] Bartlett noted that while the Supreme Court's decision in *Alexander v. Gardner-Denver Co.*[2] refused to foreclose the bringing of Title VII actions in federal court to employees who had initially pursued their claims in arbitration, the Court did recognize, in its famous footnote 21, that a prior arbitration award could play a role in a court's decision in the subsequent litigation.

The arbitration process, Bartlett concluded, is rife with characteristics that may hinder the adjudication of employment discrimination claims. The competence level of arbitrators varies widely.[3] The mechanics of an arbitration proceeding itself may preclude adequate consideration of the grievant's claim. Hearings are relatively informal: there is no jury, formal rules of evidence are not closely adhered to, written transcripts are not always taken, and arbitrators do not always issue opinions with their awards.[4] Moreover, the employee must rely upon a union representative, often uneducated in the subtleties of employment discrimination law, to act as his "attorney."[5] Finally, arbitrators frequently rely upon a "just cause" standard without regard to public law in arriving at their decisions,[6] although the Supreme Court has stated that arbitrators may look to many sources for their awards while their awards must draw their "essence" from the collective bargaining agreement.

Despite these shortcomings, Bartlett was optimistic in light of the progress the arbitral community has made in overcoming these deficiencies. Arbitrators are increasingly relying upon Title VII case law in writing their opinions. The American Arbitration Association has fashioned a set of model rules to guide arbitration proceedings where employment discrimination claims are to be heard. And many arbitrators themselves are striving to become educated in employment discrimination law and practice.[7] As a result of these developments, Bartlett speculated that the Supreme Court might change course and decide to endorse the deferral of employment discrimination claims to arbitration.[8]

In 1981, Michelle Hoyman and Lamont Stallworth gathered data on the impact of *Gardner-Denver* on subsequent relitigation of Title-VII-related arbitral awards.[9] By analyzing the opinions of attorneys who represented management and/or labor in employment discrimination related grievance arbitration proceedings, the authors attempted to assess the reactions of attorneys to the practice of relitigation of the same issues which had been previously arbitrated, the frequency and results of relitigation, the relative evidentiary weight of the arbitrator's decision by the reviewing body, and the resultant proposed changes in contract grievance procedures inspired by the *Gardner-Denver* decision.

The support for the judicial shift from deferral to arbitration to review on the merits was found by the authors to depend on whether the surveyed attorneys represented labor or management in such disputes. While 60.3 percent of those responding disagreed with the Supreme Court's decision in the *Gardner-Denver* case, 62.8 percent of the management representatives, but only 28.1 percent of the labor representatives, disagreed with the decision.[10] Additionally, 58 percent of the union attorneys maintained the view that the arbitrator should apply the external law, as opposed to 37 percent of the management attorneys who responded.[11] Only about 7.2 percent of those responding stated that "great evidentiary weight" had been accorded the relitigated arbitral decisions in the post–*Gardner-Denver* years, and in fact 56.4 percent indicated that "the award had been given either no weight or little evidentiary weight."[12]

After noting the volume of Title-VII-related breach of duty of fair representation actions since *Gardner-Denver*, the authors suggested that the granting of greater participation in the resolution of discrimination claims by the individual may be a reasonable approach. A large percentage of surveyed attorneys (71.5%) either strongly favored or favored granting the individual third party intervention status if a legally binding waiver of future relitigation remedies were executed by that individual.

With regard to incidence of review of employment discrimination related arbitral decisions, Hoyman and Stallworth concluded that the impact of the ruling appeared to have more of a procedural effect than a substantive effect in the process, since the study results indicated that a substantial amount of review activity of arbitral awards post *Gardner-Denver* had led to the reversal of only a very small fraction of all discrimination arbitration findings by reviewing bodies. Because relitigation had not occurred in the majority of cases, the authors maintained that "the arbitration still serves as a viable dispute settlement device for the resolution of Title-VII-related grievances."[13]

Charles B. Craver examined the scope of judicial intervention in public sector grievance arbitration.[14] Craver found that in public sector cases, courts are less respectful, prior to arbitration, of the parties' agreement to arbitrate, and less deferential in reviewing arbitral awards.

Prior to arbitration, courts are generally more reluctant to compel arbitration when public sector parties refuse to comply with their collective bargaining agreements and submit to arbitration. In ruling on substantive arbitrability, courts have refused to interpret the agreement broadly, as is usually done in private sector cases.[15] For example, in *Acting Superintendent of Schools v. United Liverpool Faculty Association*,[16] the New York Court of Appeals stated that "the agreement to arbitrate must be express, direct and unequivocal as to the issues or disputes to be submitted to arbitration; anything less will lead to a denial of arbitration."

Upon review, courts are more likely to overturn an arbitrator's decision in a public sector dispute. While private sector awards are normally only nullified in cases of fraud, obvious partiality, or where the arbitrator exceeded his contractually defined authority in public sector cases, courts will not so confine themselves. An award may be overturned if "clearly erroneous" or if based upon past practice rather than specific contractual language.[17] In addition, many awards may be rejected under the vague standard of "contrary to public policy."[18] Finally, some management decisions are viewed as being so closely linked to government policy that to allow an arbitrator to reverse such decisions is viewed as an unauthorized delegation of a public official's authority. Arbitration awards rescinding decisions regarding the appointment and retention of employees have been the most frequent victim of this doctrine.[19]

William J. Isaacson and William C. Zifchak analyzed the National Labor Relations Board's policy, first set forth in *Spielberg Manufacturing*[20] and *Collyer Insulated Wire*,[21] of deferral to arbitration.[22] In certain cases, the Board will suspend action on an unfair labor practice pending arbitration of the dispute.

The authors acknowledged that in cases where the union itself is a claimant, such as refusal to bargain or unilateral action on the part of the employer, Board deferral is appropriate. In such cases, the fact that the claimant is a party to the collective bargaining agreement makes it likely that the claimant's interests will be fairly represented at arbitration. However, when a claim is brought by an individual employee whose interest is not shared by the union, fair representation before the arbitrator cannot be guaranteed. Thus, in cases where employer-union collaboration is charged or the unfair labor practice charge/grievance is brought by a union dissident, the authors argue that deferral is not warranted.[23]

This concern was recognized by the Board when in *General American Transportation Corp.*,[24] it refused to defer to the contractual arbitration machinery in cases alleging violations of sections 8(a)(1), 8(a)(3), 8(b)(1)(A), or 8(b)(2). With a new Board, however, came a new policy. In 1984, the Board reversed itself and allowed such deferral, substantially broadening the scope of cases in which the Board will defer to arbitration.

The Board adopted new standards in 1984 regarding the deference to be accorded to arbitration awards. In *Olin Corp.*[25] the Board said that it would conclude that the arbitrator had "adequately considered" the unfair labor practice issue if "(1) the contractual issue was factually parallel to the unfair labor practice issue, and (2) the arbitrator was presented generally with the facts relevant to resolving the unfair labor practice." The Board took the position that under *Spielberg* an award would not have to be totally consistent with Board precedent in order to avoid violating the "clearly repugnant" standard. Said the Board: "Unless the award is 'palpably' wrong, i.e., unless the arbitrator's decision is not susceptible to an interpretation consistent with the Act, we will defer."[26]

On the so-called *Collyer Insulated Wire* issue in *United Technologies Corp.*,[27] the Board took the position that it would defer to the party's own procedures prior to their invocation by either side at the pre-arbitration stage unless the union's position could be expected to be adverse to that of the employee, or the employer's conduct constituted a rejection of the principles of collective bargaining.

The time and cost savings of the process of expedited arbitration were studied by Marcus H. Sandver, Harry R. Blaine, and Mark N. Woyan.[28] Under the most popular model of expedited arbitration, no briefs are filed or transcripts made, formal rules of evidence are suspended, the local parties themselves rather than attorneys present the case, and the arbitrator is required to render a decision within forty-eight hours of the hearing.[29] The authors examined the expedited arbitration systems prevailing in basic steel, at the Long Island Railroad, at the Kelsey-Hayes Corporation, at International Paper Company, and among several Columbus, Ohio employers. Based on this data, they concluded that expedited arbitration has significantly reduced the time and money spent in the disposition of routine, non-policy-oriented grievances.[30]

Finally, Clyde Summers, an early advocate of protecting all workers from unjust discipline regardless of whether or not they are unionized, recommended incorporating the standards and procedures existing in our current arbitration system into a wrongful discharge statute.[31] Summers noted that a cadre of well-trained arbitrators is available, as are procedures for selecting them. Furthermore, a standard for reviewing discharges, that of "just cause," is firmly entrenched in arbitral "jurisprudence," and a body of "law" that defines the boundaries of just cause already exists.[32]

Summers suggested requiring each of the parties to pay a $100.00 flat fee in order to avoid frivolous claims, with the state bearing the remainder of the costs of arbitration.[33] Protection should extend to all but probationary employees and upper level management who have employment contracts in which statutory protection could be waived.[34] The statute should reach all forms of disciplinary action, not just discharge.[35] Unionized employees whose union refuses to take their grievances to arbitration should also be allowed to pursue statutory relief. However, if a disciplinary action has already been arbitrated under a collective bargaining agreement, the employee should not get a second "bite of the apple."[36] Finally, Summers advocated granting arbitrators the same scope and flexibility in determining appropriate remedies that is currently available to arbitrators under collective bargaining agreements.[37]

There has been some recent support for Summers' position. As wrongful discharge has emerged as a valid cause of action under the common law nationwide, so have statutory proposals to deal with the problem of growing litigation and enormous damage awards. One such proposal, offered by the Ad Hoc Committee on Termination at Will and Wrongful Discharge appointed by the California State Bar, has recommended arbitration as an alternative forum for the disposition of wrongful discharge claims.[38]

NOTES

1. Bartlett, "Employment Discrimination and Labor Arbitrators: A Question of Competence," 85 W. Va. L. Rev. 873 (1983).

2. 415 U.S. 36 (1974). *See generally* Gould, "Labor Arbitration of Grievances Involving Racial Discrimination," 118 U. Penn. L. Rev. 40 (1969).

unions which had struck earlier and actually been penalized under the law—namely the welfare and the ferry boat workers—are asking to be exempted too.

The weaknesses in Taft-Hartley, combined with the provocative theatrics of Mike Quill, resulted on the national level in President Johnson's State of the Union call for amendments to its emergency strike provisions. Suggestions for revising the Taft-Hartley Act, which stipulates an 80-day "cooling-off" period in strikes affecting the country's "health and safety," are commonplace and normally one does not pay much attention to them. But the President does not seem content to let the matter drop with his indictment of the New York transit package as "inflationary." And it should be remembered that before joining the Kennedy Administration in 1961, Secretary of Labor W. Willard Wirtz proposed some very sensible procedures to deal with emergency strikes.

Whether employers like the New York City Transit Authority would be affected by Taft-Hartley revision is another matter. This law does not now cover public employment or local emergency strikes against private employers, and the President

has correctly stated that Federal legislation must take into account the legitimate prerogatives of state and local government. Indeed, for Washington to dictate how states must operate public services would contravene the trend toward greater state responsibility fostered by reapportionment.

But the Federal government can and should guarantee the right of public employes to join unions. Such an assertion of national labor policy, desirable in itself, would also serve as a *quid pro quo* to the unions for the restrictions the states are already imposing on the right to strike. In New York State, the immediate onus remains on the Legislature in Albany.

WHAT, THEN, can the New York Legislature do? It is clear that the sanctions Condon-Wadlin invokes against strikers—i.e., automatic dismissal and no pay raise for three years—are unduly harsh, have no relevance to the real causes of labor disputes, and most important, are simply not enforced against strong unions. Whatever new sanctions are enacted—and sanctions are necessary in some industries—they should be directed against the offending union rather

than against individuals. But even so, sanctions that are too stringent will prove self-defeating. For instance, legislation outlawing the union shop and company checkoff of union dues, or making unions more vulnerable to the raids of rivals, would lead to instability and frustration—and probably increase the potential for intolerably burdensome and bitterly intractable strikes.

Nor is it sensible for state lawmakers to give equal weight to all public employe strikes. Even a walkout by the groundskeepers at the governor's mansion would outrage a good many citizens. But can anyone compare this to similar conduct by policemen or firemen? Should a strike by the employes of state-owned liquor stores be treated in the same manner as a transit dispute? Actually, more industries with real emergency potential—such as electric and telephone—are in private rather than public hands. Moreover, some strikes—say, in the schools—may not threaten the public health, safety or welfare if they last for a very short period, while a week-long teachers' strike would be intolerable. The legislatures should cut through the propaganda that every public strike constitutes an emergency. The question of

states passing laws affecting private industries is one Congress must decide, since Taft-Hartley precludes state action in this area.

Legislatures or Congress also must determine what protection for employes should be established if the right to strike is restricted. Public employment is increasing and so is its importance in the economy. Labor unions should not be arbitrarily restricted in this sector. And legislatures should not be tempted by bills that would require unions to take secret strike votes. Such bills, in trying to divide the unions from employes, actually will compel labor leaders to conduct political campaigns when they should be bargaining.

In the final analysis, damages and fines are the only weapons the law can provide against an illegal strike. But, as New York's Mayor and the Transit Authority very quickly discovered, it is difficult to penalize someone while attempting to bargain with him. Therefore mediatory procedures, *to be observed prior to the contract's expiration date,* should be incorporated into law by state legislatures regardless of what is done about sanctions. Legislation of this kind might resemble the "choice of procedures" law advocated by Secretary Wirtz, and in one form already enacted in Massachusetts. In New York, for example, the law might run as follows:

1. A party wishing to modify or terminate a labor contract shall notify the other party and the Commissioner of Labor 60 days before the contract expires.

2. If the Commissioner is not notified that an agreement has been reached within 30 days, a three-man panel of mediators should assist the disputants. (This panel might be chosen by the governor or mayor; or the union and employer might each choose one member, with the third picked by the two men already selected.

3. If the Commissioner of Labor is not notified of a settlement 15 days prior to the contract's expiration, the governor or mayor might instruct the mediators to: (a) issue public recommendations: (b) issue private recommendations to the parties and, if there was no settlement after that, make the recommendations public; (c) issue a public report on the positions of the parties; (d) in a case of severe intransigence, issue a binding arbitration award.

Except in extreme circumstances, these measures should bring about a settlement—sometimes under the

W. WILLARD WIRTZ

weight of public opinion. Compulsory arbitration would be a last resort. The possible constitutional objection to handing over budgetary decisions to outside third parties can be solved, if necessary, by amending the New York Constitution. Having accepted the feasibility of "advisory" arbitration or third-party fact-finding, it is difficult to argue against a stronger dose of the same medicine in extreme cases.

IT IS DOUBTFUL that compulsory arbitration or any other form of governmental influence during emergency strikes can impose the

wage-restraints guideposts enunciated by the Council of Economic Advisors. Unions and employers could be required by law to bargain in terms of productivity or the guideposts. But the proposals outlined would work best if the mediators make awards or recommendations similar to those the parties would accept after a strike, rather than when preoccupied with the abstract welfare of the national economy.

Finally, the "cooling off" period after the termination of a contract has never worked under the present Taft-Hartley emergency provisions, although it might be useful during a period of political transition such as New York underwent this year. Normally, however, the cooling off period proves to be a "heating up" period during which both parties—without benefit of some form of fact-finding—rely on the same strategy which impelled them to disagree before the contract ended. Both sides attempt to rally outside support for themselves rather than bargain in good faith.

The "choice of procedures" encourages collective bargaining more than any other scheme of governmental involvement. Since the alternatives are not entirely predictable, they should not give the parties a crutch to lean on. (The governor or mayor can be authorized to do nothing in cases where settlement is close but one party thinks it will gain by intervention.) This approach, permitting the government to remain flexible and adapt itself to each case, may yet be incorporated in Taft-Hartley when it is revised.

The American penchant for passing laws has saddled us with some very foolish ones in the past. The question here is not whether there should be a new law, but under what conditions it will be enacted: during a period of relative calm, or during a crisis like New York's transit strike, which outrages labor's friends as well as its enemies.

Bibliographic Essay on Managing Emergency Strikes

While some of my comments in the article "Managing Emergency Strikes" have been borne out in the nineteen years that have passed since the article was published, others have not. The Condon-Wadlin Law was indeed repealed and replaced by the Taylor Law[1] and the New York City Collective Bargaining Law.[2] And although the Federal government has not guaranteed the right of public employees to join unions, most states have done so by statute.[3] Surprisingly, however, Title II of the Taft-Hartley Act, while continually criticized, has not been altered. There have been legislative proposals to amend both Title II and the emergency dispute procedures of the Railway Labor Act of 1926, but none have come to fruition.[4]

A substantial literature has developed relating to these topics. While it would be impossible to recognize all of these efforts, I shall endeavor to summarize a representative sample.

THE TAYLOR LAW

The Taylor Law, New York's legislative response to the ineffectiveness of Condon-Wadlin, has been severely criticized on several accounts since its passage in 1967. Theodore W. Kheel concluded that the then two-year-old law may have "exacerbated" several public sector contract disputes.[5] By prohibiting strikes, Kheel argued, the Taylor Law "made the march to jail a martyr's procession and a badge of honor for union leaders." It hardened bargaining positions by requiring public acceptance or rejection of fact-finder recommendations. And it clearly failed to do what it was meant to do: prevent public employee strikes.[6]

Kheel also expressed concern that support of compulsory arbitration as a final step in public employee interest disputes was ill-advised. Kheel noted the legal problems in allowing arbitrators to make decisions that are solely the province of elected officials. He stated that arbitration was only effective when the issues were sharply focused and there were clear standards of reference upon which to base a decision, attributes that are normally lacking when public sector disputes are submitted to arbitration. He also warned that the parties would begin to depend on arbitration rather than relying upon "hard" collective bargaining to settle their disputes. Kheel emphasized that primary reliance should be placed on such bargaining to settle contract disputes.[7]

Kheel's comments proved to be prophetic in this respect insofar as New York is concerned. In 1974, the New York State Legislature amended the Taylor Law to provide for compulsory arbitration as the terminal procedure in contract disputes involving police and firefighters. Thomas A. Kochan and Jean Baderschneider found some evidence to support Kheel's statement that parties may develop a dependence on compulsory arbitration.[8] Kochan and Baderschneider analyzed the negotiating experience of police and firefighter units in New York between 1968 and 1976. Their results indicated that the proportion of impasses definitely increased over this period and that the adoption of compulsory arbitration in 1974 resulted in a marginal increase in the probability of impasses small and medium-sized cities. Thus, there was some indication of a growing dependence not only on arbitration, but on other impasse procedures as well.[9] However, as noted elsewhere (pp. 37-43) the experience in other jurisdictions does not evidence a universal addiction to such procedures.

THE RIGHT TO STRIKE

The failure of Congress to explicitly recognize the right of public employees to join unions has not presented a major hindrance to organization in the public sector, in light of the willingness of state legislatures and the Federal courts to make such a recognition. The right of public employees to strike, however, has met with much greater resistance. Only eleven state legislatures have recognized even a limited right to strike.[10] The Supreme Court of California has held that the Legislature's enactment of modern labor legislation applicable to the public sector underlines the common law prohibition of the public employee strike and that, in the absence of legislation on the issue, it is not unlawful for public employees to strike unless it has been determined that the stopage poses an imminent threat to health or safety.[10a] But this remains a minority view.

Professor Kurt L. Hanslowe and John L. Acierno have explored the legal basis for this antipathy towards public sector strikes and found it lacking.[11] Hanslowe and Acierno questioned the argument that public strikes are incompatible with democratic processes, noting that several states have, in fact, granted public employees some limited right to strike. They also argued that certain market constraints comparable to the private sector, such as the employee's loss of wages during a strike, the ability to subcontract certain services, and the public's concern with increasing tax rates, would enable public officials to resist unreasonable demands.[12] Finally, they relied on Judge Skelly Wright's concurring opinion in *United Federation of Postal Workers v. Blount*[13] in arguing that the right to strike is so closely related to the constitutionally protected right to organize that it too should receive some degree of constitutional protection.[14]

This antipathy towards the right to strike is shared by the Federal government, whose employees are equally prohibited from striking.[15] This was made no clearer than in the case of the 1981 air traffic controllers' strike, described by Bernard D. Meltzer and Cass R. Sunstein.[16] Meltzer and Sunstein have concluded that President Reagan and the Department of Justice both acted within the letter of the law in their response to the strike. They contended that Reagan, as he himself said, was required to discharge all reliably identified strikers, and that the Department of Justice, in selectively prosecuting certain outspoken strike leaders, acted properly because their objective was one of deterrence rather than suppression of free speech.[17]

Meltzer and Sunstein also suggested that the controllers' willingness to strike was a misjudgment of the administration and influenced by a belief that, as in the past, the anti-strike policy would not be strictly enforced.[18] This miscalculation by the controllers points to one of the weaknesses of the anti-strike policy. The administration is under enormous pressure: if they apply the policy too vigorously they will be (and have been) criticized for ignoring the resulting human and social costs; if they vacillate in their response, on the other hand, they will be criticized for being timid and encouraging such illegal actions. Moreover, the enormous costs to not only the strikers, but to the air transport industry, the government, and the public as well, raise some legitimate questions regarding the effectiveness of discharging strikers.[19]

Meltzer and Sunstein, however, stopped short of endorsing an alternative policy. Rather, they suggested that if the federal anti-strike policy is to be retained, employees must be made to understand the rationale for such a policy, politicians must not use "bureaucrats" as scapegoats if the policy fails, and administrators must be sensitive to the grievances of employees so as to avoid fueling the fires of pro-strike sentiment.[20]

TAFT-HARTLEY AND THE RAILWAY LABOR ACTS

The emergency strike procedures of both Title II of the Taft-Hartley Act and The Railway Labor Act have attracted considerable scholarly attention in the last eighteen years. Professor Benjamin Aaron reviewed some of the proposals made to amend these provisions and offered his own alternative proposal.[21] Although careful to point out that there is no "right" answer to the problem of rational emergency disputes, Aaron suggested relying upon one procedure to cover all industries, including the railways and airlines. He endorsed the use of an emergency board to hold hearings and submit recommendations on procedures to settle the dispute, rather than substantive contractual terms. The board's recommendations would then be transmitted to Congress and the parties by the President, with or without his own recommendations. Congress, rather than the President, would then have ultimate control over the utilization of further procedures.[22]

Aaron also recommended that the President retain the discretion of deciding when a dispute has reached national emergency proportions. However, only disputes that are truly national in scope should be subject to the President's discretion, and local disputes in both the public and private sector should be left to state or local authorities.[23]

Charles Rehmus[24] rejected the 1970 Nixon proposals to amend the Railway Labor Act emergency strike provisions.[25] Rehmus noted the shortcomings of the three options available to the President under the proposal: providing an additional thirty-day cooling off period may simply prolong the inevitable; partial operation may be both economically and operationally infeasible; and final offer arbitration is largely untested and not suited for the disposition of non-economic issues.[26]

Rehmus did not, however, contend that these options would be ineffective in all circumstances. He endorsed a more flexible approach, allowing the President to choose from among these options as well as other dispute mechanisms such as arbitration. he concluded that "a broad choice of procedures seems most likely to preserve the benefits of the existing Act, to receive majority support, and to be the most effective on the public interest."[27]

Finally, John Ackerman evaluated the application of Title II procedures to the 1977-78 bituminous coal strike.[28] Ackerman analyzed weekly surveys of large employers in several coal-dependent states, conducted by the Bureau of Labor Statistics during the course of the strike. He found that the employers' predictions of widescale layoffs were greatly exaggerated and that no emergency really existed in light of conservation methods, equitable coal distribution among the states, and temporary suspension of clean air regulations, which allowed the most efficient use of existing coal reserves.[29] He concluded, therefore, that President Carter's decision to invoke the Title II procedures resulted more from political pressure than the existence of an actual emergency.[30]

NOTES

1. N.Y. Civ. Serv. Law, § 200 *et seq.* (McKinney 1973, amended 1983).
2. N.Y. City Charter Ch. 54; N.Y. City Admin. Code § 1173-1.0 *et seq.* (1967), amended 1975).

3. Arizona, Colorado, Mississippi, North Carolina, South Carolina, Utah, Virginia, and West Virginia are the only states with no statutes explicitly recognizing the right of at least some public employees to join a union. However, the federal courts in most of the these states, have recognized such a right as protected by the First Amendment. *See,* e.g. *Atkins v. City of Charlotte,* 296 F. supp. 1068 (D.N.C. 1969).

4. While President Johnson criticized Title II, in his 1966 State of the Union address, he never made specific recommendations to Congress for its amendment. *See* Cullen, *National Emergency Strikes* 81-82 (1968). In 1970, however, President Nixon proposed discontinuing the emergency strike provisions of the Railway Labor Act and placing the railroads and airlines under the jurisdiction of the Taft-Hartley Act. Under the President's proposal, upon exhaustion of the normal Title II procedures, the President would be given three options. He could:

1. Extend the non-strike cooling-off period for as long as 30 days;

2. Require partial operation of the relevant industry;

3. Invoke final offer arbitration (where the arbitrator would be forced to choose one of the party's proposals without modification).

The Nixon proposal died in Congress. *See* Rehmus, "Railway Labor Act Modifications: Helpful or Harmful," 25 Ind. & Lab. Rel. Rev. 93-4 (1971).

5. Kheel, "Strikes and Public Employment," 67 Mich. L. Rev. 931 (1969).

6. *Id.* at 935-36.

7. *Id.* at 939-40.

8. Kochan and Baderschneider, "Dependence on Impasse Procedures: Police and Firefighters in New York State." 31 Ind. & Lab. Rel. Rev. 431 (1978).

9. *Id.* at 447-48.

10. Alaska Stat. § 23.40.200 (a) (1981) (exceptions: police and firefighters, prison guards and other correctional institution employees, and hospital employees); Hawaii Rev. Stat. § 89-12 (a) (1976 & Supp. 1981) (exceptions: "essential" employees); Idaho Code § 44-1811 (Supp. 1980) (prohibition against firefighter strikes is limited to those that occur during the term of an agreement; no mention of right to strike with respect to other public employees); Illinois Public Labor Relations Act, P.A. No. 1012 (1983) (effective July 1, 1984) (exceptions: correctional institution employees, state police and firefighters); Minnesota Stat. Ann. § 179.64 (West Supp. 1981) (exceptions: confidential, essential, managerial and supervisory employees, principals and assistant principals); Montana Code Ann. § 39-31-201 (1981) (Montana Supreme Court has interpreted the Montana Public Employees Collective Bargaining Act as providing for the right to strike; exceptions: firefighters, certain health care facility employees); Ohio Rev. Code Ann. § 4117 (Page, 1983) (effective Apr. 1, 1984) (exception: "essential" employees); Oregon Rev. Stat. § 243.736 (1979) (exceptions: police, firefighters and guards at correctional or mental institutions); Pennsylvania Stat. Ann. Tit. 43, § 1101. 1001 (Purdon, 1970) (exceptions: elected officials, gubernatorial appointees, managerial and confidential employees, clergymen, police and firefighters); Vermont Stat. Ann. tit. 21, § 1730 (1978) (providing a limited right to strike for municipal employees); Wisconsin Stat. Ann. § 111.70 (4) (cm) (6) (West Supp. 1980) (exceptions: firefighters and law enforcement personnel).

10a. *County Sanitation district No. 2 of Los Angeles v. SEIU local 660* 119 LRRM 2433 (California Supreme Court, May 13, 1985). The Court's plurality indicated that the right to strike has some constitutional protection. Chief Justice Bird would have directly confronted the constitutional issue and found the strike to be constitutionally protected.

11. Hanslowe and Acierno, "The Law and Theory of Strikes by Government Employees," 67 Corn. L. Rev. 1055 (1982). *See also* Comment, "Public Employee Strikes: Legalization Through Elimination of Remedies," 72 Calif. L. Rev. 629 (1984); *San Diego Teachers Assn. v. Superior Court* 24 Cal. 3d 1 (1979); *El Rancho Unified School District v. National Education Association* 115 LRRM 2235 (1983); *Local 1245 IBEW v. City of Gridley* 113 LRRM 3729 (1983).

12. *Id*. at 1068-69.

13. 325 F. Supp. 879 (D.D.C.) *aff'd*, 404 U.S. 802 (1971).

14. Hanslowe and Acierno, *supra* note 11, at 1074-1075.

15. 5 U.S.C. § 7311 (1976).

16. Meltzer and Sunstein, "Public Employee Strikes, Executive Discretion, and the Air Traffic Controllers," 50 U. Chi. L. Rev. 731 (1983).

17. *Id*. at 792-94.

20. *Id*. at 797-98.

21. Aaron, "National Emergency Disputes: Is There a 'Final Solution'?" 1970 Wisc. L. Rev. 137 (1970).

22. *Id*. at 146.

23. *Id*. at 141-42, HS.

24. Rehmus, *supra* note 4.

25. *See supra* note 4.

26. Rehmus, *supra* note 4, at 92-3.

27. *Id*. at 94.

28. Ackerman, "The Impact of the Coal Strike of 1977-78," 32 Ind. & Lab. Rel. Rev. 175 (1979).

29. *Id*. at 182-84.

30. *Id*. at 188.

3

Public Employment: Mediation, Fact Finding and Arbitration

FOR THE PAST four years public employees throughout the country have demonstrated their dissatisfaction with existing employment conditions in unmistakably clear terms. Whether it has been the "blue flu" absences of Detroit policemen, the refusal of New York City sanitation workers to ratify agreements negotiated by their leadership, mass resignations by New York City school teachers, or walkouts by Atlanta firemen and Michigan zookeepers, the message is clear. The significance of this upheaval lies in the statistics: There are now 8.5 million workers employed by state, county and local governments, with another 4 million estimated to join their ranks by 1975. The American Federation of State, County and Municipal Employees' membership has increased by 66 per cent since 1959—and both the National Education Association and the American Federation of Teachers have enjoyed comparable success. In the sleeping giant of federal employment (where the strike weapon is still punishable as a felony) unions now hold exclusive representation rights for 45 per cent of the entire work force.

It is the right of public employees to strike that has been the center of discussion thus far.[1] But the factors which give rise to the increased reliance upon the strike weapon by public employees have received less attention. Probably nothing has been held to be more responsible for today's turmoil than the disparity in economic benefits that is said to exist between private and public employees. Unions in the private sector have negotiated a host of attractive wage and fringe-benefit packages for their increasingly affluent membership. It is an understatement to say that public workers are no longer thought to have a monopoly on employment security.[2] All of this is accentuated by the inflationary spiral that continues.

On the other hand, many public employees have received substantial—in some instances, astronomical—wage increases in recent years. In 1967, Professor George Taylor—father of New York's Taylor Law—challenged the assumption that all public employees are relatively underpaid:

It may be that the widespread belief that government employees are underpaid relates primarily to occupational categories, especially those for which there are no counterparts in the private sector. School teachers, policemen and firemen, and welfare workers who have been most militant seem to fall in this category. There is an obvious need for more information to enable one to appraise the results of using comparable wage criteria.[3]

One might note that teachers appear to be paid more than their private counterparts. (Of course, working conditions in the private schools are often better.) In any event, public workers seem to believe that they are behind—and this is more important

EDITOR'S NOTE: This article is based on a paper which the author delivered at the Thirteenth Annual Labor Management Conference at the University of Iowa on May 7, 1969.

1. See, for instance, Gould, *Managing Emergency Strikes*, The New Leader, March 14, 1966 at ; Kheel, Report to Speaker Anthony J. Travia on the Taylor Law: With a Proposed Plan To Prevent Strikes by Public Workers (February 21, 1968); Morris, *Public Policy in the Law Relating to Collective Bargaining in the Public Service*, 22 SW. L. J. 585 (1968); see generally Ross, *Those Newly Militant Government Workers*, FORTUNE, August, 1968, at 104.
2. See Collective Bargaining in the Public Sector: An Interim Report (prepared for Executive Board, AFL-CIO Maritime Trades Department, February 13, 1969).
3. Taylor, Strikes in Public Employment 8, address presented at conference held by New York State School of Industrial and Labor Relations, Cornell University, in New York City, on November 15, 1967; cf. Taylor, *Public Employment Strikes or Procedures?*, 20 IND. & LAB. REL. REV. 617 (1967).

than the actual fact. Also, it needs to be pointed out that, generally speaking, experienced workers in the public sector are behind—and this is where one finds the political wallop in the unions.

Public Employees Learning from the New Protest Tactics

Another reason for current unrest is that public employees are learning from the tactics used by others. Not only are the number of private employee stoppages in which the rank and file reject the leadership's negotiated settlement on the upswing, but there are growing numbers of people who use methods of protest and "direct action". Civil rights activists have been successful in achieving some of their objectives through demonstrations.[4] Some critics of the Vietnamese war have followed the same road. And currently student rebellions seem to know no bounds—both in tactics used and objectives which are sought. In part, anyway, public workers are responding to a general growing disrespect for authority. These are not times in which "the king can do no wrong". Antistrike laws have not seemed to persuade people not to strike.[5] The instability that flows from multiunion bargaining with the public employer does not seem to have helped matters any.[6]

Finally, in public education, we witness the growing number of male teachers with families to support.[7] Few opportunities exist for promotion into the administrative jobs. Besides unprecedented salary demands, the result is a preoccupation with policy matters that the teacher regards as within his competence as a professional. As one superintendent told me: "Most teachers in the school believe that they can do my job better than me—and maybe they can. But that attitude doesn't make for harmony."

If the problems of the public employment relationship are great and the strike weapon inappropriate (or less appropriate than in the private sector), various forms of third-party intervention may suggest themselves as a means to resolve the impasse—the is-sues on which the parties are deadlocked while negotiating a new collective bargaining agreement. But such procedures should be relied on as a last resort, when collective bargaining avenues have been exhausted, for the parties understand their own problems better than anyone else. It is they who must live with what is negotiated at the bargaining table.

Moreover, one cannot expect third-party intervention to be any kind of panacea—indeed, it may sometimes be the exact opposite. Unions and public employers act wisely and responsibly when they strive to avoid "outsiders" through dealing with their own problems and relying on their own abilities.

Of the three approaches to impasse resolution, mediation is the most tried and reliable. The skilled mediator can use his "neutral" position to good advantage in offering suggestions and proposals for compromises that are both practical and "face saving" for the parties. He may be of assistance in getting the facts straight concerning the issues in dispute.

The requisite insights can be obtained by gaining the confidence of the parties in informal off-the-record discussions and by meeting with both sides separately. But a good mediator is only able to operate successfully if he obtains the parties' trust, so that neither side believes that the mediator is the conduit for passing valuable secrets and bargaining advantages to the other side of the table.

The Federal Mediation and Conciliation Service has provided much expert assistance in the private sector. In the public sector, the New York Public Employment Relations Board has used ad hoc mediators who are not employed on a full-time basis with government. In Michigan, the Labor Mediation Board relies on its full-time staff for both private and public employee disputes.

But the success potential for negotiation is seriously limited by two factors. The first is that in these troubled times agencies like the Michigan Labor Mediation Board cannot place mediators in all of the trouble spots—particularly when school contracts are all being negotiated in August and September. The reason is an inadequate budget which results in unrealistic limitations on the amount of mediation staff to be hired and a disinclination to hire ad hoc mediators for the "busy season". To complain about strikes without providing funds with which to pay mediators defies common sense.

Second, mediation cannot achieve anything if the parties refuse to budge from their respective positions. The best of mediators cannot unsnarl recalcitrant parties and untractable issues. And unfortunately in Michigan "[i]n the crisis bargaining atmosphere of the education area, experience showed parties holding back settlement offers from the mediator for use before the fact-finder. This procedure inhibited mediators' efforts and resulted in an inordinately high number of disputes submitted to fact finding. Both employer and union recalcitrance to meet during the summer vacation period resulted in crisis bargaining for teachers' contracts."[8] It is interesting to note that in Wisconsin, where, unlike Michigan, the parties share the costs of fact finding, unions and public employers are not nearly so addicted to using the fact finder.[9]

If Mediation Fails, Then What?

If mediation fails, how is the public interest in uninterrupted services to be protected?

A number of jurisdictions have enacted statutes which provide for fact finding with recommendations to

4. Most recently, civil rights demonstrators in some instances have combined efforts with the labor union leaders to assist the organization of minority group workers. See Wooten, *14 Rights Leaders Support Strikers*, The New York Times, April 21, 1969, at 29.
5. See Goldberg, *Labor-Management Relations Laws in Public Service*, 91 MONTHLY LAB. REV. 48 (1968).
6. See Gray, *The City Unions Need One Bargaining Table*, The New York Times, December 16, 1967, at 40, col. 3.
7. See DOHERTY & OBERER, TEACHERS, SCHOOL BOARDS, AND COLLECTIVE BARGAINING (1967).
8. ANNUAL REPORT OF DEPARTMENT OF LABOR STATE OF MICHIGAN FOR 1967-68, 75-76.
9. See Stern, *The Wisconsin Public Employee Fact-Finding Procedure*, 20 IND. & LAB. REL. REV. 3 (1966).

achieve resolution of impasses.[10] Fact finding retains the principle of voluntaryism since it does not bind the disputants. The Taft-Hartley Act emergency dispute provisions do not give that statute's fact-finding board the power to make recommendations.[11] The idea that compulsion imposed upon the parties by public reaction was consistent with voluntaryism and would produce settlements encouraged Senator Taft to advocate giving the board the authority to make recommendations.[12]

The most prominent rationale for this process is the one advanced by the 1966 Taylor Report:

Fact-finding requires the parties to gather objective information and to present arguments with references to these data. An unsubstantiated or extreme demand from either party tends to lose its force and status in this forum. The fact-finding report and recommendations provide a basis to inform and crystallize thoughtful public opinion and news media comment. Such reports and recommendations have a special relevance when the public's business is involved. The public has a special right to be informed on the issues, content and merits of disputes involving public employees.[13]

Thus, if one looks to the Taylor Report for guidance, fact finding is an exercise in rationality, a careful consideration of the issues on their merits—as distinguished from their resolution through brute economic force. Presumably the public interest—as reflected in both noninflationary settlements and some bridle on the necessity to lay new taxes in order to finance the settlement —should be considered in the process.

But the problem is that the parties are not always interested in availability of good logical arguments to support their positions—and sadly enough, the same can often be said of the public itself. Indeed, newspapers and television stations sometimes refuse to report the recommendations. This may be attributable to the editor's view of what is newsworthy and, in some communities, the fact that the media disagree with the fact finder's conclusions. Thus, fact finding, at least in certain circumstances, may be substantially different from the judicial proceeding that is envisioned by the Taylor Report. My experience is that the "unsubstantiated" or "extreme" position does not necessarily ". . . lose its force and status in this [fact-finding] forum".

The fact that some unions and public members are interested in an old-fashioned practical "bargaining" —and seem insistent upon incorporating this preference into the fact-finding process—indicates that the characteristics of fact-finding will not be purely judicial. For, if one assumes that fact finding is intended to serve in lieu of the strike, then the fact finder's ability to get the parties together without economic warfare is to be a large measure of his success. Therefore, the acceptability of the fact finder's recommendation is an appropriate goal, but the recommendation should also be the most practicable and equitable answer—and these three elements are not always synonymous with one another.

In New York, the Taylor Law provides that failure to reach agreement as of sixty days prior to the budget submission date constitutes an impasse, and the fact finder's report must be submitted twenty days before the budget submission date.[14] Theoretically, this timetable is most conducive to the calm, deliberate setting which is so important to the judicial process. But in Michigan, no timetable for fact finding exists. The result is often "instant fact finding", wherein the fact finder must devise a settlement which gets the already-striking workers back on the job.[15]

Is the Fact Finder a Judge or a Mediator?

Is the fact finder's position, then, that of a judge or arbitrator, who makes a determination predicated upon purely objective criteria? Or is he more akin to the mediator, whose function is to be acceptable to the parties so that he may bring them together on an amicable basis? It is easy to see that the weight given to either of these functions may depend on the statutory timetable or lack of one.

Chairman Robert Howlett of the Michigan Labor Mediation Board has recently expressed his board's hostility toward mediation efforts by fact finders:

10. See, for instance, CONN. GEN. STAT. ANN. tit. 31, § 31-101 et seq. (1960); MASS. GEN. LAWS ANN. ch. 15A, § 1 et seq. (1958); MICH. STAT. ANN. tit. 17, § 17.6 et seq. (1960); N. Y. CIVIL SERVICE LAW § 205 (McKinney supp. 1967); WIS. STAT. ANN. ch. 111, § 111.01 et seq. (1957).
11. The emergency disputes provisions are contained in 61 Stat. 141 (1947), 29 U.S.C. §§ 157, 206-210 (1958).
12. S. 249, 81st Cong., 1st. Sess. (1949).
13. GOVERNOR'S COMMITTEE ON PUBLIC EMPLOYEE RELATIONS 53 (March 31, 1966).
14. 288 GERR F-5 (March 17, 1969).
15. Cf. ALLEN, 1967 SCHOOL DISPUTES IN MICHIGAN (1968) and SCHMIDT, OBSERVATIONS ON THE PROCESS OF FACT-FINDING IN MICHIGAN PUBLIC EDUCATION TEACHER-SCHOOL BOARD CONTRACT DISPUTES IN PUBLIC EMPLOYEE ORGANIZATION AND BARGAINING: A REPORT ON THE JOINT CONFERENCE OF THE ASSOCIATION OF LABOR MEDIATION AGENCIES AND THE NATIONAL ASSOCIATION OF STATE LABOR RELATIONS AGENCIES (1968).

This [mediation by fact-finders], we decided, was a mistake. In 1968, we instructed our fact-finders to be judges, *not mediators*. We do not rule out an "in chambers" settlement if it appears possible. In August/September, 1968, our fact-finders, particularly those with collective bargaining experience, were not always obedient to our instructions. They preferred to mediate. Some of the bargaining teams preferred it that way.[16]

In my judgment, the fact-finding process necessarily partakes of both the mediatory and judicial disciplines. While the process is a fluid one about which the drawing of hard and fast lines is still an audacious act, I am convinced that Chairman Howlett's analogy to "in chambers" settlements is a good one. For it seems difficult for the fact finder to introduce himself as a mediator, gain the parties' confidence and trust and then—having failed to bring them together without recommendations—to put on his judicial robes and hear formal testimony on the issues in dispute. The parties are bound to feel confused and betrayed by this role switching, which can result in a "judge's" reliance on information obtained through informal and frank off-the-record mediation sessions.

On the other hand, the skillful fact finder may be able to find a stage of the proceeding when, in his opinion, a settlement is near and when it is therefore propitious to adjourn the hearing for a limited period of time. Sometimes the opportunity is presented through the appearance of misunderstandings by one side of the other's position. An attempt to obtain clarification concerning the differences between the parties may give the fact finder the chance to don his mediator's hat. But, at this "in chambers" stage—as distinguished from the beginning of the hearing—the parties should have acquired some measure of respect for and confidence in the fact finder. If not, his request to adjourn for clarification or for anything else will be met with a refusal or lack of enthusiasm.

However, even when the fact finder is proceeding down the "in chambers" route, the parties are very often inclined to hold back, anticipating the possible resumption of formal hearings. The fact finder must convince the parties that he will keep the two procedures separate in his own mind. It is an understatement to note that this is not always the easiest feat to carry off.

A Marriage That's Bound To Fail

What are the basic limitations of fact finding? One of the troublesome aspects of fact finding is that all too often there is an attempt by one or both of the parties to marry the process with unfair labor practice machinery. Usually this takes the form of each or both parties excoriating the other for failing to bargain in good faith or for engaging in various other kinds of reprehensible conduct. One can appreciate the frustrations of the parties in states like New York,[17] where, prior to the 1969 amendments anyway, the Public Employment Relations Board has refused to exercise a substantial amount of unfair labor practice jurisdiction. But any attempt to merge two such processes just doesn't work.

The first reason is that acrimony ensues and the parties only heat themselves up, though one of the purposes of the fact-finding process is to get them to come together peaceably. Second, except in the most extreme cases, if the fact finder begins to "assess blame" or state in his report that one party has refused to bargain in good faith, (1) he usurps that which is more appropriately handled by an administrative agency established to deal with unfair labor practice charges, and (2) he winds up antagonizing one or both of the parties who he hopes will accept his recommendations. I do not mean to rule out a detailed statement of facts which will—without drawing conclusions in the report—make the public aware as to who is responsible for the impasse that has developed. But, for the most part, straightforward blame assessment at any stage in the process is an exercise in futility.

An institutional defect is that the process is too rigid. The prospect of a report places substantial limitations on the fact finder's mediatory skills. Once the report is issued, the positions of each side harden. If one side rejects the recommendations and the other accepts, the latter will budge precious little. Although the fact finder can be successful in a post-fact-finding-report mediation effort, all too often the parties will give vent to their hostilities and pour out their criticisms of the report and recommendations.

To cope with this general problem, Professor Hildebrand has proposed that "[i]n [its] first step the [fact-finding board] would investigate the issues and submit a confidential report to the parties, to give them a further opportunity to reach a settlement. If a settlement were not reached within a specified time, then the second stage would begin: the board would make public its findings and recommendations."[18] The 1969 amendments to the New York Taylor Law provide for making the report available to the parties before issuing it to the public.[19] Thus, the fact finder's role as mediator has received statutory recognition.

This may be one way of making the report's acceptability as a framework

16. Howlett, *Arbitration in the Public Sector*, in SOUTHWESTERN LEGAL FOUNDATION 15TH ANNUAL INSTITUTE ON LABOR LAW 249 (1969).

17. For a discussion of the New York Taylor Law and a somewhat different version of the unfair labor practice authority under that statute see Gould, *The New York Taylor Law: A Preliminary Assessment*, 18 LAB. L. J. 323 (1967).

18. Hildebrand, *The Public Sector* in FRONTIERS OF COLLECTIVE BARGAINING 146 (Dunlop & Chamberlain ed. 1967) ; for excellent discussions of the fact-finding process, see also McKelvey, *Fact-Finding in Public Employment Disputes: Promise or Illusion?*, 22 IND. & LAB. REL. REV. 528 (1969) ; Rice, *Reaching Impasses—Mediation and Fact-Finding* (unpublished 1968) ; Stern, *The*

Wisconsin Public Employee Fact-Finding Procedure, 20 IND. & LAB. REL. REV. 3 (1966) ; Zack, *Dispute Settlement in the Public Sector*, 14 N. Y. L. FORUM 249 (1968). *Cf.* Rational Public Labor Policy, New York Times, January 13, 1968, at 30.

19. See note 14 *supra*: ". . . if the dispute is not resolved at least twenty days prior to the budget submission date, the fact-finding board, acting by a majority of its members, (i) shall immediately transmit its finding of fact and recommendations for resolution of the dispute to the chief executive officer of the government involved, (ii) *may thereafter assist the parties to perfect a voluntary resolution of the dispute*, and (iii) shall *within five days of such transmission* make public such findings and recommendations . . . ."

for the settlement more likely. Public exposure would require an immediate reaction and posturing by the parties. Readjustments in the package and new avenues of compromise may suggest themselves in the interim period between private and public release of the report. In short, the process becomes more flexible.

While the New York amendments seem to contemplate one report, which is issued to the parties and the public at different times, a more sensible result is achieved if the fact finder may issue a different official report to the public if he deems it advisable. Discussions with the parties about the private report may make a revised public version desirable. Presumably, also, there is no statutory obligation in New York to release the report to the public when a settlement has been reached subsequent to the issuance of the private report and prior to the deadline for the public report.

In the Face of
Another Rejection

But what if one of the parties still rejects the recommendations in the public report? Although the unions seem to have been more prone to reject fact-finding reports and fact finding itself in New York City,[20] public employers are usually the offending parties. Since public employee unions are generally prohibited from striking, the complaint is that the public employer will simply institute its own position on employment conditions when the report is not to its liking inasmuch as the fact finder's recommendations are not binding. It is also contended that since fact finders both want to issue recommendations that are acceptable and understand that the union is shorn of power without the strike weapon, there will be a tendency on the part of the fact finder to lean toward the public employer because it is in a better position to flout the report.

The absence of finality in the fact-finding process has impelled the Taylor Committee, in its interim report, to make the following proposal:

The transmission of these recommendations, if not accepted by the parties, to

the appropriate representative body for action making them binding on the parties. Such action should be taken, unless, after due consideration, including a hearing to which the parties are summoned to show cause why that step should not be taken, the recommendations are determined to be patently unjust and arbitrary, all interests, including those of the public, considered.[21]

It may be that the "patently unjust and arbitrary" standard should be the only basis upon which a fact finder's recommendation should be nonbinding. But this comes perilously close to compulsory arbitration and thus raises most of the issues which are a part of that debate. Moreover, if this approach is taken, the pressure for statutory criteria which fact finders are obligated to follow when issuing their recommendations would properly become more persuasive. A rationale to support the report's conclusions would become a minimum requirement.[22]

If both mediation and fact finding fail to resolve public employee disputes, it is difficult to avoid thinking about the unthinkable—binding arbitration.

The American experience with arbitration is generally limited to the grievance variety, which involves an interpretation of the terms of a collective bargaining agreement—or "rights" arbitration.[23] The legal obstacles to grievance arbitration in the public sector seem to be surmounta-

ble.[24] But it is "interest" arbitration—impasse disputes concerning the terms of a new contract—which is the primary center of controversy today.[25]

Voluntary "interest" arbitration procedures agreed upon by the parties themselves have been advocated by the Taylor Report[26]—and the AFL-CIO, insofar as the federal government is concerned[27]—and they were utilized by the parties in the 1968 New York City sanitation strike.[28]

But the dissatisfaction with voluntary arbitration stems from the fact that the community is dependent upon the good sense of the parties to arbitrate and not strike when important government services are involved. The Report of the President's Review of Employee-Management Relations in the Federal Service takes the position that when either party requests the services of a new federal labor relations panel, the panel may, among other things, require the parties to submit to binding arbitrations.[29] Moreover, Rhode Island,[30] Pennsylvania,[31] Wyoming[32] and Michigan[33] have provided for compulsory arbitration in the case of unresolved "interest" disputes involving policemen and firemen.[34]

The traditional argument against any form of compulsory arbitration is that it will undermine collective bargaining because neither side will make a concession for fear of prejudicing its case in the arbitration proceeding.[35]

20. See Raskin, *Why New York Is "Strike City"*, The New York Times, December 22, 1968, (Magazine), at 7.
21. GOVERNOR'S COMMITTEE ON PUBLIC EMPLOYEE RELATIONS, INTERIM REPORT, June 17, 1968, at 28. The "show cause" proposal has been incorporated in the 1968 amendments.
22. See Rule 35 of Michigan Labor Mediation Board Rules and Regulations, which authorizes the parties to waive the requirement of a formal report to be issued by the fact finder.
23. For discussions of this issue, see Howlett, *supra* note 16; Ringer, *Legality and Propriety of Agreements To Arbitrate Major and Minor Disputes in Public Employment*, 54 CORNELL L. REV. 128 (1968). Certainly the parties to an arbitration agreement can provide that the arbitrator is not to offend existing laws.
24. *Ibid.*
25. See Perlmutter, *City and Sanitationmen To Abide By Arbitration; State Take-Over Dropped*, The New York Times, February 18, 1968, at 1, col. 8, 35, col. 1.
26. See GOVERNMENT'S COMMITTEE ON PUBLIC EMPLOYEE RELATIONS 68 (March 31, 1966).

27. 233 GERR B-1 (1968).
28. See note 25 *supra*. *Cf.* Raskin, *How To Avoid Strikes by Garbagemen, Nurses*, The New York Times, February 25, 1968, (Magazine) at 34.
29. 280 GERR (Special Supplement, January 20, 1969).
30. (Firefighters) R. I. GEN. LAWS § 28-9.1-7; (policemen) § 28-9.2-7, as amended by H. B. 1331, L. 1968, effective June 4, 1968.
31. (Firefighters and policemen) PURDON'S PENN. STAT. ANN. tit. 43, §§ 217.4, 217.7.
32. WYO. STAT. § 27-269 (firefighters).
33. (Policemen, firefighters and other municipal employees) P. A. 312 of 1969, effective October 1, 1969. This act requires compulsory arbitration on an experimental basis from October 1, 1969, through June 30, 1972.
34. Maine has enacted a statute, effective October 1, 1969, providing for the arbitration of impasse disputes if the parties agree to arbitrate. However, the award is nonbinding and merely advisory as to salaries, pensions and insurance.
35. However, the Canadian experience raises questions as to the accuracy of this claim. See remarks of H. D. Woods at Governor's Conference on Public Employment Relations, October 14, 1968.

One response to this argument is that the need for uninterrupted service justifies the impairment of free collective bargaining. But, more significantly, arbitration does not necessarily mean the end of collective bargaining if used sparingly and if the parties are not certain about its availability—or the terms under which it will be available —if collective bargaining fails. When all other procedures have been exhausted, there may be no other effective approach. And while unions might still strike against the award, public pressure for severe penalties might be greater than in the case of nonbinding fact-finding recommendations, the status of which is much lower.

The Real Confrontation— with the Taxpayers

But in public employment, there is an even more formidable objection to compulsory arbitration. For here one confronts the authority of elected officials to raise revenues and lay taxes. Putting aside the legal issues, it is questionable whether public officials and taxpayers will permit their power to be delegated away to "outsiders". Compulsory "interest" arbitration would require some modification of contemporary beliefs about representative government.

Assuming that such arbitration is a practicable idea, what criteria should the arbitrator use? For the most part, the criteria would consist of the very same factors that most fact finders take into account: (1) comparability with similar job classifications and occupations in private industry; (2) comparability with the wage patterns for the geographical labor market; (3) cost of living considerations; (4) ability to pay, both in terms of monies immediately available in the budget and the government's ability to raise revenues in the future through its tax base.[36] It seems to me that a basic prerequisite for the success of interest arbitration in public employment is that the public interest and welfare should be among the criteria to which the arbitrator is obligated to adhere. The public interest criterion, however, is at the heart of the tensions which are

built into public employment interest arbitration. One question posed by reliance on it is whether it is possible in our kind of society to deal effectively with two public interest questions in one fell swoop: (1) the strike prohibition and the importance of uninterrupted service and (2) responsible economic settlements which are not injurious to the community.

What About a Full-Time Labor Court?

Judge Samuel I. Rosenman has proposed that a full-time labor court whose judges would have life appointments should be established to adjudicate labor disputes which affect the public interest.[37] However, it is contended that arbitration can succeed only if the third party is acceptable to the parties involved at the bargaining table—that, in effect, he must be a creature of their own making, as is the case in grievance arbitration. This concept is not easily reconciled with the public interest criterion and the idea that the arbitrator must guard the treasury against the venality of avaricious unions and overly generous politicians. It is difficult to envisage the success of binding awards which take money from the public treasury and are not in some manner responsive to taxpayer interest not directly represented in the negotiations. Moreover, our urban centers are populated with many people who do not believe that public officials are generally responsive to their needs. We do not have to accept all features of the Rosenman labor court—which, after all, is intended to create public confidence in the fairness of the adjudication—to realize that the parties at the bargaining table are not the only people whose views are entitled to representation. While the arbitrator must have the understanding of the parties, his constituency must be broadly defined. To ignore this elemental principle of democratic society is to increase the risk of taxpayer revolts which veto the most properly reasoned arbitration awards.

There are no "answers" to this problem to impasse resolution in public employee labor disputes. If both sides

would sharpen their collective bargaining skills a bit, I am of the view that the legislators and judges might have less necessity for involving themselves with steps and procedures for the parties to follow.

In my judgment the following proposals flow from some of the observations that I have outlined above:

(1) The state must commit itself to use *ad hoc* mediators during the busy seasons, such as school contract negotiation season. Mediation must be available to all parties who require assistance.

(2) The costs of using fact finding should be imposed on the parties regardless of whether the parties or the state invoke the process. It may be necessary for the state to require the parties to go to fact finding in the public interest. But unions and public employers should be penalized financially for not resolving their problems earlier.

(3) A timetable—like that of the New York Taylor Law—should be established so that fact finding can be invoked in advance of either the budget submission or contract expiration date.

(4) State legislation must provide a great measure of finality as a part of the process, whether it goes under the rubric of fact finding, advisory arbitration or arbitration. If states insist that public employees do not have the right to strike, we must find a way to provide an effective and binding alternative to the strike.

But if this alternative is to be acceptable to the public as well as the parties, I am convinced that at least two reforms must be instituted outside the collective bargaining arena. One reform involves the widespread practice of making local taxes dependent upon referenda or millages. It simply does not make sense to submit an arbitration award to the public in this form. This is especially true in this age

36. See *In the Matter of Fact-Finding Between Inkster Board of Education and Inkster Federation of Teachers, Local 1068,* 236 GERR F-1 (September 23, 1968), which dramatizes the impact of the tax base upon collective bargaining in public employment.
37. *Hearings on S. 176 Before a Subcomm. of the Senate Comm. on the Judiciary,* 90th Cong., 1st Sess. 12 (1967). See generally Fleming, *The Labor Court Idea,* 65 Mich. L. Rev. 1551 (1967).

of taxpayer revolt. Public officials and the electorate must retain substantial control over what is to be expended from the public treasury—but I am not sure that the practice of millages or referenda are the most responsible forum for the exercise of this power.

Secondly, the sad truth is that, for the most part, local taxes are property taxes—and that means that they are predicated upon factors other than ability to pay through income. More-over, to the extent that the local property tax can be equated with wealth, the fact of the matter is that it becomes increasingly difficult for local officials to convince public employees they should accept less than those workers who live in another community a few miles down the road.

It will be difficult, if not impossible, to obtain taxpayer support for any process which both treats public employees equitably (and it seems to me that part of equity is comparability) and speaks in terms of finality if traditional methods of local government finance are retained. They are particularly burdensome to individuals who are on fixed incomes.

Unless we more carefully train our sights on possibilities for reform in these areas, I am fearful that the most thoughtful proposals for labor law reform will run aground on the reefs of taxpayer resistance.

Bibliographic Essay on Public Sector Collective Bargaining

One of the more ambitious efforts dealing with the peculiarities of the collective bargaining process in the public sector has been that of Harry M. Wellington and Ralph K. Winter.[1] The authors have attempted to establish a framework for collective bargaining in the public sector. While a portion of the article deals with the impact of collective bargaining on the role of government, the appropriate scope of bargaining, and the implications of allowing strikes, much of the authors' discussion is devoted to an analysis of dispute resolution mechanisms in an environment where strikes are illegal.

Wellington and Winter examined four methods of dispute resolution as alternatives to the strike: factfinding, binding arbitration, legislated settlements, and choice of procedures. They emphasized that even in the face of a legislated strike ban, strikes will best be avoided by encouraging the parties to rely on collective bargaining rather than on the impasse procedures. Should bargaining fail to result in a settlement, then the impasse procedure should serve as a means for reaching an agreement that is acceptable to the union, the executive, and the legislature.[2]

The authors contended that the "chilling effect" that the availability of such procedures will have on genuine collective bargaining could be reduced. With respect to factfinding, Wellington and Winter endorsed the use of a neutral tribunal to determine whether or not an impasse does, in fact, exist, and suggested that the procedure should be made relatively expensive to the parties.[3] To avoid the chilling effect of binding arbitration, they offered the idea of "one-or-the-other" arbitration (often referred to as "final offer" arbitration). In requiring the arbitrator to choose one or the other parties' final proposal, this method creates the risk that a party's entire position will be rejected and thereby encourages good faith bargaining.[4]

Wellington and Winter concluded, however, that it would be difficult to reduce the chilling effect that legislated settlements would have on the parties. The willingness of the parties to rely on such a procedure would depend solely on their perception of the legislative attitude. If viewed as "pro-union," the union would be more likely to abandon the bargaining table; if viewed as "anti-union," it would be the employer who would possibly forego a negotiated settlement.[5]

Finally, Wellington and Winter found that the choice-of-procedures approach offered the best chance of reducing the incidence of strikes and the least risk of chilling the collective bargaining process. Not only does it offer the flexibility to tailor the impasse procedure to the particular dispute, but in refusing to pre-ordain what procedure will be used, this approach decreases the risk of relying upon it and thereby creates an additional incentive for the parties to reach a negotiated settlement.[6]

Professor Clyde Summers characterized public sector determination of public employee terms and conditions of employment as decision-making shaped by political forces.[7] He examined the collective bargaining process and wage negotiation procedures and focused upon (1) the allocation of authority to negotiate and conclude agreements on behalf of the public employer, (2) the determination of the appropriate bargaining unit, (3) defining subjects for bargaining, and (4) defining publicity to be given to the bargaining process.

Summers maintained that collective bargaining is a prerequiste to providing employees with participation in the budget writing process. This procedure, containing within it the exclusive majority union bargaining agent within the bargaining unit, a "good faith" bargaining requirement imposed upon the public employer, a closed bilateral process that does not include other interest groups, and a binding agreement, is justified because the public employees are at a disadvantage in the political process without collective bargaining.

The highly visible claims of outnumbered public employees put them in direct confrontation with virtually all other interest groups in the budget process. When terms and conditions of employment are decided through a process of majority will, public employees must contend with both those groups opposing increased taxes and those seeking increased services. With collective bargaining the union instead confronts "rational discussion" and the "summarized and consolidated" interest of opposition groups as represented by the public employer.[8]

Summers then compared the political budget process of the independent school district model, with its own taxing authority and elected school board. Though noting the confrontation between groups who oppose increased employee wages and groups that support increased salary levels, he recognized the opportunity for a "natural alliance" between teachers and parents and stated that for this reason, bargaining for teachers may be unlike other public employee collective bargaining.[9] This analysis assumed that (1) "decisions as to general wage levels are an integral part of the budget-making process" and that (2) "most voters are taxpayers and therefore have reason to oppose increased wages which result in increased taxes."[10]

Summers outlined the effect of fragmented employee representation and employer decision-making on the political process through which terms and conditions of employment are determined. Success of of employee groups, in the absence of collective bargaining, depends upon the relative political strengths of the groups and their abilities to join with client voter groups to achieve results. High visibility settlements achieved through the collective bargaining process present the advantage of pressure for uniform treatment of bargaining units, regardless of differences in group political strengths where decisions are centralized or coordinated on the employer side. Summers contended that fragmentation of authority on the public employer side is marked by a tendency of department heads to favor the demands of employees, downplay the demands of other departments, and escape direct pressure from taxpayers in bargaining with the employee's representative, thereby greatly increasing the employee advantage. The absence of collective bargaining puts public employees at a disadvantage in the political process, while on the other hand, collective bargaining with public-employer-fragmented negotiations gives employees an advantage. Summers instead suggested that unified bargaining on the employer's side where bargaining decisions are made by a politically responsible representative would lead to a full representation of opposing interest at the bargaining table and offset to some degree the employee's special advantage.

After describing the political process where other terms and conditions of employment are the subject of bargaining (i.e., indirect wage payments, deferred wage costs, reductions and increases in service levels, goals and methods determinations, and personnel practices and administration) Summers proceeded to present his conclusions regarding an appropriate structure for determining the terms and conditions of public sector employment.

Finally, Summers advocated (1) the centralization of bargaining authority, (2) control of bargaining by a politically responsible official, (3) multiple bargaining units and pattern bargaining, (4) limitation of collective bargaining to those subject areas that inspired massed resistance from the public, and (5) distribution of negotiation status information to the general public. In order to produce fair and responsible results for public employees, Summers recommends the collective bargaining process outlined above as a suggested structure for public sector decision-making in the determination of employee wages and other conditions of employment. The aim of collective bargaining in Summers' view should be to assist those groups that are least able to exert significant influence in the normal political process and thus to equalize the political effectiveness of employee groups.

Joan McAvoy explored further the problems and promise of binding arbitration as a method of settling public sector contractual disputes.[11] After reviewing the Canadian and Australian experiences with arbitration, McAvoy considered the desirability of arbitration in the context of three basic policy questions: (1) does binding arbitration weaken our form of government?; (2) will it undermine collective bargaining?; and (3) will it inhibit strikes?

Arbitration, McAvoy concluded, may actually strengthen rather than inhibit democracy, because the settlement has been reached by a neutral who is trying to be responsive to the needs of both parties. Moreover, based on experience in Michigan and Wyoming, the availability of arbitration was not found to deter collective bargaining. A majority of disputes were settled through negotiations. Finally, the evidence also suggested that public employees would not strike in the face of an arbitration award, and that arbitration, therefore, was an effective means of discouraging public sector strikes.[12]

Peter Fenille evaluated the effectiveness of final offer arbitration in reducing the chilling effect that dispute resolution mechanisms have on good faith negotiations.[13] Fenille compared conventional binding arbitration with final offer arbitration based on the proportion of cases that went to arbitration and the median number of issues taken to arbitration in jurisdictions using those procedures. Fenille found that both the proportion of cases and the median number of issues that were submitted to arbitration were substantially lower in jurisdictions utilizing final offer arbitration. Fenille concluded, therefore, that final offer procedures were more effective in producing negotiated agreements than conventional arbitration procedures.[14]

Richard A. Lester, in an important new book[14a] concluded that experience in eight states and New York City showed that certain features and practices in public employmemt relation laws and their implementation contribute to effective functioning and achievement of the purposes of the programs. Professor Lester identified five facilitating factors which seemed evident from the experience of one or more of the nine jurisdictions:

1. Joint development and participation by labor and management—Professor Lester found that this helped explain the success of the procedures in New York City and Massachusetts;

2. The opportunity for both sides to make choices, which was evident in Minnesota, Wisconsin, New Jersey, and Massachussetts—professor Lester provided examples such as the opportunity to choose amongst various forms of arbitration or impasse procedures, participation in the choice of arbitrator and involvement through a pripartite panel, and the opportunity to determine the content of the award;

3. Med-arb was important inasmuch as it allowed for the facilitation of negotiations and agreements. Said Profesor Lester: "A tripartite arbitration panel under conventional arbitration can provide some of the advantages of med-arb but not all of those that are possible, with med-arb having, at least at the mediation stage, the leverage of last-offer-package arbitration."[14b]

4. The avilability of the right to strike, such as was present in Minnesota, often aided the parties in arriving at a voluntary settlement without undue risk of injury to orderly government.

5. The quality of the mediators and arbitrators in the staff that administered the statute and the consequent confidence in and respect for impartiality and abilities of professionals involved.

The political shortcomings of binding arbitration were explored by Joseph R. Grodin.[15] Grodin noted that when a public employer who is either elected or directly responsible to another elected official submits a dispute over the terms of a collective bargaining agreement to an arbitration, he surrenders his authority to ultimately approve or disapprove the agreement, thereby insulating policy making from ultimate political control.[16]

Grodin offered suggestions for making the arbitration more politically responsive. He recommended the use of tripartite panels rather than single neutrals. In this way, the neutral arbitrator would be forced to consider the interests of his partisan colleagues, insuring some indirect input from the electorate.[17]

Grodin rejected the idea of electing arbitrators. He pointed out that elected arbitrators, now responsible to the electorate, would lose their neutral character since the electorate is, in effect, the employer.[18] Nor did he favor making the scope of arbitration more narrow than that of bargaining. It would be impossible to establish criteria for deciding which issues should be excluded. Moreover, since arbitration is a substitute for the right to strike, unions should be able to arbitrate any issue over which it might otherwise strike.[19]

Grodin did, however, urge the delineation of specific criteria to guide an arbitrator's decision, one of which should be the employer's ability to pay.[20] Post-arbitral review should be available to insure that the arbitrator stays within the bounds of these criteria.[21] Finally, Grodin favored allowing the public employer to decide on whether an impasse will be settled by arbitration or whether a strike will be permitted instead. In this way, only truly essential employees would be prevented from striking.[22]

Richard Pegnetter examined the criteria upon which factfinders rely in the context of teacher salary disputes in New York State.[23] Pegnetter analyzed 156 factfinding reports and found that salary comparisons with nearby schools were the most frequently cited criteria. Other significant criteria were the employer's ability to pay and increases in the cost of living.[24]

Deborah M. Kolb observed several mediators, in thirty-one mediation sessions, and discovered some significant differences in the style of federal and state mediators.[25] Kolb found that federal mediators utilize joint meetings of the parties rather than separate caucuses more frequently in structuring negotiating sessions. Moreover, federal mediators rely upon the parties themselves to reduce the number of outstanding issues. While the federal mediator often initiates the idea of dropping some demands, he will not normally participate in the caucus where the parties decide which demands to abandon. The state mediator, on the other hand, will generally play a very active role in such meetings, constantly prodding the parties to compromise further. Kolb also found that federal mediators rely more heavily upon experienced negotiators to control and direct their own bargaining committees than do state mediators.[26]

These differences were reflected in the mediators' self-perceptions. State mediators saw themselves as "dealmakers," playing a fundamental role in hammering out a compromise. Federal mediators, however, viewed themselves as "orchestrators," looking only to facilitate communication between the parties rather than to strike "deals."[27]

Kolb offered several explanations for these differences. She noted that state mediators, by working previously in the public sector, were more likely to be dealing with inexperienced negotiators who were often not faced with a strike deadline. As a result, the mediator was forced to play a more active role in achieving a settlement. Kolb also recognized that the role of mediator in state agencies is often "intertwined" with that of arbitrator. Perhaps the "contract-writing" role of the arbitrator is not easily abandoned when the state neutral puts on his mediator cap.[28]

Finally, Sam and John Kagel have endorsed the use of mediation-arbitration or "med-arb" in settling contract disputes—an idea, however, that is not of recent vintage and whose themes are part of the final offer proposal.[29] In this process, the "mediator-arbiter" has several advantages: he is no longer constrained by the semi-legal posture of arbitration and he has much more "muscle" in his mediation role, since ultimately he may be called upon to determine the terms of the contract. The procedure forces the parties to disclose their "true" positions and justify them rather than playing games, as is so often the case in conventional mediation. In doing so, the chances of a negotiated settlement are greatly increased because the med-arbiter has a much better idea of where the parties truly stand.[30]

This theory was borne out in the Kagels' arbitration practice. They reported significant personal success with med-arb in several contract disputes, achieving negotiated rather than arbitrated settlements.[31]

NOTES

1. Only twelve states have failed to enact some form of legislation providing for mediation, factfinding, or arbitration in public employee disputes: Alabama,

Arizona, Arkansas, Colorado, Louisiana, Mississippi, Missouri, North Carolina, South Carolina, Utah, West Virginia and Virginia. 1 Public Employee Bargaining (CCH) § 4000 (1980).

2. H. Wellington and R. Winter, "Structuring Collective Bargaining in Public Employment," 79 Yale L. J. 805 (1970). *See generally* Anderson, "The Impact of Public Sector Bargaining: An Essay Dedicated to Nathan Feinsinger," Wisc. L. Rev. 987 (1973).

3. *Id.* at 829.

4. *Id.* at 833-834.

5. *Id.* at 838.

6. *Id.* at 833-39.

7. Summers, "Public Employee Bargaining: A Political Perspective," 83 Yale L. J. 1156 (1974).

8. *Id.* at 1168.

9. *Id.* at 1170.

10. *Id.* at 1170-71.

11. McAvoy, "Binding Arbitration of Contract Terms: A New Approach to the Resolution of Disputes in the Public Sector," 72 Colum. L. Rev. 1192 (1972).

12. *Id.* at 1208-11.

13. Fenille, "Final Offer Arbitration and the Chilling Effect," 14 Ind. Rel. 302 (1975).

14. *Id.* at 307-09.

14a. Richard A. Lester, *Labor Arbitration in State and Local Government: An Examination of Experiences in Eight States and New York City* (Industrial Relations Section, Princeton University, Princeton, N.J., 1984)

14b. *Id.* at 109

15. Grodin, "Political Aspects of Public Sector Interest Arbitration," 64 Cal. L. Rev. 678 (1976).

16. *Id.* at 681-83.

17. *Id.* at 692.

18. *Id.* at 673-94.

19. *Id.* at 696-97.

20. *Id.* at 695.

21. *Id.* at 698-99.

22. *Id.* at 700-01.

23. Pegnetter, "Fact-Finding and Teacher Salary Disputes: The 1969 Experience in New York State," 24 Ind. & Lab. Rel. Rev. 226 (1971).

24. *Id.* at 236-38.

25. Kolb, "Roles Mediators Play: State and Federal Practice," 20 Ind. Rel. 1 (1981).

26. *Id.* at 5-8.

27. *Id.* at 4.

28. *Id.* at 10, 15.

29. Kagel and Kagel, "Using Two New Arbitration Techniques," 95 Monthly Labor Review 11 (1972).

30. *Id.* at 11-12.

31. *Id.* at 12-13.

4

The Status of Unauthorized and "Wildcat" Strikes under the National Labor Relations Act

"Just as in union there is strength, in disunity there is difficulty."*

These are troubled times for the leaders of organized labor. They are compelled to adapt to their recently acquired respectability and negotiate statesmanlike economic settlements which will not injure the economy through a new self-defeating wage-price spiral.[1] But, at the same time, their flexibility at the bargaining table has become inhibited by a growing restiveness on the part of the rank-and-file.[2] The outbreak of local automobile strikes in 1964 and the membership's repudiation in 1966 of an airline agreement, negotiated under the watchful gaze of President Johnson, both demonstrate that the rank-and-file have increasingly independent notions about the bargains that are being negotiated on their behalf. Secretary of Labor W. Willard Wirtz has described the threat as "very, very dangerous for collective bargaining"[3] and has also expressed the view that such conduct might trigger increased public animosity toward the labor movement.[4] A. H. Raskin has written that:

---

* Judge Aldrich in Simmons, Inc. v. NLRB, 315 F.2d 143, 144 (1st Cir. 1963).

[1] See "Economic Report: The President's Annual Message to Congress," in 73 Weekly Compilation of Presidential Documents 105, 109-10 (January 26, 1967).

[2] See Raskin, "Rumbles From the Rank and File," The Reporter, Jan. 28, 1965, p. 27; Miller, "Surprise Strike: Not Even Top UAW Leaders Really Expected GM Walkout," Wall Street Journal, Oct. 5, 1964, p. 18, col. 4. Most recently, see "G.M. Workers End Wildcat Strike at Mansfield After Union Hearing," Daily Labor Report, Feb. 23, 1967, p. A-9; Hoffman, "G.M. Strikers in Ohio Trickle Back to Jobs at Behest of U.A.W.," N.Y. Times, March 8, 1967, p. 25, col. 1; Hoffman, "U.A.W. Takes Over Rebel Ohio Local," N.Y. Times, March 9, 1967, p. 29, col. 1.

[3] Jones, "Wirtz Upset by Workers' Rejection of Accords," N.Y. Times, Jan. 3, 1967, p. 16, col. 4.

[4] Ibid.

[C]ommunity concern about what's wrong with labor tends to operate in alternating currents and today's fuse-blower is excess power in the hands of the rank-and-file, rather than the leaders. Federal mediators report that the number of strikes from membership unwillingness to ratify pacts proposed by union negotiators has been edging upward for the last two years.[5]

Thus, it seems that the diminishing frequency of wildcat strikes,[6] believed to be a concomitant of union maturity, has failed to materialize. This development makes desirable a reexamination of the assumptions and reasoning current under the Labor Management Relations Act[7] which permit the rank-and-file to maintain its present disruptive independence. The relationship between statutory interpretation, which can encourage responsibility on the part of union leadership as well as pretermit the sometimes rash audacity of dissidents, and the national labor policy is of obvious importance. Before attempting an analysis of this relation-

---

[5] Raskin, "Why Labor Doesn't Follow Its Leaders," N.Y. Times, Jan. 8, 1967, § 4, p. 6, col. 1.

[6] The term "wildcat" strike, as used herein, is meant to be synonymous with an unauthorized strike. Sometimes a "wildcat" strike is intended to describe a strike which is in breach of contract. See Slichter, Healy & Livernash, The Impact of Collective Bargaining on Management 663-91 (1960); Magnum, "Taming Wildcat Strikes," 38 Harv. Bus. Rev. 88 (1960). However, many of the leading cases dealing with unauthorized work stoppages use the term "wildcat." See, e.g., NLRB v. Draper Corp., 145 F.2d 199, 205 (4th Cir. 1944). See also the definition contained in Roberts, Dictionary of Industrial Relations 461 (1966):

A work stoppage, generally spontaneous in character, by a group of union employees without union authorization or approval. Frequently it is called by a group of employees because of some minor problem such as the disciplining of a union member. A wildcat strike may exist where a local union has supported a strike but has not received the approval of the national or international union. A wildcat strike generally is in violation of applicable agreement.

Although it is a contention of this article that a detailed examination of a union's internal procedures in connection with wildcat strikes is improper under existing law, it becomes important to determine which entity is empowered to authorize a strike—the international or the local—along with the question of the identity of the principal bargaining representative for employees. Cf. United Packinghouse Workers v. Maurer-Neuer, Inc., 272 F.2d 647 (10th Cir. 1959); "Strike-Control Provisions in Union Constitutions," 77 Monthly Labor Review 497 (1954). Describing the general practice in connection with union authorization, Judge Sobeloff has stated the following:

The calling of a strike is such a momentous step in a labor controversy that it is usually subjected to strike control by international unions. The strike is a weapon that can bring an employer to his knees; but the effect on the employer can be too devastating for the union's own good. In addition, a strike can result in undue loss of production, harmful to the public, and a strike can waste a union's funds and otherwise weaken it in its continuing effort to better its adherents' wages and working conditions.

It is widely felt that vesting control in the international over the strike weapon assures that generally only intelligent and responsible use will be made of it after the greater interests of the international and the general economy have been considered. Such is the potential harm from indiscriminate resort to strikes that Professor Summers has commented that an international is justified in adopting severe disciplinary measures, including expulsion of individual members or revocation of a local union's charter, when an unauthorized strike has been undertaken. Summers, "Legal Limitations on Union Discipline," 64 Harv. L. Rev. 1049, 1065-66 (1951).

Parks v. International Bhd. of Elec. Workers, 314 F.2d 886, 905 (4th Cir.), cert. denied, 372 U.S. 976 (1963).

[7] Taft-Hartley Act, 61 Stat. 136 (1947), 29 U.S.C. §§ 141-87 (1964), amending National Labor Relations Act (Wagner Act), 49 Stat. 449 (1935).

ship, however, it is proper to examine the factors which may have accentuated the lack of communication between union and member.

Besides mildly inflationary economic conditions, the most apparent factors are the implications of the Landrum-Griffin Act[8] and the rise of industry-wide and multi-enterprise bargaining in this country.[9] The philosophy of Landrum-Griffin, as evidenced by the Act's protection of the individual against the union and its inevitable preoccupation with the fallibility of labor leaders, may well have precipitated, to some degree, the current restiveness of the membership. A wider unit for bargaining has intensified the international union's involvement in negotiations, and hardly anyone in the union is more out of touch with rank-and-file thinking than the international officials.[10] Ironically, past proponents of union democracy seem to have assumed that effectuation of the multi-enterprise bargaining principle would act as a *brake* on union irresponsibility exercised by an arrogant few.[11] Similarly, those who sought to atomize the union and its bargaining unit were unaware of the inflationary pressures that competitive local union wage negotiations would generate.[12] The progeny of these ideas apparently is an aroused rank-and-file and consequent industrial discontent. "[T]he rank and file once again feels itself stripped of dignity by submersion in the mass mold of factory life."[13]

I

THE LEGAL FRAMEWORK

The union, especially the international union, is the broker between interest groups—the institution that can afford a long view of the greatest good.[14] As such, it is in the best position to resolve the disputes that arise between warring factions of workers, *i.e.*, disputes concerning wage differentials for skilled and unskilled employees, the seniority districts that are to be embodied in the contract,[15] and the fringe benefits which are of varying importance to the younger and older, and the married and single, workers. Yet the outbreak of rebellion indicates the presence of both real and imaginary grievances with the system. The decisions of the National

[8] Labor-Management Reporting and Disclosure Act, 73 Stat. 519 (1959), 29 U.S.C. §§ 153, 158-60 passim (1964).
[9] Slichter, Healy & Livernash, supra note 6, at 926-30.
[10] Cf. Raskin, supra note 2.
[11] See Raskin, supra note 5.
[12] See Cox, Law and the National Labor Policy 52 (1960).
[13] Raskin, supra note 2.
[14] See Parks v. International Bhd. of Elec. Workers, 314 F.2d 886, 905, 925 (4th Cir.), cert. denied, 372 U.S. 976 (1963).
[15] See Gould, "Employment Security, Seniority and Race: The Role of Title VII of the Civil Rights Act of 1964," 13 Howard L.J. 1 (1967).

Labor Relations Board and the courts reflect the contending forces at work.

A. *Relevant Legal Principles*

There are three principles to be understood in connection with wildcat stoppages. The first is the one enunciated in *NLRB v. Washington Aluminum Co.*[16] There the Supreme Court held that a walkout by seven employees in a small and unorganized plant was protected activity under Section 7 of the Labor Management Relations Act[17] and that their employer therefore could not lawfully discharge them in retaliation for such conduct.[18] According to the Court, a discharge imposed because of "concerted activities for the purpose of collective bargaining or other mutual aid or protection"[19] would be an unfair labor practice in violation of section 8(a)(1) of the statute. Justice Black for the Court noted that the workers were protesting poor working conditions, that "they had no bargaining representative . . . of any kind to present their grievances to their employer,"[20] and that the walkout was not in breach of contract.[21] Thus, *Washington Aluminum* teaches that union activity in an established grievance procedure is not prerequisite to the exercise of statutory rights by workers under the Labor Management Relations Act. A protest against employment conditions, whether meritorious or ill-founded, is protected activity.[22]

---

[16] 370 U.S. 9 (1962).

[17] 61 Stat. 140 (1947), 29 U.S.C. § 157 (1964):
Employees shall have the right to self-organization, to form, join, or assist labor organizations, to bargain collectively through representatives of their own choosing, and to engage in other concerted activities for the purpose of collective bargaining or other mutual aid or protection, and shall also have the right to refrain from any or all of such activities except to the extent that such right may be affected by an agreement requiring membership in a labor organization as a condition of employment as authorized in section 8(a)(3) of this title.

[18] Labor Management Relations Act § 8(a), 61 Stat. 140 (1947), 29 U.S.C. § 158(a) 1964: "It shall be an unfair labor practice for an employer—(1) to interfere with, restrain, or coerce employees in the exercise of the rights guaranteed in section 7 . . . ."
Employees engaging in unprotected activity are subject to discharge. Employees who strike with economic motivations are engaged in protected activity but nevertheless may be replaced permanently. NLRB v. MacKay Radio & Tel. Co., 304 U.S. 333 (1938); cf. NLRB v. Brown, 380 U.S. 278, 283-85, 292 n.6 (1965); see especially Note, "Replacement of Workers During Strikes," 75 Yale L.J. 630 (1966). Employees who participate in strikes caused by unfair labor practices are entitled to reinstatement and back pay. Cf. NLRB v. Thayer Co., 213 F.2d 748 (1st Cir.), cert. denied, 348 U.S. 883 (1954); Local 833, UAW v. NLRB, 300 F.2d 699 (D.C. Cir.), cert. denied, 370 U.S. 911 (1962).

[19] See note 17 supra.

[20] NLRB v. Washington Aluminum Co., 370 U.S. 9, 14 (1962).

[21] Id. at 17; cf. NLRB v. Sands Mfg. Co., 306 U.S. 332, 343-44 (1938).

[22] NLRB v. Solo Cup Co., 237 F.2d 521 (8th Cir. 1956); NLRB v. Kohler Co., 220 F.2d 3 (7th Cir. 1955) (dictum); NLRB v. Marshall Car Wheel & Foundry Co., 218 F.2d 409 (5th Cir. 1955) (dictum); NLRB v. Cowles Publishing Co., 214 F.2d 708 (9th Cir. 1954); NLRB v. Southern Silk Mills, Inc., 209 F.2d 155 (6th Cir. 1953); Modern Motors, Inc. v. NLRB, 198 F.2d 925 (8th Cir. 1952); Carter Carburetor Corp. v. NLRB, 140 F.2d 714 (8th Cir. 1944); NLRB v. Peter Cailler Kohler Swiss Chocolates Co., 130 F.2d 503 (2d Cir. 1942); Firth Carpet Co. v. NLRB, 129 F.2d 633 (2d Cir. 1942); NLRB v. Brashear

The second important principle in this area has been expounded by the Court while interpreting sections 8(a)(5)[23] and 9(a),[24] both of which make it unlawful for an employer to bargain with any entity other than the exclusive bargaining representative. In this connection, the Court has said that while it is "possible" for unions and employers to leave certain areas open to individual bargaining,[25] this possibility presents the exception rather than the general rule:

[E]xcept as so provided, advantages to individuals may prove as disruptive of industrial peace as disadvantages. They are a fruitful way of interfering with organization and choice of representatives . . . . The workman is free, if he values his own bargaining position more than that of the group, to vote against representation; but the majority rules, and if it collectivizes the employment bargain, individual advantages or favors will generally in practice go in as a contribution to the collective result.[26]

Moreover, the Court has also stated:

[I]t is a violation of the essential principle of collective bargaining and an infringement of the Act for the employer to disregard the bargaining representative by negotiating with individual employees, whether a majority or a minority, with respect to wages, hours and working conditions . . . . Bargaining carried on by the employer directly with the employees whether a minority or majority, who have not revoked their designation of a bargaining agent, would be subversive of the mode of collective bargaining which the statute has ordained . . . .[27]

Despite the fact that the concept of exclusive bargaining is so far-reaching, section 9(a) limits its sweep through a proviso which permits "any individual employee or a group of employees . . . [to] have the

Freight Lines, Inc., 119 F.2d 379 (8th Cir. 1941); Golay & Co., 156 N.L.R.B. No. 123, enforced as modified, 63 L.R.R.M. 2537 (1966); Plastilite Corp., 153 N.L.R.B. 180 (1965); Tomar Prods., Inc., 151 N.L.R.B. 57 (1965); Lamar Creamery, 148 N.L.R.B. 323 (1964); Phaostron Instrument & Electronic Co., 146 N.L.R.B. 996 (1964); Schoenfeld Cordage Co., 143 N.L.R.B. 117 (1963); Delsea Iron Works, Inc., 136 N.L.R.B. 453 (1962).

23 61 Stat. 140-41 (1947), 29 U.S.C. § 158(a) (1964): "It shall be an unfair labor practice for an employer . . . (5) to refuse to bargain collectively with the representatives of his employees, subject to the provisions of section 9(a)."

24 61 Stat. 143 (1947), 29 U.S.C. § 159(a):
Representatives designated or selected for the purposes of collective bargaining by the majority of the employees in a unit appropriate for such purposes, shall be the exclusive representatives of all the employees in such unit for the purposes of collective bargaining in respect to rates of pay, wages, hours of employment, or other conditions of employment . . . .

25 J. I. Case Co. v. NLRB, 321 U.S. 332 (1944).

26 Id. at 338-39; cf. Gale Products, 142 N.L.R.B. 1246 (1963), enforcement denied, 357 F.2d 390 (7th Cir. 1964); Gould, "The Question of Union Activity on Company Property," 18 Vand. L. Rev. 73, 135-45 (1964).

27 Medo Photo Supply Corp. v. NLRB, 321 U.S. 678, 684 (1944). The union's delegation which flows from such power is a duty of fair representation to employees for whom it bargains. See Graham v. Brotherhood of Locomotive Firemen, 338 U.S. 232 (1949); Tunstall v. Brotherhood of Locomotive Firemen, 323 U.S. 210 (1944); Steele v. Louisville & N.R.R., 323 U.S. 192 (1944); Independent Metal Workers Union, 147 N.L.R.B. 1573 (1964); Miranda Fuel Co., 140 N.L.R.B. 181 (1962), enforcement denied, 326 F.2d 172 (2d Cir. 1963).

right at any time to present grievances to their employer and to have such grievances adjusted, without the intervention of the bargaining representative, as long as the adjustment is not inconsistent with the terms of a collective-bargaining contract or agreement then in effect . . . ."[28] Section 9(a) further provides that the exclusive bargaining representative must have the opportunity to be present at such an "adjustment." The uneasy accommodation that exists between the concept of an exclusive bargaining representative and the provisos to section 9(a) assumes some importance in the wildcat strike and ratification context.[29]

The third important principle is the view of Congress—as consistently interpreted by the Supreme Court[30]—that the Board and the courts are generally not authorized to regulate the economic weapons which are relied upon by either party in the union-employer relationship. In considering whether union harassing tactics could serve as the basis for a violation of the union's duty to bargain in good faith, the Court has warned against an approach which "involves an intrusion into the substantive aspects of the bargaining process . . . ."[31] Most recently, the Court has admonished the Board for attempting to shape the balance of economic power in collective bargaining relationships.[32] While addressing itself to union harassment, which the Board regarded as unlawful, the Court has said that the conduct in question must be so indefensible as to warrant "condemnation of the precise tactics involved . . . ."[33] But this requirement was enunciated in connection with an attempt by the Board to characterize economic weapons as unlawful rather than merely unprotected. The significance of an unprotected status is that employees are subject to discharge by the employer. This "no-man's land"—neither protected nor prohibited activity—is the hazy area into which the Board has been instructed not to tread. Despite the fact that the right to strike is protected by statute,[34] strikes for unlawful objectives,[35] strikes in

---

[28] 61 Stat. 143 (1947), 29 U.S.C. § 159(a) (1964); see note 24 supra.

[29] Recognition of individual rights provides a double-edged meaning for wildcat strikes. One might view this recognition as authority for activity of which the bargaining agent does not necessarily approve. But, on the other hand, § 9 establishes a peaceful method for the resolution of disputes.

[30] American Ship Bldg. Co. v. NLRB, 380 U.S. 300, 317 (1965); NLRB v. Insurance Agents' Union, 361 U.S. 477, 497-98 (1960); NLRB v. American Nat'l Ins. Co., 343 U.S. 395, 408-09 (1952).

[31] NLRB v. Insurance Agents' Union, supra note 30, at 490.

[32] NLRB v. American Ship Bldg. Co., supra note 30, at 310, 316-18.

[33] NLRB v. Insurance Agents' Union, supra note 30, at 490.

[34] Labor Management Relations Act § 13, 61 Stat. 151 (1947), 29 U.S.C. § 163 (1964): "Nothing in this Act, except as specifically provided for herein, shall be construed so as either to interfere with or impede or diminish in any way the right to strike, or to affect the limitations or qualifications on that right." See NLRB v. Fruit & Vegetable Packers, 377 U.S. 58 (1964); NLRB v. Drivers Local Union, 362 U.S. 274, 281-82 (1960); cf. Thornhill v. Alabama, 310 U.S. 88, 103-06 (1940); AFL v. Swing, 312 U.S. 321 (1941).

[35] NLRB v. Indiana Desk Co., 149 F.2d 987 (7th Cir. 1945); American News Co., 55

breach of contract,[36] "quickie" work stoppages,[37] and refusals to work overtime[38] have all been adjudged inside the boundaries of this "no-man's land" of unprotected activity.

B. *Applicable Rules of Law*

The rules of law applicable to unauthorized and wildcat stoppages, however, have been defined with far less clarity. In the leading case of *NLRB v. Draper Corp.*,[39] the union had been exclusive bargaining representative for a short period of time and had negotiated a one-year contract. But a petition, which was intended to generate opposition to the union on the theory that a pay raise would be forthcoming without its presence, had been circulated among the employees. As negotiations for a new contract began, the employer made reference to the petition in a bargaining session and, at one point, indicated that it had some doubts about the union's majority status. This attitude subsided, but some of the membership became irritated with what they regarded to be the "stalling" of negotiation sessions by the employer. Subsequent to the employer's postponement of a meeting, forty-one employees in the foundry department voted 28 to 13 to strike. These employees constituted twenty-five per cent of the work force in the bargaining unit. The employer discharged the strikers, and the union charged the employer with an unfair labor practice, alleging that the discharges interfered with employee activities protected under section 7.

The Board said that the walkout was:

[C]aused by the employees' dissatisfaction with the progress of collective bargaining negotiations between the Union and the respondent, and their

---

N.L.R.B. 1302 (1944). But see Republic Steel Corp., 62 N.L.R.B. 1008 (1945) (notice requirement of War Labor Disputes Act not complied with).

[36] NLRB v. Sands Mfg. Co., 306 U.S. 332 (1939).

[37] Cf. NLRB v. Insurance Agents' Union, 361 U.S. 477, 493 n.23, 512 n.8 (1960) (opinion of Mr. Justice Frankfurter); International Union, UAW v. Wisconsin Employment Relations Bd. (Briggs-Stratton), 336 U.S. 245 (1949); Textile Workers Union v. NLRB, 227 F.2d 409 (D.C. Cir. 1955) (dictum), modifying 108 N.L.R.B. 743 (1954). See also Home Beneficial Life Ins. Co. v. NLRB, 159 F.2d 280 (4th Cir.), cert. denied, 332 U.S. 758 (1947); Elk Lumber Co., 91 N.L.R.B. 333 (1950).

[38] C. G. Conn, Ltd. v. NLRB, 108 F.2d 390 (7th Cir. 1939); Honolulu Rapid Transit Co., 110 N.L.R.B. 1806 (1954); cf. NLRB v. Insurance Agents' Union, supra note 37, at 496 n.28. But see Dow Chemical Co., 152 N.L.R.B. 1150 (1965).

[39] 145 F.2d 199 (4th Cir. 1944); cf. Packers Hide Ass'n v. NLRB, 360 F.2d 59 (8th Cir. 1966); NLRB v. Cactus Petroleum, Inc., 355 F.2d 755 (5th Cir. 1966); NLRB v. R. C. Can Co., 328 F.2d 974 (5th Cir. 1964); Western Contracting Corp. v. NLRB, 322 F.2d 893 (10th Cir. 1963); Simmons, Inc. v. NLRB, 315 F.2d 143 (1st Cir. 1963); NLRB v. Sunbeam Lighting Co., 318 F.2d 661 (7th Cir. 1963); NLRB v. Sunset Minerals, Inc., 211 F.2d 224 (9th Cir. 1954); NLRB v. Deena Artware, Inc., 198 F.2d 645 (6th Cir. 1952); NLRB v. J. I. Case Co., 198 F.2d 919 (8th Cir. 1952); NLRB v. Warner Bros. Pictures, Inc., 191 F.2d 217 (9th Cir. 1951); Western Cartridge Co. v. NLRB, 139 F.2d 855 (7th Cir. 1943); Serv-Air, Inc., 64 L.R.R.M. 1200 (1967); Alton Box Board Co., 155 N.L.R.B. No. 94 (1965); Berger Polishing, Inc., 147 N.L.R.B. 21 (1964); American Mfg. Co., 98 N.L.R.B. 226 (1952), enforcement denied, 203 F.2d 212 (5th Cir. 1953).

desire to compel the respondent to arrange for an immediate conference. That the strike was unauthorized by the Union, that it was unprovoked by unfair labor practices and ill-advised is immaterial.[40]

The Fourth Circuit's analysis was entirely different. It observed that the Act was not passed to guarantee to employees the right to do as they please but rather to encourage the principles of collective bargaining and industrial peace.[41] While disclaiming any intention to hold that strikes could be called only by a bargaining union or that the majority of the employees must participate, the court stated that protected status for "wildcat" strikes would undermine the concept of collective bargaining through an exclusive representative which represents the majority of employees. The proviso to section 9 was cited as the proper method under which individuals or a group of employees might present grievances outside the normal bargaining process:

> Even though the majority of the employees in an industry may have selected their bargaining agent and the agent may have been recognized by the employer, there can be no effective bargaining if small groups of employees are at liberty to ignore the bargaining agency thus set up, take particular matters into their own hands and deal independently with the employer. The whole purpose of the act is to give to the employees as a whole, through action of a majority, the right to bargain with the employer with respect to such matters as wages, hours and conditions of work.[42]

The *Draper* rationale is that unauthorized stoppages inherently derogate the union, since the employer is obligated to bargain with it and not with the individual employees, and that since the majority of the employees have designated the union to represent them, a protected status for the wildcat strike dishonors their own choice. While Congress approved *Draper* in enacting the Taft-Hartley amendments,[43] the Board, as we shall see, has zealously attempted to limit its implications. Moreover, Professor Cox, without advocating an analysis in lieu of *Draper*, has indicated misgivings about that case's desirability in the absence of evidence demonstrating that the strike has interfered with collective bargaining. Some of Professor Cox's disagreements with *Draper* relating to the rank-and-file's position in the bargaining process are of interest in light of the current discussion:

> It is easy to agree with the court's conviction that the wildcat strike is a harmful and demoralizing form of industrial strife. Even where its purpose

---

[40] Draper Corp., 52 N.L.R.B. 1477, 1478 (1943).
[41] NLRB v. Draper Corp., 145 F.2d 199, 202-03 (4th Cir. 1944).
[42] Id. at 203.
[43] H.R. Rep. No. 245, 80th Cong., 1st Sess. 27 (1947). Draper is cited with apparent approval by the Supreme Court in International Union, UAW v. Wisconsin Employment Relations Bd., 336 U.S. 245, 257 (1949), and Atkinson v. Sinclair Ref. Co., 370 U.S. 238, 246 (1962).

is not to thwart the desire of the majority expressed through their designated representative, it may disrupt plant relationships and interfere with the normal processes of collective bargaining. But the considerations are not all on one side. Much can be said in favor of aggressive unions whose leaders are constantly pricked to action by militant minorities. It may be sound policy not to submerge the interests of minority groups into the policies or inertia of the union hierarchy until the collective agreement is negotiated—or at least until the union has formally adopted a position. The choice between the conflicting considerations requires a policy judgment as to how the institution of collective bargaining should operate.[44]

In light of the above discussion of the case law and the principles underlying it, this article will analyze the status of wildcat strikes occurring in three situations: (1) during contract negotiations; (2) during the term of the collective bargaining agreement; and (3) when a rival union seeks recognition (a special case that could arise under either (1) or (2)). Consideration will then be given to the problem of what approach or approaches are preferable to those taken by the Board and the courts.

II

STRIKES DURING CONTRACT NEGOTIATIONS

Wildcat strikes commonly occur when the union and employer are negotiating a contract.[45] As *Draper* indicates, the position of the union may often be less than secure and this creates uneasiness for all parties concerned.

A. *The Sunbeam Decision*

In *Sunbeam Lighting Co.*,[46] the IBEW was certified early in 1960 as collective bargaining representative for a unit of 125 employees. A few months later, the union and the employer began to meet regularly in an effort to negotiate the first contract. A good number of employees became dissatisfied with the progress of negotiations and began to ask the bargaining team almost daily about retroactive wage increases.

Prior to a May 2 meeting, the international representative warned the employer of the workers' dissatisfaction and stated that during the previous week a walkout had almost occurred. The employer indicated that striking employees would lose their jobs. At the May 2 meeting, the employer put forward its "final" offer. The international representative agreed to take this offer to the membership, but expressed the view that the employees would not accept. The representative then informed the

---

[44] Cox, "The Right To Engage in Concerted Activities," 26 Ind. L.J. 319, 332 (1951).
[45] The problem also arises in pre-election situations. See New French Benzol Cleaners & Laundry, Inc., 139 N.L.R.B. 1176 (1962); cf. Philianz Oldsmobile, Inc., 137 N.L.R.B. 867 (1962).
[46] 136 N.L.R.B. 1248 (1962), enforcement denied, 318 F.2d 661 (7th Cir. 1963).

employee bargaining committee that the employer's proposals should be kept secret until he returned from international offices. Apparently his instructions were not followed, because a walkout involving 75 to 80 employees took place the next day; however, 28 to 30 of these employees quickly returned to work. Upon learning of the strike, the international representative telegrammed the chairman of the bargaining committee, stating that "there will be no further union or negotiating meeting while the unauthorized work stoppage continues." The employer discharged the striking employees, and the union charged it with unfair labor practices in violation of sections 8(a)(1) and (3).

The Board held the walkout to be protected, noting that the bargaining agent had not taken the "final action which is within its sole authority," and that the employees, having participated in the initial formulation of contract proposals, had the right of "final approval or rejection of any tentative agreement reached."[47] The Board brushed aside the fact that the strike preceded a "formal submission" of the contract terms to the membership, characterizing as artificial a distinction between the walkout in *Sunbeam* and one which followed a "formal" expression of employee views. As to the argument adopted in *Draper*—that unauthorized strikes would undermine collective bargaining—the Board, noting the absence of a dissident group, said there was no disagreement between the union and its members. It reasoned that, because the union did not condemn the strike immediately, the employee committee could infer approval of the decision to strike. The fact that the majority of employees participated in the walkout at its inception was also relied upon.[48]

By divided vote, the Seventh Circuit reversed the Board's ruling that the employer had committed an unfair labor practice. The court, drawing heavily upon the reasoning of the dissenting opinion of Members Rodgers and Leedom,[49] said that the strike was not authorized or sanctioned by the union, and that it was necessarily at odds with the union's representative capacity. Therefore, the activity of the employees was not protected, with the result that the employer did not commit an unfair labor practice by discharging the strikers. In dissent, Judge Swygert asserted that the strike was not a "wildcat," and that *Washington Aluminum* was authority for the proposition that the "rubrics of a formal strike vote or formal authorization by a union representative is [not] pre-

---

47 Id. at 1253.
48 The Board, while emphasizing majority participation, said that "even if less than a majority of all the employees participated in the strike, that fact does not necessarily remove the strike from the protection of Section 7." Id. at 1255-56.
49 Id. at 1258 (dissenting opinion).

requisite to gaining section 7 protection for concerted activity."[50] His opinion noted that the majority of employees had clearly rejected the employer's final offer. Moreover, contrary to the majority opinion and the general tenor of the Board's opinion, Judge Swygert stated that majority participation was not necessary to a conclusion that a strike was a protected activity. According to his dissent, minority walkouts are protected when good faith bargaining has produced "a stalemate."[51]

B. The R. C. Can Decision

The Fifth Circuit, considering the rights of employees dissatisfied with the union's conduct of negotiations, seems to have departed somewhat from both the majority and dissenting viewpoints of the Seventh Circuit. In NLRB v. R. C. Can Co.,[52] bargaining negotiations subsequent to certification had been proceeding without much success. As in Draper, there were difficulties in arranging the time and place for convenient meetings. The international union representative, in collaboration with the three-man employee negotiating committee, called a meeting to discuss the lack of progress. Although the international representative reported that, in his opinion, the employer was not interested in reaching an agreement, he recommended that a strike not be called. No strike vote was taken, nor was any conclusion reached as to what course of action should be taken in the future. The next morning, two members of the bargaining committee instigated a walkout of eight of the fifty employees in the bargaining unit. When the international representative discovered what had happened, he expressed the "wish" that the strike had not taken place and advised employees to return to work unconditionally. But he still characterized the strike as "protected," despite his lack of enthusiasm for it. The Fifth Circuit articulated its understanding of the Act's philosophy on wildcat strikes in the following dicta:

> Since the employer is required to bargain with the representatives of the worker, it must have some assurance, first, as to the identity of that agent. More important, however, it must be able to deal with that agent as the responsible spokesman for the employees of the unit. There cannot be bargaining in any real sense if the employer has to deal with individuals or splinter groups. And just as attempted negotiations with such groups or individuals would make a mockery out of bargaining, so, too, must bargaining negotiations by a single agency be kept free from divisive pressures generated by dissident elements. On the other hand, a union is, or at least should be, a democratic device. The very reason for its existence is the existence of its members and others for whom the law says it acts. Con-

---

[50] NLRB v. Sunbeam Lighting Co., 318 F.2d 661, 666 (7th Cir. 1963) (dissenting opinion).
[51] Ibid.
[52] 328 F.2d 974 (5th Cir. 1964).

sequently, the law should be slow to declare that members cannot speak effectively in behalf of their own organization and the aims and objectives which it collectively seeks to assert in their behalf. In these conflicting policies, there may be found a basis for resolution: is the action of the individuals or a small group in criticism of, or opposition to, the policies and actions theretofore taken by the organization? Or, to the contrary, is it more nearly in support of the things which the union is trying to accomplish? If it is the former, then such divisive, dissident action is not protected. . . . If, on the other hand, it seeks to generate support for and an acceptance of the demands put forth by the union, it is protected so long, of course, as the means used do not involve a disagreement with, repudiation or criticism of, a policy or decision previously taken by the union such as, for example, a no strike pledge, a cooling off period, or the like during negotiation.[53] [Citations omitted.]

Pointing out that the employer was in no "quandary" about the identity of the bargaining representative, the court concluded that the strike was protected activity:

There was no real difference between what these men were after and what the Union sought. The Union . . . was trying to get the Employer to sit down and talk. That, too, was the aim of these men. Although it is true that at the Union meeting there was no vote to strike, it is equally true there was no formal vote not to strike. In any event, the consensus that the Union would not strike at the present time was not communicated to the Employer. . . . And one thing seems quite clear. The moment Lee [the international representative] learned of the action, he expressed a disappointment that the men had taken it. But in no way did he repudiate it.[54]

It should be noted that, Judge Swygert's dissent in *Sunbeam* notwithstanding, the Board has never relied upon *Washington Aluminum* to support the notion that an exclusive bargaining agent need not be involved with a strike by employees which it represents. It is to be recalled that Justice Black, speaking for the Court in that case, regarded the workers' plight as a difficult one because of the *absence* of a union. But where a union is certified or recognized, it seems that union identification with the strike is crucial in determining the status of the wildcat strikers.[55] In deciding whether such identification exists, the Board apparently relies on two factors: the object of the strikers' dissatisfaction and the identity of their goals with those of the union.

C. *Board's Indicia of Union Identification With the Wildcat Strike*

Object of Employee Dissatisfaction: Union or Employer? In general the Board, unlike the Fifth Circuit, is prone to focus on the supposed *object* of employee dissatisfaction. The question it poses is whether the

53 Id. at 978-79.
54 Id. at 979.
55 See text accompanying notes 39-42 supra.

object of dissatisfaction is the union or the employer. If it is the former, the strike is unprotected; if the latter, it is protected. This inquiry not only compels the Board to tamper with the realities of industrial relations but also puts it in the unenviable position of recasting *Draper* in an unrecognizable mold so that it may be distinguished from future cases. In *Sunbeam*, for instance, the Board characterized *Draper* as a case in which the "union agreed to postpone negotiating meeting to a new date and employees struck to compel an earlier meeting,"[56] thereby presenting it as an example of employee dissatisfaction with the union. But in fact it was the *employer* which had dictated postponement of the meeting. The union had no choice other than to accept the *fait accompli*. There had been past antiunion rumblings in *Draper*, but there was no suggestion in the trial examiner's findings that the walkout was attributable to the same dissidence.

The truth, of course, is that employee dissatisfaction of the type under discussion arises out of frustration with the bargaining progress itself. Rarely is the employer an innocent party in the situation. Management's unwillingness or inability to compromise to an extent acceptable to the union is a necessary ingredient of employee dissatisfaction. Unless one finds the unusual case where employees rebel against the excesses and unreasonableness of their union, the Board's scope of inquiry becomes an investigation of which party holds the weight of economic power. In the absence of a union's negligence in its representative capacity or its illicit collusion with an employer,[57] the workers who "put heat" on the union reflect their own irritation with the bargaining agent's lack of power to dictate change[58]—at least quickly enough for their own satisfaction. This group of workers strikes and finds itself unprotected because of the object of their dissatisfaction—the union. If, on the other hand, the union possesses more bargaining strength, it can use the weapons of economic warfare itself rather than leaving all of the combat to individuals or groups of employees. To be sure, some unions (both responsible and timid) which possess bargaining power would not strike in the most trying circumstances. But dissidents are most apt to be present where the bargaining table cannot produce results because of the union's economic failings. Political realities are quickly understood by both the responsible and the timid and, providing some semblance of

---

[56] Sunbean Lighting Co., 136 N.L.R.B. 1248, 1253 n.12 (1962), enforcement denied, 318 F.2d 661 (7th Cir. 1963).

[57] See Labor Management Relations Act § 8(a)(2), 61 Stat. 140 (1947), 29 U.S.C. § 158(a)(2) (1964); cf. Gem Int'l, Inc. v. NLRB, 321 F.2d 626 (8th Cir. 1963).

[58] See Harnischfeger Corp. v. NLRB, 207 F.2d 575, 576-77 (7th Cir. 1953).

power is available, an aroused membership is not to be ignored by leaders who are interested in survival.

Therefore, if the Board interprets the Act so as to exclude from its protection those who pressure the union rather than the employer, it is likely to favor—perhaps inadvertently[59]—employee groups with strong bargaining agents. This is not a very desirable result for a statute which eschews interpretation based on assumptions of economic power in the labor-management sphere. Even more importantly, the Board's preoccupation with the object of dissatisfaction defies common sense, for independent strike action during collective bargaining does not occur unless there is discontent with the system. This means discontent *with both parties*—union and employer. The Board's inclination to distinguish cases on the "object" basis is a fiction which beclouds the real problem, thereby bringing the national labor laws into disrespect.

Identity of Goals Between Union and Employees. An equally deficient factor upon which the Board relies is the identity of goals between the union and striking employees. This, it is to be recalled, is the criterion enunciated by the Fifth Circuit in *R. C. Can.* Under one variant of this criterion—what one may label the "Cox approach"[60]—individual employees may express themselves democratically through use of the strike weapon until the union takes a firm position. But public policy as reflected in the Act is contrary to the proposition that internal union debate may so easily spill over into the area of industrial strife.[61] Further, this

---

[59] We have already noted the Supreme Court's hostility towards a role for the Board which involves it in the conscious balancing of economic power. Without specific evidence of antiunion animus, the Supreme Court has held that employer conduct to be violative of § 8(a)(3)—which prohibits the encouragement and discouragement of union membership—must inherently discourage union activity. See NLRB v. Erie Resistor Corp., 373 U.S. 221 (1963); Radio Officers' Union v. NLRB, 347 U.S. 17 (1954). The Court seems to have applied a roughly equivalent standard to both § 8(a)(1), which prohibits employer interference, restraint, and coercion of § 7 rights, and § 8(a)(3). American Ship Bldg. Co. v. NLRB, 380 U.S. 300, 308 (1965); NLRB v. Brown, 380 U.S. 278, 283, 286-87 (1965); cf. Republic Aviation Corp. v. NLRB, 324 U.S. 793 (1945). But see the standard employed for § 8(a)(1) violations without 8(a)(3) being considered in NLRB v. Burnup & Sims, Inc., 379 U.S. 21 (1964); NLRB v. Washington Aluminum Co., 370 U.S. 9 (1962); NLRB v. Babcock & Wilcox Co., 351 U.S. 105 (1956). See also Getman, "Section 8(a)(3) of the NLRA and the Effort To Insulate Free Employee Choice," 32 U. Chi. L. Rev. 735 (1965); Comment, 32 U. Chi. L. Rev. 124 (1964).

In any event, it would seem that the Board assumes a heavy burden in attempting to establish that retaliation against a strike called without union approval discourages union membership and violates section 8(a)(3). See the dissenting opinion of Judge Gewin in NLRB v. R. C. Can Co., 328 F.2d 974, 982-87 (5th Cir. 1964).

[60] See note 44 supra and accompanying text.

[61] Cf. United Steelworkers v. Enterprise Wheel & Car Corp., 363 U.S. 593 (1960); United Steelworkers v. Warrior & Gulf Nav. Co., 363 U.S. 574 (1960); United Steelworkers v. American Mfg. Co., 363 U.S. 564 (1960). Further, it can be said that Congress, through enactment of Landrum-Griffin, intended individual grievances and dissatisfaction with the union to be resolved in the courts and not through industrial disputes.

sort of thinking is at odds with the concept of an exclusive bargaining representative.

A narrower approach to the *R. C. Can* criterion is that an unauthorized strike is permissible when it is triggered by the same problems as those with which the union has dealt.[62] The theory here is that employees who strike over issues which are off the bargaining table defy the union, intentionally or otherwise, just as those whose protests deal with the same subject matter under discussion support their representative. The trouble with this theory is that a competing faction, *e.g.*, skilled workers, may seek to impose its will on the entire unit when the union, demanding *in public* the same benefits as the. faction, is more likely to compromise in the general interest of the entire group.

A third variation of the *R. C. Can* criterion would be to require that the union and individual employees be seeking the same substantive contractual terms. We have already seen how difficult this can become because of the "huffing and puffing" at the bargaining table. As a practical matter, a union will settle for less than its press releases proclaim. This is an accepted fact to everyone except those members who may take their union's proposal seriously and, more importantly, those members who may be anxious to combat any talk of compromise. But problems remain even where the goals of the union and its members can be said to be identical. Quite often, as in *Sunbeam*, the issue is simply more money. Both the union and membership are agreed on proposals which are far apart from those submitted by management. The union, of course, desires an agreement incorporating its demands and knows that such an agreement would solve all problems with the membership. Not finding itself in a position to realize this option, the union holds out with the membership in the hope that a face-saving compromise will be achieved. The problem here is that one is dealing with a politically charged atmosphere where the union may be fenced in by its own promises. Is the Board acting intelligently in observing that the union and its individual members are after the same goals, if, in fact, the employees have taken the union newspaper too literally? Is the Board's function to rescue a beleaguered bargaining agent from an unauthorized stoppage when the stoppage is the product of fired-up emotions which cannot await the union strike approval?

It seems apparent, then, that the analysis of union promises—some of them made in the heat of the Board-conducted certification elections—should not be a basis for determining what is protected and what is not

---

[62] Western Contracting Corp. v. NLRB, 322 F.2d 893 (10th Cir. 1963).

protected. In my opinion, such an analysis would be unmanageable as well as unauthorized by the statute. As indicated above, the fact that the demands and goals of the union and its membership are identical means nothing. This approach, therefore, should not be utilized by the Board to prop up cases that may not meet the standards of section 7.

Likewise, the Board should discard the thesis that disagreement about when a strike is to be called does not equal disagreement about its goals. Ever so subtly, this idea was advanced in *Sunbeam* when the Board argued that a formal strike ratification was not required, and in *R. C. Can*, where the Board adopted the trial examiner's opinion, stating that the international representative's "reservation concerning the walkout appears to relate to its tactical wisdom."[63] Such arguments give too little weight to the fact that the timing of the strike is one of the most important questions in any bargaining situation. In 1958 the United Automobile Workers worked without a contract for three months after the expiration, in June, of the previous one. The leadership wisely chose to make September the month for increased bargaining pressure and strike threats, as September was the month for the model change-over when auto manufacturers could not afford to be without labor.[64] It would be foolish to contend that an unauthorized stoppage in July for the same economic package sought by the leadership would have been consistent with the UAW approach. A July strike would have been far more distasteful to the union than, for instance, a strike by skilled workers with the objective of achieving UAW press release demands. Yet, under the Board's rationale, both would be treated in the same manner, the July walkout representing merely an unimportant dispute over tactics and timing. Thus, such a strike would be protected activity. The Board would pay no heed to the havoc created for union policy. In connection with the skilled workers' walkout, it would be satisfied that the strike conformed to the economic package, naively unaware that the leadership's hand was being forced.[65]

---

[63] R. C. Can Co., 140 N.L.R.B. 588, 596 (1963).

[64] Note the importance that the timing of an employer lockout assumed in American Ship. Bldg. Co. v. NLRB, 380 U.S. 300, 302-04 (1965).

[65] Curiously enough, a strike for demands in excess of those supported by the international union might constitute a bargaining lever by the international itself which would use the threat of an aroused membership to increase the economic settlement for all members. This, of course, simply fortifies what has been said above: the Board will find it difficult to appreciate the reasoning of the inner councils and to arrive at decisions based on speculation about such reasoning.

See also in this regard, Office of the General Counsel, NLRB, Quarterly Report on Case Developments, November 1, 1966 at 12, wherein the General Counsel relied upon the fact that a strike had been "contemplated" at the previous Executive Board meeting to support union involvement and protected activity. Cf. R. C. Can Co., supra note 63. But it is possible that any number of inferences could be drawn from this fact. The union's leadership might well have viewed the strike with extreme reluctance.

Union's Internal Procedure. This analysis indicates that the major factors relied upon by the Board, object of dissatisfaction and identity of goals, represent a search for a substitute for formal union enforcement or authorization to strike. As noted, such a search requires knowledge of the union's internal proceedings. Many unions have elaborate procedures, some of which are set forth in their constitutions,[66] whereby employees vote to ratify and to strike, and under which the international union may release strike funds to the employees. Without knowledge of these procedures, and without access to union meetings and discussions, the Board's rationale indicated in the wildcat strike cases is based on mere speculation. Its only answer to this criticism would be that it has attempted to find out what has transpired in union meetings and strikes. In *Sunbeam*, for example, the Board noted that employees had participated in the initial formulation of contract demands and, without citing any provisions of the contract or union constitution, that the employees had the power to reject or approve any tentative agreement. In *Draper*, the Fourth Circuit, while viewing the strike as unprotected, mentioned the fact that a department had voted to strike. Finally, in *R. C. Can*, both the Board and court pointed out that no strike vote was taken and that no future course of action was prescribed by ballot.

It is surprising that so much attention is given to internal union voting practices when one considers that the weight of authority places union internal affairs—especially of the type under discussion—beyond the coverage of the Labor Act. The Supreme Court has held that it is an unfair labor practice for an employer to bargain to the point of impasse about a pre-strike voting procedure, since this is an internal union affair and therefore not a proper subject for mandatory bargaining.[67] And the Board has held that it is an unfair labor practice for an employer to insist upon ratification of the contract before signing it,[68] even when ratification is a condition to the agreement.[69] Moreover, in collective bargaining sessions an employer may not rely upon its assessment of whether internal union requirements for an authorized strike have been

---

[66] "Strike-Control Provisions in Union Constitutions," 77 Monthly Labor Rev. 497 (1954).

[67] NLRB v. Wooster Division, Borg-Warner Corp., 356 U.S. 342 (1958). See also Allen Bradley Co. v. NLRB, 286 F.2d 442 (7th Cir. 1961); Allis-Chalmers Mfg. Co. v. NLRB, 213 F.2d 374 (7th Cir. 1954); cf. International Union, UAW v. O'Brien, 339 U.S. 454 (1950); NLRB v. Darlington Veneer Co., 236 F.2d 85 (4th Cir. 1956); NLRB v. Deena Artware, Inc., 198 F.2d 645, 652 (6th Cir. 1952).

[68] North County Motors, Ltd., 146 N.L.R.B. 671, 673-74 (1964); cf. Roesch Transp. Co., 157 N.L.R.B. No. 32 (March 7, 1966); Houchens Market, 155 N.L.R.B. No. 59 (Nov. 12, 1965). See also Operating Eng'rs Union, 123 N.L.R.B. 922, 927-31 (1959); Sheet Metal Workers, 120 N.L.R.B. 1678 (1958).

[69] M & M Oldsmobile, Inc., 156 N.L.R.B. No. 91 (Jan. 17, 1966).

satisfied, since the Board and the courts, when the question comes before them, may be precluded from making any such assessments in determining the status of the strike.[70] These holdings that ratification is not the proper concern of the employer conflict with the Board's approach to the wildcat strike cases, where it has become deeply involved with meetings and votes among union members.

Not only is the Board's emphasis on internal union affairs a departure from its general rule, but in the wildcat strike situation it actually encourages the risk of employer interference *inside* the union and bargaining unit. This tends to divide the union from the employees and to exaggerate the possibility that employers will lend their aid *sub rosa* to opposition groups against a union leadership which antagonizes management. Indeed, employers can assert, with a great deal of justification, that they must make it their business to know what goes on at union meetings. Otherwise, it will be said, it is not possible for management to react to unauthorized strikes, since an employee may be properly discharged only if he has engaged in unprotected activity and the status of the activity depends upon what takes place in the union's inner councils.

Nevertheless, there are some circumstances in which internal union procedures might have relevance to unauthorized stoppages. It is to be recalled that in *R. C. Can* the Fifth Circuit noted that the "consensus" not to strike reached at the union meeting was not conveyed to the employer. Moreover, in the cases protecting internal union processes, it was always the employer (or an individual employee)[71] who initiated the forbidden probe. Drawing together these two points, one may conclude that internal union procedures may be considered relevant to the protected status of unauthorized strikes *if it is the union itself which brings the matter into the bargaining sessions with the employer.* Thus, when the union takes the position that the agreement is subject to ratification or disapproval procedures and outlines those procedures, it embodies the union constitution, or whatever is proposed, within the collective bargaining subject matter. The employer, upon accepting the appropriateness of the mechanism, has a right to rely on its execution. As a practical matter, this approach would serve to restrict the ambit of protected strikes when unions emphasize their unruly membership as a ploy for greater concessions.

Moreover, in the same context, the failure of the union to endorse

---

[70] E.g., Pullman Co. v. Railway Conductors, 52 L.R.R.M. 2829 (7th Cir. 1963).
[71] Cf. Allis-Chalmers Mfg. Co. v. NLRB, 61 L.R.R.M. 2498 (7th Cir. 1966).

publicly the proposals which it takes back to the membership[72] should, in the absence of an affirmative showing to the contrary, be deemed to indicate lack of union involvement in a strike which occurs as a result of dissatisfaction with the package. This result should be reached because unions are not designated as bargaining agents to serve as mere conduits between employer and employees; they should either endorse or reject the proposal. Responsible leadership is needed which will provide information of an objective nature not always available to the average employee. Therefore, the Board should not protect strikes which exploit internal union procedures for the purpose of extracting more demands, for the unions should be encouraged to take a genuine position in favor of that for which it asks the employees to vote. Unless the union brings ratification and strike votes to the bargaining table, however, internal regulations of the union should not be considered in connection with wildcat strikes.

It is permissible, and in some instances desirable, for union officials to override the wishes of the membership or not consult the members at all.[73] One cannot propose that the union stand up to an irresponsible membership and, at the same time, decide whether conduct is protected or not on the basis of the membership's votes or expressed sentiments. Through its misguided efforts to interpret the Act in a manner which will achieve the reinstatement of individual strikers, the Board has unreasonably undercut the authority of labor organizations over their own membership and their position with employers with whom they deal.

III

STRIKES DURING THE COLLECTIVE BARGAINING AGREEMENT

Strikes in breach of contract are unprotected activity.[74] Moreover, contract clauses prohibiting strikes are common in view of the Board's adherence to the Supreme Court's *Lucas Flour*[75] doctrine that a no-strike clause is implied where the grievance arbitration provision is a broad one.[76] In *Mastro Plastics Corp. v. NLRB*,[77] however, the Supreme Court

---

[72] See Sunbeam Lighting Co., 136 N.L.R.B. 1248, 1250 (1962).

[73] See Dunlop, The Social Utility of Collective Bargaining 19 (prepared for American Assembly, Oct. 27-30, 1966): "[I]nternational union officers should be expressed [sic] authorized, with the approval of the international executive board, to sign collective bargaining agreements without ratification of the employees directly affected." Presumably, the value would be psychological. No statute prohibits the practice which Professor Dunlop advocates.

[74] NLRB v. Sands Mfg. Co., 306 U.S. 332 (1939).

[75] Local 174, Teamsters v. Lucas Flour Co., 369 U.S. 95 (1962).

[76] Id. at 104-06; see NLRB v. Dorsey Trailers, Inc., 179 F.2d 589, 592 (5th Cir. 1950); United Elastic Corp., 84 N.L.R.B. 768, 770-71 (1949); National Elec. Prods. Corp., 80 N.L.R.B. 995, 999 (1948); Joseph Dyson & Sons, Inc., 72 N.L.R.B. 445, 446-47 (1947); cf. Scullin Steel Co., 65 N.L.R.B. 1294, 1317-18 (1946); cases cited in note 61 supra.

[77] 350 U.S. 270 (1956).

held that a no-strike clause was not intended to prohibit strikes during the contract's term if it did not contemplate a strike which responded to employer unfair labor practices. Hence a strike which flows from unfair labor practices[78]—illegalities which are "destructive" of the "foundations" of the contract—is protected unless specifically waived in the no-strike clause.[79] Since the strike in *Mastro* fell within the sixty-day negotiation period set forth in section 8(d) of the Act,[80] the Court was required to explain that where the strike was not for a "termination or modification" of the contract, workers would not lose their status as "employees" under section 8(d) and thus would retain the protection of the Act.[81]

In *Arlan's Department Store*[82] the Board apparently limited the scope of *Mastro Plastics*. Over Member Fanning's strong dissent,[83] the majority of the Board held that the protection afforded workers in *Mastro Plastics* becomes operative only where "serious, unfair labor practices" have been committed by the employer.[84] A no-strike clause which is not literally applicable to wildcat stoppages, therefore, usually can be relied upon as a basis for discharging employees when the unlawful activity by the employer is not serious.[85]

Some of the cases present rather close questions regarding the existence of contractual prohibitions. In *Western Contracting Corp. v. NLRB*,[86] for instance, the Tenth Circuit ruled that a no-strike clause

---

[78] Cf. Arlan's Department Store, 133 N.L.R.B. 802, 803-04 (1961).

[79] Mastro Plastics Corp. v. NLRB, 350 U.S. 270, 281-83 (1956).

[80] 61 Stat. 142 (1947), 29 U.S.C. § 158(d) (1964):

[W]here there is in effect a collective-bargaining contract covering employees in an industry affecting commerce, the duty to bargain collectively shall also mean that no party to such contract shall terminate or modify such contract, unless the party desiring such termination or modification— (1) serves a written notice upon the other party to the contract of the proposed termination or modification sixty days prior to the expiration date thereof, or in the event such contract contains no expiration date, sixty days prior to the time it is proposed to make such termination or modification;

(2) offers to meet and confer with the other party for the purpose of negotiating a new contract or a contract containing the proposed modifications;

. . . .

(4) continues in full force and effect, without resorting to strike or lock-out, all the terms and conditions of the existing contract for a period of sixty days after such notice is given or until the expiration date of such contract, whichever occurs later . . . .

[81] Mastro Plastics Corp. v. NLRB, supra note 79, at 284-86.

[82] 133 N.L.R.B. 802 (1961).

[83] Id. at 811-18 (dissenting in part).

[84] Id. at 804; cf. General Motors Corp., 134 N.L.R.B. 1107 (1961); Young Spring & Wire Corp., 138 N.L.R.B. 643 (1962); Mid-West Metallic Prods., Inc., 121 N.L.R.B. 1317 (1958). But see Danner Press, Inc., 153 N.L.R.B. 1092 (1965), enforcement denied, 64 L.R.R.M. 2623 (6th Cir. 1967); San Juan Lumber Co., 154 N.L.R.B. 1153 (1965); Ford Motor Co., 131 N.L.R.B. 1462 (1961).

[85] See the no-strike clause at issue in Arlan's Department Store, 133 N.L.R.B. 802, 803 (1961); cf. Plasti-Line, Inc. v. NLRB, 278 F.2d 482 (6th Cir. 1960); compare Complete Auto Transit, Inc., 134 N.L.R.B. 652 (1961).

[86] 322 F.2d 893 (10th Cir. 1963).

written to prohibit stoppages arising out of the introduction of new equipment was inapplicable to a strike protesting the employer's failure to install winter heaters in trucks.[87] In an entirely different spirit, the Fifth Circuit ruled that a strike called to protest the discharge of employees who had stopped working because of unsafe working conditions, which was eventually ratified by the international union, was unprotected.[88] In spite of the fact that the parties had not entered into a collective bargaining agreement, the court relied upon a clause, agreed upon in the course of negotiations, which would establish the peaceful and exclusive means for settling such disputes. The decision appears to be erroneous because there was no binding agreement in effect between the parties and because no attention was given to the relevance of binding arbitration and no-strike clauses which had not yet been incorporated into the agreement being negotiated. Moreover, the question of stoppages protesting intolerable conditions is specifically covered by a statutory provision. Section 502 of the Act states that "the quitting of labor by an employee or employees in good faith because of abnormally dangerous conditions for work . . . [shall not be] deemed a strike under this Act."[89] The Board, with court approval, has interpreted this provision to mean that the "quitting of labor," while not a "strike," is protected concerted activity for the "mutual aid and protection" of the employees.[90] Thus, strikes supporting such a protected "quitting of labor" should also be protected. The existence of a no-strike clause does not alter this conclusion.[91]

IV

RIVAL UNIONS

When employees challenge the wisdom of the exclusive bargaining representative's policy, their conduct is protected activity so long as there are indications that an initial attempt has been made to influence the union.[92] Although there are NLRB procedures under which the

[87] Id. at 900.

[88] NLRB v. American Mfg. Co., 203 F.2d 212 (5th Cir. 1953).

[89] 61 Stat. 162 (1947), 29 U.S.C. § 143 (1964).

[90] Knight Morley Corp., 116 N.L.R.B. 140, 146 (1956), enforced, 251 F.2d 753 (6th Cir. 1957); Metco Plating Co., 113 N.L.R.B. 204 (1955), enforced, 239 F.2d 642 (6th Cir. 1956); Fruin-Colnon Constr. Co., 139 N.L.R.B. 894, 906 (1962).

[91] But the no-strike clause governs where the work is "highly unpleasant" rather than "abnormally dangerous." Curtis Mathes Mfg. Co., 145 N.L.R.B. 473, 475 (1963). An objective test is now used to determine whether the employment conditions are "abnormally dangerous." Redwing Carriers, Inc., 130 N.L.R.B. 1208, 1209 (1961); cf. Stop & Shop Inc., 161 N.L.R.B. No. 5, 63 L.R.R.M. 1228 (1966).

[92] E. W. Buschman Co., 153 N.L.R.B. 699 (1965); Cooper Alloy Corp., 120 N.L.R.B. 586 (1958); Roadway Express, Inc., 119 N.L.R.B. 104 (1957), enforced, 257 F.2d 948 (4th Cir. 1958); Roadway Express, Inc., 108 N.L.R.B. 874 (1954), enforced sub nom. NLRB v. International Bhd. of Teamsters, 227 F.2d 439 (10th Cir. 1955); Nu-Car Carriers, Inc., 88 N.L.R.B. 75 (1950), enforced, 189 F.2d 756 (3d Cir. 1951).

dissident employees can attempt to rid themselves of a bargaining representative which is not to their liking,[93] the Board, in light of the principle that the majority representative must speak collectively for all employees in the appropriate unit,[94] is loath to countenance dissident activity during a union's term as bargaining representative. At the same time, it ordinarily is unlawful for an employer to bargain with a union which represents a minority of the employees.[95] This principle of majority rule[96] is reflected not only through the regulation of individual grievances in section 9(a),[97] but also in statutory provisions which make it unlawful for a union to strike for the purpose of recognition when another union is certified,[98] or lawfully recognized,[99] or where a representation election has been conducted within the past twelve months.[100] These provisions must be considered in attempting to resolve questions of protected activity, including the status of the wildcat strike, harmoniously with the general objectives of the Act.

The Board has made it clear that individuals may not choose any representative they wish to process grievances for them under the authority of the section 9(a) proviso,[101] for that section was not intended

---

[93] See Labor Management Relations Act §§ 9(b)(2), 9(c)(1)(A), 61 Stat. 143, 144 (1947), 29 U.S.C. §§ 159(b)(2), 159(c)(1)(A) (1964).

[94] See note 27 supra and accompanying text.

[95] International Ladies' Garment Workers Union v. NLRB, 366 U.S. 731 (1961). See note 96 infra.

[96] An exception to the majority rule principle exists where a majority union is certified but then loses its majority status. In this situation § 8(b)(7)(B) (quoted in part in note 100 infra) accords the minority union the right to represent the employees for one year from the date of the election which led to its certification. In this narrow area, the principle of stability in labor representation seems to outweigh that of majority rule.

[97] Quoted in part in note 24 supra.

[98] Labor Management Relations Act § 8(b)(4)(C), 61 Stat. 141-42 (1947), as amended, 73 Stat. 542-43 (1959), 29 U.S.C. § 158(b)(4)(C) (1964):
It shall be an unfair labor practice for a labor organization or its agents— . . . to engage in, or to induce or encourage any individual employed by any person . . . to engage in, a strike or a refusal in the course of his employment to use, manufacture, process, transport, or otherwise handle or work on any goods, articles, materials, or commodities or to perform any services; or . . . to threaten, coerce, or restrain any person . . . where in either case an object thereof is . . . forcing or requiring any employer to recognize or bargain with a particular labor organization as the representative of his employees if another labor organization has been certified as the representative of such employees under the provisions of Section 9 . . . .

[99] Labor Management Relations Act § 8(b)(7)(A), 61 Stat. 141-42 (1947), as amended, 73 Stat. 544 (1959), 29 U.S.C. § 158(b)(7)(A) (1964):
It shall be an unfair labor practice for a labor organization or its agents— . . . to picket or cause to be picketed, or threaten to picket or cause to be picketed, any employer where an object thereof is forcing or requiring an employer to recognize or bargain with a labor organization as the representative of his employees, or forcing or requiring the employees of an employer to accept or select such labor organization as their collective bargaining representative, unless such labor organization is currently certified as the representative of such employees: . . . where the employer has lawfully recognized in accordance with this Act any other labor organization and a question concerning representation may not appropriately be raised under section 9(c) of this Act . . . .

[100] Labor Management Relations Act § 8(b)(7)(B), 73 Stat. 544 (1957), 29 U.S.C. § 158(b)(7)(B): "where within the preceding twelve months a valid election under section 9(c) of this Act has been conducted . . . ."

[101] Quoted in part in note 24 supra.

to provide a forum for disruptive clashes between rival unions.[102] Similarly, the Board has held that a strike or picketing conducted by an outside union to resolve the grievances of employees is not necessarily a strike for recognition, which is protected, as opposed to one for economic purposes which is unprotected under section 9(a).[103] The considerable difficulties in determining the purpose of the strike are well reflected in the Board's recent decision in *National Packing Co.*[104]

In this case the Board was confronted with the question of whether picketing within twelve months of a union's defeat in a representation election violated section 8(b)(7)(B), which makes picketing for recognition an unfair labor practice "where within the preceding twelve months a valid election under section 9(c) . . . has been conducted . . . ." Emphasizing the right of employees to engage in concerted activities as set forth in section 7 and the right to strike protected by section 13, and assuming, *arguendo*, that the picketers constituted a "labor organization," the Board held that the strike was not organizational in nature and therefore not unlawful.

The decision can be distinguished from those involving wildcat strike situations on two grounds: (*1*) There was no exclusive bargaining representative; hence the Board was under no obligation to protect the stability of an existing relationship. (*2*) The Board was only considering what is prohibited under the Act and not, as with wildcat strikes, what is protected and unprotected. Nevertheless, *National Packing* is significant in that the Board's discussion impliedly accepted the assertion that a violation of 8(b)(7)(B) provides the employer with a defense to charges of a section 7 violation.[105]

This interplay between section 7 and the protection of an incumbent union against a rival is also demonstrated by the interesting decision of the First Circuit in *Simmons, Inc. v. NLRB.*[106] In that case the Board had found that a strike sponsored by an employee committee was not an unfair labor practice even though it had as its object recognition for

---

[102] See Hughes Tool Co. v. NLRB, 147 F.2d 69, 73 (5th Cir. 1945); NLRB v. North American Aviation, Inc., 136 F.2d 898 (9th Cir. 1943); Federal Tel. & Radio Co., 107 N.L.R.B. 649, 652 (1953); cf. Elgin, J. & E. Ry. v. Burley, 325 U.S. 711 (1945); Southern Conference of Teamsters v. Red Ball Motor Freight, Inc., 64 L.R.R.M. 2545 (5th Cir. 1967); McGuire v. Humble Oil & Ref. Co., 355 F.2d 352 (2d Cir. 1966); Black-Clawson Co. v. Int'l Ass'n of Machinists, 313 F.2d 179 (2d Cir. 1962); Modine Mfg. Co. v. Grand Lodge Int'l Ass'n of Machinists, 216 F.2d 326 (6th Cir. 1954). But see Douds v. Local 1250, Retail Wholesale Dep't Store Union, 173 F.2d 764 (2d Cir. 1949).
[103] Hotel Union, 147 N.L.R.B. 1060, 1069 n.21 (1964); District 65, Retail & Wholesale Dep't Store Union, 141 N.L.R.B. 991, 999 (1963); Waiters & Bartenders Local 500, 140 N.L.R.B. 433, 441 (1963); Local 259, UAW, 133 N.L.R.B. 1468 (1961).
[104] 62 L.R.R.M. 1260 (June 8, 1966).
[105] Id. at 1261.
[106] 315 F.2d 143 (1st Cir. 1963).

the committee and the ouster of the incumbent bargaining representative, the committee's parent body.[107] The First Circuit vacated the Board's order dismissing the employer's complaint.[108] Subsequently the Board decided that a strike to force reinstatement of the unlawful strikers was protected activity despite lack of authorization from the certified international union.[109] The First Circuit again denied enforcement, stating:

> It seems to us that there is a substantial difference . . . between a strike by the employees because of the company's improper attempt to interfere with their certified representative, and a strike which is disapproved by the certified representative and which is for the most part to obtain reinstatement of dissident employees who had illegally sought to replace the certified union. . . . [This] loads [the scales] . . . not only against the company, but against the certified union.[110]

While the stoppage to obtain reinstatement was not a continuance of the unfair labor practice strike, the First Circuit, unlike the Board, seemed willing to consider the fact that the initial dispute between the two organizations might taint conduct which follows closely thereafter and make it unprotected activity. The fact that the second strike is not a continuance of the first illegality should not automatically raise it to the status of protected activity.

As a general rule, then, the employee's section 7 rights are subordinate to the principle of majority rule. *Draper*,[111] *Sunbeam*,[112] and *R. C. Can*[113] therefore cannot protect a strike by an organized dissident group which attempts to deal with the employer in employment relations matters. When an outside union actively seeks to control the bargaining process,[114] or when a group attempts to sever or remove itself from the bargaining unit through the strike threat,[115] its activity is clearly unprotected. Of course, it is possible that an overwhelming majority of the employees might indicate their decision to pick a different bargaining representative,[116] and in such a case the Board should treat the incumbent as defunct[117] and protect the strike when used on behalf of the new union's

---

[107] Comite de Empleados de Simmons, Inc., 127 N.L.R.B. 1179 (1960).

[108] Simmons, Inc. v. NLRB, 287 F.2d 628 (1st Cir. 1961).

[109] Simmons, Inc., 134 N.L.R.B. 1038 (1961).

[110] Simmons, Inc. v. NLRB, 315 F.2d 143, 147-48 (1963).

[111] See notes 39-44 supra and accompanying text.

[112] See notes 46-51 supra and accompanying text.

[113] See notes 52-54 supra and accompanying text.

[114] NLRB v. Kearney & Trecker Corp., 237 F.2d 416 (7th Cir. 1956).

[115] General Motors Corp., 134 N.L.R.B. 1107 (1961); Ford Motor Co., 131 N.L.R.B. 1462 (1961); Dazey Corp., 106 N.L.R.B. 553 (1953); cf. NLRB v. Kaiser Aluminum & Chem. Corp., 217 F.2d 366 (9th Cir. 1954).

[116] For an analysis of majority participation as an indicia of whether a wildcat strike should be protected, see notes 125-31 infra and accompanying text.

[117] See NLRB v. Lundy Mfg. Corp., 316 F.2d 921 (2d Cir.), cert. denied, 375 U.S. 895 (1963); Louis Rosenberg, Inc., 122 N.L.R.B. 1450 (1959).

objective.[118] Similarly, where the Board finds that the employer has unlawfully assisted or dominated the incumbent union, perhaps engaging in "sweetheart" deals so as to violate section 8(a)(2) of the Act,[119] or where the employer or the incumbent has engaged in serious unfair labor practices against the outsider, a retaliatory strike in protest of such conduct should be interpreted as protected activity under the Act. The Board should adhere to this rule regardless of whether the contract contains a no-strike clause.[120]

V

THE POSITION OF THE EMPLOYER

More often than not, the employer is more seriously damaged by an unauthorized strike than is the bargaining agent for the employees. Even where the union's authority is undercut, it may choose to move with the tide and adopt a politically defensible position as its own. It is relatively simple for the union to act in such a manner when there are no contractual liabilities, *i.e.*, a no-strike clause, which would require a more statesmanlike stand. As already indicated, the Board can discourage this conduct through its power to determine what is protected and unprotected activity. It is, moreover, often the employer's fate to be pushed into the difficult and sometimes illegal posture of dealing with more than one group or organization. This is the evil which was condemned in *Draper*, the injustice of which is indisputable. Because of the likelihood of serious harm, it is important that the employer be able to decide whether a strike is unprotected. What objective factors may be relied upon in making this determination?

A. *Union Involvement*

The first and simplest factor is union involvement. The employer would know what type of conduct was involved if an unequivocal union authorization were given by some union official. The cases, however, speak of both union authorization and union ratification of strikes as constituting union involvement sufficient to meet the standards of protected activity. While ratification may be the equivalent of authorization as a matter of agency law, in the context of industrial relations this principle— insofar as relevant to the instant discussion—is most questionable. The Board has held that an unauthorized stoppage is protected if ratification

---

[118] See cases cited in note 117 supra.

[119] Cf. Confectionary & Tobacco Drivers Union v. NLRB, 312 F.2d 108 (2d Cir. 1963); NLRB v. Summers Fertilizer Co., 251 F.2d 514 (1st Cir. 1958).

[120] See Arlan's Department Store, 133 N.L.R.B. 802 (1961), discussed at text accompanying notes 82-84 supra.

takes place "within a few weeks."[121] Surely the decision concerning a strike's authorization cannot be permitted to wait so long. Unable to ascertain the strike's status, the employer is in a quandary, while his business is subjected to economic loss. And, as noted above, it would be inconsistent with existing labor policies to impose a requirement that the employer investigate internal union proceedings.

B. *Notification From Union Officials*

The better rule would be for the Board to presume that a strike is unauthorized and therefore unprotected where the employer does not receive some form of notice, from the certified bargaining agent or the entity—international or local—which normally conducts negotiations, that the strike decision emanates from responsible union officials. The internal union debate as to the strike's wisdom should not be permitted to leave the question of protected activity unresolved for an unreasonably long period of time subsequent to the strike's inception. Ratification after such an unreasonably long period, no matter how vocal it is, should not suffice to bring the conduct within the ambit of section 7.

The objection to this rule would be that it resurrects the concept of notification which has been viewed with disfavor in regard to strikes not authorized by the union,[122] and declared irrelevant by the Supreme Court in *Washington Aluminum*. In this writer's opinion, however, *Washington Aluminum* can be distinguished, and notification can be properly viewed as an implied obligation of the incumbent union. In the first place, the Court's opinion in *Washington Aluminum* indicates that enough had been done to constitute notice. Moreover, the Court specifically noted the absence of a bargaining representative. A union representing the employees could be expected to assume a heavier burden than unorganized workers. Some form of notification, therefore, is not an unreasonable obligation to be imposed on the union.

C. *Wildcat Strike Before or After Impasse in Bargaining*

Absent notification, it would seem best for the Board to devise a rule along the lines suggested by Judge Swygert's dissenting opinion in *Sunbeam*. The Board might rule that the parties must have bargained to the point of impasse before an unauthorized strike will be protected. This approach might be of value when the union returns to the members with the negotiated package or the last offer of the employer. If one assumes that the union has in good faith settled on what it recommends or takes to the membership, a walkout—whether authorized or not—does not

---

[121] Berger Polishing, Inc., 147 N.L.R.B. 21, 40 n.64 (1964).
[122] See NLRB v. Ford Radio & Mica Corp., 258 F.2d 457 (2d Cir. 1958).

unduly disrupt the bargaining process. There are three problems with this suggestion: (1) unions very often anticipate more bargaining after this stage and, even though they should not be encouraged to count on "post-impasse" bargaining, their attitude may be completely justified in certain cases; (2) more bargaining may take place which would be upset by any type of walkout; (3) the notion of impasse bargaining should more properly relate to union or employer conduct which can be controlled by the parties themselves, *i.e.*, the employer's unilateral change of working conditions.[123] Hence, in the absence of a future ruling that strikes are protected activity only if they arise after the parties have bargained to the point of impasse,[124] it seems preferable to require notification.

D. *Majority Participation in Walkout*

At the Board's urgings, employers have based decisions on a strike's protected status upon whether a majority of employees participated in the walkout. Although hedging to some degree, the Board indicated in *Sunbeam* that it is at least strongly influenced by this consideration.[125] It strenuously argued the importance of majority participation before the Tenth Circuit in *Western Contracting*, and the court found this position to be a persuasive one.[126] On the other hand, the First Circuit has reserved opinion on this question,[127] and while *Draper* alludes to the fact that only twenty-five per cent of the employees walked out, the Fourth Circuit did not appear to rely on this factor.

A number of reasons exist, however, for discarding the majority participation factor in the usual case. Since a majority of employees are not necessary to the exercise of section 7 rights in other situations,[128] why should this be necessary here? Although some exceptions should be demarcated, it is sensible in most instances to assume that a majority of employees has exercised its choice of a bargaining representative and has thereby negated any intention to permit each and every decision

---

[123] See NLRB v. Crompton-Highland Mills, Inc., 337 U.S. 217 (1949).

[124] The fact that the Supreme Court has, in American Ship Bldg. Co. v. NLRB, 380 U.S. 300, 315 (1965), seen fit to characterize the strike and lockout as "correlative" might indicate that the concept of bargaining to the point of impasse could become applicable to strikes.

[125] Sunbeam Lighting Co., 136 N.L.R.B. 1248, 1255-56 (1962). Cf. Shook & Fletcher Insulation Co., 130 N.L.R.B. 519 (1961).

[126] Western Contracting Corp. v. NLRB, 322 F.2d 893, 897-98 (10th Cir. 1963); see Brief for the National Labor Relations Board, pp. 9-10, Western Contracting v. NLRB, supra: "In . . . [Harnischfeger and Draper], a clear *minority* of the employees dissatisfied with the course of negotiations, then in progress between their union and the employer staged a spontaneous walkout . . . . [T]he *minority* action was held to be unprotected by section 7 of the Act." [Emphasis by the Board.]

[127] "Although . . . we intimate no views, it may be that, standing alone, a strike contrary to the wishes of a certified union is to be protected if a majority rather than a minority go out." Simmons, Inc. v. NLRB, 315 F.2d 143, 147 (1st Cir. 1963).

[128] See, e.g., Vogue Lingerie, Inc., 123 N.L.R.B. 1009 (1959).

—whether or not it may be as important as a strike or ratification decision—to be determined by majority vote, let alone majority participation. Moreover, the cases themselves demonstrate the impracticability of the "majority participation" requirement. In *Sunbeam*, for instance, a majority of employees were involved in the walkout at its inception, but this majority was quickly converted into a minority when a number of workers returned to their jobs. At what point then is majority participation critical? The Board and the Seventh Circuit disagree. If one waits for a period of time to elapse, as the Seventh Circuit seemed to do, the employer's hand may be strengthened—especially if the workers' jobs are threatened by replacements. On the other hand, if one focuses on majority participation at the strike's inception, the employees become the object of excessive favoritism because it is easy for them (and harassing to the employer) to engage in a quickie work stoppage.[129]

A second weakness of the majority participation factor is demonstrated by *Western Contracting*, where a majority of the employees on *a particular shift* walked out, but their number did not constitute a majority of the total employee complement. Similarly, in *Draper* an overwhelming percentage of employees in a particular department, the foundry, walked out. An unauthorized stoppage, being necessarily spontaneous in nature, may not involve workers in all shifts and departments, especially if there are considerable distances between the departments. In these situations, part of the reasoning behind the use of the majority participation factor appears to be that, where a stoppage is spontaneous and without union sanction, yet eventually achieves the support of most of the workers, it is deserving of section 7 protection. Implicit in this thinking is the incumbent union's negligence, inattentiveness, or, as we have noted earlier, economic weakness. Thus, although it should reject the majority participation factor as a general rule, the Board would be on solid ground if it were to hold that an overwhelming endorsement of the strike in the absence of authorization, coupled with some evidence of company assistance to the incumbent or "sweetheart" collusion, constitutes protected activity.

A third reason for rejecting majority participation is that it would condemn as unprotected a protest strike by a minority group of Negro employees, for instance, against racially discriminatory practices.[130] By the same token, a majority of white employees who walked out to enforce those same discriminatory practices would be protected. This absurd

---

[129] Cf. International Union, UAW v. Wisconsin Employment Relations Bd., 336 U.S. 245 (1949).
[130] Cf. NLRB v. Tanner Motor Livery, Ltd., 349 F.2d 1 (9th Cir. 1965).

result, so utterly contrary to public policy, highlights the flimsy thinking which has gone into the Board's approach to this matter.[131]

E. *Interference With Bargaining Process*

Finally, one returns to the argument advanced by Professor Cox, that a wildcat strike, to be unprotected, should in fact interfere with the bargaining process. The best rule incorporating this idea would be that wildcat strikes are protected so long as they occur after the parties bargain to the point of impasse. However, as observed earlier, this idea proceeds upon an assumption which it is best to discourage—that the wildcat strike should be used as a bargaining ploy for greater concessions than those for which the uninitiated employer settled. This, like some of the ideas already adopted by the Board, permits debates among employees to be carried on at the expense of the employer.

CONCLUSION

For a society which values both industrial peace and employee free choice, the resolution of strikes which do not have union sanction is difficult. Majority rule, valuable to both the union and employer, has an important status in this country's regulation of labor-management relations. But the employee, whether resisting an unresponsive union or an employer's damage suit, must also be considered.

If a decision is to be made which provides for the regulation of union internal procedures in the interest of dealing with a rebellious rank-and-file, that decision is for Congress and not the Board or the courts. The Board must repress its excessively protective approach to unauthorized stoppages, an approach which both encourages involvement in the union's internal affairs and, at the same time, makes union statesmanship more unlikely. A shift in Board decisions which alters the latter consideration may produce a difficult period of getting tough with unreasonable dissident elements. Whatever the result, a vehicle in support of membership revolts as well as union liability for the same conduct is not to be found in the Labor Management Relations Act.

---

[131] See cases cited in Gould, "The Negro Revolution and the Law of Collective Bargaining," 34 Fordham L. Rev. 207, 253 n.277 (1965).

Bibliographic Essay on "'Wildcat' Strikes"

Two court of appeals decisions issued subsequent to "'Wildcat' Strikes" have demonstrated more caution in declaring protected status for dissident employee economic pressure. In *NLRB v. Shop Rite Foods, Inc.,*[1] the Fifth Circuit took the position that dissidents or walkout strikers had to give the union an opportunity to consider what position to embrace and what action to undertake before worker conduct could be characterized as protected. If such prerequisites were not imposed, said the court, the collective bargaining process and resolution of grievances through it could be frustrated.

In a case discussed in "'Wildcat' Strikes" when it was at Board level, *NLRB v. Tanner Motor Livery, Ltd.,*[2] the Ninth Circuit concluded that regardless of the identity of goals between the workers and the union the employees engaged in picketing, which was designed to protest alleged discriminatory employment practices, were required to resort to the union before engaging in such action. The Ninth Circuit specifically adopted the view that the Fourth Circuit's *Draper* decision was more in accord with the statutory scheme than the decision of the Fifth Circuit in *R.C. Can.*

In addition to the literature, there have been at least two important judicial decisions[3] and one more from the Board since *Emporium.* In *Energy Coal Income Partnership 1981,*[4] the Board held a strike to be unprotected where the union was "strongly opposed" to a strike, "so informed the dissidents both before and after ther [unanimous] vote [to strike]," and made "persistent, although unsuccessful, attempts to persuade the strikers to quit the picket line." The Board contrasted these facts with those present in cases like *R.C. Can* and echoed the view expressed by the Fifth Circuit, i.e., that *R.C. Can* should be applied with "great care."[5] Board Member Dennis noted that the *R.C. Can* doctrine had not "met with universal approval" and that she found it unnecessary to pass on the validity of the doctrine.[6]

The Court of Appeals for the Sixth Circuit held that the attempt by two workers to confront company officials about a work break "despite repeated admonitions" from both the union and company that the matter was a subject for collective bargaining constituted a "blatant contravention" of the union's exclusive bargaining representative status.[7] The Seventh Circuit, in *East Chicago Rehabilitation Center v. NLRB*[8]—a case involving 1974 amendments to the NLRA that require strike notification by "labor organizations" representing health care employees—deemed strike activity protected where the union protested the same work rules at which the strike was aimed and the strikers returned to work immediately when told to do so by the union. The court also noted that the strikers were not aware that the issue in dispute was under discussion between the union and the company. Said Judge Posner, writing for a 2-1 majority,

By demonstrating to the union the passions that had been aroused by the new lunch rule, the strike led the union to demand that the employer rescind the rule, and in effect he did . . . and there is no evidence that in demanding rescision the union was merely yielding to pressure from a vocal minority and giving up alternative demands more important to the bargaining unit as a whole.[9]

In "Black Power in the Unions: The Impact Upon Collective Bargaining Relationships,"[10] an article written two years after " 'Wildcat' Strikes," I took the position that, where alleged discriminatory conditions were protested, public policy considerations warranted the provision of protected status for dissident employees where the exclusive bargaining agent or the negotiated grievance arbitration machinery was not capable of resolving the issue raised. In part, my views were based upon ideas articulated in another article of mine appearing in the same year, "Labor Arbitration of Grievances Involving Racial Discrimination."[11]

The United States Supreme Court, however, over Justice Douglas' lone dissent, concluded in *Emporium Capwell v. NLRB*[12] that dissident employees' picketing, which protested allegedly discriminatory practices, was unprotected by Section 7. The Court, speaking through Justice Marshall, concluded that the issue before them in *Emporium* was whether a group of minority employees could "bargain with their employer over issues of employment discrimination" and held that separate bargaining was not necessary to eliminate discrimination, and that it would be likely to induce strife and deadlock within the bargaining unit. Accordingly, the Court held that the objectives of Title VII of the Civil Rights Act of 1964, which prohibits discrimination on account of race, sex, religion, and national origin, could not be pursued at the expense of the orderly collective bargaining process promoted by the National Labor Relations Act.

Professor Charles B. Craver's article discussed the D.C. Circuit Court's *Emporium* decision rendered prior to the Supreme Court decision and its extension of NLRA protection to the unauthorized concerted activity of dissident picketers aimed at racial discrimination allegedly practiced by the company.[13] Craver examined the general policies underlying the exclusivity doctrine under § 9(a) of the NLRA and the protection against discrimination afforded by Title VII of the Civil Rights Act of 1964 and their impact on the right of employees' independent concerted conduct.

After delineating the *Emporium*[14] factual situation, Craver traced the historical development of selected cases of unauthorized employee conduct and the evolution and application of "exclusivity" protection of the authority and status of majority bargaining representatives and concluded that "the Emporium decision actually constitutes a significant departure from the weight of judicial precedent."[15] The author termed "novel" the D.C. Court's mandate that the NLRB determine whether "the union was actually remedying the discrimination to the fullest extent possible, by the most expedient and efficacious means," which Craver maintained represented a deviation from precedent and a shift of focus from the effect of the unauthorized dissident group activity to the conduct of the labor organization.[16] Craver asserted that since the court found no evidence of bad faith and the union proceeded in a manner which it reasonably believed would produce the optimal results, the court's decision in *Emporium* was not sustainable on constitutional grounds.

Craver viewed the actions of the dissident employees as attempts to negotiate with the company and stated that such actions transcended the narrow "grievance" right afforded by the proviso to Section 9(a), disrupted the collective bargaining process, and should be denied NLRA protection. The author rejected protection of unauthorized employee pressure, even in support of the union's bargaining position.

Craver's analysis of NLRA policy considerations underlie his contention that where there exists no evidence of union bad faith, there is no breach of union duty of fair representation and that unauthorized concerted minority activity should only be protected where such breach has in fact occurred. In concluding that the *Emporium* D.C. Circuit's holding was not supported by NLRA, Title VII, or constitutional considerations, Craver asserted that the ruling was unwarranted in view of the "many non-disruptive, remedial alternatives available to minority dissidents" and that the "result achieved by the D.C. Circuit should not be sustained."[17]

Professor Norman Cantor, in "Dissident Worker Action, After The Emporium,"[18] was critical of the Supreme Court *Emporium* decision and stated that "unauthorized employee protests should not be equated with a demand for separate bargaining."[19] My own judgment is that Professor Cantor was correct in his assessment and that the Court improperly assumed that employee protests were a request for bargaining.

Professor Cantor went on to stress the complexity of cases involving dissident or unauthorized employee protest and alluded to the factors previously referred to in " 'Wildcat' Strikes," i.e., (1) consistency between union and employee objectives, (2) the timing of the dissident action and its compatibility with union goals in this regard, (3) the special nature of employment discrimination complaints and other protests involving public policy, and (4) the various forms that employee protests could take. Professor Cantor concluded that the *Emporium* decision must be confined to its appropriate bounds.[20] He advocated the right, under the proviso to Section 9(a), of workers to present complaints independently to management, despite the contrary dictum in *Emporium*, and the idea that workers who undertake spontaneous concerted action should not be subject to permanent discipline until the union had an opportunity to address the issues raised by the workers.

NOTES

1. 430 F. 2d 786 (5th Cir., 1970).

2. 419 F. 2d 216 (9th Cir., 1969).

3. See also *NLRB v. A. Lasaponau & Sons, Inc.,* 541 F. 2d 992 (2d Cir., 1976); *Dreis & Krump Mfg. Co. v. NLRB,* 544 F. 2d. 320 (7th Cir., 1976).

4. 269 NLRB No. 137 (1984).

5. *NLRB v. Shop Rite Foods, Inc.*, 430 F. 2d 786 (5th Cir., 1970).

6. Note 15 supra at p. 5, n. 6. Member Dennis relied in part upon *Lee A. Counsaul Co. v. NLRB*, 469 F. 2d 84 (9th Cir., 1972).

7. *NLRB v. Architectural Research Co.*, 117 LRRM 3299 (6th Cir., 1984).

8. 113 LRRM 3241 (7th Cir., 1983).

9. *Id.* at 3243.

10. 79 Yale L. J. 46 (1969).

11. 118 U. Penn. L. Rev. 40 (1969).

12. 420 U.S. 50 (1975).

13. Craver, "Minority Action versus Union Exclusivity: The Need to Harmonize NLRA and Title VII Policies," 26 Hastings L. J. 1 (1975).

14. *Id.* at 2, note 5.

15. *Id*. at 40.

16. *Id.*

17. *Id*. at 51.

18. 29 Rutgers L. Rev. 35 (1976).

19. *Id.* at 56.

20. *Id*. at 72.

5

On Labor Injunctions, Unions, and the Judges: The Boys Market Case

> . . . whatever may be a union's ad hoc benefit in a particular case, the meaning of collective bargaining for labor does not remotely derive from reliance on the sanction of litigation in the courts. . . . But a union, like any other combatant engaged in a particular fight, is ready to make an ally of an old enemy, and so we also find unions resorting to the otherwise much excoriated labor injunction. Such intermittent yielding to expediency does not change the fact that judicial intervention is illsuited to the special characteristics of the arbitration process in labor disputes; nor are the conditions for its effective functioning thereby altered.[1]

On June 1, 1970, the Supreme Court decided *Boys Market, Inc. v. Retail Clerks Union*[2] and held, 5 to 2,[3] that federal courts were not precluded from issuing injunctions against strikes in violation of collective bargaining agreements negotiated between unions and employers. In contrast to current events in Great Britain,[4] time has

---

[1] Mr. Justice Frankfurter, dissenting, in Textile Workers Union v. Lincoln Mills, 353 U.S. 448, 462–63 (1957).

[2] 398 U.S. 235 (1970).

[3] Mr. Justice Marshall did not participate. Mr. Justice Blackmun was not yet a member of the Court.

[4] The British attitude was aptly summarized by Sir Winston Churchill in 1911 when he said: "It is not good for trade unions that they should be brought in con-

now nearly blurred the debate about the role of law and judges in American labor-management relations. On this side of the Atlantic the unions are no longer resentful of the courts and their potential for harmful meddling in affairs of which they know little.[5] But it is perhaps more than arguable that *Boys Market* will stir up the embers of this well-worn argument and thus revive serious questions about judicial competence in dealing with unions.

At the same time, the transformation in the labor movement's thinking is reflected in the fact that some union leaders and lawyers may greet the *Boys Market* holding as a weapon to tame an increasingful unruly and rebellious rank and file.[6] Some unions may find the task of urging members to return to work pursuant to court order less difficult than a situation in which equally meaningful sanctions are absent. But the decision's emphasis on adherence to contractual responsibility as a paramount aspect of national labor law may exaggerate the inherent tensions between industrial peace

---

tact with the courts, and it is not good for the courts." Quoted in Milne-Bailey, Trade Union Documents 380 (1929). See generally Royal Commission on Trade Unions and Employers' Associations 1965–1968, Cmnd. No. 3623 (1968) [hereinafter cited as Donovan Report]; *In Place of Strife: A Policy for Industrial Relations*, Cmnd. No. 3888 (1969); Conservative Political Centre, Fair Deal at Work: A Conservative Approach to Modern Industrial Relations (1968). See also Grunfeld, *Donovan—the Legal Aspects*, 6 Brit. J. Ind. Rel. 316 (1968); Wigham, *Tough Path to the "Fair Deal,"* The Times (London), July 7, 1970, p. 27, col. 1. *Compare* McCarthy, *The Nature of Britain's Strike Problem*, 8 Brit. J. Ind Rel. 224 (1970), *with* Turner, Is Britain Really Strike Prone? (1969). I have summarized some of the recent developments in Gould, *Book Review*, 48 Texas L. Rev. 987 (1970).

[5] See *e.g.*, Rice, *Collective Labor Agreements in American Law*, 44 Harv. L. Rev. 572 (1931); Gregory, *The Law of Collective Agreement*, 57 Mich. L. Rev. 635 (1959). For more recent handling of industrial relations problems by the Supreme Court as they relate to economic pressures, see National Woodwork Mfrs. Ass'n v. NLRB, 386 U.S. 612 (1967) (product boycotts); NLRB v. Fruit & Vegetable Packers & Warehousemen, 377 U.S. 58 (1964) (consumer picketing); American Ship Building Co. v. NLRB, 380 U.S. 300 (1965) (lockouts).

[6] See Gould, *The Status of Unauthorized and "Wildcat" Strikes under the National Labor Relations Act*, 52 Corn. L. Q. 672 (1967); Raskin, *Rumbles from the Rank and File*, The Reporter Jan. 28, 1965, at 27; Federal Mediation & Conciliation Service, 18th Annual Report 13 (1965); 21st Annual Report 13 (1968). For some of the factors that are responsible for this phenomenon in the automobile industry, see Gooding, *Blue-Collar Blues on the Assembly-Line*, Fortune Magazine 69 (July, 1970). This phenomenon is not restricted to the United States. See Farnsworth, *Europe's Militant Unions Leaving Leaders Behind*, N.Y. Times, May 4, 1970, p. 1, col. 2. Even the model of industrial peace, Sweden, seems to be no exception. See Samuelsson, The Ironminers Walkout—Signal of Change? (Jan. 28, 1970) (Swedish Information Service).

and emerging opposition to the claims of union leadership for the authority to discipline their membership.[7] Moreover, while the Court's ruling presents formidable difficulties for the unions (as well as the judges who are now moved further into the tricky business of labor contract interpretation), it is conceivable that the majority opinion's reasoning may evolve contractual rights as well as obligations for the workers' representatives.

I. The Law of § 301 before Boys Market

Mr. Justice Frankfurter's quoted warnings were directed against the Supreme Court's conclusions in *Textile Workers Union v. Lincoln Mills*,[8] *i.e.*, that § 301 (a) of the National Labor Relations Act (NLRA), which provides that "[s]uits for violation of [labor] contracts . . . may be brought in any district court of the United States having jurisdiction of the parties, without respect to the amount in controversy or without regard to the citizenship of the parties,"[9] authorized the federal courts to "fashion a body of federal law for the enforcement of . . . collective bargaining agreements" and that specific performance of promises to arbitrate grievances under such collective agreements was part of the federal law.[10] In essence, *Lincoln Mills* stated that § 301 articulated contract obligations for employers as well as unions. And the fear was—and one not held by Mr. Justice Frankfurter alone—that the judges would be unequipped for the task and, even less charitably, that a judicial bias against the unions which had been evidenced in the earlier part of the century could return under § 301.[11] Rebuttal to

---

[7] *Cf.* NLRB v. Allis Chalmers, 388 U.S. 175 (1967); Parks v. IBEW, Local 24, 314 F.2d 886, 905 (4th Cir. 1963); Atleson, *Union Fines and Picket Lines: The NLRA and Union Disciplinary Power*, 17 U.C.L.A. L. Rev. 681 (1970); Gould, *Some Limitations upon Union Discipline: The Radiations of Allis Chalmers*, paper delivered at Seventeenth Annual Institute on Labor Law, Southwestern Legal Foundation, Oct. 15, 1970; Summers, *Legal Limitations on Union Discipline*, 64 Harv. L. Rev. 1049 (1951).

[8] See note 1 *supra*.   [9] 29 U.S.C. § 185.

[10] 353 U.S. at 451. *Cf.* Kramer, *In the Wake of Lincoln Mills*, 9 Lab. L.J. 835 (1958).

[11] See Cox, *Reflections upon Labor Arbitration*, 72 Harv. L. Rev. 1482 (1959); Shulman, *Reason, Contract, and the Law in Labor Relations*, 68 Harv. L. Rev. 999 (1955). *Cf.* Bickel & Wellington, *Legislative Purpose and the Judicial Process: The Lincoln Mills Case*, 71 Harv. L. Rev. 1 (1957).

dissenters' criticisms was provided by the *Steelworkers Trilogy*,[12] which declared that the inexpertness of judges was to be carefully circumscribed by rules that doubts about arbitrability were to be resolved in its favor by the courts and that, unless clear infidelity to the agreement was evidenced, the awards of arbitrators were to be enforced by the courts. Accordingly, the status of the arbitration process as a means to resolve labor disputes was considerably enhanced. The *Steelworkers Trilogy* reiterated a theme which had initially been articulated in *Lincoln Mills:* "Plainly the agreement to arbitrate grievance disputes is the *quid pro quo* for an agreement not to strike. [Section 301] . . . expresses a federal policy that federal courts should enforce these agreements on behalf of or against labor organizations and that industrial peace can best be obtained only in that way."[13]

Although the Court spoke more qualifiedly about the *quid pro quo* concept at a later date,[14] this approach was reiterated in *United Steelworkers v. Warrior & Gulf Navigation Co.* where Mr. Justice Douglas said:[15]

> The present federal policy is to promote industrial stabilization through the collective bargaining agreement. . . . A major factor in achieving industrial peace is the inclusion of a provision for arbitration of grievances in the collective bargaining agreement.
> . . . arbitration is the substitute for industrial strife. . . .
> . . . the parties' objective in using the arbitration process is primarily to further the common goal of uninterrupted production under the agreement. . . .

Subsequently, the Court held that state courts that had theretofore heard breach of contract labor cases as well as federal tribunals were to retain jurisdiction over collective agreement disputes to articulate a uniform federal labor law of contract.[16] Under such federal labor

---

12 United Steelworkers v. American Mfg. Co., 363 U.S. 564 (1960); United Steelworkers v. Warrior & Gulf Navigation Co., 363 U.S. 574 (1960); United Steelworkers v. Enterprise Wheel & Car Corp., 363 U.S. 593 (1960).

13 353 U.S. at 455.

14 See Drake Bakeries, Inc. v. Local 50, American Bakery & Confectionery Workers, 370 U.S. 254, 261 n. 7 (1962); Local 721, United Packinghouse Workers v. Needham Packing Co., 376 U.S. 247 (1964).

15 363 U.S. at 578, 582.

16 Charles Dowd Box Co. v. Courtney, 368 U.S. 502 (1962); Teamsters, Local 174 v. Lucas Flour Co., 369 U.S. 95 (1962).

law, a union refusal to arbitrate could be remedied by damages in the instance of either a no-strike clause or a broad arbitration clause through which the no-strike obligation was implied.[17] But, if the federal labor policy was to encourage the peaceable resolution of industrial disputes and if the no-strike pledge and the grievance-arbitration machinery were properly viewed as an exchange as the Court had stated in *Lincoln Mills* and the *Steelworkers Trilogy*, the question whether an employer could obtain an injunction against the no-strike violation remained clouded. This was so because the Norris-LaGuardia Act, enacted by Congress in 1932, prohibited, except in enumerated instances, the issuance of injunctions by federal courts.[18] More specifically, Norris-LaGuardia provides that federal courts shall not have jurisdiction to issue an injunction in a "labor dispute" so as to prohibit any person from "[c]easing or refusing to perform any work or to remain in any relation of employment."[19]

In essence then, the federal judiciary was confronted with a fundamental dilemma in an attempt to reconcile two diverse statutes. Norris-LaGuardia, on the one hand, was representative of a strong congressional desire to remove the courts from labor disputes on the theory that they had acted in a biased and uninformed manner, thus exposing the judiciary to a disrespect and contempt that independent judges cannot afford in a democracy.[20] There had been serious abuses in connection with the issuance of such injunctions,[21] albeit for the most part outside the context of labor contract litigation. Moreover, it was thought important to take away from federal judges the power effectively to resolve labor disputes according to their own view of social and economic philosophy—

---

[17] Teamsters, Local 174 v. Lucas Flour Co., 369 U.S. 95 (1962). The British courts seem more cautious about the articulation of such judge-made law because there is no comparable statutory authority. See Ford Motor Co. v. Amalgamated Union of Eng'rs & Foundry Workers, [1969] 1 W.L.R. 339. But see Selwyn, *Collective Agreements and the Law*, 32 Mod. L. Rev. 377 (1969).

[18] 29 U.S.C. § 104.   [19] *Ibid.*

[20] *Compare* Bickel, The Supreme Court and the Idea of Progress (1970), *and* Bickel, The Least Dangerous Branch (1962), *with* Black, The People and the Court (1960).

[21] See Frankfurter & Greene, The Labor Injunction (1930); Aaron, *Labor Injunctions in the State Courts: Part II—A Critique*, 50 Va. L. Rev. 1147 (1964); Comment, *Labor Injunctions and Judge-Made Labor Law: The Contemporary Role of Norris-LaGuardia*, 70 Yale L.J. 70 (1960).

particularly where, as in the case of strikes, what purported to be temporary relief had the effect of finality.[22] As Mr. Justice Harlan said: ". . . this judge-made law of the late 19th and early 20th centuries was based on self-mesmerized views of economic and social theory."[23] But subsequent to Norris-LaGuardia, Congress had begun to move in another direction. The passage of the NLRA in 1935[24] had put the NLRB, and eventually the federal courts,[25] into the middle of industrial disputes. In effect, the policy of laissez faire —or "collective laissez faire," as Professor Kahn-Freund would have it[26]—was implicitly rejected by a statute that invoked the courts and which, particularly through its 1947 Taft-Hartley amendments of which § 301 was a prominent part, seemed to invite a measure of judicial activism. The approach taken by the Court in *Lincoln Mills* and the *Steelworkers Trilogy* accentuated the dilemma all the more. For these cases articulated the *quid pro quo* approach that meant, if it meant anything, that employers could enforce the no-strike obligation against unions. Despite the broad prohibitory language of Norris-LaGuardia, the Court had reconciled the statute with the grievance machinery of the Railway Labor Act (RLA) in *Brotherhood of Railroad Trainmen v. Chicago & Indiana R.R.*,[27] where it held that strikes called over an issue properly submitted to the National Railroad Adjustment Board (NRAB) could be enjoined. Thus, where the RLA was involved, the Norris-LaGuardia hurdle was not too high for the Court to jump in order to enjoin a strike.[28] In 1962 Mr. Justice Black, speaking for the Court, attempted to deal

---

[22] On the nature of the injunction, see FRANKFURTER & GREENE, note 21 *supra*, at 53–60.

[23] Brotherhood of Railroad Trainmen v. Jackson Terminal Co., 394 U.S. 369, 382 (1969). See also Marine Cooks v. Panama S.S. Co., 362 U.S. 365, 369 (1960).

[24] 49 Stat. 449 (1935).   [25] 29 U.S.C. § 160(f).

[26] Kahn-Freund, *Labor Law*, in LAW AND OPINION IN GREAT BRITAIN IN THE 20TH CENTURY 227 (Ginsberg ed. 1959). See also in this connection GRUNFELD, MODERN TRADE UNION LAW (1966); KAHN-FREUND, LABOR LAW; OLD TRADITIONS AND NEW DEVELOPMENTS (1968); WEDDERBURN, THE WORKER AND THE LAW (1965); WEDDERBURN & DAVIES, EMPLOYMENT GRIEVANCES AND DISPUTES PROCEDURE IN BRITAIN (1969).

[27] 353 U.S. 30 (1957).

[28] For an excellent analysis of this decision see Cox, *Current Problems of the Law of Grievance Arbitration*, 30 ROCKY MOUNT. L. REV. 247, 252 (1958). Subsequently, the Court declined the opportunity to undertake a more difficult accommodation in NLRB v. Drivers Local 639, 362 U.S. 274 (1960).

with the same problem in the context of the NLRA in *Sinclair Refining Co. v. Atkinson.*[29]

In *Sinclair*, by a 5 to 3 vote,[30] the Court rejected the argument that § 301 of the act could be said to have "impliedly repealed" § 4 of the "pre-existing Norris-LaGuardia Act." In that case the collective bargaining agreement provided for binding arbitration of "any difference regarding wages, hours or working conditions between the parties hereto or between the Employer and an employee covered by this working agrement which might arise within any plant or within any region of operations." The contract also imposed a flat prohibition upon slowdowns, strikes, or work stoppages for "any cause which is or may be the subject of a grievance."[31] The complaint alleged that a number of work stoppages and strikes had been undertaken in violation of the contract. The company claimed that in such circumstances there was no adequate remedy at law that would protect its contractual rights and therefore requested injunctive relief. The unions sought dismissal of the complaint on the ground that the controversy was a "labor dispute" within the meaning of the Norris-LaGuardia Act and that therefore a federal court was without jurisdiction to issue the injunction requested.

The majority opinion of the Court concluded that since the strike constituted a "labor dispute" within the meaning of Norris-LaGuardia, the statute barred an injunction. Conceding the argument that the injunction might be sensible and sound labor policy, Mr. Justice Black said for the majority:[32]

> We cannot ignore the plain import of a congressional enact-
> ment, particularly one which, as we have repeatedly said, was

---

[29] 370 U.S. 195 (1962). See *Report of Special Atkinson-Sinclair Committee*, 1963 ABA Section of Labor Relations Law, pt. II, 226–40.

[30] Mr. Justice Frankfurter did not participate. Mr. Justice Stewart was part of the *Sinclair* majority but switched his position in *Boys Market*. Mr. Chief Justice Burger, not a member of the Court at the time of *Sinclair*, was also a part of the *Boys Market* majority.

Chief Justice Burger had earlier indicated an impatience with stare decisis in the area of labor law by joining the concurring opinion of Mr. Justice White in Longshoremen v. Ariadne Co., 397 U.S. 195, 201–02 (1970), which announced a desire to reconsider some of the preemption doctrine. This opinion, together with the Chief Justice's concurring opinion in Taggart v. Weinacker's, Inc., 397 U.S. 223, 227–28 (1970), evoked a memorandum from Mr. Justice Harlan stressing adherence to prior judgments, even in those cases in which he had dissented.

[31] 370 U.S. at 197.   [32] *Id.* at 203.

deliberately drafted in the broadest of terms in order to avoid
the danger that it would be narrowed by judicial construction.
. . . Upon consideration, we cannot agree with [the view that
Norris-LaGuardia has been narrowed by the subsequent enactment of § 301] and agree instead with the view . . . that § 301
was not intended to have any such partially repealing effect
upon such a longstanding carefully thought out and highly
significant part of this country's labor legislation as the Norris-
LaGuardia Act.

The Court stated that the failure of Congress expressly to repeal
Norris-LaGuardia when enacting § 301 made it unlikely that Congress intended to repeal the former statute's anti-injunction features
—particularly in light of the fact that Congress had repealed Norris-
LaGuardia for other purposes in the NLRA where it sought to
prohibit certain kinds of economic pressure by unions.[33] Moreover,
the Court rejected the employer argument that, even if Congress
did not intend to repeal Norris-LaGuardia, it was willing to confer
a power upon the courts to "accommodate" the provisions of
seemingly contrary statutes.

Mr. Justice Brennan, speaking also for Justices Douglas and Harlan, dissented in *Sinclair* and stated that the majority's conclusions
were inconsistent with the federal labor policy favoring arbitration
as articulated in *Lincoln Mills* and the *Steelworkers Trilogy*. Conceding the fact that Congress did not repeal Norris-LaGuardia
insofar as § 301 was concerned, Mr. Justice Brennan contended
that such a conclusion did not preclude judicial inquiry into the
question of accommodation. The dissenting opinion thus concluded
that merely because Congress did not wish to permit the wholesale
abandonment of Norris-LaGuardia in contract actions, it was not
necessarily logical to conclude that § 301 and its approach were to
be subservient to Norris-LaGuardia. Further, the dissenting opinion
stated that the anti-injunction features of Norris-LaGuardia were
not vital to the ends of federal labor policy where the underlying
dispute which gave rise to the strike was itself arbitrable and thus

---

[33] *Id.* at 204–05. The Court specifically referred to the fact that Congress had
amended Taft-Hartley and repealed Norris-LaGuardia so as to permit the board
some latitude to seek injunctions and the Attorney-General to enjoin national
emergency strikes. 29. U.S.C. §§ 160, 178. One obvious distinction between these
provisions and § 301 is that government rather than private employers requests
injunctive relief in the former situations. *Cf.* Sears, Roebuck & Co. v. Carpet Layers
Local 419, 397 U.S. 655 (1970).

capable of resolution through preferred procedures, *i.e.*, arbitration, as implied in the NLRA.[34]

Mr. Justice Brennan had other objections to the majority opinion in *Sinclair*. He noted that the practical effect of *Sinclair* forced on the Court the choice between two equally undesirable alternatives. On the one hand, the uniformity of federal labor law governing the collective agreement argued for the proposition that injunctive relief must be denied in state as well as federal courts. If the Court was to hold that federal and state courts were bound by the same rules, § 301 would then deprive employers of a state remedy that they had enjoyed prior to the passage of the 1947 amendments. This seemed inconsistent with § 301 because the statute had clearly been designed to create a greater contractual responsibility on the part of unions and the Court would thus be articulating a rule that would have the opposite effect.

On the other hand, if state courts were to retain the ability to issue injunctions where no state "baby" Norris-LaGuardia Acts were in existence,[35] state courts would then become the "preferred instruments to protect the integrity of the arbitration process."[36] Thus, the state judiciary would become dominant in an area of law that was to be both uniform and federal. Disparate rules of law that would result, depending upon the particular jurisdiction in which the strike took place, would be clearly inconsistent with the Court's prior pronouncements on the desirability of uniformity in labor-management contractual relationships.

Mr. Justice Brennan also noted that unions might attempt to remove such injunction suits to federal courts, although he was of the view that removal would not be allowed. But "if it is allowed, the result once again is that § 301 will have had the strange consequence of taking away a contract remedy available before its enactment."[37]

---

[34] "Final adjustment by a method agreed upon by the parties is declared to be the desirable method for settlement of grievance disputes arising over the application or interpretation of an existing collective-bargaining agreement." 29 U.S.C. § 173(d).

[35] "Almost half the states have such provisions." Aaron, *Strikes in Breach of Collective Agreements: Some Unanswered Questions*, 63 COLUM. L. REV. 1027, 1036 n. 67 (1963). See also Bartosic, *Injunctions and Section 301: The Patchwork of Avco and Philadelphia Marine on the Fabric of National Labor Policy*, 69 COLUM. L. REV. 980, 1001–11 (1969).

[36] 370 U.S. at 226.   [37] *Id.* at 227.

And, indeed, in *Avco Corp. v. Aero Lodge No. 735*[38] the majority of the Court approved removal.

In *Avco* the complaint stated that employees were engaging in work stoppages and a walkout because of disputes "allegedly subject" to the grievance procedure in the face of a no-strike clause. The state court issued an *ex parte* injunction. The respondents then moved in the federal district court for removal of the case. Mr. Justice Douglas, speaking for the Court,[39] held that the action was removable. He said, however, that "the nature of the relief available after jurisdiction attaches is, of course, different from the question whether there is jurisdiction to adjudicate the controversy."[40] Thus, the power of federal courts as well as the question whether state court injunctions were to be dissolved in such removal proceedings was left open. Similarly, the Court avoided the question of state court authority to issue injunctive relief, independent of the removal question, in light of *Sinclair*. Mr. Justice Stewart, concurring, joined by Justices Harlan and Brennan, said: "[T]he Court expressly reserves decision on the effect of *Sinclair* in the circumstances presented by this case. The Court will, no doubt, have an opportunity to reconsider the scope and continuing validity of *Sinclair* upon an appropriate future occasion."[41]

That future occasion turned out to be the case of *Boys Market*. Appropriately, the task of delivering the majority opinion fell to Mr. Justice Brennan, who had written the dissent in *Sinclair*. In *Boys Market*, the union protested the assignment of certain work to the employer's supervisors and other nonbargaining unit employees. The union representative insisted that certain food cases be stripped of all merchandise placed there by such non-unit employees and restocked by workers whom the union represented. When the employer resisted this demand, the union called a strike despite a broad arbitration clause that purportedly covered the dispute in question. A separate clause, entitled "work stoppages," stated that "matters subject to the procedures of this Article shall be settled and resolved in the manner provided herein," and went on to prohibit

---

[38] 390 U.S. 557 (1968). Cf. Lesnick, *State-Court Injunctions and the Federal Common Law of Labor Contracts: Beyond Norris-LaGuardia*, 79 HARV. L. REV. 757 (1966).

[39] Mr. Justice Douglas had previously reiterated his views on the *Sinclair* problem in Local 1219, ILA v. Philadelphia Marine Trade Ass'n, 389 U.S. 64, 77 (1967).

[40] 390 U.S. at 561.   [41] *Id.* at 562.

stoppages or lockouts except where "the other party refuses to perform any obligations under this Article or refuses to abide by, accept or perform a decision or award of an arbitrator or board."[42]

The employer, upon seeking a temporary restraining order in a state court, simultaneously sought to invoke the grievance and arbitration procedures so as to resolve the underlying dispute. The state court issued both a temporary restraining order forbidding continuation of the strike and an order to show cause why a preliminary injunction should not be granted. The union then removed this action to federal district court and made a motion to quash the state court's temporary restraining order. The employer, in turn, moved for an order compelling arbitration and enjoining the continuation of the strike.

The federal district court ordered the parties to arbitrate and enjoined the strike, but the Ninth Circuit reversed upon the authority of *Sinclair*.[43] The Supreme Court, in *Boys Market*, undertook to "re-examine" the *Sinclair* holding and concluded that "*Sinclair* was erroneously decided and that subsequent events have undermined its continuing validity."[44]

II. THE ACTIVIST RATIONALE OF BOYS MARKET

The primary reason given for such a re-examination was the fact that *Sinclair* "stands as a significant departure from our otherwise consistent efforts upon the congressional policy to promote the peaceful settlement of of labor disputes through arbitration."[45] But a preliminary question not touched by any of the opinions in *Boys Market* is whether the Court's efforts in the *Steelworkers Trilogy* had made any contribution to the achievement of industrial peace and, thus, whether abandonment of the stare decisis principle could be justified in terms of the overriding importance of § 301 as a central part of national labor policy. Although the impact of the law upon industrial relations is quite difficult to measure in most instances, the argument that the Court's work is irrelevant to the presence of work stoppages, if accepted, would make rejection of the prohibitory language of Norris-LaGuardia all the more difficult. If it were, accommodation between the two statutes would be hardly worth the candle.

---

[42] 398 U.S. at 239 n.3.

[43] 416 F.2d 368 (1969).

[44] 398 U.S. at 238.

[45] *Id*. at 241.

Professor Wellington made such an argument. He contended that the increased number and percentage of strikes recently occurring during the terms of labor contracts prove that the *Trilogy* has "had no effect" in contributing to labor peace.[46] Moreover, he continued, where there are issues that are critical to the parties, they are simply postponed for resolution through warfare subsequent to the expiration of the contract. One can hardly dispute the existence of an extreme tenacity by the parties which is sufficient in a number of instances merely to postpone the confrontation to a later date. The subcontracting issue in the automobile industry provides a more than adequate example.[47] The United Automobile Workers Union has continuously attempted to restrict managerial authority in this area through both arbitration and contract negotiation.

This thesis of despair, however, ignores the fact that the contractual strike prohibition may serve as a cooling-off period and thus lend a measure of rationality to the resolution of disputes. The allocation of a specific time for disputes, *i.e.*, the expiration of the collective agreement, releases the union from pressure to threaten the stoppage over every grievance that arises, improves management's ability to meet business orders and delivery dates and, if one can judge from the British experience, probably induces a better atmosphere for productivity increases.[48]

Moreover, the fact that breach-of-contract stoppages appear to be on the upswing since the *Trilogy* hardly proves Professor Wellington's point. In the first place, *Sinclair*—the governing law for the past eight years—deprived management of its most effective remedy for breach of a no-strike clause. It is at least possible that *Boys Market* may have improved this situation to some extent and thus made breach-of-contract stoppages less likely. But, more important, an analysis of the *Trilogy* and strike statistics that fails to take account of other factors operating during the past decade is necessarily superficial. The most obviously relevant consideration is the phenomenon of relatively full employment and inflation—both of which may

---

[46] WELLINGTON, LABOR AND THE LEGAL PROCESS 119–20, 353–54 n.62 (1968).

[47] See Ford Motor Co., 42 Lab. Arb. 220 (1964). Ford Motor Co., unreported (June 9, 1967). See, most recently, on the subject, Erikson, *Ford's Contract Workers Come under Fire*, Detroit News, Aug. 1, 1970, p. 5A, col. 5.

[48] See Donovan Report; FLANDERS, COLLECTIVE BARGAINING: PRESCRIPTION FOR CHANGE (1967); FLANDERS, INDUSTRIAL RELATIONS: WHAT IS WRONG WITH THE SYSTEM? (1965).

encourage restiveness under a contract of fixed duration or, for that matter, under any other system.[49] And it would be interesting to speculate (and it would be no more speculative than the attack upon the *Trilogy* under discussion) about the extent to which the very considerable number of rank and file rejections of negotiated contracts during recent years would have taken the form of wildcat or breach-of-contract strikes if the no-strike obligation did not have some legal sanctions behind it.[50] Explosive discontent in the work place may have been channeled into another forum that appears to be less disruptive. If so, one can find the § 301 rationale substantially intact, thus justifying the reconciliation of the no-strike mandate to its purposes.

Because Mr. Justice Black had assented to both *Lincoln Mills* and the *Steelworkers Trilogy*,[51] the above rationalization would not have been to his liking—although it must be pointed out that Mr. Justice Black has remained the most consistent critic of the Court's decisions in the arbitration area.[52] Stymied by the industrial peace objectives interpretation previously placed upon § 301, Mr. Justice Black apparently felt obliged to focus his attack on the weak points of the majority opinion of Mr. Justice Brennan in *Boys Market*.

At the outset of the majority opinion, the Court brushed aside the doctrine of stare decisis as a rule that did not necessitate mechanistic adherence to prior decisions. As Mr. Justice Stewart said in a separate concurring opinion quoting Mr. Justice Frankfurter: "Wisdom

---

[49] For a more detailed critique of Professor Wellington's views, see Gould, *Book Review*, 16 WAYNE L. REV. 384 (1969); Shapiro, *Book Review*, 22 STAN. L. REV. 657 (1970).

[50] See Salpukas, *Young Workers Raising Voices for Factory and Union Changes*, N.Y. Times, June 1, 1970, p. 23, col. 1, where it is indicated that younger workers wish to remove the no-strike clause, "want faster changes and sometimes bypass their own union leaders and start wildcat strikes." The 1970 Steelworkers convention also demonstrated a growing demand for the elimination of no-strike clauses. See Conti, *U.S.W. Convention Echoes with Strike Talk for Next July*, Wall St. J., Oct. 2, 1970, p. 8, col. 2.

[51] Indeed, Mr. Justice Black joined with Mr. Justice Douglas in his dissenting opinion in Association of Westinghouse Salaried Employees v. Westinghouse Elec. Corp., 348 U.S. 437 (1965), in a view which was eventually to become the majority opinion in *Lincoln Mills*.

[52] See Mr. Justice Black's dissenting opinions in Teamsters Local 174 v. Lucas Flour Co., 369 U.S. 95 (1962); Smith v. Evening News Association, 371 U.S. 195, 201 (1962); Carey v. Westinghouse Elec. Corp., 375 U.S. 261, 273 (1964); Vaca v. Sipes, 386 U.S. 171, 203 (1967); Republic Steel Corp. v. Maddox, 379 U.S. 650, 659 (1965).

too often never comes, and so one ought not to reject it merely because it comes late."[53] Moreover, the Court stated that the mere silence of Congress was an insufficient reason to refuse to reconsider *Sinclair*. The most important factor in the Court's decision was the *Steelworkers Trilogy* and its policy in favor of arbitration. Said the Court: "Furthermore, in light of developments subsequent to *Sinclair*, in particular a decision in *Avco Corp.,* . . . it has become clear that the *Sinclair* decision does not further but rather frustrates realization of an important goal of our national labor policy."[54] Mr. Justice Brennan then noted that "*Avco*, viewed in the context of *Lincoln Mills* and its progeny, . . . produced an anomalous situation which . . . makes urgent the reconsideration of *Sinclair*."[55]

The urgency resulted from the destruction of state court jurisdiction over breach of no-strike clause cases. Since *Avco* permitted removal and *Sinclair* precluded federal district court injunctions, said the Court, the state courts were now effectively ousted from this field. But this, in turn, was inconsistent with the Court's previously announced holding that federal jurisdiction for breach of contract cases was to supplement the pre-existing jurisdiction of state courts and not to intrude upon this area.[56] Said the Court: "It is ironic indeed that the very provision which Congress clearly intended to provide additional remedies for breach of collective-bargaining agreements has been employed to displace previously existing state remedies."[57] Mr. Justice Brennan agreed that labor law issues could not be "administered identically in all courts," but, where so significant a remedial device as the injunction was involved, "its availability or non-availability in various courts will not only produce rampant forum-shopping and maneuvering from one court to another, but will also greatly frustrate any relative uniformity in the enforcement of arbitration agreements."[58] Since some state courts permitted injunctions to be issued in the *Sinclair–Boys*

---

[53] 398 U.S. at 255. Frankfurter's statement quoted by Mr. Justice Stewart is from a dissenting opinion in Henslee v. Union Planters Bank, 335 U.S. 595, 600 (1949).

[54] 398 U.S. at 241.   [55] *Id.* at 244.

[56] "The clear implication of the entire record of the congressional debate in both 1946 and 1947 is that the purpose of conferring jurisdiction upon the federal courts was not to displace, but to supplement, the thoroughly considered jurisdiction of the courts of the various States over contracts made by labor organizations." Charles Dowd Box Co. v. Courtney, 368 U.S. 502, 511 (1962).

[57] 398 U.S. at 245.   [58] *Id.* at 246.

Market type of cases,[59] and since this had obviously created forum-shopping,[60] the Court's observations seem to have been well justified.

Mr. Justice Brennan, however, was not content to rest on lack of uniformity and the implications of *Avco*. The *Boys Market* opinion further stated—in response to the argument that *Sinclair* should be made applicable to the states so as to avoid the uniformity problem[61]—that such a resolution of the dilemma would have "devastating implications," since, under such a scheme, equitable remedies would not be available in any forum. Said the Court: "Any incentive for employers to enter into such an [arbitration and no-strike] arrangement is necessarily dissipated if the principal and most expeditious method by which the no-strike obligation can be enforced

[59] See, for instance, Perry & Sons v. Robilotto, 39 Misc.2d 147 (N.Y. Sup. Ct. 1963); McCarroll v. Los Angeles County District Council of Carpenters, 49 Cal.2d 45 (1957). The argument was made, however, that § 301 and the Court's decision in *Sinclair* precluded the issuance of injunctions in labor disputes by state courts because *Sinclair* was federal substantive labor law. See Shaw Elec. Co. v. IBEW, Local 98, 418 Pa. 1, (1965). The cases are collected in Bartosic, note 35 *supra*, at 1102, nn. 136, 137, 138. The Supreme Court had reserved decision on this matter both in *Avco*, 390 U.S. at 560 n.2; and in *Dowd Box*, 368 U.S. at 514 n.8. *Cf.* Ruppert v. Engelhofer, 3 N.Y.2d 576 (1958).

[60] American Dredging Co. v. Local 25, Int'l Union of Operating Eng'rs, 338 F.2d 837 (3d Cir. 1964). For a thorough and excellent discussion of this matter see Bartosic, note 35 *supra*, at 987–96.

[61] Presumably state courts may issue injunctions under appropriate circumstances in labor disputes even without statutory authorization. Of course, the employer may circumvent any difficulties on this score by simply filing a request for injunctive relief under *Boys Market* in federal district court. But the rule ought to be the same in state courts—even in those jurisdictions which have baby Norris-LaGuardia Acts —so as to preserve both federal and state jurisdiction and to reduce the incentive to utilize only federal tribunals. In effect, *Boys Market* ought to require a second accommodation at the level between § 301 and state statutes. See Teamsters Local 174 v. Lucas Flour Co., 369 U.S. 95 (1962); Charles Dowd Box Co. v. Courtney, 368 U.S. 502 (1962). But see McCarroll v. Los Angeles County Dist. Council of Carpenters, 49 Cal. 2d 45 (1957). This would delimit both the automatic issuance of injunctions without consideration of such factors as whether the dispute itself was arbitrable, see, *e.g.*, Construction & Gen. Laborers Local 246 v. Jordan Co., 75 L.R.R.M. 2201 (Ga. 1970) as well as mandate the modification of "baby" Norris-LaGuardia statutes to conform with *Boys Market*. Professor St. Antoine does not appear to be so certain. See St. Antoine, *Interventionism, Laissez-Faire, and Stare Decisis*, Address before ABA Section of Labor Relations Law, Aug. 10, 1970. The federal courts will probably revise state court injunctions at variance with *Boys Market* requirements. See Holland Construction Co., Inc. v. International Union of Operating Engr's, 74 L.R.R.M. 3087 (D. Kan. 1970). *Cf.* Atlantic Coast Line R.R. v. Locomotive Engineers, 398 U.S. 281 (1970).

is eliminated."[62] The Court did not, however, cite any empirical data or authority to support this proposition. Most probably, this portion of the Court's rationale falls short of the mark since all evidence is that arbitration clauses have gained increasingly wider acceptance during the past eight years, *i.e.*, since *Sinclair* has been the law.[63] Thus, this aspect of the *Boys Market* rationale, though its logic is sound, is not in tune with the practicalities of industrial relations.

Mr. Justice Brennan hedged against the possibility of such criticism when he stated that even if management were not encouraged to resist arbitration agreements by *Sinclair*, it was improperly deprived of the most effective weaponry to deal with no-strike violations. The Court's opinion did not assess the effectiveness of the more traditional remedies utilized by management, *i.e.*, discharge and discipline, nor did it deal with the possibility of encouraging parties voluntarily to adopt "quickie" or expeditious grievance-arbitration machinery equipped to deal with stoppages, perhaps through the use of a permanent umpire rather than an ad hoc arbitrator.[64] But the Court did address itself to the availability of damages under § 301 and state breach-of-contract cases:[65]

> While it is of course true, as respondent contends, that all other avenues of redress, such as an action for damages, would remain open to an aggrieved employer, an award with damages after a dispute has been settled is no substitute for an immediate halt to an illegal strike. Furthermore, an action for damages prosecuted during or after a labor dispute would only tend to aggravate industrial strife and delay an early resolution of the difficulties between employer and union.

Here the Court is on undeniably sound ground. Employers are unlikely to sue and certainly not to continue such legal action subse-

---

[62] 398 U.S. at 248.

[63] Approximately 94 percent of the collective bargaining agreements negotiated between unions and employers contain arbitration clauses. U.S. Bureau of Labor Statistics, BULL. No. 1425-1, *Grievance Procedures*, p. 1 (1964). It would appear that the *Sinclair* rule did not deter employers from entering into contracts with arbitration clauses. See also Jones & Smith, *Management and Labor Appraisals and Criticisms of the Arbitration Process: A Report with Comments*, 62 MICH. L. REV. 1115 (1964).

[64] But see 398 U.S. at 244 n. 10.   [65] *Id.* at 248.

quent to a strike settlement.[66] Indeed, the price of settlement is often
a promise by management to withdraw damage suits that are pending or about to be instituted. A contrary practice would detract
from the achievement of sound industrial relations.[67] Moreover, the
measure of damages to which the employer is entitled is vague and
debatable.[68]

If, however, the injunction is indeed the most effective remedy
and the damage actions will simultaneously produce the discord that
is so antithetical to our national labor policy, the Court was nevertheless still left with the problem of the Norris-LaGuardia bar
against enjoining "labor disputes." The Court concluded that since
congressional emphasis in dealing with labor unions had changed
from the days of Norris-LaGuardia as labor organizations "grew in
strength and developed toward maturity,"[69] equitable remedies that
protected collective bargaining procedures and arbitration could be
accommodated by Norris-LaGuardia. Indeed, said the Court, since
the purpose of Norris-LaGuardia was to encourage and foster the
growth of labor organizations, equitable remedies of the kind articulated in *Boys Market* were hardly inconsistent with the "core purpose"[70] of that statute.

In dissent, Mr. Justice Black stated that stare decisis, while not of
overbearing importance in the constitutional arena where ultimate
responsibility rests with the Court, ought to foreclose re-examination of past decisions where the primary responsibility lies with
Congress, unless there were exceptional circumstances presented.[71]

---

[66] See *Report of Special Atkinson-Sinclair Committee*, note 29 *supra*, at 242; Cox,
note 28 *supra*, at 255; Warren, C. J., dissenting, in UAW v. Russell, 356 U.S. 634,
647 (1958).

[67] This practice prevails in Great Britain as well. See WEDDERBURN & DAVIES, note
26 *supra*, at 49. At the same time, it should be noted that the possibility of a damage
action has some deterrent effect. And equally important is the fact that some of the
courts have imposed bonds upon unions that cannot be negotiated away at the
bargaining table. See Tanker Service Committee, Inc. v. Masters Local 14, 269 F.
Supp. 551 (E.D. Pa. 1967), *aff'd* 394 F.2d 160 (3d Cir. 1968); Ormet Corp. v. United
Steelworkers, 72 L.R.R.M. 2268 (W.D. Pa. 1969), *injunction suspended pending
appeal*, 72 L.R.R.M. 2510 (3d Cir. 1969). An obvious benefit to be derived from this
conditional damage remedy is speed. But, query, is this reconcilable with Drake
Bakeries v. Bakery Local 50, 370 U.S. 254 (1962), which remits damage questions
to arbitration?

[68] See cases cited *infra*, at note 126. See Cox, note 28 *supra*. But see, *e.g.*, International Brotherhood of Teamsters Local 25 v. W. L. Mead, Inc., 230 F.2d 576 (1st Cir.
1956); United Steelworkers of America v. CCI Corp., 395 F.2d 529 (10th Cir. 1968).

[69] 398 U.S. at 251.   [70] *Id*. at 253.   [71] *Id*. at 255.

Mr. Justice White relied upon the majority opinion in *Sinclair* in his separate dissent.[72]

Perhaps, where highly volatile and controversial issues like strikes and labor contracts are involved, Congress should be charged with final responsibility to adjust the delicate balance after the Court has placed interpretative gloss upon the statute as it did in *Sinclair*. Trade unionists who regard *Boys Market* as a logical extension of the *Steelworkers Trilogy* (and there are many such union advocates) might have hoped to fashion a political compromise in Congress that would have removed some of the Taft-Hartley amendments far more onerous to organized labor. Such an approach, however, overlooks the argument that error—particularly an error which is an egregious departure from national labor policy articulated by the Court—ought to be corrected. Moreover, if the criticism is made that the Court has become too activist and usurped the authority of Congress, it would seem that that kind of critique is more properly leveled at *Lincoln Mills* and its rather extraordinary assumption of authority to fashion federal labor law.[73] There must be no mistake about the fact that *Boys Market* is judicial policy making. But it was *Lincoln Mills* that called upon the courts to make use of their "judicial inventiveness."[74] And I should think that, in terms of both legislative intent and judicial precedent, the foundation of *Boys Market* is more firmly established than that upon which *Lincoln Mills* rested. In 1947 Congress was most concerned to discipline trade unions which exhibited a lack of contractual responsibility.[75]

The Court, having made its quantum jump in *Lincoln Mills* hardly could have retained a doctrine that was contrary to the direct implications of that decision as well as the *Trilogy*. After all, it was *Lincoln Mills* that properly assumed the applicability of § 301 to labor unions. The difficult question, decided affirmatively in that case, was whether liability was to be imposed upon

---

[72] *Id.* at 261.

[73] Mr. Justice Douglas said in *Lincoln Mills:* "The legislative history of § 301 is somewhat cloudy and confusing. But there are a few shafts of light that illuminate our problem." 353 U.S. at 452. See Bickel & Wellington, note 11 *supra*.

[74] 353 U.S. at 457. For an application of this approach to another area of labor arbitration, see Gould, *Labor Arbitration of Grievances Involving Racial Discrimination*, 118 U. Pa. L. Rev. 40 (1969). See also in this regard Shapiro, *Some Thoughts on Intervention before Courts, Agencies and Arbitrators*, 81 Harv. L. Rev. 721 (1968).

[75] 398 U.S. at 245 n.12. See the discussion of legislative history in *Lincoln Mills*, 353 U.S. at 452–57.

employers as well. Moreover, as the majority noted in *Boys Market*, primary reliance upon damages (as well as the unmentioned remedy of discharge and discipline) is most often an irritant, inappropriate to mature union-employer relationships, and thus at odds with the national labor policy that favors the achievement of industrial peace. *Boys Market* can then be said to be in step with a common law of labor relations that is "dynamic and adaptable to changing times [predicated upon] legislatively based principles . . . to the extent it is in the law developed during the more than thirty years of administering our most comprehensive national labor scheme, the National Labor Relations Act."[76]

One other factor not mentioned by the Court in *Boys Market* is that an employer who sought damages or disciplinary action would normally proceed to arbitration. This course of action is required by the Court's decision in *Drake Bakeries*[77] handed down at the time of *Sinclair*. If the hearing were to take place in the midst of the stoppage or while the underlying issue which had given rise to it was still unresolved, the setting would more often be counterproductive than not. In the midst of a strike or its immediate aftermath, emo-

---

[76] 394 U.S. at 383.

[77] 370 U.S. 254 (1962). In *Drake Bakeries*, the Court held that the proper forum for adjudication of a no-strike violation was arbitration rather than the courts. *Cf.* Atkinson v. Sinclair Refining Co., 370 U.S. 238 (1962). The Court also held that a strike in violation of the contract did not necessarily repudiate the arbitration clause through which the alleged no-strike violation might be heard. See Local 721, United Packing House, Food & Allied Workers v. Needham Packing Co., 376 U.S. 247 (1964). On the *Drake Bakeries* rule, see generally, Fluor Corp. v. Carpenters District Council, 424 F.2d 283 (5th Cir. 1970); Johnson Builders, Inc. v. United Bhd. of Carpenters and Joiners, 422 F.2d 137 (10th Cir. 1970); Howard Elec. Co. v. IBEW, Local 570, 423 F.2d 164 (9th Cir. 1970); Local 748, IUE v. Jefferson City Cabinet Co., 314 F.2d 192 (6th Cir. 1963); Los Angeles Paper Bag Co. v. Printing Specialties and Paper Products Union, 345 F.2d 757 (9th Cir. 1965); District 50, United Mine Workers of America v. Chris-Craft Corp., 385 F.2d 946 (6th Cir. 1967). For cases granting stay of proceedings pending arbitration, see IT&T v. Communication Workers, 422 F.2d 77 (2d Cir. 1970); Scalizitti Co. v. Operating Eng'rs., Local 150, 351 F.2d 576 (7th Cir. 1965); Franchi Construction Co. v. Hod Carriers, Local 560, 248 F. Supp. 134 (D. Mass. 1965); United States Steel Corp. v. Seafarers, 237 F. Supp. 529 (E.D. Pa. 1965); Clothing Workers v. United Garment Mfg. Co., 338 F.2d 195 (8th Cir. 1964); Fifth Ave. Coach Lines v. Transport Workers, 235 F. Supp. 842 (S.D. N.Y. 1964); Swartz & Funston v. Bricklayers, 319 F.2d 116 (3d Cir. 1963); Gilmour v. Lathers Union, Local 74, 223 F. Supp. 236 (N.D. Ill. 1963); Yale & Towne Mfg. Co. v. Local 1717, IAM, 299 F.2d 882 (3d Cir. 1962). For cases denying stay of proceedings pending arbitration, see G. T. Schjeldahi Co. v. Local 1680, IAM, 393 F.2d 502 (1st Cir. 1968); Simonds Construction Co. v. Hod Carriers, Local 1330, 315 F.2d 291 (7th Cir. 1963); Boeing Co. v. UAW, 234 F. Supp. 404 (E.D. Pa. 1965).

tions run high. Here again, *Sinclair,* by permitting the strike to continue, could be viewed as an aberration.

Nevertheless, the unease with which many both in and out of the house of labor view *Boys Market* has substantial historical basis. One must recall that the issuance of an injunction as a result of *Boys Market* is dependent upon the existence of an arbitrable grievance that gave rise to the strike. The Court's holding is a "narrow one." As Mr. Justice Brennan said in dissent in *Sinclair:*[78]

> ... the employer should be ordered to arbitrate, as a condition of his obtaining an injunction against the strike. Beyond this, the District Court must, of course, consider whether issuance of an injunction would be warranted under ordinary principles of equity—whether breaches are occurring and will continue, or have been threatened and will be committed; whether they have caused or will cause irreparable injury to the employer and whether the employer will suffer more from the denial of an injunction than the union will from its issuance.

Labor experience with injunctions before 1932 was extremely bad.[79] Among the abuses were frequent use of *ex parte* injunctions against strikes and picketing, issuance of injunctions on the basis of vague and generalized affidavits, and general unwillingness by the judiciary to reverse, at the permanent injunction stage, a decision already made by the judge in issuing a temporary restraining order. Once the injunction was handed down, contempt penalties were often meted out against individual strikers as well as union representatives by the same judge who had issued the decree at the outset.[80] Moreover, prior to Norris-LaGuardia, judicial intervention

---

[78] 370 U.S. at 228. See Teamsters, Local 795 v. Yellow Transit Freight Lines, 370 U.S. 711 (1962), and General Electric Co. v. Local 191, IUE, 398 U.S. 436 (1970), *vacating and remanding* 413 F.2d 964 (5th Cir. 1969), where the underlying disputes were not arbitrable. On the *Sinclair* debate prior to *Boys Market,* see generally Aaron, note 35 *supra;* Bartosic, note 35 *supra;* Isaacson, *The Grand Equation: Labor Arbitration and the No-Strike Clause,* 48 A.B.A.J. 914 (1962); Dunau, *Three Problems in Labor Arbitration,* 55 VA. L. REV. 427 (1969); Givens, *Section 301, Arbitration and the No-Strike Clause,* 11 LAB. L. J. 1005 (1960); Wellington, *The No-Strike Clause and the Labor Injunction: Time for a Re-Examination,* 30 U. PITT. L. REV. 293 (1968); Keene, *The Supreme Court, Section 301 and No-Strike Clauses: From Lincoln Mills to Avco and Beyond,* 15 VILL. L. REV. 32 (1969); Stewart, *No-Strike Clauses in the Federal Courts,* 59 MICH. L. REV. 673 (1961).

[79] See generally, FRANKFURTER & GREENE, note 21 *supra;* Wellington & Albert, *Statutory Interpretation and the Political Process: A Comment on Sinclair v. Atkinson,* 72 YALE L.J. 1547 (1963).

[80] On the right to trial by jury as it may relate to contempt proceedings in *Boys Market* injunctions, see Bloom v. Illinois, 391 U.S. 194 (1968); Frank v. United

in labor disputes carried with it the so-called objectives test. This test, through which the courts could evaluate the legitimacy of the objectives of strikers, was used by a heavy-handed and pro-employer judiciary to suppress worker protest without remedying the serious injustices that were to be found in the employer-employee relationship. Its apogee was *Duplex Printing Press Co. v. Deering*,[81] where the Court enjoined a secondary boycott in the teeth of the supposedly ameliorative provisions of the Clayton Act.[82] Norris-La-Guardia was the answer to such abuses, destroying federal court jurisdiction in the labor dispute arena.

A short answer to this forecast of doom based on history is that the Court's holding in *Boys Market* is not one-sided. The employer must demonstrate a willingness to arbitrate the underlying dispute. Further, accommodations between antitrust legislation and Norris-LaGuardia are undertaken elsewhere in order to reconcile two statutory policies.[83] The task of harmonizing Title VII of the Civil Rights Act of 1964 as well as other civil rights legislation on employment[84] with the NLRA and the RLA policies against work stoppages has been undertaken by the judiciary.[85] And while con-

---

States, 395 U.S. 147 (1969); Duncan v. Louisiana, 391 U.S. 145 (1968). See also *In re* Green, 369 U.S. 689 (1962). The early summary contempt cases often involved the unions. See *In re* Debs, 158 U.S. 564 (1895); Gompers v. United States, 233 U.S. 604 (1914).

[81] 254 U.S. 443 (1921). See also, in this regard, Loewe v. Lawlor, 208 U.S. 274 (1908); Lawlor v. Loewe, 235 U.S. 522 (1915). The British analogue appears to be Taff Vale Ry. v. A.S.R.S., [1901] A.C. 426.

[82] 15 U.S.C. §§ 12 *et seq.* Apparently the Clayton Act, rather than restricting the injunction, stimulated its use. See FRANKFURTER & GREENE, note 21 *supra*, at 99. "This [the Clayton Act] introduces no new principle into the equity jurisprudence of those courts. It is merely declaratory of what is the best practice always." American Foundries v. Tri-City Council, 257 U.S. 184, 203 (1921).

[83] Note, *Accommodation of Norris LaGuardia Act to Other Federal Statutes*, 72 HARV. L. REV. 354 (1958). See Apex Hosiery Co. v. Leader, 310 U.S. 469 (1940); United States v. Hutcheson, 312 U.S. 219 (1941); Allen Bradley v. Local 3, IBEW, 325 U.S. 797 (1945); Amalgamated Meat Cutters v. Jewel Tea Co., 381 U.S. 676 (1965); Ramsey v. UMW, 416 F.2d 655 (6th Cir. 1969), *cert. granted*, 397 U.S. 1006 (1970).

[84] See 42 U.S.C. § 1981. *Cf.* Jones v. Alfred H. Mayer Co., 392 U.S. 409 (1968); Waters v. Wisconsin Steel Works, 2 FEP Cases 574 (7th Cir. 1970). See also Exec. Order No. 11246, 3 C.F.R. 339 (1964–65).

[85] See Gould, *Black Power in the Unions: The Impact upon Collective Bargaining Relationships*, 79 YALE L.J. 46 (1969). *Cf.* NLRB v. Tanner Motor Livery Ltd., 419 F.2d 216 (9th Cir. 1969). On the accommodation issue, see especially Waters v. Wisconsin Steel Works, note 84 *supra*.

ceding the revived threat of judicial decrees based upon personal philosophy, Professor Cox has said: "Making an exception [to Norris-LaGuardia] for strikes in breach of contract would carry out fairly specific legislative enactment without inviting judicial determination of labor policy."[86]

Most significant is the improved position in which labor unions now find themselves in the United States. The relationship between organized labor and capital can no longer be generalized into one involving unequal parties in an atmosphere of bitter social strife.[87] Indeed, in some instances, it is the unions which now hold the cards of power.[88] The labor movement cannot evade the responsibility of contractual sanctions when it has voluntarily entered into the collective agreement for the benefit of its members. And the fact of the matter is that the abuses that prompted Norris-LaGuardia had little to do with breach of contract stoppages or the interpretation of collective agreements.

At the same time, it must be acknowledged that the injunctive power now in the hands of federal and state courts in labor disputes in all parts of the country may contain a potential for abuse that Norris-LaGuardia was devised to correct, particularly where unions are weak. This is less an argument against *Boys Market* than it is a call upon the federal courts to draw upon that "judicial inventiveness" which Mr. Justice Douglas prescribed in *Lincoln Mills*. Special rules upon which *Boys Market* injunctions are to be conditioned must be enunciated by the Court.[89] And finally, the good sense of the *Boys Market* conclusion is also demonstrated by the fact that, despite Norris-LaGuardia, injunctions have been issued against both employers and unions so that a substantial number of limitations upon Norris-LaGuardia have already been set forth by the courts. The order of specific enforcement in *Lincoln Mills* was one in-

---

86 Cox, note 28 *supra*, at 256.

87 For a description of the situation in 1930, see FRANKFURTER & GREENE, note 21 *supra*, at 81.

88 See Cox, LAW AND THE NATIONAL LABOR POLICY 48–52 (1960); *cf.* Gould, *Taft-Hartley Revisited: The Contrariety of the Collective Bargaining Agreement and the Plight of the Unorganized*, 13 LABOR L.J. 348 (1962).

89 For instance, in the preemption area, the Court in Linn v. United Plant Guard Workers, Local 114, 383 U.S. 53 (1966), borrowed from the constitutional rules articulated in New York Times Co. v. Sullivan, 376 U.S. 254 (1964). Thus, the Court in *Linn* held that state jurisdiction over libel actions arising out of labor disputes could be maintained where the statement was made with deliberate or reckless untruth. See also note 80 *supra*.

stance.[90] And, under the RLA, a similar order was entered against an employer who refused to recognize the lawful representative of its workers.[91] The duty of fair representation (now carried over into the NLRA)[92] was imposed upon the unions through equity.[93] Most recently, stoppages by white workers aimed at perpetuating racially discriminatory practices have been enjoined.[94]

Nor has the injunctive power been utilized only against stoppages for racial discrimination or for enforcement of recognition rights. In *Chicago River*,[95] Chief Justice Warren, speaking for a unanimous Court, held that where a minor dispute under the RLA involving the interpretation of the labor contract was submitted to the NRAB, the Court might lawfully enjoin the union from striking to defeat the jurisdiction of the board. The Court stated that the Norris-La-Guardia Act could not be read alone when dealing with matters under the RLA. The Court differentiated the controversy arising under Railway Labor Act machinery from the kinds of labor disputes that had triggered Norris-LaGuardia: "Such controversies, therefore, are not the same as those in which the injunction strips labor of its primary weapon without substituting any reasonable alternative."[96] As Professor Cox has said: "... there is much the same kind of conflict between the Norris-LaGuardia Act's blanket restriction and the policy of Section 301 as there was in the *Chicago*

---

[90] "The kinds of acts which had given rise to abuse of the power to enjoin are listed in § 4. The failure to arbitrate was not a part and parcel of the abuses against which the act was aimed. Section 8 of the Norris-LaGuardia Act does, indeed, indicate a congressional policy to a settlement of labor disputes by arbitration, for it denies injunctive relief to any person who has failed to make 'every reasonable effort' to settle the dispute by negotiation, mediation, or 'voluntary arbitration.'. . . we see no justification in policy for restricting § 301 (a) to damages suits, leaving specific performance of the contract to arbitrate grievance disputes to the inapposite procedural requirements of the Act." Douglas, J., in *Lincoln Mills*, 353 U.S. at 458.

[91] Virginia R. Co. v. System Federation, 300 U.S. 515 (1937); *cf.* Texas & N. O. R.R. v. Brotherhood of Ry. & S.S. Clerks, 281 U.S. 548 (1930).

[92] NLRB v. Local 1367, ILA, 368 F.2d 1010 (5th Cir. 1966); Local 12, United Rubber Workers v. NLRB, 368 F.2d 12 (5th Cir. 1966).

[93] Graham v. Brotherhood of Locomotive Fireman & Enginemen, 338 U.S. 232 (1949).

[94] State v. Baugh, 2 FEP Cases 271 (W.D. Wash. 1969); United States v. Local 189, United Papermakers & Paperworkers, 282 F. Supp. 39 (E.D. La. 1968); Central Contractors Ass'n v. Local 46, IBEW, 2 FEP Cases 189 (W.D. Wash. 1969); United States v. Building & Const. Tr. Coun. of St. Louis, 271 F. Supp. 447 (E.D. Mo. 1966).

[95] Brotherhood of R.R. Trainmen v. Chicago River & Indiana R. Co., 353 U.S. 30 (1957).

[96] *Id.* at 41.

River case between the blanket restrictions of the Norris-LaGuardia Act and the obligation to submit grievances to the Adjustment Board. From the standpoint of practical labor relations the two situations are exact parallels."[97]

The majority opinion in *Boys Market* relied heavily upon *Chicago River*. In *Sinclair*, the Court had held that *Chicago River* was distinguishable from § 301 contract law for two reasons: (1) the "affirmative duty" imposed upon unions under the RLA which compelled submission of disputes to the NRAB as an "exclusive method"; (2) the rejection by Congress of a Norris-LaGuardia repeal in the case of no-strike violations under the NLRA.[98] But *Boys Market* treated the *Chicago River* doctrine as "equally applicable" to § 301. To the arguments put forth by Mr. Justice Black in *Sinclair*, Mr. Justice Brennan responded thus:[99]

> To be sure, *Chicago River* involved arbitration procedures established by statute. However, we have frequently noted, in such cases as *Lincoln Mills*, the *Steelworkers Trilogy*, and *Lucas Flour*, the importance which Congress has attached generally to the voluntary settlement of labor disputes without resort to self-help and more particularly to arbitration as a means to this end.

Thus, the *Chicago River* principle of accommodation governs § 301 as well. As noted above, the distinction between the RLA and NLRA articulated by *Sinclair* has always seemed strange. For, aside

---

[97] Cox, note 28 *supra*, at 255.   [98] 370 U.S. at 210–12.

[99] 398 U.S. at 52.

Professor St. Antoine has pointed out that the Court's language in *Boys Market* can be interpreted so as to permit injunctions where grievance procedures exist without arbitration. See St. Antoine, note 61 *supra*. Section 203 of the NLRA, although it does not mention arbitration speaks of "final adjustment." It is therefore possible that an employer can convince a court that final adjustment which places authority in the employer's hands short of arbitration is consistent with the *quid pro quo* concept for *Boys Market* purposes.

Query, can the employer and union agree in their collective bargaining agreement to permit the employer to obtain a *Boys Market* injunction even where the underlying dispute is non-arbitrable? May the parties widen the accommodation between Norris-LaGuardia and § 301 and thus in effect confer jurisdiction upon the court under § 301 contract law? This is obviously quite different from a situation where the parties might seek to oust the court of jurisdiction. Cf. United Electrical Radio & Machine Workers of America v. NLRB, 409 F.2d 150 (D.C. Cir. 1969). See also IUE v. General Elec. Co., 407 F.2d 253, 259 (2d Cir. 1968), on the question whether the parties may nullify by collective agreement the *Warrior* presumption on arbitrability. Prior to *Boys Market* the courts held that the parties were able to confer jurisdiction for injunctive relief under *Sinclair*, albeit there in the context of grievance-arbitration machinery. See cases in note 115 *infra*. Moreover, it is possible

from the fact that resort to the NRAB is specifically provided by the statute, neither statutory procedure may be properly said to be more compulsory or exclusive than the other. Under the RLA—as is the case under the NLRA—one party must trigger machinery in order to have it utilized. Moreover, just as the Court in *Boys Market* has indicated that an employer unwilling to proceed to arbitration cannot obtain the fruits of the injunctive decree against a labor union, so also under the RLA there is doubt that the *Chicago River* doctrine is applicable where a submission has not been made to NRAB.[100] Because *Boys Market* relied so heavily upon *Chicago River* as well as "ordinary principles of equity" in the issuance of injunctions, the attention of the courts confronted with requests for injunctive relief under § 301 will undoubtedly focus upon experience to date under the Railway Labor Act.

A. STATUS QUO IN EMPLOYMENT CONDITIONS

Probably, one of the first issues to be presented will be whether the employer has an obligation to freeze existing working conditions

---

for a party to waive meritorious objections in equity. See McCLINTOCK ON EQUITY, 101–02 (2d ed. 1948). The case would be the least compelling where the union had only grievance machinery and not an arbitration clause available to it or where the arbitration clause was carefully circumscribed. Moreover, it is possible that the court may focus upon the question whether the no-strike clause itself is arbitrable, Stroehmann Bros. Co. v. Local 427, 74 L.R.R.M. 2957 (M.D. Penna. 1970), inasmuch as meritorious defenses to the no-strike obligation would be raised, or whether the matter in dispute is susceptible to arbitration as part of an actual employment condition that is involved in the employment relationship. An obvious example of a case not susceptible to arbitration, but which ought to be a leading candidate for *Boys Market* injunctive relief where the parties have so provided by contract, is where a union engages in stranger picketing and the dispute is unrelated to the employment relationship of the workers at that particular plant. See, generally, Johnson Builders, Inc. v. United Brotherhood of Carpenters, 422 F.2d 137 (10th Cir. 1970); Carney & Florsheim, *The Treatment of Refusals to Cross Picket Lines: "Bypaths and Indirect Crookt Ways,"* 55 CORN. L. REV. 940 (1970); Comment, *Picket Line Observance: The Board and the Balance of Interest,* 79 YALE L.J. 1369 (1970). All of this would comport with national labor policy insofar as it emphasizes freedom of contract considerations. See NLRB v. Insurance Agents' International Union, 361 U.S. 477 (1960); NLRB v. American Nat. Ins. Co., 343 U.S. 395 (1952). Cf. Phelps Dodge Corporation, 184 N.L.R.B. No. 106 (1970). On the question of waiver through management rights and zipper clauses, see note 133 *infra,* and Long Lake Lumber Co., 182 N.L.R.B. No. 65 (1970); see Standard Trucking Co., 183 N.L.R.B. No. 67 (1967); Cello-Foil Products, Inc., 178 N.L.R.B. No. 103 (1969); Century Electric Motor Co., 180 N.L.R.B. No. 174 (1970).

[100] Cf. Manion v. Kansas City Terminal Ry., 353 U.S. 927 (1957); Louisville & N. R.R. v. Brown, 252 F.2d 149 (5th Cir. 1958).

pending the outcome of the arbitration proceeding. In *Brotherhood of Locomotive Engineers v. Missouri-Kansas-Texas Railroad Co.*,[101] the Court dealt with the question whether a *Chicago River* injunction might be granted which conditioned its enforcement upon the employer's preservation of the status quo in working conditions. The Court, in *M-K-T*, held that a district court is empowered to exercise the "typical" powers of a court of equity and therefore may, in appropriate circumstances, require the maintenance of the status quo by the employer. A contrary result, said the Court, could only be justified by an abuse of discretion by the trial court when balancing the equities or by the "clearest legislative direction," inasmuch as such relief was sometimes "essential to insure that extraordinary equitable remedies [injunctions against strikes] will not become the engines of injustice."[102]

Since § 301 contains no legislative guidance to the contrary, it would appear that *Boys Market* may justify federal court intervention in the underlying dispute that gave rise to the stoppage at the time of the request for injunction. Indeed, the lower courts operating under § 301, and anticipating an issue which *M-K-T* did not resolve,[103] have issued temporary injunctive relief against employers,

---

[101] 363 U.S. 528 (1960). See generally Comment, 60 COLUM. L. REV. 381 (1960); *cf.* Elgin, J. & E. Ry. Co. v. Burley, 325 U.S. 711 (1945); Order of Conductors v. Pitney, 326 U.S. 561 (1946); Slocum v. Delaware, L. & W.R. Co., 339 U.S. 239 (1950); Order of R.R. Telegraphers v. Chicago & North Western Ry. Co., 362 U.S. 330 (1960). See Meltzer, *The Chicago & North Western Case: Judicial Workmanship and Collective Bargaining*, 1960 SUPREME COURT REVIEW 113.

[102] 363 U.S. at 532.

[103] In *M-K-T* the Court said: "We did not decide in *Chicago River*, and we do not decide here, whether a federal court can, during the pendency of a dispute before the Board, enjoin a carrier from effectuating the changes which gave rise to and constitute the subject matter of the dispute, *independent'y of any suit by the railroad for equitable relief*. As we read the order of the District Court, this case does not involve independent relief for the union." *Id.* at 531 n. 3. (Emphasis added.)

Lower courts have, however, granted injunctions requested by unions to preserve the status quo pending resolution of the merits by the NRAB. See Railroad Yardmasters v. St. Louis–San Francisco Ry., 231 F. Supp. 986 (N.D. Tex. 1964), *app. dismissed*, 345 F.2d 18 (5th Cir. 1965); Spokane, P. & S. Ry. v. Order of Ry. Conductors & Brakemen, 265 F. Supp. 892 (D.D.C. 1967). And see Westchester Lodge 2186 v. Railway Express Agency, Inc., 329 F.2d 748 (2d Cir. 1964). Relief has been denied where there is no evidence of irreparable injury. Brotherhood of R.R. Trainmen v. Boston & Maine R.R., 244 F. Supp 378 (D. Mass. 1965).

For cases arising under the NLRA involving remedial authority of the board, see NLRB v. Tidee Products, Inc., 426 F.2d 1243 (D.C. Cir. 1970); United Steel-

independent of any request for relief against a strike, where preservation of the status quo was necessary to protect the union and employees from irreparable injury.[104] For instance, where an employer sought to remove certain operations from Washington, D.C., to Chicago, temporary relief to the union was granted pending the outcome of arbitration, since the balance of convenience was weighted in favor of the employees.[105] In this connection, the court noted that "human considerations" were to be carefully taken into account.[106] Moreover, without considering the contract provisions relied upon by the union, the court noted that the employer's delay in selecting the arbitration panel, albeit a "plausible" and "perfectly reasonable one," caused potential harm to the workers since the arbitration process could not be completed prior to the contemplated business rearrangement. Thus, a preliminary injunction was granted by the court. Still another court, without discussing contract provisions, preserved the status quo where an employer planned to move to an-

workers v. NLRB, 74 L.R.R.M. 2747 (D.C. Cir. 1970); cf. NLRB v. Gissel Packing Co., 395 U.S. 575 (1969), and see note 104 *infra*.

On the problem of the status quo in the context of federal government employment, see United States v. Plasch, 75 L.R.R.M. 2331 (7th Cir. 1970).

[104] Local 38, RWDSU v. American Bakeries Co., 305 F. Supp. 624 (W.D. N.C. 1969); Local 328, IBT v. Armour & Co., 294 F. Supp. 168 (W.D. Mich., 1968); International Union, UAW v. Seagrave Fire Apparatus Division, 56 L.R.R.M. 2874 (S.D. Ohio 1964); Local Div. 1098, Amalgamated Ass'n of St. Elec. Ry. & Motor Coach Employees of America, AFL-CIO v. Eastern Greyhound Lines, 225 F. Supp. 28 (D. D.C. 1963); International Union, UAW, Local 408 v. Crescent Brass & Pin Co., 46 L.R.R.M. 2975 (E. D. Mich. 1960). But see Wolko v. Highway Truck Drivers, 232 F. Supp. 594 (E.D. Pa. 1964); Electrical Workers v. General Elec. Co., 332 F.2d 485 (2d Cir. 1964). On some of the general remedial problems in labor law, see St. Antoine, *A Touchstone for Labor Board Remedies*, 14 Wayne L. Rev. 1039 (1968). Under the RLA there is a status quo requirement for so called "major" disputes; the minor disputes are referred to the National Railroad Adjustment Board. See Detroit & Toledo Shore Line R.R. v. United Transportation Union, 396 U.S. 142 (1969). Cf. Bhd. Locomotive Fireman v. Bangor & Aroostook Railroad Co., 420 F.2d 77 (D.C. Cir. 1969); Chicago & N.W. Ry. Co. v. UTU, 422 F.2d 979 (7th Cir. 1970); Piedmont Aviation, Inc. v. Air Line Pilots Ass'n, 416 F.2d 633 (4th Cir. 1969). The question of status quo arrangements for employment conditions is under debate in Great Britain. See Hanna, *Scanlon Key to Pact or Chaos*, Sunday Times (London), June 28, 1970, p. 54, col. 4; Shakespeare, *Engineering "Summit" on Labour Dispute*, The Times (London), June 19, 1970, p. 23, col. 1; Shakespeare, *Engineering Disputes Row Vital to Future*, The Times (London), Apr. 24, 1970, p. 23, col. 4.

[105] Amalgamated Ass'n of St. Elect. Ry. & Motor Coach Employees v. Eastern Greyhound Lines, 225 F. Supp. 28 (D.D.C. 1963).

[106] See also Slote, Termination: The Closing at Baker Plant (1969).

other state.[107] Because the inconvenience to the employer in this case was more than "a few weeks delay" in moving facilities, thus entailing "substantial monetary losses," injunctive relief would be denied, said the court, if the company furnished a bond in the amount of $400,000 to protect the union should it prevail in arbitration.

Where an injunction is issued under *Boys Market*, the argument on behalf of a status quo arrangement as the price of enjoining the union's stoppages becomes more compelling. But the range of cases may be relatively narrow. Presumably, cases where management is engaging in a plant closure[108]—a large subcontracting operation, or massive discharges or layoffs of workers where that is protested—present the kind of situation in which the *M-K-T* remedy may be appropriate.

There are two principal difficulties with this approach. First, it will be contended that federal courts will become unduly enmeshed in the merits of labor disputes, a result which was heartily condemned by the Court in the *Steelworkers Trilogy*. The Court's answer to this allegation that in effect the authority of the arbitrator—or in the case of the RLA, the NRAB—would be usurped, is only partially satisfactory:[109]

> It is true that a District Court must make some examination of the nature of the dispute before conditioning relief since not all disputes coming before the Adjustment Board threaten irreparable injury and justify the attachment of a condition. . . . But this examination of the nature of the dispute is so unlike that which the Adjustment Board will make of the merits of the same dispute, and is for such a dissimilar purpose, that it could not interfere with the later consideration of the grievance by the Adjustment Board.

The federal courts operating under § 301 have been successful in avoiding this pitfall. Moreover, the standard for judicial examination may be somewhat instructive for federal and state courts in determining whether the strike should be enjoined.[110]

A second, related consideration is that, where substantial interference with managerial prerogatives and economic decisions is involved, the courts may be reluctant to act. Indeed, Professor Kroner

---

[107] International Union, UAW v. Seagrave Fire Apparatus Division, 56 L.R.R.M. 2874 (S.D. Ohio 1964).

[108] But see Textile Workers Union v. Darlington Mfg. Co., 380 U.S. 263 (1965); cf. Fibreboard Paper Products Corp. v. NLRB, 379 U.S. 203 (1964).

[109] 363 U.S. at 533–34.   [110] See text *infra*, at notes 125–38.

has asserted that this has been the experience under the RLA.[111] And in many respects the cases arising under the RLA are the most attractive candidates for status quo relief since delays before the NRAB have been scandalously long. The federal judiciary may approach the question of enjoining plant removals and subcontracting with a great deal of trepidation. Despite the fact that reinstatement of employees improperly discharged is an appropriate and common remedy, the courts may be somewhat reluctant to impose this kind of relief pending the outcome of arbitration, especially where there is a personal employer-employee relationship.[112]

Moreover, such a utilization of *Boys Market*, in anything less than the most extreme kind of case involving arbitrary action by an employer, runs against the grain of a substantial amount of arbitral precedent which has been evolved over the past twenty-five years. The conventional wisdom remains that management has the authority to move first and that it is the union's function to challenge but not to interfere with a decision before it is made.[113] Thus, the broad latitude of the *M-K-T* principle might put the courts on a collision course with the everyday expectations of management and labor. On the other hand, it may be said that injunctions against strikes arising out of labor disputes are so extraordinary because of Norris-LaGuardia, that equally unusual decrees are well justified. Yet, the courts may be reluctant to condition the injunction in the absence of some procedure to protect the employer against burdensome delay and consequent economic injury. The dilemma is perhaps best demonstrated by the facts of *Boys Market* itself. For, in that case,

---

[111] Kroner, *Interim Injunctive Relief under the Railway Labor Act: Some Problems and Suggestions*, 18TH ANNUAL N.Y.U. CONFERENCE ON LABOR 179; Kroner, *Minor Disputes under the Railway Labor Act: A Critical Appraisal*, 37 N.Y.U. L. REV. 41 (1962). See also Comment, note 101 *supra*.

[112] Proposals have been put forward (and have been incorporated in some collective bargaining agreements) to the effect that unless the discharge involves some particularly troublesome offense such as stealing, dishonesty, drunkenness on the job, etc., the employee should be permitted to work until the discharge is resolved in arbitration. Alternatively, it has been advocated that if management is in error about the discharge and the arbitrator holds that some other penalty such as a suspension was the proper method of dealing with the worker, full back pay as well as reinstatement be provided. The theory is that the power to discharge and to await the outcome of a lengthy arbitration proceeding places too much authority in the hands of management, may deter employees from engaging in legitimate activity, and places all of the burden of inconvenience upon the worker.

[113] Of course, this is especially true where employees are given orders to follow. See Fleming, *Arbitrators and the Remedy Power*, 48 VA. L. REV. 1199, 1222 (1962).

if union allegations prove accurate, workers are being deprived of employment to which they are entitled. Over a period of time during which final adjudication is pending, damages can be substantial. But, in my judgment, it would be difficult to convince most judges that the situation is unusual enough to warrant relief of the *M-K-T* variety.

All of this then suggests an alternative scope of inquiry under the *Boys Market* doctrine hinted at by some of the § 301 cases that have granted injunctions to preserve the status quo. The judicial experience with so-called "quickie" arbitration procedures may be instructive. Before such an examination of the relationship between the law on this subject and status quo remedies, it is necessary to examine the law that had developed in this area prior to *Boys Market* and the implications of the Court's decision in that case for such cases.

B. "QUICKIE" ARBITRATION ON THE STRIKE IN BREACH OF CONTRACT

In *New Orleans Steamship Association v. General Longshore Workers*,[114] an employers' association brought an action to enforce an arbitration award directing two local unions and their members to cease and desist work stoppages in violation of a collective bargaining agreement. The arbitrator, serving as one of six permanent arbitrators selected by the parties for the duration of the contract, was notified by the employer that the local unions had engaged in work stoppages and was requested to hold a hearing within seventy-two hours as provided by the contract. Within seventy-two hours a hearing commenced which lasted four days and an award was entered approximately two months later in which the arbitrator found that the stoppages had occurred in violation of the agreement. The arbitrator therefore directed the unions, their officers, agents, representatives, and members to cease and desist from work stoppages in violation of their contract. The district court dismissed the complaint which sought an enforcement of the award, relying principally upon *Sinclair* and its interpretation of the Norris-LaGuardia Act. In effect, the district court held, as did other federal courts,[115]

---

[114] 389 F.2d 369 (5th Cir. 1968).

[115] See Marine Transport Lines, Inc. v. Curran, 65 L.R.R.M. 2095 (S.D. N.Y. 1967); Gulf & South American S.S. Co. v. National Maritime Union, 360 F.2d 63 (5th Cir. 1966). But see Philadelphia Marine Trade Ass'n v. Local 1291, ILA 368 F.3d 932 (3d Cir. 1966), *rev'd on other grounds*, 389 U.S. 64 (1967); Pacific Maritime Ass'n v. International Longshoremen .& W. U., 304 F. Supp. 1315 (N.D. Cal.

that the employer was attempting to gain indirectly that which *Sinclair* declared unobtainable because of Norris-LaGuardia. Under this view, enforcement of the arbitration award was regarded as a kind of injunctive decree which was prohibited by *Sinclair*.

A unanimous Fifth Circuit reversed. The court stated that, if an arbitrator were to issue such a ruling "absent jurisdiction," one would be confronted with an attempt to gain a federal injunction against a work stoppage contrary to the *Sinclair* rule. But the court refused to find that such a situation was to be found in the facts of *New Orleans Steamship Association*. The court correctly noted that *Sinclair* did not involve an arbitration award but rather an injunction to enforce a no-strike clause where "strikes were ensuing but where there had been no arbitration."[116] Therefore, said the court, *Sinclair* did not govern the precise issue involved. The court then turned to *Lincoln Mills* and the *Steelworkers Trilogy* and the interpretation of § 301 of the NLRA given in those cases. Not to enforce the award by injunction, said the court, would be to discourage arbitration. The no-strike clause and arbitration were a *quid pro quo* and the parties having submitted their dispute to arbitration under a specified procedure with articulated remedies, the losing party might—absent the injunction—ignore the award and continue the stoppage. This case, said the court, was distinguishable from *Sinclair*. Such a result could not be imputed to Congress:[117]

> In this case the parties agreed to the remedy of a desist order by the arbitrator. Such an order was entered and breached. The court in enforcing such order or award, although injunctive in nature, would be doing no more than enforcing the agreement of the parties. This not unusual action on the part of the court will lie unless the court has been deprived of jurisdiction by the Norris-LaGuardia Act.
>
> . . . We have before us a contract wherein the parties have ceded their remedy of self-help in a labor dispute to arbitration

1969); Ruppert v. Engelhofer, 3 N.Y.2d 576 (1958); *In re* Local 28, Sheet Metal Workers, 53 L.R.R.M. 2590 (N.Y. Sup. Ct., N.Y. Co., 1963); F & M Schaefer Brewing Co. v. Hoh, 72 L.R.R.M. 2529 (N.Y. Sup. Ct., Kings Co. 1969); Ford Motor Co. Chicago Stamping Plant, 41 Lab. Arb. 619 (1963); *In re* Ford Motor Company, 41 Lab. Arb. 621 (1963). See generally, Givens, *Injunctive Enforcement of Arbitration Awards Prohibiting Strikes*, 17 Lab. L.J. 292 (1966); McDermott, *Enforcing No-Strike Provisions via Arbitration*, 18 Lab. L.J. 579 (1967). The quickie arbitration clause is a mandatory subject of bargaining within the meaning of § 8(a)(5), § 8(b)(3), and § 8(d) of the act. See United Electrical Radio and Machine Workers of America v. NLRB, 409 F.2d 150 (D.C. Cir. 1969).

[116] 389 F.2d at 371.   [117] *Id.* at 372.

even to the point of permitting the arbitrator to grant a desist order.

The force of Mr. Justice Brennan's reasoning in *Boys Market* applies in even greater measure to the *New Orleans Steamship* fact situation. A contrary result would have been inconsistent with a policy supporting voluntry arbitration. Even if, contrary to what was asserted in *Boys Market*, employers might not be renouncing arbitration procedures because of a failure to obtain adequate remedies to enforce the *quid pro quo*, it is difficult to envisage any inducement for employers to negotiate quickie arbitration procedures with all the inconvenience and hardship involved for both parties, if the union or dissident workers might flaunt the award without fear of its judicial enforcement and contempt penalties. The Fifth Circuit's holding must therefore be viewed as more nearly harmonious with the national labor policy than the opposing position urged upon that tribunal.

The rules articulated in *New Orleans Steamship*, however, present both pitfalls and opportunities for the courts confronted with *Boys Market* applications for injunctions. On the negative side is the real likelihood that impatient employers may run to the courts and thus bypass arbitration and, perhaps even more important, the negotiation of expeditious no-strike procedures. This availability of the judicial avenue may, exaggerated by other factors besides the *Boys Market* result, prove too attractive to employers. The unions too may be moved away from quickie arbitration—at least as it applies to the strike issue—because the Supreme Court has held that an injunction is appropriate only in the case of an arbitrable dispute. But the no-strike clause itself is generally not so limited,[118] and there was no indication in the Fifth Circuit's opinion that the enforcement of an arbitrable award had any such qualifications.[119] If it is possible that an employer might obtain relief under a quickie or

---

[118] There are, however, many exceptions to the broad prohibitions contained in no-strike provisions. See U.S. BUREAU OF LABOR STATISTICS, BULL. No. 1425-1, *Arbitration Procedures* 56 (1966). The limited nature of many no-strike clauses was a point emphasized in brief for the AFL-CIO, as amicus curiae, in *Boys Market* case, at pp. 21-23.

[119] See Gulf & South American Steamship Co. v. National Maritime Union, 360 F.2d 63, 65 (5th Cir. 1966), where the court refused enforcement of an arbitration award prohibiting a strike where it was clear that the underlying issue which triggered the stoppage was arbitrable but was not decided by the arbitrator.

seventy-two-hour arbitration procedure without regard to the question whether the underlying dispute is arbitrable, unions will soon shun the arbitral route because management's resort to the judiciary will produce a better result in this regard under *Boys Market, i.e.,* an injunction only in the case of an arbitrable dispute that triggered the stoppage. *Boys Market* provides for arbitration of this issue almost simultaneous with injunctive relief against the union. Indeed, for reasons enumerated below,[120] equity might well dictate a judicial decree requiring a speedy arbitral resolution of the issue that caused the strike or an order that arbitration with regard to both the underlying and no-strike issue proceed simultaneously. Here again, labor unions will benefit by channeling the strike issue to the courts rather than the arbitrator.

This then would be an undesirable and obviously unintended byproduct of *Boys Market.* It is antithetical to the doctrine of a limited role for the judiciary in labor arbitration matters stated by the Court in the *Steelworkers Trilogy.* And, ironically, if the situation were to develop as stated above, the criticism echoes that which the Court itself gave to *Sinclair* in the *Boys Market* opinion, *i.e.,* that the former case was an inconsistent departure from § 301 as interpreted by the Court. The effect of *Boys Market* could produce an anomaly of equal proportions, *i.e.,* to discourage the utilization of voluntary arbitration procedures.

To counter such a situation, the ruling in *New Orleans Steamship* might be modified so as to comport with *Boys Market.* The argument against this is that the parties themselves have provided both a no-strike obligation and arbitration as well as the remedy which the arbitrator is to impose through the collective bargaining process. According to this view, cease and desist orders might issue in enforceable form in those instances where the parties themselves have provided for them. Otherwise, both freedom to bargain collectively and the growth of arbitration are obstructed through any approach that would impose judge-made rules of law.[121] On balance, it seems that such considerations are outweighed by the imminent erosion of arbitral adjudication of no-strike issues. Here judicial involvement

---

[120] See text *infra,* at note 124.

[121] This, of course, is not to say that judge-made rules of law are entirely inappropriate. See *Lucas Flour Co.,* 369 U.S. 95 (1962). See generally Summers, *Collective Agreements and the Law of Contracts,* 78 YALE L.J. 525 (1969). *Cf.* Gulf & South American Steamship v. National Maritime Union, 360 F.2d 63, 65 (5th Cir. 1966).

contains within it the seeds of abuse and error.[122] It ought to be effectively limited—to the extent possible—in the spirit of the *Steelworkers Trilogy*.

At the same time, two factors remain unaltered by the re-evaluation of *New Orleans Steamship* described above. Employers will feel more secure moving to the courts for injunctive relief rather than to arbitration, even where expeditious procedures are available. In part, this explains the absence of any clear pattern of arbitration procedures to deal with the strike in breach of contract. Management is fearful of the tendencies of arbitrators in this area. And, as the facts in *New Orleans Steamship* demonstrate, arbitrators, sensitive to industrial tensions and factors such as morale and productivity in the plant community, are reluctant to put themselves in the position of commanding unusual remedies that might interfere with the parties' traditional expectations.[123] To some extent, this reluctance may be charged to arbitrators' alleged concern with their own self-preservation.[124] But this reluctance can be more easily understood when one recalls the status quo controversy and the *M-K-T* remedy. In the absence of the most clearly articulated grant of authority, an arbitrator would not require an employer to retain a worker on the payroll during an interim period while the merits of his discharge were resolved. As noted above, the expectation is that management has the authority to act subject, of course, to the union's challenge. In sensitive areas like this and the strike issue, arbitrators are cautious.

The unions, generally, have not been favorably impressed by the process. Although a speedy cease and desist order can often relieve the union of the hard and unpopular task of urging an aroused membership back to work, the union is faced with the one-sidedness of the procedure. There are inherent difficulties in explaining to the rank and file the reason for a special procedure to deal with strikes different from other breaches of the contract[125] even if the fact is

---

122 See text *infra*, at notes 128–41.

123 "In general, caution should certainly be the password on arbitral inventiveness in this area." Fleming, note 113 *supra*. For a discussion of this problem, see Gould, note 74 *supra*.

124 See Hays, Labor Arbitration: A Dissenting View (1966). *Cf.* Fleming, The Labor Arbitration Process (1965).

125 I am somewhat skeptical of the view that simply because the stoppage is a wildcat, the union will be willing and anxious to attempt to get the workers back

that other alleged contract violations, which may also entail the issuance of extraordinary remedies, require a more lengthy hearing, and detailed investigation and analysis.

At this point, analysis of *M-K-T* and *New Orleans Steamship* tends to converge. As Professor Kroner has noted, the small number of reported decisions imposing temporary injunctive relief where employer conduct has produced irreparable injury to workers reflects a deep-seated reluctance to interfere with managerial decisions that involve substantial business rearrangements motivated by economics. Moreover, as the Court properly noted in *M-K-T*, the function of the judiciary is not to examine the merits but only to determine whether expeditious relief is necessary. The inescapable problem is that the employer has no remedy for interference with efficiency and other factors, even though management's position may eventually prevail on the merits. This, of course, enforces the reluctance to move into this area where long delays and interference with implementation of such managerial decisions are involved.

The issuance of an injunction is not, however, an automatic process.[126] It is a function of judicial discretion and involves considerations of equity. Where the union may suffer irreparable injury as a result of employer action involving, for instance, plant closures or removal, it may be inequitable to enjoin the strike in violation of contract even though arbitration will be required and the award will issue long after the action has been taken, thus making it increasingly unlikely that the union can obtain a meaningful remedy as a practical matter. Taking a cue from *M-K-T*, courts—where equities are balanced properly and the unions are not themselves guilty of footdragging in pursuing grievance-arbitration machinery—might pose this alternative to the employer: (1) the status quo until arbitration is completed; (2) speedy arbitration procedures[126a] on

---

on the job. At the same time the union may adopt this posture so as to avoid a potential for damages liability. See Bartosic, note 35 *supra;* Dunau, note 78 *supra.*

[126] *Cf.* Crestwood School District v. Crestwood Education Ass'n, 382 Mich. 577 (1969); School District for the City of Holland v. Holland Education Ass'n, 380 Mich. 314 (1968). See 398 U.S. at 253–54.

[126a] Judge Frankel in American Tel. & Tel. Co. v. Communications Workers, 75 L.R.R.M. 2178 (S.D. N.Y. 1970), ordered the parties to select an arbitrator from the very day of the no-strike injunction and further ordered that the "arbitrator so selected shall be required by the parties in the submission to render his award by noon on Aug. 24, 1970 [six days after his selection]." *Id.* at 2180. Although such speed is unusual in the arbitration process, the arbitrator was selected according

the underlying issues as well as discharge, discipline, and damages issues that may arise out of the violation of the no-strike clause itself. Presumably, management would opt for the latter and this would then have the desirable effect of encouraging the use of voluntary arbitration procedures that are expeditious. More important, if this kind of rule is articulated as a matter of federal labor law, the parties might begin to address themselves to speedy arbitration measures concerning both no-strike issues and, at least, substantial managerial rearrangements. This would then take both the no-strike and other underlying issues away from the courts and put them into the hands of the arbitrators. The inducement for the unions would be that relief would be forthcoming on matters that seriously affect workers' security. The employers would avoid the distasteful status quo requirement of substantial duration as the price of judicially obtained remedies. This would make the courts a less inviting place to proceed and presumably would encourage the peaceful resolution of labor disputes by more appropriate processes.

III. THE JUDICIAL ROLE

In the *Steelworkers Trilogy* the Court instructed federal district courts to order parties to arbitrate unless it could be said with positive assurance that the matter was not arbitrable. In one of these three landmark cases, *United Steelworkers v. American Mfg. Co.*,[127] the Court, in rationalizing this doctrine, examined the no-strike clause and said: "There is no exception to the 'no-strike' clause and none therefore should be read into the grievance clause, since one is *quid pro quo* for the other."[128]

As previously noted, however, a literal application of the *quid pro quo* approach has not found favor with the Court. Further, where the no-strike clause is not unqualified as it was in *American Manufacturing*, the courts have not altered their analysis from that employed in the *Steelworkers Trilogy* in determining whether arbitration ought to be compelled.[129] This in itself undermines the simplistic view that would resolve all doubts in favor of enjoining

---

to the court order and the award appears to have been rendered within the deadline. See American Tel. & Tel. Co., Daily Lab. Rep. 170 (1970).

[127] 363 U.S. 564 (1960).   [128] *Id.* at 567.

[129] See, *e.g.*, Akron Typographical Union 182 v. The Beacon Journal Publishing Co., 72 L.R.R.M. 2362 (N.D. Ohio 1968), *aff'd*, 416 F.2d 969 (6th Cir. 1969); IUE v. General Elec. Co., 332 F.2d 485 (2d Cir. 1964); Lodge 913, IAM v. General Elec.

strikes on the theory that the same judicial attitude must be taken to both portions of the exchange between labor and management rather than having the courts reserve such decrees for issuance only where it can be said with reasonable certainty that the no-strike obligation is being violated. The first of these two paths would produce an indiscriminate reliance upon the injunctive process that would indeed nullify the purpose of Norris-LaGuardia as well as give an aura of legitimacy to the notion that the judiciary is inherently biased in labor disputes. But, as the Court has said in *Boys Market*, injunctions are to be issued with care. One is not confronted with an exception to the rule that the equities are to be balanced. On the other hand, if one does not resolve all doubts in favor of judicial intervention, as in the *Steelworkers Trilogy*, the courts are faced with what was so artfully avoided in those cases, contract interpretation.

The dangers involved, at least with regard to no-strike issues, have been somewhat exaggerated.[130] First, it should be a relatively easy matter for a judge to determine whether a stoppage, or a strike or slowdown or other kind of interruption of production contrary to the union's commitment to industrial peace, has taken place and is prohibited by the contract. The evidentiary hearing will not be lengthy in most cases. Moreover, in those few instances where the employer will have been found to have repudiated the no-strike clause through violations of the contract, including the arbitration provisions, the courts are not adrift, since the issue has been before them in connection with motions to compel arbitration.[131] If the Court holds that the *Lucas Flour* rule establishing an implied no-strike liability on the basis of a broad arbitration clause is carried over, the effort of a trial court ought to be, in these kinds of cases, a relatively simple one.

The web becomes a bit more tangled when the courts are confronted with the numerous conditional no-strike clauses. For instance, the collective agreement may state that the union and/or employee cannot strike unless and until grievance procedure has

---

Co., 57 L.R.R.M. 2526 (S.D. Ohio 1964); IUE v. Westinghouse Elec. Corp., 53 L.R.R.M. 2923 (S.D. N.Y. 1963); United Steelworkers of America, AFL-CIO v. General Elec. Co., 211 F. Supp. 562 (N.D. Ohio 1962).

[130] See Dunau, note 78 *supra*, at 466 n.105.

[131] See especially United Packinghouse Workers v. Needham Packing Co., 376 U.S. 247 (1964); Ice Cream Drivers v. Borden, Inc., 75 L.R.R.M. 2481 (2d Cir. 1970).

been exhausted. The NLRB, although not primarily concerned with contract interpretation, has faced up to this issue.[132] The courts are not so unequipped as to disqualify them outright for a similar role.[133] If the arbitrator finds that the conditions do not prohibit the strike, the injunction must be dissolved. The same holds true where the

---

[132] On the board's authority, see NLRB v. Strong Roofing & Insulating Co., 393 U.S. 357 (1969); NLRB v. Acme Indus. Co., 385 U.S. 432 (1967); NLRB v. C & C Plywood Corp., 385 U.S. 421 (1967). The board's authority over unfair labor practices is plenary. See Carey v. Westinghouse Elec. Corp., 375 U.S. 261, 268 (1964); Smith v. Evening News Ass'n, 371 U.S. 195, 197–98 (1962); cf. United Steelworkers v. American Int'l Aluminum Corp., 334 F.2d 147 (5th Cir. 1964); Amalgamated Ass'n of St. Employees v. Trailways of New England, Inc., 232 F. Supp. 608 (D. Mass. 1964), aff'd, 343 F.2d 815 (1st Cir. 1965). The board must interpret conditional no-strike clauses. See, e.g., Young Spring & Wire Corp., 138 N.L.R.B. 643 (1962); Mid-West Metallic Prods., Inc., 121 N.L.R.B. 1317 (1958).

The board's considerations of strikes during the term of a contract generally arise under § 8(d) prohibitions against a strike or lockout to terminate or modify the terms of a collective bargaining agreement without providing proper notice prior to contract expiration. Speaking about this statutory provision, the board has said: "Our interpretation preserves the right to strike in all circumstances where the parties have provided in their agreement for negotiating substantial changes in its provisions—if the statutory requirements of § 8(d) are met. Moreover, our decision has no bearing on the right to strike for reasons and purposes other than to obtain contract modification or termination." Lion Oil Company, 109 N.L.R.B. 680, 684 (1954), aff'd, NLRB v. Lion Oil Company, 352 U.S. 282 (1957). See also Mastro Plastics v. NLRB, 350 U.S. 270, 284–89 (1956); United Furniture Workers of America v. NLRB, 336 F.2d 738 (D.C. Cir. 1964); McLeod v. Compressed Air, 292 F.2d 358 (2d Cir. 1961). The § 8(d) "cooling off" period for which notice must be given may not be waived by the parties' contract. See Rocky Mountain Prestress, Inc., 172 N.L.R.B. No. 87 (1968). The question whether a stoppage is arrived at to enforce a different interpretation of the contract is a difficult one to resolve. See General Elec. Co., 181 N.L.R.B. No. 111 (1970); International Union, UMW v. NLRB, 257 F.2d 211 (D.C. Cir. 1958); Kaynard v. Communications Workers of America, 72 L.R.R.M. (E.D. N.Y. 1969). The scope of bargaining during the term of the contract remains wide. See NLRB v. C & C Plywood Corp., 385 U.S. 421 (1967); UAW v. General Motors Corp., 381 F.2d 265 (D.C. Cir. 1967); NLRB v. Jacobs Mfg. Co., 196 F.2d 680 (2d Cir. 1952); Equitable Life Ins. Co., 133 N.L.R.B. 1675 (1961); Proctor Mfg. Corp., 131 N.L.R.B. 1166 (1961); cf. Tidewater Associated Oil Co., 85 N.L.R.B. 1096 (1949); LeRoy Mach. Co., 147 N.L.R.B. 1431 (1964); New York Mirror, 151 N.L.R.B. 834 (1965). See generally Cox & Dunlop, Regulation of Collective Bargaining by the National Labor Relations Board, 63 HARV. L. REV. 389 (1950). Where a stoppage during the term of the agreement is in breach of contract, the strikers are subject to discharge and discipline inasmuch as their conduct is unprotected activity. See NLRB v. Sands Mfg. Co., 306 U.S. 332 (1939); Artim Transportation System, Inc. v. NLRB, 396 F.2d 359 (7th Cir. 1968); Sillbaugh v. NLRB, 74 L.R.R.M. 2955 (D.C. Cir. 1970); A. Borchman & Sons Co., 174 N.L.R.B. No. 38 (1969); McLean Trucking Company, 175 N.L.R.B. No. 66 (1969).

[133] See, e.g., Forrest Industries, Inc. v. Local 3-436, Int'l Woodworkers of America, 381 F.2d 144 (9th Cir. 1967); Rothlain v. Armour & Co., 268 F. Supp. 545 (W.D. Pa. 1967); General Elec. Co. v. Local 761, IUE, 62 L.R.R.M. 2782 (W.D. Ky. 1966).

arbitrator determining the question of arbitrability for himself[134] holds that the underlying dispute is not arbitrable. Yet, this problem becomes more complicated and the sanctions less attractive when, for instance, certain subject matter is exempted from the no-strike obligation. In the automobile industry, production standards and the pay rates for new jobs, health and safety matters, are all outside the strictures of the no-strike clause.[135] But much to the consternation of employers, such clauses often act as stalking horses for dissatisfaction over other issues or protests where two or more are inescapably intertwined. This is the kind of no-strike case that can be difficult to sort out, especially for a court. Although the problem grows in the automobile industry, the companies have been reluctant to press the issue in arbitration. But a legal remedy may prove more tempting to management now that the Court has spoken in *Boys Market*. Here again, one notes the movement away from arbitration into the courts, an undesirable result from the vantage point of preserving industrial self-government.

Such problems are troublesome, but hardly insurmountable. In the first place, while the court is required to determine whether the strike is in breach of contract, such a ruling ought not to foreclose a hearing de novo on the strike issue before an arbitrator. Since a number of arbitrators have held that damages may be awarded under the contract in the case of a no-strike violation,[136] the issues relating to contract interpretation, including union responsibility for the stoppage, could be raised anew at that time. Here again, the theme

---

134 In the *Warrior* case the arbitrator considered the question of arbitrability anew. See Warrior & Gulf Navig. Co., 36 Lab. Arb. 695 (1961). Of course, the courts must also examine under the *Warrior* standard in the first instance. See Atkinson v. Sinclair Refining Co., 370 U.S. 238, 241 (1962); Wiley v. Livingston, 376 U.S. 543 (1964).

135 See, *e.g.*, Agreement between Ford Motor Company and UAW (Oct. 25, 1967), pp. 24, 56, which exempts production standards, health and safety, and new job rates from the no-strike clause subsequent to the exhaustion of the grievance procedure. See Agreement between Chrysler Corp. and UAW (Nov. 10, 1967), pp. 7-8, 41-42. Agreement between General Motors Corp. and UAW (Dec. 15, 1967), pp. 85-87, 36-40.

136 On damages for no-strike clause violations, see Drake Bakeries, Inc. v. Local 50, 370 U.S. 254, 265-66 (1962). See Roger J. Air & Son, Inc., unreported (May, 1970); Vulcan Mold & Iron Co., 53 Lab. Arb. 869 (1969); Forest City Publishing Co., 50 Lab. Arb. 683 (1968); Pinchaven Sanitarium, Inc., 49 Lab. Arb. 991 (1967); Cleveland Newspaper Publishers Ass'n, 49 Lab. Arb. 1043 (1967); Bradlees Family Circle Stores, 47 Lab. Arb. 567 (1966); American Pipe & Construction Co., 43 Lab. Arb. 1126 (1964); Publishers Ass'n of New York, 42 Lab. Arb. 95 (1964); Booth Newspapers, Inc., 43 Lab. Arb. 785 (1964). See also Fleming, note 113 *supra*.

is one previously expressed in connection with both status quo relief for unions and the conclusory nature of the court's adjudication of the arbitrability question. An injunction issued under the authority of *Boys Market* is essentially temporary relief for the employer because of both irreparable injury and the inadequacy of alternate remedies. This and the clear thrust of the *Steelworkers Trilogy* mean that arbitrators ought to review both arbitrability and the no-strike violation and the courts must keep entirely clear of the merits on both issues when one party seeks to enforce an award or to dissolve the injunctions as the result of the arbitrator's holding. This the court cannot do upon request for temporary relief under *Boys Market*. Accordingly, the price of the Court's holding is that a union may have imposed upon it (for a considerable period of time unless more speedy arbitration processes are devised) an injunctive decree because, in the court's view, it can be said with reasonable certainty that the no-strike clause has been violated— and the union is thereby restrained from use of its most effective weapon until the arbitrator has rendered an award to the contrary. Of course, one should not fudge and say that the treasuries of the unions are exposed to employer actions only in the instance of arbitration. Quite obviously, resistance to the *Boys Market* injunction can produce contempt sanctions—and where the injunction must be dissolved subsequent to an arbitrator's award, the resulting inequities are particularly glaring. Obstreperous trade unionists have discovered that, in cases where Norris-LaGuardia prohibitions have not been found to be applicable, judicially imposed fines can be substantial indeed.[137] If the courts may issue injunctions under *Boys Market*, their decrees will have to be enforced.

---

[137] Both the United Mine Workers and its former president, John L. Lewis, were fined large sums for contempt of court. See United States v. UMW, 330 U.S. 258 (1947). See also N.Y. Times, Aug. 4, 1970, p. 27, col. 6, and see *id.*, Aug. 5, 1970, p. 38, col. 1, for account that the union and officers were fined $25,000 per day for contempt for a stoppage directed against an arbitrator's award. In this case, however, the company bargained away the contempt fine. The trial judge then asked that criminal contempt proceedings be brought against the union. See Whitney, *U.S. Acts on Union in Parcel Strike*, N.Y. Times, Sept. 24, 1970, p. 61, col. 1. Criminal contempt proceedings raise the problem of right to jury trial. See cases cited in note 80 *supra*. Moreover, the specter of both civil and criminal contempt sanctions is present even where the injunction is later found to be invalid. See Walker v. City of Birmingham, 388 U.S. 307, 316 n. 6 (1967). The Court has held, however, that if state jurisdiction had been preempted, the injunction can be properly defied if there is an attempt to challenge the injunction's validity. *In re* Green, 369 U.S. 689 (1962).

At the same time, the federal law of labor injunctions under § 301 can be articulated so as to guard against the judicial abuses of the past. The Court has borrowed from constitutional law principles to determine the extent to which state courts may entertain suits for libel in cases arising from labor disputes.[138] There is no reason why the same cannot be done in connection with labor injunctions. For instance, the Court has held that, where First Amendment rights are involved, restraining orders cannot be issued *ex parte* and without a full hearing on the merits.[139] The Court would be wise to adopt a similar rule for both federal and state judges in the case of § 301 injunctions. This is in the spirit of *Boys Market*. The uniform federal labor law of § 301 must provide adequate safeguards against repetition of our experience with judicial abuses in connection with labor injunctions, even if, as the Court in *Boys Market* has noted, unions have matured and gained strength and the judicial treatment of labor cases is far more progressive than it was forty years ago.

The difficulty inherent in judicial involvement grows where the courts must not merely interpret the no-strike clause, but also other portions of the contract as well. In the pristine *Boys Market* case, the question whether the underlying dispute is arbitrable can be resolved within the guidelines set forth in the *Steelworkers Trilogy*. But suppose that the parties then proceed to the arbitration, and the arbitrator renders an award, the effect of which the parties disagree about. The union might then strike to enforce its interpretation of the award. Indeed, the no-strike provision in *Boys Market* itself states that "this [no strike] limitation shall not be binding upon either party hereto if the other party [refuses to arbitrate] . . . or fails to abide by, accept or perform a decision or award of an arbitrator or board."[140] In such a case, the parties' clear preference is to resolve the refusal to abide by an award or the disagreement as to its interpretation through industrial warfare. This then, unlike the situation in *New Orleans Steamship*, where the Fifth Circuit was able to enjoin a stoppage because of the reconciliation of such action with the parties' intent, or the *Boys Market* litigation

---

[138] See Linn v. United Plant Guard Workers, Local 114, 383 U.S. 53 (1966).

[139] See Carroll v. President & Comm'rs of Princess Anne, 393 U.S. 175 (1968), which held unconstitutional temporary restraining orders issued without notice or opportunity to be heard, on the ground that it denied the First Amendment right to speak.

[140] 398 U.S. at 239 n.3.

where the no-strike clause appeared to cover the dispute in question, since the employer wished to invoke the grievance-arbitration machinery, poses a more difficult question for the courts.

Where the parties, as in *Boys Market*, indicate quite clearly that an exception to the no-strike clause is intended where one of the parties refuses to abide by the award, the argument in favor of not issuing an injunction becomes a strong one. After all, the parties have themselves designated the method of dispute resolution. Moreover, the courts would be deciding whether the parties had complied with the award in the teeth of a mandate against judicial intervention.

Suppose, however, that there is no contract provision such as that contained in the *Boys Market* agreement. Should the result be the same? The parties have not bargained their way out of the courts, but the difficulties involved in determining compliance remain. The Third Circuit, in *Philadelphia Marine Trade Association v. ILA, Local 1219*,[141] held that where stoppages were called to protest an arbitrator's award, confirmed in that case in a federal district court, the union could be enjoined from thwarting enforcement of the award by the imposition of contempt sanctions. But the question whether the union is actually resisting the award—before or after its confirmation in court[142]—is more difficult than determining whether the court ought to enforce the award itself. There is a risk of erroneously construing the arbitrator's award in terms of the particular work stoppage engaged in. It would seem proper, therefore, and compatible with Norris-LaGuardia (especially where there are any exceptions to the scope of the no-strike clause which make the lawfulness of the strike an important issue), to enjoin the stoppage only where it is patent that its intent or effect is to undermine the award. In the absence of such a finding, a court of equity might well refer the matter back to the arbitrator to obtain further clarification or, alternatively, order the parties to proceed to arbitration on the merits of the issue or the scope of the no-strike clause or both. Where, however, there is no issue about the no-strike aspect, an injunction would undoubtedly issue under the standards of the *Boys Market* doctrine.

---

[141] 365 F.2d 295 (3d Cir. 1966), 368 F.2d 932 (3d Cir. 1966), *rev'd on other grounds*, 389 U.S. 64 (1967).

[142] See Dunau, note 78 *supra*, at 476–77.

There is one final issue which will undoubtedly come before the courts more often in the future. This is the question of union responsibility for the stoppage and the standard to be imposed upon the union under contract language in existence.[163] This is a most important issue in terms of guarding or raiding (depending upon one's vantage point) the union treasury, but also because, if union responsibility is not established, the courts are up against the most untidy consequence of *Boys Market:* the enforcement of judicial decrees against individual workers or groups of workers (which may constitute a dissident organization) who call or are involved in unauthorized stoppages.

It has been said that the principal contribution of *Boys Market* is that the decision will make available the more potent remedy of injunction to deal with wildcat or unauthorized stoppages.[164] In one sense, this assessment of the Court's decision is an accurate one in that union leaders will find it easier to stand up to the rank and file and to adhere to contract commitments. The court issuing the injunction becomes the political scapegoat rather than the international or local union officers. With rank and file protests on the upswing, *Boys Market* may provide a much needed palliative to cope with the unauthorized stoppages in breach of contract. Yet, this analysis is superficial for a number of reasons.

In the first place, a collective bargaining agreement may impose a mere passive responsibility on the part of the international or local union, *i.e.,* the union must not sanction or encourage the stoppage. Thus, the no-strike clause may simply require the union not

---

163 See FAIRWEATHER, EMPLOYER ACTIONS AND OPTIONS IN RESPONSE TO STRIKES IN BREACH OF CONTRACT 129 (1966). *Compare* United Constr. Workers v. Haislip Baking Co., 223 F.2d 872 (4th Cir. 1955), *with* United Textile Workers v. Newberry Mills, 238 F. Supp. 366 (W.D. S.C. 1955). See Cox, *Some Aspects of the Labor Management Relations Act, 1947,* 61 HARV. L. REV. 274, 302–12 (1948).

164 See Unkovic, *Enforcing the No-Strike Clause,* 21 LAB. L.J. 387 (1970). Of course, if rank and file pressure makes a substantial impact upon union leadership, the price of the no-strike clause itself as well as other costs imposed upon the employer may go higher. I am advised of one situation where the union relinquished wage increase demands in order to obtain removal of the no-strike clause and the *Boys Market* remedy.

to encourage such unauthorized activity rather than to impose a more severe affirmative action obligation to see that the stoppage is discontinued. Perhaps the courts will read no-strike clauses broadly so as to require the union to engage in a good faith effort to get the workers to return to the job.[165] Broad contract construction would be compatible with the policy of federal labor law of encouraging industrial peace in the *quid pro quo* concept which might otherwise be thwarted by irresponsible rank and file activities. And it would not conflict with either the standard previously advocated for a judicial finding of no-strike violation, *i.e.*, that the violation be reasonably clear, or final adjudication of liability and violation questions by the arbitrator.

Even if the union is responsible for bringing an end to the stoppage, difficulties remain. The union cannot be regarded as a guarantor to supply labor in all instances.[166] Some of these problems are highlighted by Judge Judd's recent opinion in *REA Express v.*

---

[165] For the variety of no-strike clauses and arbitral awards regarding them, see, *e.g.*, Vulcan Mold & Iron Co., 53 Lab. Arb. 869 (1969); Forest City Publishing Co., 50 Lab. Arb. 683 (1968); Merchant's Frozen Foods Div., 34 Lab. Arb. 607 (1960); Cleveland Newspapers Ass'n, 49 Lab. Arb. 1043 (1967); Master Builders Ass'n, 49 Lab. Arb. 1157 (1967); Electric Autolite Co., 40 Lab. Arb. 522 (1963); Crawford Clothes, Inc., 12 Lab. Arb. 1104 (1949); Motor Products Corp., 12 Lab. Arb. 49 (1949). *Cf.* GOULDNER, WILDCAT STRIKE (1965); Leahy, *Arbitration, Union Stewards and Wildcat Strikes*, 25 ARB. J. 150 (1970). The court order must be based upon contract. *Cf.* Cox, note 163 *supra*, at 311.

[166] *Cf.* NLRB v. Norfolk Shipbuilding & Drydocking Corp., 195 F.2d 632, 636 (4th Cir. 1952). Even if the affirmative action obligation is not present, the union's withdrawal of support has some impact upon employee action: "By pledging that it will not support a wildcat strike a Union makes it clear that it will not make [strike assistance] . . . payments. A contract usually allows the employer to stop paying the premiums for employee insurance coverage during the strike, and so the Union pays the premiums to keep the coverage intact. In a no-support type no-strike pledge, however, the Union makes it clear that it will not finance such premiums. Most importantly, in a no-support type clause the Union pledges that it will not use its talent and resources in planning and waging any strike that occurs. Often an international union gives a strike a whole new dimension by contacting the customers of a struck employer with whom it has collective bargaining relationships and asking them, in consideration of their good relationship, to discontinue purchasing from the struck employer during the strike. This cannot happen where the international has pledged no support. Nor can an international use its often extensive communications media in aid of a strike where it has signed a promise of no support. The international may not plan strategy or tactical moves to assist the strikes in their resort to self-help. Finally, the international may not use its very considerable strength with other international unions to solicit financial and tactical support for the strikers." Brief for International Union, UAW and Local Union No. 758, pp. 44–45, in Vulcan Mold & Iron Co., 53 Lab. Arb. 869 (1969).

Brotherhood of Railway, Airline & Steamship Clerks,[167] where the court issued an injunction against the international union as well as the local. Although the international had not authorized the strike, the international had not taken disciplinary action against those responsible for the stoppage. Said the court:[168]

> There is no evidence that BRAC [the international union] ever took any action to penalize those responsible for illegal work stoppages. The penalties in the BRAC constitution for illegal strikes may be so severe that they are reluctant to apply them. The only specific penalties mentioned are expulsion of participating members, which it is the duty of the local Lodge to enforce promptly, and revocation of the charter of any lodge which does not proceed with the members transferred to other lodges. . . . BRAC should be able, however, to find some powers lurking in the 171 pages of constitution, statutes, and protective laws which it could use to protect itself against violations by its members of obligations which it has assumed as the bargaining agent for all employees.

In effect, this is the approach that the Trades Union Congress has agreed to undertake to regulate "unofficial" stoppages in Great Britain.[169] But it is much easier to talk about such actions than to impose them, for the political facts of life may make it difficult

---

[167] 74 L.R.R.M. 2346 (E.D. N.Y. 1970).

[168] *Id.* at 2439. But see Boeing v. Local Lodge 751 and IAM, 91 F. Supp. 596 (W.D. Wash. 1950), where it was held that the international was subject to several rather than joint liability where both the international and local were party to the collective agreement. Thus, unless stated to the contrary, the contract does not automatically obligate the international for the local's conduct. Section 301 makes federal labor law dependent upon traditional rules of agency. *Cf.* United Broth. of Carpenters and Joiners v. United States, 330 U.S. 395 (1947); UMW v. Gibbs, 383 U.S. 715, 736 (1966); Flaherty v. McDonald, 178 F. Supp. 544, 548 (S.D. Cal. 1959). One kind of international union discipline is placing the local under trusteeship. But this raises problems under § 302 of Landrum Griffin. See Jolly v. Gorman, 74 L.R.R.M. 2706 (5th Cir. 1970). Whether the union violates § 8(b)(1)(A) of the NLRA when it disciplines nonstriking members seems to turn on whether the union stoppage is lawful. Thus a strike in breach of contract by the union makes the collection of union imposed fines unlawful "restraint" and "coercion." See National Grinding Wheel Company, Inc., 176 N.L.R.B. No. 89 (1969); Stark Glass, Inc., 177 N.L.R.B. No. 37 (1969); Rocket Freight Lines Co. v. NLRB, 74 L.R.R.M. 2452 (10th Cir. 1970); *cf.* National Tea Company, 181 N.L.R.B. No. 116 (1970).

[169] See Wood, *Anti-Strike Bill Abandoned by Wilson: Agreement Heals Breach in the Labour Movement*, The Times (London), June 19, 1969, p. 1, col. 1. See also note 4 *supra;* Carr, *The Unions: What the Tories Would Put in Place of Strife*, Sunday Times (London), June 1, 1969, p. 12, col. 1; Shanks, *Reforming the Unions by*

for internationals to penalize local union officers who may then be tempted to move to another union in competition for the same members. Although such considerations are tempered by the very judicial intervention which has been temporarily rejected in Britain, these problems are now exaggerated in this country by the withdrawal of the UAW and International Brotherhood of Teamsters from the AFL-CIO and the consequent potential for increased raiding among the unions.[170] And much the same factors are present where the local union moves against individual workers. These workers may opt for a more politically acceptable choice in the form of a rival union. On the other hand, if the court is requiring the international or local officers to take action of a fairly reasonable nature, *i.e.*, trusteeship rather than expulsion or fines, and the instances in which such sanctions are imposed remains limited to cases in which there is defiance of court orders, or a strong potential for such, damage to both organized labor and the courts may be minimized. And perhaps it may be said that even the transferral of allegiance to another union may be desirable from the point of view of public policy if the competing union decides to behave properly. But, of course, the price or by-product of such success may be the irrational resolution of grievances, exorbitant and inflationary settlements (in the case of interest disputes), or an indiscriminate sanction of employee claims—all of which are risks whenever reduction of strikes becomes a primary goal in labor-management policy.

If legal action against the unions is unsuccessful, there is only one other approach that could be taken through the courts, *i.e.*, an employer suit against the individual striker or groups of strikers. This approach has been adopted in Sweden,[171] but employers rarely sue individual employees because of the disruptive effect upon a harmonious industrial relations policy. Moreover, the Swedish statute specifically limits the amount of damages that can be collected to a relatively small amount, thus striking the same kind of

---

Contract, The Times (London), Nov. 13, 1967, p. 21, col. 3. For some of the recent decisions by British courts on the right to strike, see Daily Mirror Newspapers v. Gardner, [1968] Q.B. 762; Torquay Hotel Co. v. Cousins, [1968] 3 W.L.R. 540; Stratford & Son v. Lindley, [1965] A. C. 269; Rookes v. Barnard, [1964] A.C. 1129.

[170] See Loftus, *AFL-CIO Drops Automobile Union for Dues Arrears*, N.Y. Times, May 17, 1968, p. 1, col. 3; Janson, *U.A.W. and Teamsters Form Political and Organizing Team*, N.Y. Times, July 24, 1968, p. 51, col. 1.

[171] See SCHMIDT, THE LAW OF LABOUR RELATIONS IN SWEDEN 117 (1962).

contorted balance adopted by the New York legislature in 1967 in the Taylor Law[172] with regard to public employees. Whether injunctive decrees or damage suits may be maintained against employees pursuant to § 301 has not yet been resolved by the Supreme Court. The Court has held, in *Atkinson v. Sinclair Refining Co.,*[173] that union agents may not be sued individually under § 301 inasmuch as the act was intended to render the union liable as an entity for breach of contract. But *Atkinson* dealt with suits against individuals where the responsibility belonged to the union and therefore the relief sought against union agents was essentially duplicative. In *Atkinson*, the Court specifically reserved ruling on the question whether damage suits against individuals may be entertained under § 301.[174]

V. Conclusion

> An enforced shut-down caused by a strike in a small plant in a quite different part of the country may hit the earnings of . . . a highly capitalised firm very hard. Its willingness to accept the risks of heavy investment in the production of specialised products dependent on the chain of other operations will be influenced by the view that it takes of the reliability of the engagements made by its suppliers of essential goods and services. If the flow is constantly subject to unpredictable interruption, business initiative in important fields of activity is likely to be discouraged. There is also the effect on wage-earnings; the demand for total autonomy by a work group

---

[172] N.Y. Civ. Serv. Law, § 200 *et seq.* (McKinney Supp. 1969), imposes penalties upon individual workers, § 210(2)(f) (one year's probation while serving without tenure); § 210(2)(g) (payroll deduction of twice daily rate for each day in violation of act); § 210(3)(g) (no compensation paid to those engaged in strike).

[173] 370 U.S. 238, 246–49 (1962).

[174] *Id.* at 249 n.7. See also in this connection Louisville & N.R.R. v. Brown, 252 F.2d 149 (5th Cir. 1958); Givens, *Responsibility of Individual Employees for Breaches of No-Strike Clauses,* 14 IND. & LAB. REL. REV. 595 (1961); Comment, *Liability of Employees under State Law for Damages Caused by Wildcat Strike: The Brown Case,* 50 COLUM. L. REV. 177 (1959); Gilmour v. Wood Wire & Metal Lathers International Union, Local 74, 223 F. Supp. 236 (N.D. Ill. 1953). But two state courts have enjoined strike activity by individuals. See American Device Mfg. Co. v. Machinists, 105 Ill. App.2d 299 (1969); Armco Steel Corp. v. Perkins, 411 S.W.2d 935 (Ky. Ct. App. 1967). Query, does an injunction against individuals raise constitutional questions? See International Union, UAWA v. W.E.R.B., 336 U.S. 245, 259 (1949); Dorchy v. Kansas, 272 U.S. 306, 311 (1926). See also Hughes v. Superior Court, 339 U.S. 460, 465 (1950).

which has banded together to stop or slow down production in one place results in the loss of wages and the disruption of the working lives of many times their number elsewhere. These workers and their employers both have a right to expect the effective intervention of trade unions in plants where labour is organised, to ensure that frivolous or minor disputes are not allowed to cause excessive damage.[175]

So said Andrew Shonfield, in a Note of Reservation to Great Britain's Donovan Report of 1968. In effect, the arbitration system in the United States is an answer to the problem to which Mr. Shonfield was addressing himself in Britain, although the American system's success may be extolled beyond actual practice in the plant.[176] Of course, it is axiomatic that the democratic society cannot eliminate strikes, whether they occur during the term of the contract or at its expiration. As a matter of fact, the short-run impact of *Boys Market* may actually increase the incidence of stoppages over the terms of a new contract in industries like auto and steel where the rank and file rumblings about elimination of the no-strike clause during the term of the agreement are the greatest. *Boys Market* could impel union leadership to press hard for the removal of the strike prohibition even to the point of striking for this demand at the expiration of the contract. But the interdependent nature of a technologically advanced economy requires modernized industrial relations and this necessitates changes which may be abrasive to private parties.[177] The labor unions do not stand immune from that rule of life. (Indeed, the labor movement's willingness to obey Taft-Hartley national emergency dispute injunctions indicates its recognition of this.) Section 301, as interpreted by the Court in *Lincoln Mills* and its progeny, seeks to make the law responsive to these conditions.

And yet, to paraphrase Santayana, one cannot ignore history and risk repetition of its mistakes. Mr. Justice Frankfurter's dissent in *Lincoln Mills* was largely undercut by the *Steelworkers Trilogy*.

---

[175] Donovan Report, 288, 289. See also the expansive approach taken toward enjoining jurisdictional stoppage in the United States (partially on the authority of *Boys Market*), in Plasterers Local Union No. 79 v. NLRB, 74 L.R.R.M. 2575 (D.C. Cir. 1970).

[176] See Kuhn, Bargaining in Grievance Settlement (1961).

[177] See Galbraith, The New Industrial State (1967); Crosland, The Future of Socialism (1956).

But his views loom larger when one considers the problems bound up with *Boys Market*. The nature of judicial scrutiny in connection with the injunction gives Frankfurter's dissenting opinion a more prophetic quality. Nevertheless, while conceding the existence of a specter now somewhat enlarged, on balance, I am of the view that judicial resiliency is sufficient to evade most of the traps that once brought the unions to distrust so severely the law and the courts.

6

On Labor Injunctions Pending Arbitration: Recasting *Buffalo Forge*

The proper role of the federal courts in the settling of labor-management disputes has been a concern of Congress and the courts throughout this century.[1] The courts originally took an activist role, indiscriminately issuing injunctions against the activities of labor unions. Congress responded with the Norris-LaGuardia Act in 1932 to shelter the organizational efforts of unions by prohibiting federal court issuance of injunctions in "labor disputes."[2] With the growth of unionism and increased concern about the power of unions, subsequent legislation narrowed the restriction on federal court labor injunctions.[3] Courts were left the task of reconciling the anti-injunction provisions of the 1930's legislation and the conflicting provisions of later laws.

In a series of cases[4] culminating in *Buffalo Forge Co. v. United*

The author wishes to thank Seth Goldberg, Stanford 1978, for his research, insightful criticism and thoughtful reviews of an earlier draft of this Article. Mr. Goldberg's indispensable assistance helped the author achieve a greater clarity of expression in the final manuscript. The author also would like to thank Bert Slonim, Stanford Law School teaching fellow 1976-77, Simon Klevansky, Stanford 1977, and Barbara Yanni, Stanford 1979, for their valuable research and assistance. The author also is grateful for a grant from the National Science Foundation.

1. *See, e.g.,* F. FRANKFURTER & N. GREENE, THE LABOR INJUNCTION (1930); Gould, *On Labor Injunctions, Unions, and the Judges: The Boys Market Case*, 1970 SUP. CT. REV. 215; Comment, *Labor Injunctions and Judge-Made Labor Law: The Contemporary Role of Norris-LaGuardia*, 70 YALE L.J. 70 (1960).

2. Norris-LaGuardia Act of 1932, ch. 90, 47 Stat. 70 (codified at 29 U.S.C. §§ 101-115 (1970)).

3. Labor-Management Reporting and Disclosure Act of 1959, Pub. L. No. 86-257, 73 Stat. 519 (codified at 29 U.S.C. §§ 401-531 (1970)); Labor Management Relations (Taft-Hartley) Act, 1947, ch. 120, 61 Stat. 136 (codified at 29 U.S.C. §§ 141-187 (1970)).

4. *See, e.g.,* Gateway Coal Co. v. UMW, 414 U.S. 368 (1974); Boys Mkts., Inc. v. Retail Clerks Local 770, 398 U.S. 235 (1970); Sinclair Ref. Co. v. Atkinson, 370 U.S. 195 (1962); Textile Workers Union v. Lincoln Mills, 353 U.S. 448 (1957); Brotherhood of R.R. Trainmen v. Chicago River & Ind. R.R., 353 U.S. 30 (1957).

Steelworkers,[5] the Supreme Court has tried to settle the role of the federal courts in labor-management disputes. *Buffalo Forge* held that certain strikes could not be enjoined by federal courts pending arbitration of the strike's permissibility under the collective bargaining agreement.

Part I of this Article traces the development of judicial enforcement of collective bargaining agreements over the last 20 years. During this period, the willingness of courts to issue injunctions against violations of collective bargaining agreements steadily increased. Initially, the Court permitted injunctions compelling employers to arbitrate disputes with labor unions.[6] The Court next enjoined strikes pending arbitration of whether the strike breached an express no-strike clause in a collective bargaining agreement.[7] Prior to *Buffalo Forge*, this trend had reached its zenith.[8] This Article argues that the federal court policy of freely issuing injunctions precipitated an ill-conceived retreat in *Buffalo Forge*.

Part II analyzes the *Buffalo Forge* decision and argues that the majority's standard for distinguishing between strikes that may be enjoined pending arbitration, and those that may not, not only fails to alleviate the problems relating to the issuance of injunctions that existed prior to *Buffalo Forge*, but also creates additional difficulties. This Article favors an alternative standard that has now been adopted by Justice Steven's dissenting opinion in *Buffalo Forge*. Finally, Part III discusses the potential impact of *Buffalo Forge* on union pleas for injunctions against employers. This Article argues that although courts have interpreted *Buffalo Forge* to apply to this issue, that case, whether rightly or wrongly decided, should have no effect on the resolution of this question.

I. The Availability of Injunctive Relief in Labor Disputes Before the Federal Courts

In the early years of organized labor, prior to the emergence of industrial unionism, the federal courts demonstrated a pro-employer bias in handling labor relations. The courts sought to thwart the growth of labor unions through a variety of measures, the most

---

5. 428 U.S. 397 (1976).

6. *E.g.*, United Steelworkers v. Enterprise Wheel & Car Corp., 363 U.S. 593 (1960); United Steelworkers v. Warrior & Gulf Navigation Co., 363 U.S. 574 (1960); United Steelworkers v. American Mfg. Co., 363 U.S. 564 (1960); Textile Workers Union v. Lincoln Mills, 353 U.S. 448 (1957).

7. *E.g.*, Boys Mkts., Inc. v. Retail Clerks Local 770, 398 U.S. 235 (1970).

8. *E.g.*, Gateway Coal Co. v. UMW, 414 U.S. 368 (1974).

prominent being the indiscriminate issuance of anti-labor injunctions.[9] The Norris-LaGuardia Act of 1932[10] embodied a congressional reaction against the federal judiciary's partiality.[11] The central purpose of the Act was to allow individual workers freedom from "interference, restraint, or coercion of employers of labor, or their agents" in designating their representatives and organizing and engaging in concerted activities.[12] Section 4 achieves this purpose by depriving federal courts of jurisdiction to enjoin any person from "[c]easing or refusing to perform any work or to remain in any relation of employment."[13]

In the years since the Act was passed, both Congress and the courts have narrowed the broad Norris-LaGuardia prohibition of injunctions in labor disputes. Through the Labor Management Relations (Taft-Hartley) Act[14] and the Labor-Management Reporting and Disclosure Act[15] Congress exempted temporary and preliminary injunctive relief sought by the National Labor Relations Board in several situations.[16] Section 301(a) of the Labor Management Relations Act[17] allowed federal courts with jurisdiction over a union

---

9. *See, e.g.*, Bedford Cut Stone Co. v. Journeymen Stone Cutters' Ass'n, 274 U.S. 37 (1927); Hitchman Coal & Coke Co. v. Mitchell, 245 U.S. 229 (1917). For a discussion of court practices, see F. FRANKFURTER & N. GREENE, *supra* note 1, at 17-81.

10. Norris-LaGuardia Act of 1932, ch. 90, 47 Stat. 70 (codified at 29 U.S.C. §§ 101-115 (1970)).

11. *See* 75 CONG. REC. 4915 (1932) (policy and purpose of Act is to ensure that government, particularly the courts, is neutral in labor disputes) (remarks of Sen. Wagner); Gould, *supra* note 1, at 219-20.

12. 29 U.S.C. § 102 (1970). One of the main purposes of the Act was to prevent federal court intervention in union strike activities. For a further discussion of the Act's policies, see H.R. REP. NO. 669, 72d Cong., 1st Sess. 3-11 (1932); S. REP. NO. 163, 72d Cong., 1st Sess. 7-18 (1932); Comment, *supra* note 1, at 74-76.

The ease with which courts issued injunctions against strikes prior to Norris-LaGuardia had the practical effect of eliminating the strike as a union weapon. The injunctions would remain in force until the permissibility of the strike was determined, leaving the employer free to continue efforts to defeat the strike. As a result, by the time a strike ultimately might be declared legal by the court and an injunction dissolved, the employer and passing events had often undermined the union's power to call an effective strike. F. FRANKFURTER & N. GREENE, *supra* note 1, at 201.

13. 29 U.S.C. § 104(a) (1970).

14. Labor Management Relations (Taft-Hartley) Act, 1947, ch. 120, tit. I, § 101(8)(b), 61 Stat. 141 (codified at 29 U.S.C. § 158(b) (1970)).

15. Labor-Management Reporting and Disclosure Act of 1959, Pub. L. No. 86-257, § 704(a), (c), 73 Stat. 542 (codified at 29 U.S.C. § 158(b)(4), (7) (1970)).

16. These situations include secondary boycotts, 29 U.S.C. § 158(b)(4)(B) (1970), jurisdictional disputes, 29 U.S.C. § 158(b)(4)(D) (1970), and organizational and recognitional picketing, 29 U.S.C. § 158(b)(7) (1970).

17. Labor Management Relations (Taft-Hartley) Act § 301(a), 29 U.S.C. § 185(a) (1970) ("Suits for violation of contracts between an employer and a labor organization representing

and employer to enforce their collective bargaining agreement. In *Textile Workers Union v. Lincoln Mills*,[18] the Supreme Court reintroduced judicial involvement in labor-management disputes by interpreting section 301(a) as authorizing federal courts to "fashion a body of federal law for the enforcement of . . . collective bargaining agreements."[19]

In *Lincoln Mills*, the union sought an injunction to compel the employer to arbitrate grievances under a collective bargaining agreement that contained both no-strike and arbitration clauses. The Court reasoned that "[p]lainly the agreement to arbitrate grievance disputes is the *quid pro quo* for an agreement not to strike. . . . [Section 301(a)] expresses a federal policy that federal courts should enforce these agreements on behalf of or against labor organizations and that industrial peace can be best obtained only in that way."[20] An injunction compelling the employer to arbitrate did not violate the Norris-LaGuardia prohibition of injunctions in labor disputes, the Court ruled, because injunctions against employer refusals to arbitrate were not "a part and parcel of the abuses" that were the target of Norris-LaGuardia.[21]

The Supreme Court reaffirmed the policy favoring the settlement of labor disputes through arbitration in the *Steelworkers Trilogy*.[22] In two of these three cases, a union sought to compel an employer to arbitrate a dispute. The Court did not decide whether the disputes fell within the scope of the arbitration clause; instead, it ordered the employer to submit this issue to arbitration so long as there was contractual basis to do so.[23] The arbitrator was to make a de novo finding on the issue of arbitrability[24] and, if the dispute was

---

employees in an industry affecting commerce . . . may be brought in any district court of the United States having jurisdiction of the parties . . . .").

18. 353 U.S. 448 (1957).

19. *Id.* at 451.

20. *Id.* at 455. For an analysis of the Court's assertion that the agreement to arbitrate grievance disputes is the quid pro quo for a no-strike clause, see Comment, *The Lincoln Mills Case and Specific Enforcement of No-Strike Clauses in the Federal Courts*, 25 U. CHI. L. REV. 496, 499-502 (1958).

21. 353 U.S. at 458.

22. United Steelworkers v. Enterprise Wheel & Car Corp., 363 U.S. 593 (1960); United Steelworkers v. Warrior & Gulf Navigation Co., 363 U.S. 574 (1960); United Steelworkers v. American Mfg. Co., 363 U.S. 564 (1960).

23. United Steelworkers v. Enterprise Wheel & Car Corp., 363 U.S. 593, 596 (1960) (by implication); United Steelworkers v. Warrior & Gulf Navigation Co., 363 U.S. 574, 585 (1960); United Steelworkers v. American Mfg. Co., 363 U.S. 564, 567-68 (1960).

24. If one of the parties to a collective bargaining agreement resists arbitration, and the other party initiates a judicial proceeding to compel the process, the court must find a

within the arbitrator's jurisdiction, to rule upon the merits. The arbitrator's award was specifically enforceable in court and was not to be overturned unless it "manifested an infidelity" to the collective bargaining agreement itself.[25] Thus, the Court advanced the policy favoring arbitration by creating two presumptions: First, courts must resolve all doubts about the arbitrability of a dispute in favor of arbitration;[26] second, an arbitrator's award is presumptively valid.[27] The effect of these presumptions was to exclude the judiciary from deciding the merits of labor disputes.

Lincoln Mills and the *Steelworkers Trilogy* involved injunctions compelling employers to arbitrate. In *Sinclair Refining Co. v. Atkinson*,[28] the Court confronted for the first time the question whether Norris-LaGuardia prohibits an injunction against a *union* striking in

---

contractual basis in the collective bargaining agreement to compel arbitration. John Wiley & Sons, Inc. v. Livingston, 376 U.S. 534, 546-47 (1964); Atkinson v. Sinclair Ref. Co., 370 U.S. 238, 241 (1962); United Steelworkers v. Warrior & Gulf Navigation Co., 363 U.S. 574, 582 (1960). Because any contractual basis will suffice, the court's interpretation of arbitrability may differ from that which an arbitrator would make when considering the merits of the dispute. With respect to this issue, some courts have held that a judicial decision on arbitrability precludes the arbitrator from deciding that the dispute is not arbitrable under the contract. *See* Piano & Musical Instrument Workers Local 2549 v. W.W. Kimball Co., 239 F. Supp. 523 (N.D. Ill. 1965); Claremont Painting & Decorating, 46 Lab. Arb. 894 (1966) (Kerrison, Arb.) The better view is that the arbitrator, who is expert at such determinations, may review arbitrability de novo subsequent to a court's determination in granting a motion to compel arbitration. *See* Gulf States Utilities Co., 69-1 Lab. Arb. Awards 3110 (1969) (Ray, Arb.); J.C. Wattenbarger & Sons, 66-2 Lab. Arb. Awards 5141 (1966) (Robert, Arb.); Warrior & Gulf Navigaton Co., 36 Lab. Arb. 695, 696-99 (1961) (Holly, Arb.). *Cf.* Georgia-Pacific Corp., 40 Lab. Arb. 769 (1963) (Leflar, Arb.) (arbitrator to decide whether there was a "management function"); Sidele Fashions, Inc., 36 Lab. Arb. 1364, 1368 (1961) (Dash, Arb.) (arbitrator to review compliance with procedure invoking arbitration). This second view is consistent with my position that the arbitrator hears all arbitrable issues de novo in both *Boys Markets* and *Buffalo Forge* proceedings. Despite the fact that judicial inquiry must be exacting when enjoining strikes, *see* notes 106-09 *infra* and accompanying text, arbitrators should be able to decide all issues de novo in *Boys Markets* and *Buffalo Forge* injunction proceedings because of their expertise, which the Court recognized in *Steelworkers Trilogy*.

25. United Steelworkers v. Enterprise Wheel & Car Corp., 363 U.S. 593, 597 (1960); United Steelworkers v. Warrior & Gulf Navigation Co., 363 U.S. 574, 568-69 (1960); United Steelworkers v. American Mfg. Co., 363 U.S. 564, 568 (1960).

26. *E.g.*, United Steelworkers v. Warrior & Gulf Navigation Co., 363 U.S. 574, 582-83 (1960) ("An order to arbitrate the particular grievance should not be denied unless it may be said with positive assurance that the arbitration clause is not susceptible of an interpretation that covers the asserted dispute. Doubts should be resolved in favor of coverage."). Professor Cox was an early advocate of judicial restraint in determining the arbitrability of a dispute. For his seminal discussions of the roles of judge and arbitrator, see Cox, *Current Problems in the Law of Grievance Arbitration*, 30 ROCKY MTN. L. REV. 247, 258-66 (1958) and Cox, *Reflections upon Labor Arbitration*, 72 HARV. L. REV. 1482, 1507-15 (1959).

27. *E.g.*, United Steelworkers v. Enterprise Wheel & Car. Corp., 363 U.S. 593, 597 (1960).

28. 370 U.S. 195 (1962).

violation of a no-strike clause. Despite the quid pro quo relationship between the arbitration and no-strike provisions, and prior case law holding that arbitration clauses were specifically enforceable against employers,[29] *Sinclair* held that injunctions against striking unions would violate the anti-injunction provisions of Norris-LaGuardia.[30] The Court, over a vigorous dissent by Justice Brennan, concluded that Congress, and not the Court, would have to repeal section 4 of the Norris-LaGuardia Act[31] in order for an injunction to issue against unions.[32]

Eight years later, *Boys Markets, Inc. v. Retail Clerks Local 770*[33] overruled *Sinclair* on the ground that the earlier decision represented a "significant departure from our otherwise consistent emphasis upon the congressional policy to promote the peaceful settlement of labor disputes through arbitration."[34] Emphasizing the quid pro quo analysis, the Court noted that the availability of effective injunctive relief to enforce a no-strike clause could function as the principal incentive for an employer to accept grievance-arbitration machinery.[35] According to this view, an employer bargains for continuous work production throughout the life of the collective bargaining agreement in return for accepting an arbitration clause.[36] The Court also implied, citing *Lincoln Mills*, that the availability of injunctive relief against labor organizations for the breach of the no-strike clause was not "part and parcel" of the abuses against which Norris-LaGuardia was aimed.[37] For these reasons, the Court con-

---

29. *E.g.*, Textile Workers Union v. Lincoln Mills, 353 U.S. 448, 451 (1957).

30. 370 U.S. at 203.

31. 29 U.S.C. § 104 (1970); *see* text accompanying note 13 *supra*.

32. 370 U.S. at 214-15.

33. 398 U.S. 235 (1970). For a discussion of *Boys Markets* and cases preceding it, see Gould, *supra* note 1.

34. 398 U.S. at 241.

35. *Id.* at 248.

36. Textile Workers Union v. Lincoln Mills, 353 U.S. 448, 454-55 (1957).

37. 398 U.S. at 241-42; *see* note 12 *supra*.

An additional reason for overruling *Sinclair* was that the decision was in conflict with § 301(a) of the Labor Management Relations Act, 29 U.S.C. § 185(a) (1970). Prior to *Sinclair*, injunctions against strikes in violation of no-strike clauses had been available in state courts. 398 U.S. at 243-44. *Sinclair*, coupled with the ready removal by unions of labor cases from state to federal courts, *see, e.g.*, Avco Corp. v. Aero Lodge 735, 390 U.S. 557 (1968), eliminated the availability of this state remedy to employers. Congress, however, by conferring jurisdiction over labor disputes upon federal courts through § 301(a) had intended to supplement preexisting state remedies, not to extinguish such remedies. Charles Dowd Box Co. v. Courtney, 368 U.S. 502, 511 (1962). *Boys Markets* found *Sinclair* to be inconsistent with this congressional intent. 398 U.S. at 245. *Cf.* William E. Arnold Co. v. Carpenters Dist. Council, 417 U.S. 12 (1974) (state jurisdiction over collective-bargaining disputes not limited to dam-

cluded that the pro-arbitration policies of section 301(a) outweighed the anti-injunction policies of Norris-LaGuardia.[38] This decision allowed courts to enjoin strikes pending the arbitrator's decision of whether the strike was barred by the collective bargaining agreement. The Court also indicated the standards that district courts should use to decide whether to issue injunctions.[39]

At the same time, the Supreme Court was fashioning a new federal common law of labor contract. In *Local 174, International Brotherhood of Teamsters v. Lucas Flour Co.*,[40] the Court held that even absent an express no-strike clause, courts could award damages against unions for strikes when the collective bargaining contract contained a broad arbitration clause.[41] The Court inferred a no-strike obligation from the union's agreement to arbitrate all issues, without considering whether parties normally bargain for an explicit no-strike provision.[42] *Gateway Coal Co. v. UMW*[43] coupled the *Lucas Flour* "constructive no-strike agreement" to the *Boys Markets* approval of injunctions against unions. In *Gateway Coal*, the Court implied a no-strike clause from the existence of a broad arbitration provision in the collective bargaining agreement and, despite a "substantial question of contract interpretation" concerning the scope of the no-strike clause,[44] enjoined the strike. The standard

---

ages); McCarroll v. Los Angeles Dist. County Council of Carpenters, 49 Cal. 2d 45, 63, 315 P.2d 322, 332 (1957) (state courts not deprived of power to grant relief by Norris-LaGuardia Act or § 301 of the Labor Management Relations Act).

38. 398 U.S. at 252-53.

39. Justice Brennan, the author of the *Boys Markets* majority, cited his dissenting opinion in *Sinclair* to indicate the appropriate standards: "A District Court entertaining an action under § 301 may not grant injunctive relief against concerted activity unless and until it decides that the case is one in which an injunction would be appropriate despite the Norris-LaGuardia Act. When a strike is sought to be enjoined because it is over a grievance which both parties are contractually bound to arbitrate, the District Court may issue no injunctive order until it first holds that the contract *does* have that effect; and the employer should be ordered to arbitrate, as a condition of his obtaining an injunction against the strike. Beyond this, the District Court must, of course, consider whether issuance of an injunction would be warranted under ordinary principles of equity—whether breaches are occurring and will continue, or have been threatened and will be committed; whether they have caused or will cause irreparable injury to the employer; and whether the employer will suffer more from the denial of an injunction than will the union from its issuance." *Id*. at 254.

40. 369 U.S. 95 (1962).

41. *Id*. at 105.

42. *Id*. at 105-06.

43. 414 U.S. 368 (1974). For an excellent discussion of some of the issues raised in *Gateway*, see Atleson, *Threats to Health and Safety: Employee Self-Help Under the NLRA*, 59 MINN. L. REV. 647 (1975).

44. *Id*. at 384. The Court framed the question of the judicial power to enjoin strikes in terms of "whether the union was under a contractual duty not to strike." *Id*. at 380. However,

announced in this case and its use in the *Lucas Flour* context increased the potential for the issuance of injunctions against strikes and walkouts.[45]

The frequent issuance of injunctions placed courts on a collision course with the unions. This problem was particularly acute in the coal mines, where the sympathy strike is a deeply established tradition.[46] The United Mine Workers union, which was involved in

---

following the *Lucas Flour* decision, the contractual duty not to strike was implied from the agreement to arbitrate. *Id.* at 381-82. Whether the dispute was arbitrable centered on an interpretation of a mine safety committee provision in the contract. The mine safety committee was empowered to make decisions, binding upon management and the union, to close down unsafe areas. *Id.* at 382-83. If properly invoked, the provision could have been an express contractual exception to the duty to arbitrate, which would overcome the presumption of arbitrability. *See* notes 22-27 *supra* and accompanying text. The Court implied the duty not to strike from the agreement to arbitrate. Thus, whether the union had properly invoked the safety committee procedure that would have removed the dispute from arbitration became a contractual issue that determined the applicability of the no-strike clause—an issue the Court left for the arbitrator. 414 U.S. at 384. As a result, *Gateway Coal* may be seen as empowering the courts to enjoin strikes even absent a clear contractual no-strike duty based upon a broad arbitration clause. *See* 63 GEO. L.J. 275, 279-83 (1974).

45. *See* Lowden & Flaherty, *Sympathy Strikes, Arbitration Policy and the Enforceability of No-Strike Agreements—An Analysis of Buffalo Forge*, 45 GEO. WASH. L. REV. 633, 658-59 (1977); Note, *The Applicability of* Boys Markets *Injunctions to Refusals to Cross a Picket Line*, 76 COLUM. L. REV. 113, 122-23 (1976).

In addition, *Gateway Coal* may have increased the potential for issuance of injunctions by an implicit weakening of the ordinary equitable standards applied in *Boys Markets, see* note 39 *supra*. 63 GEO. L.J. 275, 287-88 (1974).

After *Gateway Coal*, courts reached conflicting results on the issue of whether a sympathy strike—the refusal of a union to cross another union's picket line—could be enjoined on the basis of a broad arbitration clause and in the absence of an explicit no-strike clause. In one line of cases, federal courts enjoined sympathy strikes pending arbitration of the strike's permissibility on the basis of broad arbitration clauses and in the absence of explicit no-strike clauses. *E.g.*, Island Creek Coal Co. v. UMW Dist. 2, 507 F.2d 650 (3d Cir.), *cert. denied*, 423 U.S. 877 (1975); Armco Steel Corp. v. UMW, 505 F.2d 1129 (4th Cir. 1974), *cert. denied*, 423 U.S. 877 (1975); Inland Steel Co. v. Local 1545, UMW, 505 F.2d 293 (7th Cir. 1974). *Contra*, Plain Dealer Publishing Co. v. Cleveland Typographical Union No. 53, 520 F.2d 1220 (6th Cir. 1975), *cert. denied*, 428 U.S. 909 (1976).

In a second line of cases, federal courts enjoined sympathy strikes only when the collective bargaining agreement contained an arbitration clause and an explicit no-strike clause. *E.g.*, Associated Gen. Contractors v. Operating Eng'rs Local 49, 519 F.2d 269 (8th Cir. 1975); Valmac Indus. v. Food Handlers Local 425, 519 F.2d 263 (8th Cir. 1975), *vacated and remanded*, 428 U.S. 906 (1976); NAPA Pittsburgh, Inc. v. Automotive Chauffeurs Local 926, 502 F.2d 321 (3d Cir.) (en banc), *cert. denied*, 419 U.S. 1049 (1974); Pilot Freight Carriers, Inc. v. International Bhd. of Teamsters, 497 F.2d 311 (4th Cir.), *cert. denied*, 419 U.S. 869 (1974); Monongahela Power Co. v. Local 2332, IBEW, 484 F.2d 1209 (4th Cir. 1973). *Contra*, Hyster Co. v. Independent Towing & Lifting Mach. Ass'n, 519 F.2d 89 (7th Cir. 1975), *cert. denied*, 428 U.S. 910 (1976); Gary Hobart Water Corp. v. NLRB, 511 F.2d 284 (7th Cir.), *cert. denied*, 423 U.S. 925 (1975); Amstar Corp. v. Amalgamated Meat Cutters, 468 F.2d 1372 (5th Cir. 1972).

46. *See also* text accompanying notes 62-63 *infra*.

Gateway Coal, believed that its failure to negotiate a no-strike clause meant that it had not made a no-strike pledge. Findings by federal courts that sympathy strikes violated implied no-strike provisions tended to escalate tension with the federal judiciary that has produced widespread union disobedience of injunctions and a lingering controversy about the right of coal miners to strike during the term of the collective bargaining agreement.[47]

My concern with the issuance of injunctions pending arbitration—both 8 years ago[48] and today—is twofold. First, the judicial inquiry into no-strike violations should be far more exacting and critical than the inquiry employed in the *Steelworkers Trilogy* to determine if a party resisting arbitration has breached an arbitration clause.[49] Courts should be reasonably certain that the union has engaged in a violation of the no-strike clause before issuing a *Boys Markets* injunction.[50] A lesser standard might defeat the policies embodied in Norris-LaGuardia.[51] This concern was not shared by the Court in *Gateway Coal*, where a more flexible standard was set forth.[52]

Second, whenever a *Boys Markets* injunction issues, it should be conditioned on the willingness of both parties to accede to expedited arbitration procedures.[53] .Under such procedures, the arbitrator decides in a few days or hours whether the union has breached the no-strike clause, as well as whether the employer has violated the agreement in connection with the underlying grievance that precipitated the strike. Thus, expedited arbitration limits the duration of the court's injunction and preserves the role of arbitration as the

---

47. *See, e.g.*, Carbon Fuel Co. v. UMW, 517 F.2d 1348 (4th Cir. 1975); Peabody Coal Co. v. Local 1734, UMW, 484 F.2d 78 (6th Cir. 1973); Bethlehem Mines Corp. v. UMW, 476 F.2d 860 (3d Cir. 1973); Proceedings, 47th Consecutive Constitutional Convention, United Mine Workers of America 556–58 (Sept. 23-Oct. 2, 1976); Raskin, *Arbitration in the Mines has Created More Disputes*, N.Y. Times, Dec. 4, 1977, § E, at 5, col. 1. The same problem has emerged in other countries. *See, e.g.*, Gould, *Taft-Hartley Comes to Great Britain: Observations on the Industrial Relations Act of 1971*, 81 YALE L.J. 1421 (1972).

48. *See* Gould, *supra* note 1.

49. *See* text accompanying notes 22-27 *supra*.

50. *See* Gould, *supra* note 1, at 251.

51. *Id*. Forbidding the enjoining of permissible strikes was a goal of the Act. *See* H.R. REP. NO. 669, *supra* note 12, at 3-9; S. REP. NO. 163, *supra* note 12, at 21; Comment, *supra* note 1, at 74.

52. 414 U.S. at 377-80; *see* text accompanying note 44 *supra*.

53. Parties commonly bargain for expedited arbitration of many issues arising under the collective bargaining agreement. *See* Cohen, *The Search for Innovative Procedures in Labor Arbitration*, 29 ARB. J. 104 (1974); Zalusky, *Arbitration: Updating a Vital Process*, AFL-CIO AM. FEDERATIONIST, Nov. 1976, at 1. Thus, the suggestion in the text is consistent with existing practices.

dispute-settlement mechanism. Although most *Boys Markets* cases are not reported, it does not appear that many courts have required expedited arbitration coupled with a de novo hearing as a condition of injunctive relief.[54] The failure of courts to adopt these two proposals has contributed substantially to an avalanche of *Boys Markets* cases and problems relating to union worker disobedience.[55]

These wrong turns taken by the Court in *Lucas Flour* and *Gateway Coal* influenced it to take a subsequent major detour, erroneous in my view, from *Boys Markets*. In *Buffalo Forge Co. v. United Steelworkers*,[56] the Court, emphasizing caution at the expense of promoting arbitration, held that injunctive relief against sympathy strikes could not be issued by federal district courts because of the language and policy of the Norris-LaGuardia Act.[57] The more appropriate course of action would have been to tighten the standards announced in *Gateway Coal*[58] and reverse the use of the *Lucas Flour* implied no-strike obligation in cases involving injunctions against strikes.

II. THE *BUFFALO FORGE* DECISION

In *Buffalo Forge Co. v. United Steelworkers*, a 5-4 majority of the Supreme Court held that a federal court could not enjoin a sympathy strike pending an arbitrator's decision of whether the strike is forbidden by the express no-strike clause contained in the collective bargaining contract.[59] The United Steelworkers union, representing production and maintenance workers, was party to two separate collective bargaining agreements, containing arbitration provisions applicable to disputes over the meaning of the agreement and iden-

---

54. *See, e.g.*, Inland Steel Co. v. Local 1545, UMW, 505 F.2d 293 (7th Cir. 1974). *But see, e.g.*, Gateway Coal Co. v. UMW, 414 U.S. 368, 372-73 (1974); Bethlehem Mines Corp. v. UMW, 494 F.2d 726, 740 (3d Cir. 1974).

55. *See* note 47 *supra* and accompanying text.

56. 428 U.S. 397 (1976).

57. *Id.* at 409-11. For other discussions of the history leading up to *Buffalo Forge*, see Lowden & Flaherty, *supra* note 45, at 635-48; Smith, *The Supreme Court, Boys Markets Labor Injunctions, and Sympathy Work Stoppages*, 44 U. CHI. L. REV. 321, 323-30 (1977).

58. *See* note 44 *supra* and accompanying text.

59. 428 U.S. at 404-11. The Labor Law Reform Bill, H.R. 8410, 95th Cong., 1st Sess. (1977), supported by the Carter Administration, was passed by the House of Representatives last October and contains an amendment that apparently would reverse *Buffalo Forge*. *See House Passage of Labor Law Reform Bill*, 96 LAB. REL. REP. (BNA), News and Background Information 121-22 (1977). Representative Frank Thompson's (D., N.Y.) substitute amendment would have authorized the NLRB to seek injunctive relief against stranger picketing or wildcat strikes not authorized by a union certified by the NLRB for the affected employees. For a general discussion of the legislation prior to House passage, see Gould, *The Unions and Carter: Prospects for Labor Law Reform*, 224 THE NATION 466 (1977).

tical no-strike clauses.[60] The union also had been certified to act as bargaining agent for the employer's clerical and technical workers. After months of negotiations, the union and employer had failed to arrive at a first collective bargaining agreement for this group of employees.[61] The failure of these negotiations sparked a strike by clerical and technical employees, who then established picket lines.[62] After a few days, the union directed the production and maintenance workers to honor the picket lines.[63]

The employer filed suit in federal district court, claiming that the production and maintenance workers' sympathy strike violated the no-strike clause in their collective bargaining agreement and that the court should enjoin the strike pending the arbitrator's resolution of that issue.[64] The district court reasoned that *Boys Markets* established a "narrow exception" to section 4 of the Norris-LaGuardia Act and denied the preliminary injunction on the ground that the sympathy strike was not over an arbitrable grievance.[65] The Second Circuit affirmed, agreeing that *Boys Markets* permitted injunctions only against strikes "*over a grievance* which the union has agreed to arbitrate."[66] The Supreme Court affirmed.[67]

A.   *The Reasoning of the Majority*

Justice White, writing for the Court, attempted to establish two basic points to justify the result in *Buffalo Forge*. First, the Court noted that the dispute in *Boys Markets* "was of the kind subject to the grievance and arbitration clauses contained in the collective-bargaining contract, and it was also clear that the strike violated the no-strike clause accompanying the arbitration provisions."[68] The sym-

---

60. *Id.* at 399-400.

61. *Id.* at 400.

62. *Id.*

63. *Id.* at 400-01.

64. The employer also requested damages, a temporary restraining order and an order requiring the submission of any "underlying dispute" to the contractual grievance-arbitration machinery. *Id.* at 401-02.

65. Buffalo Forge Co. v. United Steelworkers, 386 F. Supp. 405 (W.D.N.Y. 1974).

66. Buffalo Forge Co. v. United Steelworkers, 517 F.2d 1207, 1210 (2d Cir. 1975).

67. Buffalo Forge Co. v. United Steelworkers, 428 U.S. 397, 404 (1976). Chief Judge Peckham has applied the *Buffalo Forge* reasoning to employer petitions for injunctive relief arising under the Railway Labor Act and thus has created an exception to the Court's holding in Brotherhood of R.R. Trainmen v. Chicago River & Ind. R.R., 353 U.S. 30 (1957). *See* Trans Int'l Airlines, Inc. v. International Bhd. of Teamsters, 96 L.R.R.M. 2766, 2768–70 (N.D. Cal. 1977).

68. *Id.* at 406. The Court did not address a second possible distinction between *Buffalo Forge* and *Boys Markets* based on the difficulty of determining whether the union breached the

pathy strike in *Buffalo Forge* was distinguished on the ground that it was not "*precipitated* by a dispute between union and management that was subject to binding arbitration under the provisions of the contracts."[69]

The majority's second point was that the policies underlying *Boys Markets* did not reasonably call for allowing federal courts to enjoin sympathy strikes. The Court began this argument by noting that:

> The driving force behind *Boys Markets* was to implement the strong congressional preference for the private dispute settlement mechanisms agreed upon by the parties. Only to that extent was it held necessary to accommodate § 4 of the Norris-LaGuardia Act to § 301 of the Labor Management Relations Act and to lift the former's ban against the issuance of injunctions in labor disputes. Striking over an arbitrable dispute would interfere with and frustrate the arbitral processes by which the parties had chosen to settle a dispute. The *quid pro quo* for the employer's promise to arbitrate was the union's obligation not to strike over issues that were subject to the arbitration machinery. . . . Otherwise, the employer would be deprived of his bargain and the policy of the labor statutes to implement private resolution of disputes in a manner agreed upon seriously would suffer.[70]

The Court then argued that in *Buffalo Forge* "neither [the strike's] causes nor the issue underlying it [was] subject to the settlement procedures provided by the contracts between the employer and respondents. The strike had neither the purpose nor the effect of denying or evading an obligation to arbitrate or of depriving the employer of his bargain."[71] Justice White asserted that the denial of the requested relief did not deprive the employer of its quid pro quo because the collective bargaining agreement did not provide for judicial review of fact and law pending arbitration of a strike *over a non-arbitrable issue*.[72] The Court then stated that the policy con-

---

no-strike clause. In *Boys Markets* the strike clearly breached the no-strike clause. *Id*. In *Buffalo Forge* this issue may have presented a more difficult question of contract interpretation. *See* text accompanying notes 98-103 *infra*.

69. 428 U.S. at 406 (emphasis added). As Justice White points out, *id*. at 406-07, the *Boys Markets* Court expressly adopted the principles enunciated by the dissent in *Sinclair*, including the proviso that "[w]hen a strike is sought to be enjoined because it is over a grievance which both parties are contractually bound to arbitrate, the District Court may issue no injunctive order until it first holds that the contract *does* have that effect," Sinclair Ref. Co. v. Atkinson, 370 U.S. 195, 228 (1962) (Brennan, J., dissenting). For a full statement of the principles enunciated in the *Sinclair* dissent and adopted in *Boys Markets*, see Boys Mkts., Inc., v. Retail Clerks Local 770, 398 U.S. 235, 254 (1970); note 39 *supra*.

70. 428 U.S. at 407.

71. *Id*. at 407-08.

72. *See id*. at 408-09, 411. The Court suggested that an injunction would not issue because the parties had not provided for injunctive relief prior to the decision of the

siderations central to *Boys Markets* were not applicable in *Buffalo Forge* and therefore it was no longer necessary to accommodate section 4 of Norris-LaGuardia to section 301(a) of the National Management Relations Act.[73]

The Court also expressed concern that issuance of an injunction in *Buffalo Forge* would encourage federal courts to enjoin other breaches of contract pending the exhaustion of grievance-arbitration contract provisions.[74] The potential involvement of federal courts in contractual interpretation and factfinding in labor disputes might defeat the congressional policy of promoting arbitration.[75] The litigation of issues prior to arbitration, argued the Court, would influence the arbitrator's decision, discourage parties from relitigating before the arbitrator and often permanently settle the issue.[76] Such a level of federal court involvement "would cut deeply into the policy of the Norris-LaGuardia Act."[77] These considerations led the Court to find that the admittedly arbitrable issue in *Buffalo Forge*— the permissibility of the sympathy strike under the terms of the collective bargaining agreement—must be resolved by the arbitrator before an injunction would issue.

B. *Criticism of the* Buffalo Forge *Decision*

Justice White's opinion in *Buffalo Forge* has many shortcomings. Even if the decision is correct, it ignores the fundamental problems created by *Gateway Coal* and creates an inflexible rule that may frustrate the intent of the parties. Further, the Court's failure to enjoin the strike based on the absence of an underlying arbitrable dispute improperly applies the policies developed in earlier decisions. The only possible rationale for the decision turns upon the proposition that the question of whether or not a sympathy strike violates a no-strike clause is somehow more difficult than the ques-

---

arbitrator. *Id.* at 411. The Court's statement may refer to a clause requiring quick arbitration of the permissibility of strikes over non-arbitrable disputes, rather than a clause permitting injunctions of the same disputes prior to arbitration.

73. *Id.* at 407-08.

74. *Id.* at 410. Yet courts have considered enjoining "other breaches of contract" both before and after *Boys Markets* in instances of unions seeking temporary or preliminary injunctions against employers pending arbitration of grievances. Unions have petitioned for injunctions in instances of planned work-site relocations, subcontracting or contracting out of work, technological innovations, and safety disputes. *See* notes 114-19 *infra*. For a more complete discussion of this aspect of federal court jurisdiction to issue injunctions in labor disputes, see text accompanying notes 113-31 *infra*.

75. 428 U.S. at 410-11.

76. *Id.* at 412.

77. *Id.* at 410.

tion presented in *Boys Markets*. But even this logic, which is not articulated in the opinion, cannot support the per se rule announced in *Buffalo Forge*.

1. *Shortcomings of the* Buffalo Forge *decision*.

Buffalo Forge is an inappropriate response to the problems created by the low standards for issuing injunctions announced in *Gateway Coal*.[78] The threat remains that courts will influence or frustrate the arbitral process, because *Buffalo Forge* does not alter the standards developed in earlier cases.[79] Rather, that standard has been eliminated in a small number of cases.

Under this exception, federal courts generally will no longer issue injunctions against sympathy strikes, regardless of their certainty that the strike breached the no-strike clause, until the arbitrator makes this finding. This per se rule denies employers who bargained for a no-strike clause intended to cover sympathy strikes the benefits of fully uninterrupted production. In addition, *Buffalo Forge* suggests that strikes aimed at altering the terms of existing contracts, albeit in the teeth of an explicit no-strike clause, cannot be enjoined unless a court finds that the strike-precipitating issue is arbitrable.[80] Thus, courts may be unable to enjoin a strike or some other form of economic pressure designed to influence management's product-pricing policies or its advertising programs,[81] policies and programs that may affect the employment opportunities and conditions of bargaining-unit workers. The decision may dictate the same result when the union activity involves South African racial policies, for instance, and the strike is an attempt by the union to pressure its employer to cease its business relationships with other companies or governments involved in racially discriminatory practices.[82] Strikes in these situations present no less

---

78. *See* notes 43-45 *supra* and accompanying text.

79. For a discussion of the standards developed in earlier cases, see notes 18-45 *supra* and accompanying text. These standards remain applicable in most injunction cases because *Buffalo Forge* only applies to sympathy strikes or other strikes over non-arbitrable disputes. *See* Smith, *supra* note 57.

80. *See* 428 U.S. at 409-12; 15 DUQ. L. REV. 315, 326 (1976-77).

81. Often parties do not place these types of issues within the scope of an arbitration clause in a collective bargaining agreement or refer to them in any other portion of the agreement. *Cf.* Fibreboard Paper Prods. Corp. v. NLRB, 379 U.S. 203, 217 (1964) (Stewart, J., concurring) (employer's subcontracting practices not included in the original collective bargaining agreement between the parties).

82. *See* United States Steel Corp. v. UMW, 519 F.2d 1236 (4th Cir. 1966); W. GOULD, BLACK WORKERS IN WHITE UNIONS: JOB DISCRIMINATION IN THE UNITED STATES (1977);

potential for undermining the parties' contractual expectations than the strike in *Boys Markets*.

The decision in *Buffalo Forge* to base federal labor policy on the presence or absence of an underlying *arbitrable* dispute is likely to cause a related issue to arise in a multi-employer or single-employer master-contract context: Can the unity of interests between two groups of employees cause a sympathy strike to be enjoinable? Suppose that employee grievances have accumulated in two plants and that the workers are members of the same international union but different locals. Suppose further that employees of Plant *A* walk out over an arbitrable grievance in violation of a no-strike clause and that subsequently they are joined by employees of Plant *B*, who refuse to cross *A*'s picket line when delivering goods and then join the strike with roving pickets. If employees of Plant *B* have similar grievances, is there a unity of interest between the two groups such that Plant *B*'s employees are in fact striking over a grievance that is an "underlying one" to the arbitration process within the meaning of *Boys Markets*? Does it make any difference if Plant *B*'s employees engage in their own strike which itself could be enjoined? In this connection, it is interesting to note that the workers involved in the sympathy strike in *Buffalo Forge* were members of the same international union, but neither the Court nor the parties considered the implications of that fact.[83] This would be an important factor to take into account in this example, as would the commonality of interests attested to by the same collective bargaining agreement in the plants and the accumulation of grievances in both situations. Much of the language in *Buffalo Forge* supports the view that the Court is unwilling to enjoin strikes in situations involving unity of interests.[84] Yet the closeness of the vote coupled with a stronger unity of interests than in *Buffalo Forge* argues persuasively for a different result.

Thus, *Buffalo Forge* is both unresponsive to the problem of low standards for issuing injunctions created by *Gateway Coal* and may

---

Gould, *Multinational Corporations and Multinational Unions: Myths, Reality, and the Law*, 10 INT'L L. 655, 660-61 (1976); Gould, *Black Power in the Unions: The Impact on Collective Bargaining Relationships*, 79 YALE L.J. 46 (1969); Gould, *The Status of Unauthorized and "Wildcat" Strikes Under the National Labor Relations Act*, 52 CORNELL L.Q. 672 (1967). *See generally* NLRB v. ILA, 332 F.2d 992 (4th Cir. 1964); Harrington & Co. v. ILA Local 1416, 356 F. Supp. 1079 (S.D. Fla. 1973).

83.   428 U.S. at 429 n.25 (Stevens, J., dissenting). Two courts have rejected the unity-of-interest approach to *Buffalo Forge* cases. *See* Ziegler Coal Co. v. Local 1870, UMW, 96 L.R.R.M. 3360 (7th Cir. 1977); Southern Ohio Coal Co. v. UMW, 551 F.2d 695 (6th Cir. 1977).

84.   *See id.* at 406, 409 (majority opinion); *id.* at 429 n.25 (Stevens, J., dissenting).

frustrate the intent of the parties in negotiating a no-strike clause. The decision also evidences little sensitivity to the ever present and unavoidable tension between the courts and arbitrators, which flows from both the *Steelworkers Trilogy* and *Boys Markets*.[85]

2.   *Applying the policies underlying* Boys Markets *to* Buffalo Forge.

The *Boys Markets* exception to section 4 of the Norris-LaGuardia Act should not be limited to enforcing a no-strike clause pending arbitration of that issue *only when the strike is over an underlying arbitrable dispute*. The presence or absence of an underlying arbitrable dispute is not a sound distinction for federal labor policy and has no statutory basis. The issuance of an injunction in *Buffalo Forge* is supported by the two policy considerations that led the Court to the *Boys Markets* decision:[86] promotion of the arbitration process[87] and uninterrupted production during the term of the collective bargaining agreement.[88] With respect to the policy of uninterrupted production, it is difficult to understand Justice White's attempt to distinguish the effect of the breach of the no-strike clause in *Buffalo Forge* from the effect of the strike in *Boys Markets*.[89] He apparently assumed that the parties had "bargained" for an injunction against strikes in breach of the no-strike clause only when there was a strike over an arbitrable issue.[90] As Justice Stevens indicated in his dissent, there was no basis in law or in the parties' agreement for such a conclusion.[91] Not only is this "bargained for" assumption an invention that is not based upon actual labor contracts, but it is doubtful whether Norris-LaGuardia, which presumably lies at the bottom of Justice White's opinion, can be contractually modified in this manner. Given the similar effects on the employer in both cases and the

---

85. Gould, *supra* note 1.

86. Boys Mkts., Inc. v. Retail Clerks Local 770, 398 U.S. 235, 241-42 (1970).

87. *Id.* at 242-43 (1970); John Wiley & Sons, Inc. v. Livingston, 376 U.S. 543, 549 (1964); Local 174, Int'l Bhd. of Teamsters v. Lucas Flour Co., 369 U.S. 95, 105 (1962); United Steelworkers v. Warrior & Gulf Navigation Co., 363 U.S. 574, 577-78 (1960); Textile Workers Union v. Lincoln Mills, 353 U.S. 448, 458-59 (1957).

88. Boys Mkts., Inc. v. Retail Clerks Local 770, 398 U.S. 235, 241 (1970); John Wiley & Sons, Inc. v. Livingston, 376 U.S. 543, 549 (1964); Local 174, Int'l Bhd. of Teamsters v. Lucas Flour Co., 369 U.S. 95, 105 (1962); United Steelworkers v. Warrior & Gulf Navigation Co., 363 U.S. 574, 578 (1960); Textile Workers Union v. Lincoln Mills, 353 U.S. 448, 454 (1957).

89. Justice Stevens argued in his dissent that an employer is just as effectively deprived of its quid pro quo—uninterrupted production for a period of time—by a sympathy strike situation as by a strike over an arbitrable dispute. 428 U.S. at 417-19.

90. *Id.* at 407 ("The *quid pro quo* for the employer's promise to arbitrate was the union's obligation not to strike *over issues that were subject to the arbitration machinery*." (emphasis added).

91. *Id.* at 418-19 (Stevens, J., dissenting).

unsoundness of the "bargained for" argument, Norris-LaGuardia should not have blocked the *Buffalo Forge* injunction.[92] Section 301(a)'s design to make labor contracts binding and enforceable should control.[93] Finally, Justice White's reliance upon Norris-La-Guardia as a bar to *Buffalo Forge* injunctions is undercut by the Court's willingness to enforce arbitration awards that declare sympathy strikes to be a violation of the labor contract.

The other policy asserted by the Court in *Boys Markets*, promotion of the arbitration process,[94] is also applicable to *Buffalo Forge*. Although the Court in *Buffalo Forge* ignored the role of arbitration in that case, the disputed contractual provision—the no-strike clause—will be placed before the arbitrator for review just as both disputed issues—the underlying grievance and no-strike clause—are placed before the arbitrator in a *Boys Markets* case. There is no basis in logic or law for concluding that Norris-LaGuardia is offended by the issuance of an injunction in *Buffalo Forge* because only one issue, the meaning of the no-strike clause, will be placed before the arbitrator. It is the possibility of judicial error in issuing injunctions that offends Norris-LaGuardia[95] and that risk is not significantly greater in *Buffalo Forge*. In addition, Justice White's argument that an injunction in *Boys Markets* promotes arbitration because it insures that a dispute will be resolved in the method agreed upon by the parties[96] applies equally to the dispute in *Buffalo Forge* over the meaning of the no-strike clause. Although arbitration may not be promoted to as great an extent by issuing injunctions in *Buffalo Forge* cases as in *Boys Markets* cases, the differences between the two fact patterns do not justify a different result in the *Buffalo Forge* case.[97]

3. *An alternative interpretation of* Buffalo Forge:
   The unarticulated assumption.

A second possible interpretation of *Buffalo Forge* is that federal courts may not issue injunctions against sympathy strikes pending

---

92. *See* text accompanying note 38 *supra*.

93. *See* Smith, *supra* note 57, at 340-44.

94. Boys Mkts., Inc. v. Retail Clerks Local 770, 398 U.S. 235, 241 (1970); *see* note 87 *supra* and accompanying text.

95. *See* note 12 *supra*.

96. 428 U.S. at 410-11.

97. Justice Stevens, in his dissenting opinion in *Buffalo Forge*, persuasively argued that an injunction should issue even though arbitration was promoted less by the injunction in *Buffalo Forge* than in *Boys Markets*. 428 U.S. at 424-32. To reach this conclusion he closely analyzed the importance of the promotion of arbitration in the *Boys Markets* decision. *Id.*

arbitration of the strikes' permissibility because the question of whether a sympathy strike violates a no-strike clause involves unusual risks of judicial interference with labor-management relations.[98] Under this interpretation of *Buffalo Forge*, the risk of federal court injunctions of *permissible* strikes, a concern of Norris-LaGuardia,[99] is minimized. Justice White hinted at this reasoning when he argued that the sympathy strike question was for the arbitrator, not the court.[100] Yet, he also recognized that a court could enforce the arbitrator's decision with an injunction against the strike once the arbitrator determined that the sympathy strike violated the collective bargaining contract.[101] The Court's argument suggests that Norris-LaGuardia blocks only the risk of interference with the parties' method of dispute settlement and not eventual equitable relief. The Court did not address the question of whether the risks of interference in *Buffalo Forge* were greater or less than those in *Boys Markets*.

The decision in *Buffalo Forge* may be based on the unarticulated assumption that the risks of enjoining a permissible strike were

---

98. *See id.* at 410-13.

99. *See* note 12 *supra*.

100. 428 U.S. at 405. Justice Stevens disagreed with the majority's view that the potential for the issuance of an erroneous injunction or usurpation of the arbitrator's function was greater in *Buffalo Forge* than in *Boys Markets*. "In each of these cases [*Boys Markets* and *Gateway Coal*] . . . the choice was between interpretation of the agreement by the court or interpretation by the arbitrator; a decision that the dispute was not arbitrable, or not properly arbitrated, would have precluded an interpretation of the agreement according to the contractual grievance procedure. In the present case, an interim determination of the no-strike question by the court neither usurps nor precludes a decision by the arbitrator. By definition, issuance of an injunction pending the arbitrator's decision does not supplant a decision that he otherwise would have made. Indeed, it is the ineffectiveness of the damages remedy for strikes pending arbitration that lends force to the employer's argument for an injunction. The court does not oust the arbitrator of his proper function but fulfills a role that he never served." *Id.* at 428 (Stevens, J., dissenting).

The union's rejoinder was that speed is of the essence and that by the time an arbitrator reverses an erroneously issued injunction, the strike or its impetus will have been lost or dissipated. *Id.* The dissent, in referring to the union's argument that a temporary injunction can quickly end a strike, replied: "[T]his argument demonstrates only that arbitration, to be effective, must be prompt, not that the federal courts must be deprived entirely of jurisdiction to grant equitable relief. Denial of an injunction when a strike violates the agreement may have effects just as devastating to an employer as the issuance of an injunction may have to the union when the strike does not violate the agreement." *Id.* at 428-29. Accordingly, Justice Stevens gave his support to a form of expedited arbitration in the context of *Boys Markets* injunctions. *Id.* at 431-32. For a discussion of this issue, see text accompanying notes 110-12 *infra*.

101. *Id.* at 405, 425 n.18. Ironically, an arbitrator's award prohibiting a sympathy strike may be enforced despite the strictures of Norris-LaGuardia. *See, e.g.*, Pacific Maritime Ass'n v. International Longshoremen's and Warehousemen's Union, No. C 77 2306 CFP (N.D. Cal. Oct. 14, 1977).

greater in that case than in *Boys Markets*. Although it is more difficult to determine whether a sympathy strike violates a no-strike clause than to determine whether a strike over an arbitrable dispute violates a no-strike clause,[102] arbitrators routinely decide the former by looking at the language of the no-strike clause. If the clause is worded broadly to include all strikes, work stoppages, work suspensions, and work slow downs, a sympathy strike normally is construed to be a violation.[103] The experience of arbitrators confirms that the problems involved with determining the status of sympathy strikes under no-strike clauses do not appear to be fundamentally different from the problems involved with determining the status of any other work slowdown or stoppage.

Strikes over other non-arbitrable issues, such as an employer's business practices,[104] do not present courts with complex contractual provisions to interpret. The sole issue in suits to enjoin such strikes is the scope of the no-strike clause. This issue is no more troublesome to courts than the no-strike issue presented in *Boys Markets*. Assuming that the difference between the risks of enjoining permissible strikes in *Buffalo Forge* and *Boys Markets* is the only logical basis for distinguishing the two cases, strikes over non-arbitrable disputes should be enjoined. Courts looking to *Buffalo Forge*, however, may consider an injunction in this type of case as an even more radical extension of *Boys Markets* that an injunction of a sympathy strike: First, this basis for distinguishing *Buffalo Forge* from *Boys Markets* was not articulated by the Court; second, the Court in *Buffalo Forge* viewed *Boys Markets* as a narrow exception to Norris-LaGuardia.[105]

---

102. *Compare* Amalgamated Lace Operative, 54 Lab. Arb. 140 (1969) (Frey, Arb.) (sympathy strike), *with* Elmira School Dist., 54 Lab. Arb. 569 (1970) (Markowitz, Arb.) (strike over an arbitrable issue).

103. Amalgamated Lace Operative, 54 Lab. Arb. 140, 144 (1969) (Frey, Arb.). This Article does not intend to suggest that interpreting broad contract clauses is entirely uncomplicated. Some arbitrators have held that even under a no-strike contract clause, which prohibits "other interferences by the union or by any of its employees," the arbitrator is obligated to determine whether the action is in fact a "strike." *E.g.*, Vermont Structural Steel Corp., 60 Lab. Arb. 842 (1973) (Hogan, Arb.). Other arbitrators have found that sympathy strikes are not "strikes." *E.g.*, Associated Gen. Contractors, 63 Lab. Arb. 32 (1974) (Gallagher, Arb.). Moreover, some arbitrators have concluded that language such as "other cessation of work" is necessary to prohibit a sympathy strike. The extra language resolves any ambiguity relating to this issue. Arkansas La. Gas Co., 42 Lab. Arb. 626 (1964) (Quinlan, Arb.). *Contra*, New England Master Textile Engravers Guild, 9 Lab. Arb. 199 (1947) (Waller, Arb.).

104. For a discussion of the effect of the *Buffalo Forge* decision on strikes over non-arbitrable disputes, see text accompanying notes 80-82 *supra*.

105. 428 U.S. at 406, 409-11.

C. *The Proposed Method of Resolving the* Boys Markets-
   Buffalo Forge *Issue*

This author proposed a solution to the *Boys Market-Buffalo Forge*
problem 8 years ago.[106] First, courts must be reasonably certain that
the union has breached the no-strike clause before issuing an injunction.[107] As noted by Justice Stevens in his dissenting opinion in
Buffalo Forge, a higher standard than the one currently used by the
Court would make federal judges, admittedly less expert in labor
matters than arbitrators, less likely to misconstrue the contract
pending arbitration of the no-strike issue.[108] This higher standard
furthers the policy of Norris-LaGuardia by lessening the risk that
courts will enjoin permissible strikes.[109]

Second, issuance of an injunction against a striking union should
be conditioned upon the willingness of both parties to accede to
expedited arbitration.[110] This change would minimize further the
risks of enjoining permissible strikes because arbitrators would be
able to correct errors by the court promptly.[111] The change also
would ensure that disputes are settled quickly and in the manner the
parties intended.[112]

III.   THE UNION AS PLAINTIFF

A. *Criteria for Enjoining Employers Prior to* Buffalo Forge

One of the most perplexing issues to emerge from *Buffalo Forge*
is the continued vitality of union prayers for injunctive relief against
employers violating their obligations under collective bargaining
agreements. Although few courts have considered this issue since
Buffalo Forge, one recent opinion suggests that *Buffalo Forge* bars

---

106. Gould, *supra* note 1, at 244-56.

107. *Id*. at 250-56.

108. 428 U.S. at 431 (Stevens, J., dissenting). The standard announced by Justice Stevens
was that "the judge should not issue an injunction without convincing evidence that the strike
is clearly within the no-strike clause." *Id*.

109. *See id*.; Note, *supra* note 45, at 136. *Buffalo Forge* seems to make judges more
reticent about issuing *Boys Markets* injunctions. *See, e.g.*, National Rejectors Indus. v. United
Steelworkers, 96 L.R.R.M. 2120, 2127 (8th Cir. 1977) (Lay, J., dissenting). *Cf.* Anheuser-
Busch, Inc. v. Teamsters Local 633, 511 F.2d 1097 (1st Cir.), *cert. denied*, 423 U.S. 875
(1975) (court may order arbitration without issuing preliminary injunction affecting a no-
strike clause).

110. Gould, *supra* note 1, at 244-50. Justice Stevens also favors this procedure. 428 U.S.
at 431 (Stevens, J., dissenting).

111. Gould, *supra* note 1, at 249-50.

112. *Id*.

union injunctive relief pending arbitration.[113] Unions are likely to seek injunctive relief, pending the decision of the arbitrator, in cases involving such issues as plant relocations,[114] subcontracting or contracting out,[115] technological innovation,[116] safety disputes,[117] scheduling,[118] or successorship.[119] From the union vantage point, irreparable harm may be triggered by lost work opportunitites, because backpay cannot compensate for the repossessions, foreclosures and psychological harm that might accompany job losses.[120] In this connection, three questions must be answered: Under what circumstances, if any, may such injunctions issue? To what standard

---

113. Transit Union Div. 1384 v. Greyhound Lines, Inc. (Greyhound II), 550 F.2d 1237 (9th Cir.), *cert. denied*, 46 U.S.L.W. 3216 (Oct. 4, 1977).

114. Lever Bros. Co. v. Chemical Workers Local 217, 554 F.2d 115 (4th Cir. 1976); Local 13, Int'l Fed'n of Professional and Technical Eng'rs v. General Elec. Co., 90 L.R.R.M. 2566 (E.D. Pa. 1975), *rev'd*, 531 F.2d 1178 (3d Cir. 1976); Technical Workers Local 757 v. Budd Co., 345 F. Supp. 42 (E.D. Pa. 1972); Sappington v. Associated Transp., Inc., 79 L.R.R.M. 2494 (D. Md. 1972); Rochester Indep. Workers Local 1 v. General Dynamics Corp., 76 L.R.R.M. 2540 (W.D.N.Y. 1970).

115. Pipefitters Local 91 v. Kimberley-Clark Corp., 93 L.R.R.M. 2702 (N.D. Ala. 1976); Local 32B, Serv. Employees Int'l Union v. Sage Realty Corp., 402 F. Supp. 1153 (S.D.N.Y.), *aff'd*, 524 F.2d 601 (2d Cir. 1975); IBEW Local 278 v. Jetero Corp., 88 L.R.R.M. 2182 (S.D. Tex. 1972), *aff'd and remanded*, 496 F.2d 661 (5th Cir. 1974); IUE v. Radio Corp., 77 L.R.R.M. 2201 (D.N.J. 1971).

116. Detroit Typografical Union No. 18 v. Detroit Newspaper Publishers Ass'n, 81 L.R.R.M. 2797 (E.D. Mich.), *rev'd*, 471 F.2d 872 (6th Cir. 1972), *cert. denied*, 411 U.S. 967 (1973).

117. United Steelworkers v. Blaw-Knox Foundry & Mill Mach., Inc., 319 F. Supp. 636 (W.D. Pa. 1970).

118. Transit Union Div. 1384 v. Greyhound Lines, Inc. (Greyhound I), 529 F.2d 1073 (9th Cir.), *vacated and remanded*, 429 U.S. 807 (1976), *rev'd*, 550 F.2d 1237 (9th Cir.) (Greyhound II), *cert. denied*, 46 U.S.L.W. 3216 (Oct. 4, 1977); Branch 998, Nat'l Ass'n of Letter Carriers v. United States Postal Serv., 88 L.R.R.M. 3524 (M.D. Ga. 1975); National Ass'n of Letter Carriers v. United States Postal Serv., 88 L.R.R.M. 2678 (S.D. Iowa 1975); Local 174, Util. Workers Union v. South Pittsburgh Water Co., 345 F. Supp. 52 (W.D. Pa. 1972); Pittsburgh Newspaper Printing Pressmen's Union No. 9 v. Pittsburgh Press Co., 343 F. Supp. 55 (W.D. Pa. 1972), *aff'd*, 479 F.2d 607 (3d Cir. 1973); SIU de Puerto Rico v. Virgin Islands Port Auth., 334 F. Supp. 510 (D.V.I. 1971).

119. Bartenders Local 340 v. Howard Johnson Co., 535 F.2d 1160 (9th Cir. 1976); Local 228, Int'l Alliance of Theatrical Stage Employees v. Gayety Theatre, 87 L.R.R.M. 3020 (N.D. Ohio 1974); Food Employees Local 590 v. National Tea Co., 346 F. Supp. 875 (W.D. Pa.), *remanded*, 474 F.2d 1338 (3d Cir. 1972); Detroit Local Joint Executive Bd., Hotel and Restaurant Employees v. Howard Johnson Co., 81 L.R.R.M. 2329 (E.D. Mich. 1972), *aff'd*, 482 F.2d 489 (6th Cir. 1973), *rev'd*, 417 U.S. 249, *vacated and remanded*, 500 F.2d 402 (6th Cir. 1974).

120. A preliminary injunction may be granted only upon a showing that irreparable harm will otherwise occur. Societe Comptoir De L'Industrie v. Alexander's Dep't Stores, Inc., 299 F.2d 33 (2d Cir. 1962); Communications Workers v. Western Elec. Co., 430 F. Supp. 969 (S.D.N.Y. 1977). "Irreparable harm means irremediable injury that is certain and great." Flood v. Kuhn, 309 F. Supp. 793, 799 (S.D.N.Y. 1970), *aff'd*, 443 F.2d 264 (2d Cir. 1971), *aff'd*, 407 U.S. 258 (1972). In a labor context, the loss of a job may cause irreparable harm. *See* King v. Randazzo, 234 F. Supp. 388 (E.D.N.Y. 1964), *aff'd*, 346 F.2d 307 (2d Cir. 1965). *Cf.*

of proof will courts hold unions seeking injunctions against employers? And, more basically, to which question is that standard to be applied—whether there is an arbitrable dispute or whether the union will prevail on the merits?

1. *Guidelines for issuing injunctions against employers.*

The suggested high level of restraint that courts should exercise before issuing injunctions against strikes by labor unions[121] should not apply to the situation in which a union is seeking to enjoin an employer pending arbitration. Injunctions against employers are not "part and parcel" of the abuses that were the target of Norris-LaGuardia.[122] Therefore, they do not present the same problems of accommodation with section 301(a) that compel caution in enjoining strikes.[123] Rather, employers should be enjoined pending arbitration from behaving in a manner that might make later arbitration of the merits of a dispute a futile act.[124]

Before an employer is enjoined from undertaking a particular act pending arbitration, courts must decide whether the collective bargaining agreement grants the arbitrator jurisdiction to decide the permissibility of that act. Courts generally resolve this question in favor of the union on the basis of the presumption of arbitrability found in the *Steelworkers Trilogy.*[125] Once the dispute is found to be arbitrable, courts must decide whether the injunction should issue. Criteria governing the issuance of preliminary injunctions come into play in making this determination.[126]

Local 464, Am. Bakery & Confectionery Workers v. Hershey Chocolate Corp., 245 F. Supp. 748, 751 (M.D. Pa. 1965) (Irreparable harm may be caused by anything having a "detrimental effect on wages, working conditions, seniority, fringe benefits, job status, or any other rights or benefits enjoyed by the employees affected.").

121. *See* text accompanying notes 107-09 *supra.*

122. *See* note 12 *supra.*

123. *See* text accompanying notes 29-32 & 35-38 *supra.* The distinction is illustrated by the discussion of the accommodation between Norris-LaGuardia and § 301 in Gould, *supra* note 1, at 217-25.

124. The standard is well articulated in Lever Bros. Co. v. Chemical Workers Local 217, 554 F.2d 115, 123 (2d Cir. 1976) (addendum to opinion): "An injunction to preserve the *status quo* pending arbitration may be issued either against a company or against a union in an appropriate *Boys Markets* case where it is necessary to prevent conduct by the party enjoined from rendering the arbitral process a hollow formality in those instances where, as here, the arbitral award when rendered could not return the parties to the *status quo ante.*"

125. *See* text accompanying notes 22-27 *supra.*

126. *See, e.g.,* Boys Mkts., Inc. v. Retail Clerks Local 770, 398 U.S. 235, 249-53 (1970); Hoh v. Pepsico, Inc., 491 F.2d 556, 560-62 (2d Cir. 1974).

The granting or denial of a preliminary injunction is a "matter of sound judicial discretion, in the exercise of which the court balances the conveniences of the parties and possible

2. *Judicial development of the equity standard for injunctions against employers.*

Prior to *Buffalo Forge*, the basic question of whether to apply the equity standard to the merits of arbitrability or to the merits of the underlying dispute proved somewhat confusing to courts having only *Lincoln Mills* and the *Steelworkers Trilogy* as precedents.[127] In *Hoh v. Pepsico, Inc.*,[128] Judge Friendly, speaking for the Second Circuit, clearly articulated the principle that equitable standards for issuing a preliminary injunction apply not only to the question of arbitrability but also to the underlying claim:[129]

> [T]he "ordinary principles of equity" referred to as a guide in the portion of the *Sinclair* dissent that was approved in *Boys Markets* include some likelihood of success. . . . We think this must mean not simply some likelihood of success in compelling arbitration but in obtaining the award in aid of which the injunction is sought. Although courts have been directed by the *Steelworkers'* Trilogy . . . to be liberal in construing agreements to arbitrate, this instruc-

---

injuries to them according as they may be affected by the granting or withholding of the injunction." Yakus v. United States, 321 U.S. 414, 440 (1940).

Three basic principles of equity are involved in injunction cases. First, the movant must show that unless an injunction is granted, substantial and irreparable injury will result to the movant. *See* note 120 *supra*. Second, the alleged injury to the movant must be shown in all probability to outweigh the likely injury to the defendant. *E.g.*, Division 1098, Amalgamated Ass'n of St. Employees v. Eastern Greyhound Lines, 225 F. Supp. 28, 30 (D.D.C. 1963). Finally, the movant must not have an adequate remedy at law. *E.g.*, Local 328, Int'l Bhd. of Teamsters v. Armour & Co., 294 F. Supp. 168, 172 (W.D. Mich. 1968) ("[T]he affected employees, if the union prevails on the unfair labor practice complaint, would have a remedy, but it would be extremely difficult to afford them relief in the event they prevail."). Many courts would require an additional criterion, that the movant show "some likelihood of success" on the merits. Hoh v. Pepsico, Inc., 491 F.2d 556, 561 (2d Cir. 1974). *See* text accompanying notes 128-31 *infra*. *Boys Markets*, however, held that in determining whether to grant relief in these types of cases, district courts were bound by the three basic principles of equity enunciated by the dissenting opinion in Sinclair Ref. Co. v. Atkinson, 370 U.S. 195 (1962). Boys Mkts., Inc. v. Retail Clerks Local 770, 398 U.S. 235, 249 (1970); *see* note 39 *supra*.

127. *See, e.g.*, Local 328, Int'l Bhd. of Teamsters v. Armour & Co., 294 F. Supp. 168 (W.D. Mich. 1968); Local 464, Am. Bakery & Confectionery Workers v. Hershey Chocolate Corp., 245 F. Supp. 748 (M.D. Pa. 1965); Division 1098, Amalgamated Ass'n of St. Employees v. Eastern Greyhound Lines, 225 F. Supp. 28 (D.D.C. 1963).

128. 491 F.2d 556 (2d Cir. 1974).

129. *Hoh* also held that the procedural requirements of Norris-LaGuardia, as expressed in § 7, 29 U.S.C. § 107 (1970), remain applicable after *Boys Markets* to suits by a union "so far as consistent with the policies of § 301 of the Labor Management Relations Act as interpreted in the dissenting opinion in Sinclair Refining v. Atkinson . . . [and] approved in *Boys Markets*." 491 F.2d at 560. The court stated that the provisions of § 7, which require the testimony of witnesses in open court and a finding that "as to each item of relief granted greater injury will be inflicted upon complainant by the denial of relief than will be inflicted upon defendants by the granting of relief," 29 U.S.C. § 107(c) (1970), are consistent with *Boys Markets*. 491 F.2d at 560.

tion does not extend to the grant of ancillary relief; on such a matter they must continue to exercise the sound discretion of the chancellor. It would be inequitable in the last degree to grant an injunction pending arbitration which was costly to a defendant on the basis of a claim which although arguably arbitrable was plainly without merit.[130]

Following *Hoh*, the federal judiciary generally employed the standards articulated by Judge Friendly in deciding whether to issue injunctions against employers' potential violations of collective bargaining agreements pending arbitration.[131] *Buffalo Forge* may cast doubt on the continuing vitality of this approach.

B. *Possible Effects of* Buffalo Forge

If *Buffalo Forge* has any effect in the area of injunctions against employers, it will disturb the desirable standard developed by courts for use in these types of cases. Although the decision should not affect the issuance of injunctions against employers, its opaque and confusing analysis may foster erroneous interpretations. Several federal courts have considered *Buffalo Forge* relevant to union injunctions against employers[132] and at least one has denied an injunction that would have issued under *Hoh*.[133] *Transit Union Division 1384 v. Greyhound Lines, Inc. (Greyhound II)*,[134] provides a striking example of the threat posed by *Buffalo Forge*. The case can be interpreted to hold that courts should not issue injunctions against employers pending arbitration.[135]

1. *The* Greyhound II *opinion.*

In *Transit Union Division 1384 v. Greyhound Lines, Inc. (Greyhound I)*,[136] the employer notified the union that within 2 months it

---

130. 491 F.2d at 561.

131. *See, e.g.*, Transit Union Div. 1384 v. Greyhound Lines, Inc. (Greyhound I), 529 F.2d 1073, 1077-78 (9th Cir.), *vacated and remanded*, 429 U.S. 807 (1976), *rev'd*, 550 F.2d 1237 (9th Cir.) (Greyhound II), *cert. denied*, 46 U.S.L.W. 3216 (Oct. 4, 1977).

132. *See* Transit Union Div. 1384 v. Greyhound Lines, Inc. (Greyhound II), 550 F.2d 1237 (9th Cir.), *cert. denied*, 46 U.S.L.W. 3216 (Oct. 4, 1977); UMW Dist. 2 v. Rochester & Pittsburgh Coal Co., 416 F. Supp. 74 (W.D. Pa. 1976). *But see* Lever Bros. Co. v. Chemical Workers Local 217, 554 F.2d 115, 121-23 (4th Cir. 1976) (addendum to opinion); Communications Workers v. Western Elec. Co., 430 F. Supp. 969, 973-78 (S.D.N.Y. 1977).

133. Transit Union Div. 1384 v. Greyhound Lines, Inc. (Greyhound II), 550 F.2d 1237 (9th Cir.), *cert. denied*, 46 U.S.L.W. 3216 (Oct. 4, 1977).

134. 550 F.2d 1237 (9th Cir.), *cert. denied*, 46 U.S.L.W. 3216 (Oct. 4, 1977).

135. *See* 550 F.2d at 1238-39 ("While a promise to submit a dispute to arbitration may justify a finding of an implied duty not to strike, . . . such a promise does not imply a duty on the part of the employer to preserve the status quo pending arbitration.").

136. 529 F.2d 1073 (9th Cir. 1976).

planned to change the work cycles of bus drivers operating Van-couver-Seattle and Seattle-Portland runs from the existing cycles of 6-days-on, 3-days-off, and 4-days-on, 3-days-off, respectively, to a straight weekly schedule of 5-days-on and 2-days-off. The union protested this change, contending that it could not be made unilat-erally under the provisions of the collective bargaining agreement. The employer responded that its action was authorized, and the union thereupon requested immediate arbitration and maintenance of the status quo pending arbitration. Greyhound agreed to im-mediate arbitration but refused to refrain from making the sched-uled changes pending arbitration. The union then petitioned the federal district court to enjoin Greyhound from implementing the changes pending resolution of the matter through arbitration,[137] and the court granted the injunction.[138] The Ninth Circuit affirmed.[139]

The Supreme Court remanded *Greyhound I* for "further con-sideration in light of *Buffalo Forge*,"[140] and the Ninth Circuit direct-ed briefs from the parties on the questions of whether in light of *Buffalo Forge, Boys Markets* authorized the injunctive relief obtained in *Greyhound I* and whether *Buffalo Forge* required different conclu-sions of law from those entered in the previous opinion. On April 1, 1977, the panel, once again speaking through Judge Sneed, revers-ed itself.[141]

In an opinion purporting to apply the logic of the *Buffalo Forge* majority, the Ninth Circuit found that a preliminary injunction should not issue against the proposed work-schedule changes.[142] The *Greyhound II* court reasoned that a promise to maintain the status quo pending arbitration was both analogous to a no-strike pledge on the part of a union and a prerequisite to the issuance of a preliminary injunction against the employer.[143] The absence of such a clause in the parties' collective bargaining agreement therefore

137. *Id*. at 1075.
138. *Id*.
139. *Id*. at 1079.
140. Greyhound Lines, Inc. v. Transit Workers Div. 1384, 429 U.S. 807 (1976). "When the Supreme Court remands a decision for reconsideration in light of an opinion which was not in existence at the time the court of appeals made its decision, it takes no position on the merits of the case." Lever Bros. Co. v. Chemical Workers Local 217, 554 F.2d 115, 121 n.11 (4th Cir. 1976) (addendum to opinion).
141. Transit Workers Div. 1384 v. Greyhound Lines, Inc. (Greyhound II), 550 F.2d 1237 (9th Cir.), *cert. denied*, 46 U.S.L.W. 3216 (Oct. 4, 1977).
142. 550 F.2d at 1238.
143. *Id*.

precluded granting the union's motion.[144] Judge Sneed found two additional reasons why an injunction should not issue. First, an employer's actions pending arbitration generally would not frustrate the arbitral process, although a strike in the same situation would do so.[145] Additionally, the union would not suffer irreparable harm if the injunction were not granted.[146]

2. *The Ninth Circuit's untenable position.*

The *Greyhound II* opinion is easily assailable even when considered as an application of *Buffalo Forge*. It completely overlooks the glaring distinction between injunctions against employers and those against labor strikes.[147] Furthermore, none of the three rationales proffered by the Ninth Circuit adequately supports its result.

The first ground of the *Greyhound II* decision is that *Buffalo Forge* requires the presence of an explicit promise by the employer to maintain the status quo pending arbitration as a condition for an injunction against an employer's contemplated act.[148] In arriving at this holding, Judge Sneed interpreted *Buffalo Forge* as stating that the union's promise not to strike is made only in return for the employer's promise to arbitrate grievances.[149] *Buffalo Forge*, however, does not support this broad statement. That case was concerned with the availability of injunctive relief pending arbitration and not with broad pronouncements about labor contract law. According to Judge Sneed, the union's no-strike pledge is limited to strikes over underlying disputes subject to arbitration, because only then does the union receive its quid pro quo: settlement of the underlying dispute through arbitration.[150] Therefore, prior to arbitration, courts will enjoin only strikes over arbitrable disputes. Judge Sneed applied this logic to the facts of *Greyhound II*.[151] He analogized an employer's promise to preserve the status quo pending arbitration to a promise not to strike by a union.[152] He then concluded that "the Union's promise to submit the dispute to arbitration and not to

---

144. *Id.* at 1238-39.
145. *Id.*
146. *Id.* at 1239.
147. *See id.* at 1238.
148. *Id.*
149. *See* Buffalo Forge Co. v. United Steelworkers, 428 U.S. 397, 407 (1976).
150. *See* notes 70-73 *supra* and accompanying text.
151. 550 F.2d at 1238.
152. *Id.*

strike could not have been given in exchange for an express promise by Greyhound to preserve the status quo because no such promise was made."[153]

Judge Sneed's approach in *Greyhound II* fails to recognize the basic difference between that case and *Buffalo Forge*. The issuance of injunctions against employers does not raise the fundamental concerns of Norris-LaGuardia as does the issuance of injunctions against strikes.[154] Therefore, no basis exists in *Buffalo Forge* for abandoning the equity criteria previously adopted for issuing injunctions against employers or for requiring any provisions paralleling a no-strike clause as a prerequisite to such relief.[155]

Judge Sneed's insistence that an injunction against an employer will only issue if the parties bargained for a status quo ante clause is an attempt to require a provision parallel to the no-strike clause which the Court required as a prerequisite to injunctive relief in *Boys Markets*. Even if *Buffalo Forge* makes the quid pro quo rationale developed in cases involving injunctions against strikes applicable to injunctions against employers, Judge Sneed draws an improper analogy between the no-strike clause and a status quo ante clause. A no-strike clause does not directly address either the preservation of the status quo or the speed with which relief will be granted. A status quo ante clause does deal directly with the speed of relief and is therefore more correctly analogized to a "quickie" arbitration clause, which contains both a promise not to strike and an agreement to arbitrate within a very short period the contractual propriety of a strike.[156] The Court did not require a "quickie" clause in *Boys Markets* as a prerequisite to a preliminary injunction against a strike pending arbitration. Therefore, the *Boys Markets* requirement of a no-strike clause is not authority for the status quo ante clause required by Judge Sneed in *Greyhound II*.

---

153. *Id.*

154. *See* note 12 *supra. But see* Hoh v. Pepsico, Inc., 491 F.2d 556, 560 (2d Cir. 1974) (Section 7 of the Norris-LaGuardia Act, 29 U.S.C. § 107 (1970), is sometimes applicable.).

155. No court prior to *Greyhound II* required a status quo clause before issuing an injunction against an employer. *See, e.g.*, Local 328, Int'l Bhd. of Teamsters v. Armour & Co., 294 F. Supp. 168 (W.D. Mich. 1968); Local 464, Am. Bakery & Confectionery Workers v. Hershey Chocolate Corp., 245 F. Supp. 748 (M.D. Pa. 1965); Division 1098, Amalgamated Ass'n of St. Employees v. Eastern Greyhound Lines, 225 F. Supp. 28 (D.D.C. 1963).

156. One example of the operation of a "quickie" arbitration clause occurred in New Orleans S.S. Ass'n v. ILA Local 1418, 389 F.2d 369 (5th Cir. 1968). There, the employer notified the arbitrator that the union was striking in violation of the collective bargaining agreement. The arbitrator commenced a hearing within 72 hours on the issue of the strike's permissibility. When the arbitrator issued an award against the strike 2 months later it was enforceable in court. *See* Gould, *supra* note 1, at 244-45 & n.115.

In *Buffalo Forge*, Justice White was troubled by the absence of a provision in the no-strike clause permitting parties to seek injunctive relief pending arbitration.[157] Justice White may have confused this type of provision with a "quickie" no-strike arbitration clause. If Justice White had intended to require the latter clause, Judge Sneed's requirement of a status quo clause gains some support. A "quickie" arbitration clause, if honored by the courts, would influence the speed and significance of the relief. Even the "quickie" no-strike arbitration clause, however, is not a precise analog to the status quo provision Judge Sneed discusses. Assuming that *Buffalo Forge* required a "quickie" no-strike clause as a prerequisite for the issuance of an injunction against a strike over a non-arbitrable grievance, Judge Sneed's reasoning is not compelling. Judge Sneed does not explain why *Buffalo Forge*, rather than *Boys Markets*, should govern injunctions against employers. Whatever the ambiguities of *Buffalo Forge, Boys Markets* did not require a "quickie" no-strike arbitration clause.[158]

Judge Sneed's second rationale in *Greyhound II* was that a status quo ante clause need not be implied, unlike a no-strike clause,[159] because "a strike pending arbitration generally will frustrate and interfere with the arbitral process while the employer's altering the status quo generally will not."[160] Judge Sneed fails to address the hardships, such as a loss of bargaining-unit jobs,[161] that can accompany an employer's action. These hardships, like the economic hardships that accompany strikes, may cause disputes to be resolved through economic pressure rather than through arbitration.

Judge Sneed gave an alternative basis for the *Greyhound II* decision, that the union would not suffer irreparable injury if the injunction failed to issue.[162] This finding contradicts two earlier findings in the case. The district court in *Greyhound* concluded that irreparable harm would result if the employer's action was allowed to proceed[163] and the Ninth Circuit adopted the district court's conclusion in *Greyhound I*.[164] Despite these shortcomings, this finding provides the most sound basis for the result in *Greyhound II*.

---

157. *See* note 72 *supra* and accompanying text.

158. *See* Boys Markets, Inc. v. Retail Clerks Local 770, 393 U.S. 235 (1970).

159. *See* text accompanying notes 40-42 *supra*.

160. 550 F.2d at 1238-39.

161. *See* note 120 *supra* and accompanying text.

162. 550 F.2d at 1239.

163. Transit Union Div. 1384 v. Greyhound Lines, Inc. (Greyhound I), 529 F.2d 1078, 1078-79 (1976).

164. *Id.*

C. *Possible Implications of* Greyhound II

Although the reasoning in *Greyhound II* is flawed, it is based upon an interpretation of *Buffalo Forge* that other courts may follow. In addition, if *Buffalo Forge* stands for less judicial interference with the collective bargaining agreement,[165] then arguably the problems posed by the sympathy-strike question may be posed by other disputed contractual provisions in the context of a union plea for injunctive relief. Organized labor therefore may have lost more than it gained by the prohibition against enjoining sympathy strikes pending arbitration. It is difficult to evaluate the magnitude of *Buffalo Forge*'s effect on injunctions against employers except to note that every reported decision involving a union-sought injunction against employer action since *Buffalo Forge* has considered its effect.[166] One of these cases suggests that courts may be able to distinguish *Greyhound II* by finding irreparable injury.[167]

If courts do interpret Justice White's opinion in *Buffalo Forge* to prohibit injunctions against employers in circumstances that would have given rise to injunctions before the decision, the equitable balance developed by federal courts will disappear. The confusion in Justice White's opinion and the lack of a clearly articulated rationale for the decision make this development a real possibility.

IV. Conclusion

Buffalo Forge was wrongly decided; there is no viable basis for distinguishing it from *Boys Markets*. Equally important, a possible basis for distinguishing the case is based on an unarticulated assumption that has no basis in precedent: that the risk of enjoining permissible strikes is greater in *Buffalo Forge* cases than in *Boys Markets* cases. Confronted with "massive preliminary injunction litigation,"[168] the Court sought to limit the impact of *Boys Markets* rather than reconsider earlier cases. The error committed in so doing was compounded because the issue of contractual complexity was not different from the one courts normally confront under section 301 by virtue of *Boys Markets* itself.

Ironically, the one union benefit that came from *Boys Markets*—the increased respectability of union motions for injunctive relief

---

165. *See* text accompanying notes 98-101 *supra*.

166. *See* note 132 *supra*.

167. Lever Bros. Co. v. Chemical Workers Local 217, 554 F.2d 115, 122-23 (4th Cir. 1976) (addendum to opinion).

168. 428 U.S. at 411 n.12.

pending arbitration—may be lost. The Ninth Circuit already has sounded the retreat in *Greyhound II*, although the extent to which this case will be followed is uncertain.[169]

Perhaps the Court, or possibly Congress, will overrule *Buffalo Forge* with the same disregard for stare decisis that led to *Boys Markets*. The logic of Justice Stevens' dissent is nearly impeccable.[170] Beyond reversal of Supreme Court authority in other areas, the answer to the concerns expressed by Justice White in *Buffalo Forge* is the opportunity for de novo arbitral review of cases that are remitted to impartial neutrals, as well as the adoption of procedures to expedite the arbitration process itself. As the latter is accomplished, the persuasiveness of Justice Stevens' dissent becomes all the more apparent. The sooner that insight is revealed to a majority of the Court, the better for labor, management and the public.

---

169. *See, e.g.*, Lever Bros. Co. v. Chemical Workers Local 217, 554 F.2d 115, 122-23 (4th Cir. 1976) (addendum to opinion); Communication Workers v. Western Elec. Co., 430 F. Supp. 969, 973-78 (S.D.N.Y. 1977).

170. Justice Stevens seems to have missed the mark in contending that an injunction against a sympathy strike is to be favored because "a sympathy strike does not directly further the economic interests of the members of the striking local." Buffalo Forge Co. v. United Steelworkers, 428 U.S. 397, 429 (1976) (Stevens, J., dissenting). Antithetical considerations argue for an injunction. *See* notes 102-03 *supra* and accompanying text.

7

Employer's Remedies: Arbitration and Section 301

A. *Union Liability*

Section 301 of the Act provides that "suits for violation of contracts between an employer and a labor organization representing employees in an industry affecting commerce"[132] may be entertained in the federal courts.[133] Shortly after the enactment of section 301 in 1947, Professor Cox wrote that a union would not be liable under section 301 for an unauthorized stoppage if the union disavowed its participating stewards.[134] He expressed the view that where the international union was signatory to a no-strike clause which required it not to support such a walkout, it would be liable for a strike called by the local union if (*1*) the local "engaged in the strike at least partly for the purpose of furthering the interests of the international" and (*2*) the local's conduct was of the same "general nature" as that which it was authorized to engage in on behalf of the international.[135]

A less devious standard was followed by the Fourth Circuit in *United Constr. Workers v. Haislip Baking Co.*[136] In that case the international's

---

[132] 61 Stat. 156 (1947), 29 U.S.C. § 185 (1964).

[133] See Textile Workers Union v. Lincoln Mills, 353 U.S. 448 (1957); Local 174, Teamsters v. Lucas Flour Co., 369 U.S. 95 (1962); Charles Dowd Box Co. v. Courtney, 368 U.S. 502 (1962); United Steelworkers v. Enterprise Wheel & Car Corp., 363 U.S. 593 (1960); cf. United Steelworkers v. Warrior & Gulf Nav. Co., 363 U.S. 574 (1960); United Steelworkers v. American Mfg. Co., 363 U.S. 564 (1960).

[134] Cox, "Some Aspects of the Labor Management Relations Act, 1947," 61 Harv. L. Rev. 274, 311 (1948).

[135] Id. at 312.

[136] 223 F.2d 872 (4th Cir.), cert. denied, 350 U.S. 847 (1955). See also Garmeada Coal

regional director intervened in a strike where there was no evidence that the union had instigated or encouraged the walkout. The regional director attempted unsuccessfully to get the employees back to work and did not insist upon the immediate reinstatement of discharged employees whose firings had triggered the strike. In exculpating the union from liability, the Fourth Circuit said that "the question is not whether they did everything they might have done, but whether they adopted, encouraged or prolonged the continuance of the strike."[137]

The decision in *Haislip* is a sound one and it comports with the approach that the Board should adopt in section 7 cases. In the absence of contract language to the contrary,[138] there should be evidence of genuine union authorization in both situations.[139] Thus, the union should obtain protection for the strikers and contractual liabilities for itself under what are roughly the same standards. A departure from this approach would require both the Board and courts to immerse themselves in international union procedures and resolutions so as to determine the authority of international, local, and steward under their own constitutions and by-laws. While it would seem proper to say that a union must vigorously disavow striking stewards, section 301 cannot be read to require that the union purge itself and discipline the offending members.[140] By the same token, the Board should not view union hostility to bargaining unit strikers as a prerequisite to a finding of unprotected status.

As a matter of good sense, there are very sound reasons for a narrow concept of union liability. The union bargains for all employees in an appropriate unit, but it does not necessarily have the loyalty of all employees. Even in a union shop, the willingness to follow union leadership on economic questions, as well as matters of discipline of individual

---

Co. v. International Union, UMW, 230 F.2d 945 (6th Cir. 1956); Local 25, Teamsters v. W. L. Mead, Inc., 230 F.2d 576 (1st Cir.), cert. dismissed, 352 U.S. 802 (1956); Textile Workers Union v. Aleo Mfg. Co., 94 F. Supp. 626 (M.D.N.C. 1950); General Magnetic Co. v. United Elec. Workers, 328 Mich. 542, 44 N.W.2d 140 (1950).

[137] United Constr. Workers v. Haislip Baking Co., 223 F.2d 872, 877-78 (4th Cir.), cert. denied, 350 U.S. 847 (1955); cf. C. & D. Batteries, Inc., 16 Lab. Arb. 198 (1951).

[138] See BNA, Union Liability for Strikes, Collective Bargaining Negotiations & Contracts (1963).

[139] However, ratification would bind a union under § 301. If the proposals enumerated in this article are accepted, ratification would not be acceptable in many cases arising under § 301. See note 121 supra and accompanying text.

[140] International Union discipline and expulsion of wildcat strikers would not violate the Act. Cf. Allis-Chalmers Mfg. Co. v. NLRB, 358 F.2d 656, 662 (7th Cir.), cert. granted, 385 U.S. 810 (1966) (dissenting opinion); Parks v. International Bhd. of Elec. Workers, 314 F.2d 886 (4th Cir.), cert. denied, 372 U.S. 976 (1963); Summers, "Legal Limitations on Union Discipline," 64 Harv. L. Rev. 1049, 1065-66 (1951). But the union is more limited in affecting a worker's employment status. Radio Officers' Union v. NLRB, 347 U.S. 17 (1954); Union Starch & Ref. Co. v. NLRB, 186 F.2d 1008 (7th Cir.), cert. denied, 342 U.S. 815 (1951); see the remarks of Senators Pepper and Taft, April 29, 1947, in 2 Legislative History of the Labor Management Relations Act of 1947, at 1094.

employees, may be of varying degrees and intensity. The union may not even be in a position to discipline employees who are non-members. And it is somewhat extreme to hold the union liable for damages when it takes a position opposite to that taken by the striking employees and does not encourage the strike. On the other hand, if the union takes the side of the strikers, but draws short of committing itself to the stoppage, it would seem that the union's obligation is to do more than remain silent. Furthermore, there may be groups within the unit which are hostile to the bargaining agent. Such groups may contain a contending faction or members of a rival union which would like to have the incumbent exposed to liability. Moreover, an employer-sponsored strike is certainly not beyond the realm of possibility. Just as the debates among workers should not be protected activity under section 7 and thus provide a basis for liability against the employer, so also should the employer be precluded from taking advantage of factions within the unit.

8

Wildcat Striking Employees Are Not Liable in Damages for Breach of a No-Strike Clause

A fourth case involving dispute resolution was *Complete Auto Transit, Inc. v. Reis.*[168] The Court was presented with the question of whether an employer had a cause of action for damages against individual employees for breach of a collective bargaining agreement's no-strike provision where the stoppage was unauthorized. Almost twenty years ago the Court, in the *Atkinson*[169] case, had held that individual union representatives could not be sued under section 301 of the Act where the stoppage was union authorized or ratified. This result, said the Court, was dictated by the legislative history of the Taft-Hartley amendments and the sensitivity and concern expressed by Congress about the *Danbury Hatters*[170] judgment in which individual union members, in some instances, lost their homes because of money judgments against them arising out of strikes and boycotts found to be unlawful.[171] In *Atkinson,* the Court specifically left open the question of individual employee liability where the stoppage was not authorized by the union.[172]

This Term, in yet another opinion authored by Justice Brennan, the Court held that the same result applies where the stoppage is unauthorized, *i.e.,* that individual employees are not liable as individuals. Said the Court:

---

169. Atkinson v. Sinclair Refining Co., 370 U.S. 238 (1962).
170. Lawlor v. Loewe, 235 U.S. 522 (1915); Loewe v. Lawlor, 208 U.S. 274 (1908).
171. *See generally* W. GOULD, A PRIMER ON AMERICAN LABOR LAW (MIT Press) (to be published April 1982).

Section 301(b) by its terms forbids a money judgment entered against a union from being enforced against individual union members. . . . It is a mistake to suppose that Congress thereby suggested by negative implication that employees *should* be held liable where their union is not liable for the strike. . . . Although lengthy and complex, the legislative history of Section 301 clearly reveals Congress' intent to shield individual employees from liability for damages arising from their breach of the no-strike clause of a collective-bargaining agreement, whether or not the union participated in or authorized the illegality. Indeed, Congress intended this result even though it might leave the employer unable to recover for his losses.[173]

The Court's careful examination of the legislative history and the debate about enforceability of collective-bargaining agreements in both 1946 and 1947,[174] immediately prior to the enactment of the Taft-Hartley amendments which included section 301, seemed to make it clear that Congress was concerned about avoiding individual employee liability for breach of a labor contract. While the issue is not entirely free from doubt, it appears as though Congress, particularly Senator Taft, assumed that employers would have the remedy of dismissal against wildcat strikers[175] and that that would be sufficient. Chief Justice Burger's dissent, in which Justice Rehnquist joined, was relatively unpersuasive in its reliance upon section 301(b) establishing by negative implication that individuals would be exculpated from liability only in strikes in which unions were involved and also in its assessment of legislative history.[176] Indeed, the rather cursory examination of legislative history given by the dissent in *Complete Auto Transit* seems out of step with those critics of the Warren Court who viewed expansive statutory and constitutional interpretations as a basis for "making law" which reflected a judge's philosophy and predeliction. The dissent also seems deficient in its all

---

172.   Atkinson v. Sinclair Refining Co., 370 U.S. 238, 249 n. 7 (1962).

173.   101 S.Ct at 1840. (emphasis in original) (citations omitted).

174.   *Id.* at 1841-44. *See also* 92 Cong. Rec. 5705-06 (1946); *Id.* at 5930-32; 93 Cong. Rec. 5041-42 (1947).

175.   101 S.Ct. at 1841-43. *See generally* Gould, *The Status of Unauthorized and "Wildcat" Strikes Under the NLRA,* 52 CORNELL L. Q. 672 (1967).

176.   101 S.Ct. at 1853.

too ready assumption that common law rules of agency would automatically bind workers in damages when the union may have been
authorized to bargain without the individual's vote or full
membership.[177]

On the one hand, it might be said that industrial self-government is promoted by the holding inasmuch as *Complete Auto
Transit* keeps these kinds of disputes out of the courts and is therefore more likely to channel them into the parties' own dispute resolution machinery. (Labor and management should find the holding
preferable in this respect to both *Barrentine* and *Clayton.*) But at
the same time, adherence to contractual responsibilities, particularly
an essential part of the employer's bargain (and, most specifically,
the no-strike clause), may be undermined in some circumstances.
Because of this—and perhaps out of defensive reaction to the charge
that the Court's *Carbon Fuel*[178] decision of last Term (also authored
by Justice Brennan for a unanimous Court), which held that international unions were liable for damages for breach of contract only for
strikes which they had authorized or ratified, coupled with *Complete
Auto Transit,* make the employer's plight in wildcat strikes desper-
ate and without remedy—the majority opinion ventured to speculate
about the impact of its holding.

And the difficulty with Justice Brennan's opinion is not so much
its examination of legislative history but rather this unnecessary ex-
cursion into the practical effects of its holding. Justice Brennan referred to the "significant array of other remedies available to employers to achieve adherence to collective bargaining agreements" as
a basis for countering the argument that a damage remedy against
individual employees is "*indispensable* to preserve the integrity of
the collective-bargaining agreement and thereby to further the national labor policy of promoting industrial peace."[179] Surely, as Justice Brennan contended, "[i]t is by no means certain that an individual damages remedy will meaningfully increase deterrence of wildcat
strikes above that resulting from use of other available remedies."[180]
This cautious formulation of the proposition seems to make more
sense than Chief Justice Burger's bald assumption that the deterrent

---

177. *Id.* at 1850.
178. Carbon Fuel Co. v. UMW of America, 444 U.S. 212 (1979).
179. 101 S.Ct. at 1845 n.18 (emphasis in original).
180. *Id.*

is a significant one. It may or may not be in any number of given situations. The difficulty with Justice Brennan's position is that the alternatives do not look particularly attractive either.

In *Complete Auto Transit,* Justice Brennan referred to a damage action against the union as one remedy which is part of the "significant array."[181] As the Court noted in *Boys Markets,*[182] when injunctions against unions for no-strike violations were held to be appropriate remedies, damage actions may tend to simply "aggravate industrial strife and delay an early resolution of the difficulties" between the parties.[183] Moreover, the *Carbon Fuel*[184] decision makes it difficult in many instances to pin liability upon the union. As Justice Powell said in a particularly perceptive concurring opinion: "It is a foolish union that would invite a damages suit by explicitly endorsing a strike in this manner."[185]

Justice Brennan also referred to the fact that the employer may dismiss workers who unlawfully walk off the job.[186] But this too may be counterproductive in some circumstances, simply promoting more substantial stoppages called in protest against the dismissals themselves. As Justice Powell noted, discharge is not a "realistic remedy in most cases."[187] And, although Justice Powell did not in any way advert to this consideration, it seems extremely undesirable as a matter of policy to promote a remedy which involves loss of work and job security.

Moreover, as Justice Powell also pointed out, union discipline of strikers is unlikely, impractical, and something that the union is not legally obligated to undertake.[188] Finally, there are other decisions of

---

181. *Id.* at 1845 n.18.
182. Boys Mkts., Inc. v. Retail Clerks Union, Local 770, 398 U.S. 235, 248 (1970).
183. *Id.*
184. Carbon Fuel Co. v. UMW of America, 444 U.S. 212 (1979).
185. 101 S.Ct. at 1848 (Powell, J. concurring). *Carbon Fuel* does not explicitly govern the relationship between the local union and its rank and file nor should it necessarily govern different contract language. *See,* United Steelworkers of America v. Lorain, 616 F.2d 919 (1980); Eazor Express, Inc. v. Int'l Bhd. of Teamsters, 520 F.2d 951 (3d Cir. 1975), *cert. denied,* 424 U.S. 935 (1976); Keebler v. Bakery Workers, Local 492-A, 104 L.R.R.M. 2625 (E.D. Pa. 1980). *But see* Airco Speer Carbon-Graphite v. Local 502, IVE, 108 L.R.R.M. 2779 (W.D. Pa. 1980). *See generally,* Whitman, *Wildcat Strikes: The Unions' Narrowing Path to Rectitude?* 50 IND. L.J. 472 (1975). Of course, *Carbon Fuel* makes it difficult to reach the international treasury which is far more plentiful than that of most of its local affiliates.
186. 101 S.Ct. at 1847.
187. *Id.*
188. *Id.* at 1848.

the Board—some of which were alluded to by the concurring opinion[189] and some of which were not not[190]—which make it difficult to say that the employer's array of remedies is significant. The most mischievous of them is the recently decided *Pacemaker Yacht*[191] decision in which the Board held that a strike is not unprotected by virtue of a no-strike clause unless the subject matter which triggered the strike was explicitly contemplated by the parties as within the no-strike clause's scope. It is difficult to imagine a more extraordinary and harmful opinion—and one which is inconsistent with the *Steelworkers Trilogy*[192] and its admonition about the gaps and ambiguities that are inherent in collective agreements.

Thus, Justice Powell seems to be on much firmer ground than Justice Brennan in stating the following:

> The Court plainly is unrealistic . . . when it suggests that employers have at their disposal a battery of alternate remedies for illegal strikes. . . . The result of the absence of remedies is a lawless vacuum. Despite a no-strike clause, a plant may be closed with adverse consequences that often are far-reaching. The strike injures the employer, other companies and their employees, and consumers in general. Frequently, the strike is harmful even to the majority of strikers, who feel obligated to honor the picket line of minority wildcatters.[193]

Both *Complete Auto Transit* and *Carbon Fuel* advise employers that they have other remedies. The vacuum described by Justice Powell does not promote industrial peace and negotiated dispute resolution procedures. The underlying assumption subscribed to by both Justice Brennan and Justice Powell is that the law can play a role in deter-

---

189. South Central Bell Telephone Co., 254 N.L.R.B. 32 (1981); Miller Brewing Co., 254 N.L.R.B. 24 (1981); Precision Casting Co., 233 N.L.R.B. 183 (1977). *But see,* NLRB v. Armour-Dial, Inc., 638 F.2d 51 (7th Cir. 1981); Gould, Inc. v. NLRB, 612 F.2d 728 (3d Cir. 1979), *cert. denied,* 101 S.Ct. 247 (1980) (denying enforcement of Board policy that union officer may not be disciplined more severely than other strikers); Indiana & Mich. Elec. Co. v. NLRB, 599 F.2d 227 (7th Cir. 1979). *But see* Hammermill Paper Co. v. NLRB, 108 L.R.R.M. 2001 (3d Cir. 1981); Metropolitan Edison Co. v. NLRB, 108 L.R.R.M. 3020 (3d Cir. 1981).

190. *See* note 191, *infra.*

191. 253 N.L.R.B. 95 (1980), *enforcement denied,* 108 L.R.R.M. 2818 (3d Cir. 1981).

192. *See* note 92, *supra.*

193. 101 S.Ct. at 1848-49.

ring unlawful stoppages—and the American experience, at least, seems to make that proposition more than arguably valid. There is the not too thinly veiled assumption contained in Justice Powell's opinion that the availability of remedies to employers could be of considerable assistance to employers confronted with wildcat strikes. But modern industrialized democracies have not always had an easy time in generating foolproof legal answers to this problem.

Finally, it should be noted that *Complete Auto Transit* majority opinion leaves open a number of issues. Foremost amongst them is the question of whether an employer may seek injunctive relief against individual employees who violate the no-strike agreement.[194] Although civil contempt penalties raise some of the same concerns about money judgments against workers present in damage actions, it is possible that the Court's resolution of this issue could be different.

Further, the Court left open the question of whether an injunction could issue against individual union members in a sympathy strike situation of the kind involved in *Buffalo Forge*,[195] where the Court held that an injunction could not be obtained against the union which had pledged itself to no strikes and yet had engaged in a sympathy strike, because there was no underlying grievance that triggered the stoppage which was arbitrable. And, indeed, the Court seems to have hinted at the potential for a modification or reversal of *Buffalo Forge* itself, a decision which I always found both singularly unpersuasive and inconsistent with *Boys Markets*[196] and responsible for the mischievous extension of the coterminous interpretation[197] doctrine so as to immunize unions from damage actions when they engage in sympathy strikes in the teeth of broad no-strike clauses prohibiting all strikes and picketing during the term of the agree-

---

194. *Id.* at 1849.

195. Buffalo Forge Co. v. United Steelworkers of America, AFL-CIO, 428 U.S. 397 (1976).

196. *See,* Gould, *On Labor Injunctions Pending Arbitration: Recasting Buffalo Forge,* 30 Stan. L. Rev. 533 (1978); Gould, *On Labor Injunctions, Unions and the Judges,* 1970 Sup. Ct. Rev. 215. Of course, for the arbitration process to be utilized under the circumstances, the employer ought to be able to initiate it. *Cf.* Drake Bakeries v. Local 50, Am. Bakery & Confectionary Workers, 370 U.S. 254 (1962).

197. The doctrine appears to originate with Gateway Coal Co. v. UMW of America,

ment.[198] One must recall that Justice Brennan led the charge in this area, writing the dissent in *Sinclair* which was adopted by Justice Stewart for the Court in *Boys Markets* and dissenting with three other members of the Court in *Buffalo Forge*.

Said Justice Brennan in *Complete Auto Transit:* "It *may be* that an injunction would not issue against a participating or authorizing union in circumstances otherwise the same. . . ."[199] (emphasis supplied). In *Complete Auto Transit* the strike began over a non-arbitrable issue but was continued as a result of an arbitrable matter. Does *Boys Markets* govern—or does *Buffalo Forge?* The Court has granted certiorari on the question of *Buffalo Forge*'s continued viability.[200] Justice Stewart, part of the *Buffalo Forge* majority, departed the Court on July 3, 1981, and Justice O'Connor's views on this subject are not known. It may be that Justice Brennan will write another chapter in this area during the October 1981 Term. The holding in *Complete Auto Transit* increases the odds on serious reconsideration of *Buffalo Forge*.

---

198.   *See, e.g.,* Delaware Coca-Cola Bottling Co., Inc. v. Teamsters, Local 326, 624 F.2d 1182 (3d Cir. 1980). *But see* Amcar Division, ACF Industries v. NLRB, 641 F.2d 561 (8th Cir. 1981); NLRB v. Gould, Inc., 105 L.R.R.M. 2288 (10th Cir. 1980) (relying principally on contract language). In the unfair labor practice context providing protected status for sympathy strikers, even with a broad no-strike clause, *see* NLRB v. Southern Calif. Edison Co., 107 L.R.R.M. 2667 (9th Cir. 1981); Gary-Hobart Water Corp. v. NLRB, 511 F.2d 284 (7th Cir. 1975), *cert. denied,* 423 U.S. 925 (1975).

199.   101 S.Ct. at 1845 n.18.

200.   Jacksonville Bulk Terminals, Inc. v. Int'l Longshoremen's Ass'n., 101 S.Ct. 1737 (1981).

201.   101 S.Ct. 2546 (1981).

Bibliographic Essay on Legal Constraints on Strikes During the Term of a Collective Bargaining Agreement

In *Jacksonville Bulk Terminals, Inc. v. International Longshoreman's Assn.*,[1] a majority of the Supreme Court, in an opinion authored by Justice Marshall, concluded that the *Buffalo Forge* opinion governed the question of whether an injunction could be issued by a federal district court against a work stoppage in breach of contract aimed at inducing workers not to handle cargo bound for or coming from the Soviet Union or carried on Russian ships at the time of the Soviet Union's intervention in Afghanistan. The Court held that the stoppage was a "labor dispute" within the meaning of the Norris-LaGuardia Act and that therefore, inasmuch as the statute does not exempt "labor disputes having their genesis in political protest,"[2] the stoppage was a labor dispute immunized from traditional interference by Norris-LaGuardia. Thus the same accommodation between the competing policies of Norris-LaGuardia and Taft-Hartley involved in *Boys Market* and *Buffalo Forge* had to be struck by the Court. Although such political strikes can run afoul of the secondary boycott prohibition of the statute,[3] the Court concluded that *Buffalo Forge* required no injunction to issue because the stoppage was not triggered by an underlying grievance which was itself susceptible to arbitration.

Chief Justice Burger and Justice Powell dissented. Justice O'Connor, while concurring in the judgment, opined that the result was "inescapable" because of the Court's unwillingness to overrule *Buffalo Forge* and thus implied her willingness to join in such a reversal at a future date. Justice Brennan, who had joined Justice Stevens' dissent in *Buffalo Forge* and had authored the *Sinclair* dissent which was adopted by the majority in *Boys Market*, joined the majority here and thus presented no opportunity for a 5–4 reversal. Justice Brennan did not write a separate opinion indicating the basis for his seemingly contrary positions in *Buffalo Forge* and *Jacksonville Bulk Terminals.*

In an article written just before the issuance of *Jacksonville Bulk Terminals,* "Strikes Over Non-Arbitrable Labor Disputes,"[4] Professor Cantor took the position that *Buffalo Forge* ought not to apply to strikes in a number of circumstances. Professor Cantor argued that *Buffalo Forge* would apply regardless of the scope and precision of the no-strike clause and its coverage of sympathy strikes. But where the parties had specifically authorized a resolution of the propriety of the strike by an arbitrator prior to the strike itself, Professor Cantor stated that the reasoning of *Boys Market* ought to apply inasmuch as it could not be said that the role of the arbitrator would be usurped through the issuance of an injunction. Professor Cantor was also of the view that *Buffalo Forge* does not foreclose injunctive relief against sympathy strikers where the underlying dispute between roving pickets and other employees is itself susceptible to arbitration. Professor Cantor stated that where disputes arose outside the industry, striking workers should demonstrate some "economic interest in the underlying dispute" in order to qualify for Norris-LaGuardia protection. However, *Jacksonville Bulk Terminals* seems to doom that approach.

Further, Professor Cantor took the position that wildcat strikes could be enjoined, even though the underlying grievance was not arbitrable, on the ground that such strikes undercut the collective bargaining process, which is itself promoted by federal national labor policy. Professor Cantor also advocated that preliminary judicial findings on the question of whether the underlying grievance was arbitrable, as well as the existence of a no-strike clause violation, be made under standards more ambitious than determination of whether a "colorable" position about arbitrability or a violation of the no-strike laws was present. Finally, he took the position that a strike motivated by an attempt to obtain a contract change should not be put within the scope of *Buffalo Forge* simply because the union conceded that it would have no meritorious claim under the contract.

Contrary to most scholarly comment, Professor Mayer Freed, in "Injunctions Against Sympathy Strikes: In Defense of *Buffalo Forge*,"[5] took the position that *Buffalo Forge* is consistent with the policies contained in the statute as well as with judicial precedents. Professor Freed is of the view that attacks on *Buffalo Forge* are not accommodation arguments, but rather thinly disguised variations on the repeal argument which was rejected by the Court in *Sinclair.* Professor Freed's view is that, inasmuch as the practical effect of a position contrary to the majority in *Buffalo Forge* is to favor arbitration of all employer grievances, the policy objective is to substitute arbitration for litigation and not industrial warfare. Such a policy would differ profoundly from that announced in *Lincoln Mills* and *Steelworkers Trilogy.*

A second issue dealt with in my "Recasting *Buffalo Forge*" article was also subsequently treated by Professor Cantor in *"Buffalo Forge* and Injunctions Against Employer Breaches of Collective Bargaining Agreements."[6] In this article, Professor Cantor took the position that a preliminary injunction could be issued against an employer who breaches a collective bargaining agreement pending arbitration of the grievance in a number of instances: (1) where there is a status quo obligation which obligates the employer not to change conditions of employment while a dispute is being resolved through arbitration process or some other machinery; (2) in "extraordinary situations" where there is a showing of injury "irremediable by an arbitrator, balance of harms favoring the union, and probable success on the merits."[7] Here Cantor makes the point that "[l]ong custom holds that an employer may implement its interpretation [of the agreement] in the interim."[8] Thus he noted that the parties expectations, rather than the Norris-LaGuardia Act, limit the issuance of an injunction to limited situations despite the tension between judicial and arbitral authority. Professor Cantor notes that where the same issues are considered by both the court and the arbitrator, a converse determination on the merits by the arbitrator subsequent to a full hearing, filing of briefs, etc., is not precluded.

Although the *Boys Market* piece in the *Supreme Court Review* discussed the relationship between injunctions and expedited procedures, it did not focus upon an issue raised before the Court of Appeals for the Second Circuit in *United Parcel Service (N.Y.), Inc. v. Local 804 International Brotherhood of Teamsters.*[9] In that case the court held that Section 8 of the Norris-LaGuardia Act requires resort to voluntary arbitration machinery prior to seeking injunctive relief and that where there is expedited machinery addressed to the no-strike issue, as contained in the party's collective bargaining agreement, the employer was obliged to proceed to arbitration before seeking injunctive relief.

NOTES

1. 457 U.S. 702 (1982).
2. *Id.* at 711.
3. *International Longshoreman's Assn., AFL-CIO, et al. v. Allied International, Inc.* 456 U.S. 212 (1982).
4. 23 Bost. Coll. L. Rev. 633 (1982).
5. 54 N.Y.U. L. Rev. 289 (1979).
6. 1980 Wisc. L. Rev. 247.
7. *Id.* at 289.
8. *Id.*
9. 698 F. 2d 100 (2d Cir., 1983).

9

The Established Relationship
Between Labor and Management

A. *The* Dow Chemical Case: *A Panorama of Arbitration and the Peace Obligation*

In *Dow Chemical Co. v. NLRB*[117] the Third Circuit, for the second time in four years,[118] dealt with a case which presented a whole host of important issues. But the court, which had nearly invited the Board to fashion a federal labor law of contract in light of important Supreme Court decisions such as *Boys Markets v. Retail Clerks*,[119] marched down the hill this past fall, stating that there had been a terrible misunderstanding flowing either from its opinion in *Dow I* or in the Board's understanding of it upon remand. This seemingly never-ending saga is best understood by a brief examination of the previous holdings of the Board and the Third Circuit in *Dow I* as well as *Dow II*.

The dispute in *Dow I* involved a number of employees in the

---

[117] 105 L.R.R.M. 3327 (3d Cir. 1980).
[118] *Dow I* is found at 102 L.R.R.M. 1199 (1979).
[119] 398 U.S. 235 (1970).

company's latex department who, prior to the litigation under discussion, worked a "seven and two" schedule in that they worked seven consecutive days and then had two days off. The employer reached a decision to change the schedule to a regular five-day work week with two days off and wanted to accomplish this without laying off any of the employees. It was necessary to reduce the hourly rate of one of the senior employees whose job was being eliminated and who would be transferred to another position. Further, as the Administrative Law Judge found, "because of the reduction of hours worked and the elimination of overtime, weekend, and holiday premiums . . . [it was] estimated that other employees would earn approximately $750 less per year than they would on the seven to two schedule." The Administrative Law Judge also found that he had "no doubt that it [the decision to make the change] was premised on valid economic and business considerations," i.e., a drop in sales attributable to the loss of one of the company's large customers.

The Administrative Law Judge found that there was a series of meetings relating to the mechanics of the change before its planned institution and that the company refused to engage in negotiations about it. The union had taken the position that any change in shift schedule was a violation of the agreement between the parties. A meeting was held pursuant to the grievance procedure, which procedure culminated in nonmandatory arbitration, i.e., arbitration may be initiated as the last step of the machinery but only with the consent of both sides. When the change was instituted, the union struck despite the existence of a no strike clause, while ignoring pleas of company representatives urging them to "order the membership back to work and process the grievance through the grievance procedure provided in the existing contract between Dow Chemical Company and District 50."[120] Subsequently, successful meetings with state mediation officials were held with a view towards attempting to resolve the dispute. After these meetings the employer rescinded the collective bargaining agreement between the parties and soon thereafter terminated the employees. A week later, employer representatives received a petition signed by fifty-five hourly employees which stated that they did not "want or need" the union as a collective bargaining representative, and the em-

---

[120] Dow Chemical Co., 212 N.L.R.B. 330, 337 (1974).

ployer advised the union that it no longer recognized it as the collective bargaining representative because of lack of majority support.

The Administrative Law Judge found that the company's unilateral change of working hours was not sanctioned by the collective bargaining agreement and therefore found that the announcement and scheduling of the change violated Sections 8(a)(5) and (1) of the Act. The Administrative Law Judge also found, however, that while the parties had completed and complied with the first four steps of the grievance procedure, the final step had not been completed, and "it had been the practice of the parties to always adhere to this requirement."[121] The contract provided that a right to strike was authorized by the agreement after all the contractual prerequisites had been exhausted. Accordingly, the strike was not authorized by the agreement. Applying the doctrine of the *Mastro Plastics*[122] decision and the Board's application of it in *Arlan's Department Store of Michigan, Inc.*,[123] the Administrative Law Judge concluded that, while the employer had engaged in unfair labor practices, they were not of "such serious nature"[124] so as to be "destructive of the foundation on which collective bargaining must rest."[125] The Judge stated that "there is no evidence that Respondent held any union animous [*sic*], the parties appear to have long enjoyed a harmonious relationship, and there is no evidence to indicate that Respondent wished to 'rid itself of the union.' "[126] Since there was a contract grievance procedure available for the peaceful resolution of the dispute, the Judge held that the strike was unprotected from its inception. With regard to the rescission of the contract, the Judge, relying upon the Board's *Marathon Electric*[127] decision, held that the employer did not violate its refusal to bargain obligation under the statute when it rescinded the contract in response to the union's breach of the no-strike provisions.[128]

---

[121] *Id.* at 340.

[122] Mastro Plastics Corp. v. NLRB, 350 U.S. 270 (1956).

[123] 133 N.L.R.B. 802 (1961).

[124] Dow Chemical Co., 212 N.L.R.B. 330, 340 (1974).

[125] *Id.*

[126] *Id.*

[127] Marathon Electric Mfg. Corp., 106 N.L.R.B. 1171 (1955), *enforced*, 223 F.2d 338 (D.C. Cir.), *cert. denied*, 350 U.S. 981 (1956).

[128] Dow Chemical Co., 212 N.L.R.B. 330, 340-41 (1974).

In *Dow I*, by a 2-1 vote, a three-member panel affirmed the Administrative Law Judge's decision in its entirety, with Member Fanning dissenting in part. Member Fanning, relying upon his dissent in *Arlan's Department Store*,[129] noted that his position was that "a general no-strike clause in a contract for the term of that contract bars only the right to strike over disputes concerning the economic relationship between the employers and the employees, *i.e.*, an economic strike, and does not bar a strike to protest unfair labor practices in the absence of an express waiver, since such strike, in my view, is outside of the scope of contract."[130] In any event, Member Fanning would have found the employer's unilateral change of work schedules sufficiently serious to justify employee concerted action outside the grievance-arbitration provisions under the authority of *Arlan's*, inasmuch as "the injury suffered by employees in the bargaining unit is not limited to [their own losses]" but extended "to the union's status as bargaining representative . . . affecting all employees in the bargaining unit."[131] Member Fanning, applying the majority's "test of experience, good sense, and good judgment," and concluding that the strike was immune from the general no-strike prohibition, said:

> "Experience" informs us that wage reductions are among the most sensitive issues in labor relations. "Good sense" tells us that an unlawfully imposed wage cut will provoke employees into withholding their labor. "Good judgment" demands that before a no-strike be construed as applying to strikes protesting unfair labor practices there be clear and unmistakable language in the contract to that effect. It demands as well consideration of the fact that the Union and the employees withheld strike action and continued to utilize the grievance provisions of the contract in an attempt to force the Respondent to the bargaining table up to the time that Respondent decided to implement the announced change. Considering these circumstances, it is clear that responsibility for the strike rests more upon Respondent as perpetrator of the unfair labor practice than upon the Union and the employees who sought to utilize peaceful means of securing their statutory rights and only desisted therein when brought face to face with a *fait accompli.*[132]

The Third Circuit's approach in *Dow I*, in an opinion authored by Judge Aldisert, expressed the view that the Board had

---

[129]   133 N.L.R.B. 802 (1961).
[130]   Dow Chemical Co., 212 N.L.R.B. 330, 334 (1974).
[131]   *Id.*
[132]   *Id.*

probably considered the legal issues involved under inappropriate standards. The court stated that the "major question" presented was whether the Board should have considered the effect of the *Boys Markets* decisions. Preliminarily, the court noted that substantial evidence in the record justified the support of the Board's conclusion that the employer was not contractually justified in its unilateral implementation of the shift changes and that, therefore, the statute had indeed been violated. Moreover, the court noted that, since the union did not exhaust the grievance procedures nor file a written request for arbitration as provided by the contract, its strike was not authorized by the agreement's "limited reservation of a right to strike."[133]

Judge Aldisert stated that the court declined "the invitation to resolve this case by simply pigeon-holing it as within the rule of *Mastro Plastics* or that of *Arlan's*."[134] The court stated that these rules must be understood in terms of their legal settings and that "fundamental developments in national labor policy" since those decisions should have commanded the Board's attention. The court stated that the Board had not evaluated the question of whether the company could have avoided "abrogating the collective bargaining agreement and terminating the employees had *it* sought to arbitrate the dispute."[135] The court then discussed the development of modern labor policy as it relates to the collective bargaining agreement—the law as it has evolved since *Steelworkers Trilogy*—and said that its consideration was "on the facts of the instant case and with respect to the company's post-strike actions, the appropriate accommodation between these general principles and the older rules of *Mastro Plastics* and *Arlan's*."[136]

The court noted that both sides had resorted to "the tooth and claw of industrial warfare, rather than availing themselves of procedures provided in their collective bargaining agreement and encouraged by the congressionally mandated national labor policy."[137] The union had struck and the company had "disdained" the arbitration process and "ultimately resorted to re-

---

[133] 91 L.R.R.M. 2275, 2279 (3d Cir. 1976).
[134] *Id.*
[135] *Id.* (emphasis in original).
[136] *Id.* at 2282.
[137] *Id.*

scission of the contract." Said the court, "A more primitive, abrasive and disrupting example of labor-management relations is difficult to imagine. Indeed, the avoidance of such traumatic ruptures in industrial relations is the precise aim of the national labor policy. Yet the Board and the intervenor-company would have us hold that the national labor policy will sanction the company's ultimate actions."[138]

The court stated that, given the *quid pro quo* arbitration and no-strike provisions in the collective bargaining agreement, it would have "no difficulty in concluding that an employer's failure to seek *Boys Markets* injunctive relief would be an "appropriate factor" to consider in determining whether "subsequent action" was permissible under the statute. The court said, "[T]he availability of a *Boys Markets* injunction effects a *pro tanto* modification of the *Arlan's* rule. A contrary conclusion would be a total perversion of the national labor policy espoused by Congress and the Supreme Court."[139] However, in *Dow I* the court noted that the arbitration clause was not co-extensive with the no-strike clause and that arbitration could be obtained only where both parties gave written consent. Under the circumstances *Boys Markets* injunctive relief would not be available to the company. Compliance with the grievance procedure was nevertheless mandatory. The court noted that the company did not take action to seek specific enforcement of the grievance procedure and that, inasmuch as the underlying dispute "revolved around the interpretation of the management-rights clause," it was susceptible to resolution through the arbitration process. The court indicated that the only stumbling block to proceeding to arbitration was the consent of the parties—the union indicating its desire to arbitration, the company never affirmatively having sought abritration. The court said:

> Accordingly, we believe that, although *Boys Markets* was unavailable to the company to compel arbitration, this conclusion begs the pivotal question: whether the company, having failed to take positive steps to have the dispute resolved peacefully, can build a sanctuary for subsequent actions in derogation of its previously harmonious relationship with the union. As a practical matter, had the company sought a peaceful and orderly resolution of the underlying dispute, it is highly probable that the union would have at least

---

[138] *Id.*
[139] *Id.* at 2283.

suspended the strike.[140]

The court stated that its decision was "guided in the first instance by jurisprudential guideposts" provided by recent Court pronouncements on national labor policy. The court expressed its "grave doubts" about the Board's resort to the *Mastro Plastic-Arlan's* formula and its contribution to industrial peace. The opinion referred to the difficulties involved in predicting whether an unfair labor practice had been committed and whether it was a "serious" one, thereby creating a protected status for the strike. The court conceded that the union would still be "on the horns of a dilemma" in assessing the employer's unfair labor practice but that the company, when confronted with the strike would "know that it should take certain precautions before resorting to such self-help as cancellation of the contract, termination of employees and refusal to recognize the union."[141] The Board's role, said the court, would remain an important one because its expertise should be sought in the form of an *amicus* brief in the context of an employer's *Boys Markets* petition for injunction required by the Board's own rules. In any event, the court noted that the Board was itself deferring certain Section 8(a)(5) charges to arbitration.[142]

Finally, the court, with reference to *Marathon Electric,* disapproved the rule that a strike in breach of contract "automatically" provides the employer with the option to terminate the contract. Examining the facts of the instant case, the court noted that the company had both legal and contractual remedies available to it "short of contract termination," *i.e.,* compelling the completion of a grievance procedure, taking affirmative steps to have the dispute submitted to arbitration and filing a Section 301 damage suit. The court remanded to the Board for reconsideration of all aspects of the case except those relating to the Board's finding that the company had violated its bargaining obligation through its unilateral change in conditions of employment.

Dow II[143] contains at least four different opinions at the Board

---

[140] *Id.* at 2284.

[141] *Id.* at 2285.

[142] *Id. See also id.* at 2280 where the court cites cases in which the Board has applied the *Collyer* doctrine to defer § 8(a)(5) cases to the arbitral process where the collective bargaining agreement provides for arbitration.

[143] Dow Chemical Co., 244 N.L.R.B. No. 129 (1979).

level. While a majority of the Board retained the *Arlan's* rule,[144] two dissenters[145] would have overruled the decision. A majority of the Board, however, over one dissent, found that there was indeed a "serious unfair labor practice" within the meaning of *Arlan's* and that, therefore, protected status for the union's strike was not dependent upon completion of the grievance procedure and a written request for arbitration. On the applicability of *Boys Markets,* the Board—as had the courts previously—noted that an injunction would not be available to the employer under the circumstances. Additionally, two Board members noted that the Court had emphasized that *Boys Markets* was a "narrow holding." But, of course, the position of the Court, when it stressed the narrow holding of *Boys Markets,* was based upon the question of whether injunctive relief would be available in light of the policies of the Norris-La Guardia Act.[146] This has nothing whatever to do with the issue that was before the Board.

With regard to the unwillingness of the employer to arbitrate, the Board concluded that on the basis of

> comparative responsibility in carrying out their contractual commitments, the onus for the strike must be placed upon the Respondent. It would not have occurred but for the Respondent's adamant insistence upon implementing the unilateral shift change before the grievance procedure could be completed and before arbitration could be set in motion, if agreed to.[147]

Member Penello concurred in part and dissented in part, proclaiming his adherence to *Arlan's* and the Board's previous conclusion that the strike was unprotected under it. Member Penello rejected the court's limitation of traditional self-help measures as "improper and unwelcome intrusion[s] into the col-

---

[144] Members Penello, Murphy and Truesdale were in favor of retaining the rule. *Id.* at 5.

[145] Chairman Fanning and Member Jenkins would have overruled *Arlan's. Id.* at 5 n.8.

[146] *See id.* at 7 n.11, where the Court is quoted as saying:
Section 301 of the Act assigns a major role to the courts in enforcing collective-bargaining agreements, but aside from the enforcement of the arbitration provisions of such contracts, *within the limits permitted by Boys Markets,* the Court had never indicated that the courts may enjoin actual or threatened contract violations despite the Norris-La Guardia Act.

[147] *Id.* at 8.

lective bargaining process."[148] The Penello opinion also expressed disagreement with the view that the company had not been willing to initiate peaceful procedures as an alternative to strike.

Finally, Member Truesdale concurred, and, like Members Penello and Murphy, he adhered to *Arlan's* because of his concern that the absence of such a rule would eliminate deterrence to strike during the term of the agreement. The Truesdale opinion was alone in addressing the *Marathon Electric* rule, concluding that any unfair labor practice committed by an employer would prohibit rescission of the contract by management in response to a strike even though the strike itself was in breach of the no-strike clause. With regard to the application of the rule, however, Member Truesdale found that the employer's unfair labor practice was a serious one, in part because of the employer's "relative unwillingness to proceed with arbitration."[149] Member Truesdale stated that he regarded rescission as "inconsistent with the peculiar nature of a collective-bargaining agreement."[150]

Dow II, an opinion authored by Judge Gibbons and issued by only one of the three judges who had been on the bench in *Dow I*, has only added to the confusion in this area. In *Dow II* the court, conceding that it had addressed the *Mastro Plastics-Arlan's* formulation "with perhaps less precision than we might have, "stated that it was "proceeding on the assumption that the strike was a material breach of contract, and that our primary interest in remanding was to determine whether, assuming such a breach, *subsequent* company actions could be considered unlawful retaliation against protected activities."[151] The court stated that, had it considered the possibility that the strike at its inception was unlawful, the opinion in *Dow I* would have been written quite differently, inasmuch as the conclusion that subsequent company rescission was retaliation for protected activity would have been "inescapable."[152]

Judge Gibbons' opinion stressed the frequency with which dis-

---

[148] *Id.* at 32.
[149] *Id.* at 57 n.112.
[150] *Id.* at 57.
[151] Dow Chemical Co. v. NLRB, 105 L.R.R.M. 3327, 3332 (3d Cir. 1980) (emphasis in original).
[152] *Id.*

putes over management prerogatives clauses and potential refusal-to-bargain violations emerge and the contrast that such cases present with those involving the destruction of employee choice of bargaining representatives—the former disputes being resolved frequently and appropriately by the arbitration process. Accordingly, the court stressed its adherence to the Board's rule and emphasized the fact that the union could have sought retroactive "economic relief" through either arbitration or Board unfair labor practice charges. If, said the court, *Boys Markets* injunctive relief litigation was encouraged, the question of whether the dispute was outside the no-strike undertaking would have to be confronted by the court and would thus usurp the arbitrator's role.

The court also refused to repudiate *Marathon Electric* because, in its view, such a rule would effectively prevent the employer's attempt to hire new employees. In this connection, the court failed to take account of the fact that the employer's ability to get adequate temporary replacement may vary depending upon the labor market and type of job involved. While the court offered its *mea culpa* to the Board for the confusion that was engendered by its initial remand, its opinion was so startlingly different in *Dow II* from that in *Dow I* that in large part it can only be explained by the change in the composition of the panel. Only Judge Weiss dissented on the ground that the Board should have an opportunity to determine whether termination of the contract was justified when the company had not exhausted the available grievance procedures or refused to proceed in court.[153] The *Dow* litigation has thus ended not with a bang but a whimper—and with a highly unsatisfactory rationale at that!

B. No-Strike Obligations and Sympathy Strikes

In a series of decisions relating to the scope of no-strike clauses, both the Board and the Third Circuit have formulated a rule of labor contract law for no-strike clauses which, in my judgment, is both mistaken in all important aspects and contrary to existing arbitral precedents. In *Pacemaker Yacht Co.*,[154] the representative union had negotiated a collective bargaining agreement which provided for an employee health and welfare

---

[153] *Id.* at 3336.
[154] 253 N.L.R.B. No. 95 (1980).

benefit program under which the employer was required to pay 40 cents per hour to the Teamsters' Health and Welfare Fund of Philadelphia and Vicinity, a joint employer-union venture. The Fund, in turn, retained an independent insurance carrier to underwrite the health and welfare program. The employer had no contractual obligation with respect to the benefit program, nor was it obliged to guarantee that the Fund fulfill its commitments to the insurance carrier. In early 1978 the Fund ceased paying premiums to the insurance carrier, whereupon the carrier stopped honoring medical benefit claims submitted by employees. It was undisputed that the employer had at all times complied with its contractual duty to make contributions to the Fund. A strike and sympathy stoppage resulted from the inability to resolve this matter effectively. The agreement contained a very broad and explicit no-strike clause. The employer dismissed employees involved in the unauthorized stoppages, and an arbitrator held that they were properly terminated for violating the no-strike clause. The award, however, permitted some employees to be recalled.

The Board noted that the right to strike can only be waived when there is explicit waiver language in the contract or so-called "protective extrinsic evidence" in the form of bargaining history or other relevant conduct of the parties. Reversing the Administrative Law Judge's finding that the strike had been waived, the Board said that the fact that there was no evidence that the parties "considered or discussed whether the no-strike clause would cover the situation which arose here indicates that no clear and unmistakable waiver of the right to strike over the Fund's inaction occurred."[155] The Board said that there had been no "conscious yielding" since the matter was beyond the parties' anticipation and quoted the Administrative Law Judge in this connection. Said the Board:

> This observation only lends support to our conclusion that there was no waiver of the right to strike over the matter involved in this case. It stands to reason that the Union could not have made a clear and unmistakable waiver of the employees' right to strike to put pressure on the Fund since the parties never foresaw the possibility of such a situation. The mere fact that the parties may not be in a position to foresee that the situation may arise is certainly no reason to find . . . that if they had been able to envision the type of strike involved herein they would have included it as a situ-

---

[155] *Id.*, slip op. at 9.

ation to which the right to strike is waived.[156]

This is a remarkable and unfortunate decision. It is deeply at odds with the tenor of *Steelworkers Trilogy* itself, which highlighted the peculiar nature of collective bargaining agreements and the unforeseen contingencies and gaps that are likely to arise. One must recall that the Court stressed the fact that the collective bargaining agreement is a "generalized code to govern a myriad of cases which the draftsmen cannot wholly anticipate."[157] This is the rationale which justified—at least in part—a policy promoting arbitration as a *quid pro quo* for the no-strike clause as a matter of federal labor law. The no-strike clause in *Pacemaker Yacht* was all-embracing and thus intended to address a wide variety of unanticipated problems. The clause was not limited to arbitrable disputes, and it was fanciful for the Board to limit it as it did. The Board stated that the conclusion that a general no-strike clause did not waive this strike was "more compelling" than in the case of sympathy strikes because here the strike was "a breakdown of one of the major components of collective bargaining agreements. . . . [U]nlike the sympathy strike, the walkout here was over a matter which intimately related to the terms and conditions of employment of the striking employees."[158] But this point cuts in exactly the opposite direction. The strike was over subject matter at which most no-strike provisions are aimed.

In *Pacemaker Yacht* the Board also held, without much discussion, that sympathy strikers could strike in the teeth of the no-strike clause which prohibited "picketing" or "other interruption of a company's operations." Although this issue is a more difficult one, the result here also seems to be erroneous. In order to understand this issue, it is important to consider the Third's Circuit's *Coca Cola Bottling Co.*[159] decision, which formulated a rule for excluding sympathy strikes from the strictures of broad no-strike clauses.

In *Coca Cola* the union entered into a broad no-strike clause

---

[156] *Id.*

[157] United Steelworkers v. Warrior & Gulf Navig. Co., 363 U.S. 574, 578-80 (1960). *See* Cox, *Reflections upon Labor Arbitration* 72 Harv. L. Rev. 1482 (1959).

[158] Pacemaker Yacht Co., 253 N.L.R.B. No. 95 at 11.

[159] Coca-Cola Bottling Co. v. Teamsters Local 326, 104 L.R.R.M. 2776 (3d Cir. 1980).

which prohibited any strike or any curtailment of work or restriction of service or interference with the operation of the Company or any picketing or patrolling during the term of the agreement. The grievance-arbitration clause defined a grievance as a dispute or complaint arising between the parties thereto under or out of the agreement with the interpretation, application, performance, termination or alleged breach thereof. Accordingly, it was more limited than the no-strike clause.

Coca Cola's drivers, who had been previously employed by another employer, could not negotiate a collective bargaining agreement with the company, and thus the drivers set up a picket line. The production and maintenance unit covered by the above-referenced contract clauses refused to cross the picket line, and the employer then filed a Section 301 damage action in federal district court. In a non-jury trial, the district court concluded that the work stoppage was a sympathy strike and that the no-strike clause waived the production and maintenance employees' right to engage in sympathy strikes and awarded damages. The Third Circuit reversed on this issue.

In an opinion authored by Chief Judge Seitz, the court referred back to its own precedent,[160] in which it had held that a general and broad arbitration clause—from which a no-strike commitment was implied[161]—was not explicit enough to waive the right to a sympathy strike. In these cases the court had relied upon the notion of coterminous interpretation, *i.e.*, if the subject matter of the strike was arbitrable, then the strike itself would violate the no-strike clause. This is a logical proposition, inasmuch as the no-strike obligation is derived from the arbitration clause itself. By definition, it is difficult to see how the no-strike pledge can be broader than the arbitration clause. Characterizing the coterminous interpretation idea in *Coca Cola,* the Third Circuit said that "[t]he theory underlying this is that the no-strike clause is a *quid pro quo* for the arbitration clause. . . . In short, the obligation to not strike is read to be an obligation not to strike over arbitrable issues."[162]

---

[160] *Id.* at 2778 (citing United Steelworkers v. NLRB, 536 F.2d 550, 555 (3d Cir. 1976); United States Steel Corp. v. UMW (U.S. Steel II), 548 F.2d 67 (3d Cir. 1976).

[161] The Supreme Court first accepted this notion of a no-strike obligation in Teamsters Local 174 v. Lucas Flour, 369 U.S. 95 (1962).

[162] Coca-Cola Bottling Co. v. Teamsters Local 326, 104 L.R.R.M. 2776, 2779

In *Coca Cola*, where there was an express no-strike clause, the court nevertheless decided to apply the same principles and relied, in part, upon the Supreme Court's *Buffalo Forge*[163] decision, which held that an injunction could not issue under Section 301 against a sympathy strike where there was no underlying grievance triggering the stoppage which itself was susceptible to resolution through the arbitration process. In *Buffalo Forge*, therefore, there was no *quid pro quo* between the arbitration and no-strike clauses. Said the Third Circuit, "The *quid pro quo* rationale underlying coterminous interpretation also applies where the union actually gives up its right to strike instead of having it implied from the arbitration clause."[164]

The court emphasized the fact that the *Buffalo Forge* opinion had used the *quid pro quo* theory to arrive at its conclusion. But as noted above in connection with my discussion of reliance upon *Buffalo Forge* in *Dow II*, *Buffalo Forge* was formulated with a view towards avoiding the policy prohibiting injunctions contained in Norris-La Guardia. The court said in this connection, "Normally, the employer will not agree to arbitration unless he gets an agreement from the union that it will not strike over those arbitrable issues. In addition, in the normal case the union will not agree to a no-strike clause that extends beyond the arbitration clause."[165] But this is not so. The Third Circuit provided no evidence at all in the form of contract clause studies to demonstrate its point. And if it had looked to contract language and, indeed, the decisions of arbitrators in interpreting no-strike clauses, it would have seen that the clauses frequently are not coterminous. The no-strike clause is often broader than the arbitration clause,[166] and arbitrators have not interpreted

---

(3d Cir. 1980). While the court has fashioned a doctrine of "coterminous application," it has recognized that the "two issues [arbitration provision and no-strike obligation] remain analytically distinct." Gateway Coal Co. v. United Mine Workers, 414 U.S. 368, 382 (1974).

[163] Buffalo Forge Co. v. United Steelworkers, 428 U.S. 397 (1976). I have criticized this decision in Gould, *On Labor Injunctions Pending Arbitration: Recasting Buffalo Forge*, 30 STAN. L. REV. 533 (1978). Much of my thinking in this area was first articulated in Gould, *On Labor Injunctions, Unions, and the Judges: The Boys Markets Case*, 1970 SUP. CT. REV. 215.

[164] Coca-Cola Bottling Co. v. Teamsters Local 1326, 104 L.R.R.M. 2776, 2779 (3d Cir. 1980).

[165] *Id.* at 2780.

[166] No-strike clauses appear in 92% of all agreements. Fifty-three percent of the clauses are unconditional bans on interference with production durirg the

labor contracts in the fashion utilized in *Coca Cola.*[167] Further, the court stated that the contract here supported coterminous interpretation. It relied upon the fact that the rights of the drivers were not protected by the agreement, and thus the underlying grievance could be dealt with through arbitration. Arbitration of the dispute presumably could be had, however—but only insofar as the no-strike issue itself was involved.

Finally, the court relied upon *Mastro Plastics* and the narrow reading given to a no-strike clause in that case. While referring to *Mastro Plastics,* the court stated that the contract "taken as a whole, dealt with the economic relations between the unfair labor practice strikers and their employer, such as wages, hours, and so forth. In effect, the no-strike clause was a promise by the union not to strike over matters covered by the contract."[168] But *Mastro Plastics* was not, as the court in *Coca Cola* indicated, a hurtful analogy, inasmuch as it excluded the subject matter from the no-strike clause (1) because of its nature and inability to resolve such problems through the arbitration process; (2) because public policy indicated that interference with employee free choice would preclude strikes over such matters.[169]

The Tenth Circuit also has had a recent opportunity to deal with the sympathy strike issue in *NLRB v. Gould, Inc.*[170] The no-strike clause stated that the union agreed "that there will be no strike, work interference, or other work stoppage. . . ."[171] But it was, in the court's view, "linked to the grievance arbitration machinery," inasmuch as the clause stated that the union had given its commitment "[i]n view of the procedure for the orderly settlement of grievances. . . ."[172] The case presented the question of whether a walkout triggered by informational pickets protesting the presence of a nonunion contractor violated the

---

life of the contract, while 39% are conditional bans which permit strikes under certain circumstances. *Reported in* COLLECTIVE BARGAINING: NEGOTIATIONS AND CONTRACTS: BASIC PATTERNS CLAUSE FINDER (BNA) 77:1 (1978).

[167] *See, e.g.,* Bucyrus-Erie Co., 69 LAB. ARB. REP. (BNA) 93 (1977); Sterling Regal, Inc., 69 LAB. ARB. REP. (BNA) 513 (1977); Southern Ohio Coal Co., 66 LAB. ARB. REP. (BNA) 446 (1976).

[168] Coca-Cola Bottling Co. v. Teamsters Local 326, 104 L.R.R.M. 2776, 2780 (3d Cir. 1980).

[169] *Id.*

[170] 105 L.R.R.M. 2778 (10th Cir. 1980).

[171] *Id.* at 2789.

[172] *Id.* at 2791.

no-strike clause. An arbitrator, considering the propriety of dismissal of employees who had participated in the strike, concluded that the no-strike clause waived the right to engage in sympathy strikes. The Board disagreed, and the Tenth Circuit affirmed its conclusions.[173]

The court, noting that no extrinsic evidence had been presented to prove that the no-strike clause prohibited sympathy strikes, concluded that it was unable to infer a waiver, inasmuch as the agreement did not expressly address the issue. The court stated that the language of the no-strike clause "suggests that if the dispute involving a strike is not subject to the grievance-arbitration machinery of the contract, the strike is not prohibited by the no-strike clause."[174] Although the Tenth Circuit, like the Third, drew support for its conclusion from *Buffalo Forge,* its opinion is essentially based on the peculiar contract language involved rather than the coterminous interpretation theory so vigorously expressed in *Coca Cola.* As such, the opinion in *Gould, Inc.* is a more defensible one.

Another case presenting the same issue is *Amcar Division, ACF Industries v. NLRB.*[175] Here the Eighth Circuit stated that in considering the question of whether a right to engage in sympathy strikes has been waived by a no-strike clause, the court must "look to the language of the contract, the bargaining history, and other relevant conduct of the parties that shows this understanding of the contract."[176] Although the Third and the Tenth Circuits take the same approach, it is clear that the Eighth Circuit's assessment of the no-strike clause language is quite different. Said the court, confronted with language which was more narrow than that contained in either *Coca Cola* or *Gould, Inc.*:

> [T]his [the no-strike clause] is insufficient, in and of itself, to constitute a waiver of the right to engage in sympathy strikes. . . . [A] number of cases have interpreted general no-strike clauses to preclude sympathy strikes. The broad language of this no-strike clause, when examined in light of the bargaining history . . . and the facts surrounding the parties' actions at issue here, indicate a clear waiver of the Union's right to engage in a sympathy strike.[177]

---

[173] *Id.* at 2792.
[174] *Id.* at 2791.
[175] 106 L.R.R.M. 2518 (8th Cir. 1981).
[176] *Id.* at 2522.
[177] *Id.*

This seems to me to be the sounder view. While broad contract language is not dispositive, it should create a presumption which, along with bargaining history and conduct of the parties, prohibits sympathy strikes. It properly rejects the coterminous interpretation approach, as well as the Board's refusal to consider other conduct, such as contemporaneous statements by union officials.

A final case in the no-strike arena involved a different issue. The Third Circuit was at work again in *Pittsburgh Steel Co. v. Steelworkers,*[178] where it dealt with a problem arising in the wake of the Supreme Court's *Carbon Fuel* decision.[179] *Pittsburgh Steel* involved the violation of a no-strike pledge in an agreement to which the International Union was a party. It raised the question of whether an order directing the parties to pursue a contractual arbitration remedy should be aimed at the International when the record demonstrated that it did not instigate, support, ratify or encourage the wildcat strike by the Local in question. Indeed, the record indicated that the International had actively opposed the strike and urged the local union members to return to work and arbitrate their grievances. The district court had directed injunctive relief against the International because, despite its opposition to the strike, the view of the court was that it could be ordered to take steps to end the stoppage.

In the first place, the court noted that this case, unlike *Carbon Fuel,* was not one in which the employer sought to obtain money damages from the International for the acts of members of the Local. The Third Circuit noted that the Court's *Carbon Fuel* holding had not answered the question raised here, *i.e.,* where damage liability is foreclosed by the stance of the International, may injunctive relief nevertheless be provided? The court stated that the law of prospective contract remedies was not so "stale" as to require a result that dictated that the union was immune from injunctive relief simply because it had not committed a breach which would make it liable in damages. Said Judge Seitz for the court, "When a court has a case before it justifying an injunction to prevent a breach of contract by a party to that contract, there must be authority to issue injunctive relief even

---

[178] 105 L.R.R.M. 2198 (3d Cir. 1980).
[179] Carbon Fuel Co. v. UMW, 444 U.S. 212 (1979) (international union not liable for wildcat strikes).

against third parties where such relief is necessary, or perhaps merely helpful, in effectuating the relief against the contracting party in default."[180] But under the circumstances the court held that injunctive relief was not appropriate, even though the International's "lack of culpability" was not a bar to injunctive relief in all cases. The Third Circuit stated that the district court had made no finding which would suggest that an order directing the International to take steps to end the strike would either be necessary or helpful. There was no basis for assuming that an order directed only against the Local and its offices would be disobeyed and no record that the Local had a history of defiance of the terms negotiated on its behalf by the International. The court said:

> There may be circumstances in which the district court should direct such a parent union to take affirmative steps in aid of a valid *Boys Markets* injunction. But we do not think any such order should be entered absent findings by the district court: (1) that its own order directed to the local union and its members will not be fully effective; (2) that the steps already taken by the International are not likely to be effective; and (3) that specific additional steps, carefully specified in the order, will add significantly to the deterrent effect of the injunction against the local and its members. Even when the court has made these findings it should still consider whether, in view of the inevitable intrusion upon the internal affairs of the union, the marginal potential increase in the effectiveness of the *Boys Markets* injunction is justified.[181]

C. Discipline of Union Stewards

The Eighth Circuit in *NLRB v. Armour-Dial, Inc.*[182] dealt with another issue which involves the policy of industrial peace and the no-strike clause—the lawfulness of employer discipline of union officials for involvement in stoppages in breach of contract. The Seventh and Third Circuits have previously reversed the Board and held that such discipline does not constitute unlawful discrimination because of union activity. The Seventh Circuit has stated that deterring union officials from engaging in unlawful conduct by discipline and, in so doing, imposing a greater degree of responsibility upon them for adherence to the

---

[180] Pittsburgh Steel Co. v. Steelworkers, 105 L.R.R.M. 2198, 2202 (3rd Cir. 1980).

[181] *Id.* at 2203.

[182] 106 L.R.R.M. 2265 (8th Cir. 1981).

no-strike clause is not tantamount to discouraging union members from holding union office and, therefore, does not have an unlawful "inherently adverse" effect on employee rights.[183] Similarly, the Third Circuit has concluded that no prejudice to employee rights can result from the deterrence of involvement in illegal activity and that more severe discipline may be imposed upon those individuals who have a special duty to provide compliance with the contract, *i.e.*, union officials.[184] The Third Circuit said, "It is certainly fair to assume that usually it is the steward or some other union official close to the scene who has the power, authority and influence most effectively to quash an illegal strike during its infancy or to prolong it indefinitely. The threat of his disciplinary discharge, therefore, is a valuable option which the employer should not be prohibited from exercising where it has been contractually acquired."[185] These decisions seem to make eminently good sense because they recognize the special responsibility that is thrust upon union stewards and are compatible with arbitration awards which have generally held that more severe sanctions may be imposed upon union officials who have a greater responsibility in terms of adherence to the no-strike clause.[186]

The Seventh and Third Circuits, however, have been careful to permit such penalties to be imposed only upon union stewards who actually participate in the unlawful conduct itself. What is somewhat troubling about the Eighth Circuit's opinion in *Armour-Dial* is that it held that participation in unlawful conduct can be inferred from the conduct of union representation in meetings between the union and the company. The Eighth Circuit opinion is probably correct on the facts of the

---

[183] Indiana & Mich. Elec. Co. v. NLRB, 599 F.2d 227 (7th Cir. 1979).

[184] Gould, Inc. v. NLRB, 612 F.2d 728 (3d Cir. 1979).

[185] *Id.* at 734. The Board seems to be modifying its previous position to the extent of requiring that the same penalty be imposed on unions where a violation is found against stewards as employees; *see* Miller Brewing Co., 254 N.L.R.B. No. 24 (1981); South Central Bell Tel. Co., 254 N.L.R.B. No. 32 (1981).

[186] Provisions limiting the union's liability for violation of a no-strike pledge appear in only 35% of collective bargaining agreements, and most of these require some form of positive action by the union in order to avoid liability (for example, attempts to get the employees to return to work or public disavowal of the strike). *Reported in* COLLECTIVE BARGAINING: NEGOTIATIONS AND CONTRACTS: BASIC PATTERNS CLAUSE FINDER (BNA) 77:4 (1978).

case, inasmuch as the union leadership did seem to promote the stoppage and boycott involved in that case. But it would be extremely dangerous and counterproductive to impose sanctions simply on the basis of participation in meetings and statements which could be characterized as posturing for the rank and file. The union officials who may be dedicated to compliance with the contract obligations frequently walk a difficult line in terms both of retaining a position of leadership in the rank and file and simultaneously dissuading them from illegal conduct. The Board and the courts must handle these problems with caution and sensitivity.

Bibliographic Essay on the Established Relationship Between Labor and Management

The Court of Appeals from the Sixth Circuit, in an opinion offered by Judge Peck, concluded that the coterminus interpretation of arbitration in most strike caluses is not to be applied to damage actions brought by employers under Section 301 of the Act.[1] The court held that the doctrine of coterminus interpretation has no applicability to collective bargaining agreements that contain explicit no-strike clauses. The doctrine of coterminus interpretation is to be restricted to injunction proceedings, said Judge Peck, noting that the Court's decision in *Buffalo Forge* and *Jacksonville Bulk Terminals* had assumed that the no-strike clause in those cases was violated by a strike over a nonarbitrable issue. Said the court: "When the no-strike clause is independent from the arbitration and grievance procedure provisions, however, no principle of contract interpretation requires limitation of the scope of the no-strike clause to matters covered by the contractually provided arbitration and grievance procedures."[2] The court also noted that the contract had excluded certain issues from the scope of the no-strike clause and that therefore it could be assumed that all other issues were covered by the broad no-strike provision, whether they were arbitrable or not arbitrable.

Judge Keith dissented in an opinion joined by Judge Edwards and Judge Jones relying upon what he viewed as the "vast weight of authority [to the effect that . . . an express waiver of the right to strike cannot be read in a vacuum."[3] Said Judge Keith: "A no-strike provision must be interpreted in light of the concomitant duty to arbitrate. It would be inimical to fundamental principles of labor relations to prohibit strikes in protest of matters which cannot be resolved through arbitration."[4]

In *Metropolitan Edison Co. v. NLRB*,[5] a unanimous Supreme Court held that an employer may not unilaterally define the actions a union official is required to take to enforce a no-strike clause and penalize him for his failure to comply where the contract does not provide such an obligation. Such sanctions imposed upon union officials, as opposed to others, would violate the anti-union discrimination prohibitions contained in the NLRA. The Court, speaking through Justice Powell, declared that unions and employers could secure the integrity of the no-strike clause by requiring affirmative steps on the part of union officials. But in this case the union had not waived its statutorily protected right to engage in protected activity—even though arbitrators had held, under the previous collective bargaining agreements with the same language, that union officials did indeed have an obligation to take affirmative steps. The Court concluded that two arbitration awards imposing a more burdensome duty upon union officials did not establish a pattern "clear enough to convert the union's silence (on this issue) into binding waver."[6]

NOTES

1. *Ryder Truck Lines v. the Teamsters Freight Local No. 480* 727 F.2d 594 (6th Cir. 1984)
    2. *Id.* at 600.
    3. *Id.* at 603.
    4. *Id.*
    5. 460 U.S. 693 (1983).
    6. *Id.* at 709.

10

Taft-Hartley Comes to Great Britain: Observations on the Industrial Relations Act of 1971

"It is not good for trade unions that they should be brought in contact with the courts, and it is not good for the courts."[1]

Sir Winston Churchill

"The unions should take the position squarely that they are amenable to law, prepared to take the consequences if they transgress, and thus show that they are in full sympathy with the spirit of our people whose political system rests upon the proposition that this is a government of law, and not of men."[2]

Mr. Justice Brandeis

On this silver anniversary of the enactment of the Taft-Hartley amendments to the National Labor Relations Act of 1935,[3] one no longer hears its provisions denounced, as they were, by the leaders of organized labor as a "slave labor" act. The Act, which made collective bargaining agreements enforceable in court,[4] prohibited sec-

This article benefited from the criticisms of Sir Geoffrey Howe, Solicitor General of the United Kingdom, Professor Cyril Grunfeld, Counsel to the Commission on Industrial Relations, and Professor Norman Selwyn, University of Aston, Birmingham, England. Of course, the views expressed are my own and should not be attributed to any of the individuals mentioned.

The author wishes to express gratitude to Lynn Coe, Harvard Law School, '72, and member of the State Bar of Washington, for his generous assistance.

1. TRADE UNION DOCUMENTS 380 (Milne-Bailey ed. 1929).
2. *Congressional Record*, Senate, April 20, 1947, quoted in 2 LEGISLATIVE HISTORY OF THE LABOR MANAGEMENT RELATIONS ACT, 1947, at 1145-46.
3. Labor Management Relations Act, 1947, ch. 120, §§ 101 *et seq.*, 61 Stat. 136 [hereinafter cited as LMRA or Taft-Hartley Act] *amending* The National Labor Relations Act, 1935, ch. 372, §§ 1-16, 45 Stat. 449 [hereinafter cited as NLRA]. The NLRA has been further amended by The Labor-Management Reporting and Disclosure Act of 1959, Pub. L. No. 86-257, §§ 1 *et seq.*, 73 Stat. 519. These statutes are codified at 29 U.S.C. §§ 141 *et seq.* (1970). Compare the silver anniversary discussion of Raskin, *Taft-Hartley at 25; How It's Worked*, N.Y. Times, June 18, 1972, at 1 with views of George Meany, President of the AFL-CIO, *id.*
4. LMRA § 301, 29 U.S.C. § 185 (1970).

ondary boycotts[5] and closed shops,[6] placed authority in the Attorney General to sue to enjoin for an eighty-day period strikes which created a national emergency,[7] was anathema to the unions. When Adlai Stevenson, making the first of two losing passes at the presidency, repudiated past Democratic Party pledges, and stated that he would not repeal Taft-Hartley but would only propose its amendment,[8] he was the first Northern leader of his party to state the unthinkable, and not merely think it. The United States would never again seriously contemplate turning away from the legal regulation of trade unions in a modern interdependent economy.

What is particularly significant in this regard is trade union acceptance of the role of law in industrial relations and the labor movement's acquiescence in the propriety of some portions of Taft-Hartley as representing something quite different from a return to the bad old days which trade unionists legitimately fear. To be sure, some of the provisions adopted by the 80th Congress in 1947 still rankle—and quite properly so.[9] But organized labor in the United States is alive and well. To the extent that it has problems in organizing the unorganized, the primary blame lies with the unions themselves,[10] not with the law.

Far from evolving into repressive legislation, much of Taft-Hartley is of benefit to American trade unions. Nothing was more responsible for the "slave labor" charge than the emergency strike provisions of Taft-Hartley. Yet today, trade union leaders advocate retention of existing Taft-Hartley procedures in this area, and propose their application to public employment labor disputes.[11] Because of the comprehensiveness of the statute's unfair labor practice provisions,

---

5. NLRA § 8(6) 4(B), 29 U.S.C. § 158(b)(4)(B) (1970).
6. NLRA §§ 8(a)(3), (b)(4), 29 U.S.C. §§ 158(a)(3), (b)(4) (1970).
7. LMRA §§ 206-10, 29 U.S.C. §§ 176-80 (1970).
8. Actually, after receiving the Democratic nomination, Governor Stevenson retreated to the rhetoric of repeal, but his speeches and press conference comments reveal acceptance of some of Taft-Hartley's provisions. *See* A. STEVENSON, MAJOR CAMPAIGN SPEECHES OF ADLAI E. STEVENSON 1952, at 46, 157; N.Y. Times, July 31, 1952, at 9.
9. NLRA § 14(b), 29 U.S.C. § 164(b) (1970) permits states to prohibit any union security arrangement requiring membership or the payment of dues to the collective bargaining representative and, accordingly, precludes labor and management from making their own agreement on this subject and weakens the union as a bargaining entity. Further, some of the limitations on organizational and recognitional picketing dull union organization weaponry which are a legitimate part of the arsenal. *See, e.g.,* 29 U.S.C. § 158(b) (1970).
10. One proof of this proposition is the continued growth of the International Brotherhood of Teamsters against whom most of Taft-Hartley is aimed. *See* R. JAMES & E. JAMES, HOFFA AND THE TEAMSTERS 143-58 (1965). The Teamsters succeed simply because they do the best job of organizing workers. On weaknesses plaguing American unions, *see generally* S. BARKIN, THE DECLINE OF THE LABOR MOVEMENT (1961).
11. *See* T. Kheel, *Report to Speaker Anthony J. Travia on the Taylor Law,* Feb. 21, 1968, which was met by favorable trade union reaction.

the doctrine of pre-emption has ousted the states' jurisdiction over a wide variety of problems relating to strikes and picketing and thus removed the potential for large awards of compensatory and punitive damages against unions.[12] When it comes to the enforcement of collective agreements, it is the unions, supposedly the objects of discipline for their irresponsible failure to abide by contractual obligations, which have been plaintiffs in the overwhelming majority of court proceedings and grievants in most of the arbitrations.[13]

Last year, the British Parliament passed the first comprehensive legislation relating to labor management relations in the United Kingdom. The legislation attempted to both restrict union abuses in the collective bargaining arena and provide statutory protection for unions and employees. The Industrial Relations Act of 1971, which is more comprehensive than all of the major labor legislation enacted by Congress in 1935, 1947 and 1959 viewed together,[14] establishes a wide variety of unfair industrial practices applicable to both unions and employers,[15] prohibits the "unfair" dismissal of employees,[16] introduces an obligation requiring employers to bargain with an exclusive or "sole" bargaining representative[17] and prohibits the right to strike in a number of contexts. It makes collective agreements legally enforceable for the first time,[18] and it puts great pressure on the unions to "register"[19] with the government, and thereby to specify which union officers shall be liable for breaches of collective contracts and of statutory obligations. An abiding theme of the Act is the encouragement of central union authority which, in turn, will be more attuned to responsibilty and orderliness in its dealings with employers.[20]

Thus, from an almost exclusive reliance on "voluntarism," *i.e.*, the promotion of negotiating procedures drawing at most indirectly upon law, Great Britain has now imposed upon the conduct of unions and

12. *See* Garner v. Teamsters Local 66, 346 U.S. 485 (1953); San Diego Bldg. Trades Council v. Garmon, 359 U.S. 236 (1959); Teamsters Local 20 v. Morton, 377 U.S. 252 (1964). *But see* Internat'l Union v. Russell, 356 U.S. 634 (1958); United Constr. Workers v. Laburnum Constr. Corp., 347 U.S. 656 (1954).

13. *See, e.g.*, Aaron, *Judicial Intervention in Labor Arbitration*, 20 STAN. L. REV. 41 (1967).

14. See note 3 *supra*. On American and European labor law generally see Summers, *American and European Labor Law: the Use and Usefulness of Foreign Experience*, 16 BUFFALO L. REV. 210 (1966).

15. Industrial Relations Act 1971, c72 [hereinafter cited as Ind. Rela. Act 1971], §§ 5, 13(2), 16, 22, 33(3), 36, 54, 55, 66, 70, 96-98, 130. I have discussed the Conservative Government Industrial Relations Bill prior to amendment in Gould, *Unions on a Legal Leash*, The Guardian Weekly (Manchester) Jan. 23, 1971, at 7, col. 1.

16. Ind. Rela. Act 1971, §§ 22-26.

17. Ind. Rela. Act 1971, §§ 50, 55.

18. Ind. Rela. Act 1971, § 34.

19. *See* pp. 1437-40 *infra*.

20. *See, e.g.*, Ind. Rela. Act 1971, § 36(2).

employers more formal and far-reaching regulations than those characterizing the U.S. system, a system which British experts traditionally regarded as excessively law-ridden. Moreover, where the U.S. system represents a gradual accretion of statutory and ever-changing case law, and where gradualness has allowed labor and management here to adapt to the system, the British have attempted an abrupt, mammoth, one-step codification. The suddenness of change contributed to causing political and social upheaval. The summer of 1972 in Great Britain was one of nearly unprecedented bitterness and tumult. Not since the Conservative Government's repeal of the Trade Disputes Union Act of 1913 in 1927, and the Labor Government's repeal of the 1927 law in 1946, has labor law figured so prominently in the national political arena.[21] Not since the General Strike of 1926 has Britain moved so near a total collapse of civility.[22] While government ineptness in administering the statute, an unfavorable judicial ruling,[23] and ever-worsening unemployment and inflation have aggravated the turmoil, the hard feeling arising out of the summer's railway and dock strikes is largely attributable to the Act itself. Although some prominent beneficial by-products of statutory intervention in industrial relations are already visible—*i.e.*, an accord between labor and management establishing a conciliation and arbitration service[24]—the unions remain totally committed to avoiding all involvement with the Act's institutions and, along with the British Labor Party, to pressing for repeal of the statute.[25] The jailing of five dockers for contempt of court[26]

21. The Conservative Party, however, had spoken of repealing the Labor Party's 1946 repeal. *See* H. LASKI, TRADE UNIONS IN THE NEW SOCIETY 57 (1950).

22. See the worried comments of both Lord Devlin and the London Times: Devlin, *Politics and the Law: A Matter of Judgment,* The Sunday Times (London), August 6, 1972, at 14, col. 2; *Yes, We Are In Danger,* The Times (London), July 28, 1972, at 17, col. 1.

23. *See* the Court of Appeal's decision in Heaton's Transport Ltd. v. Transport and General Workers Union, [1972] 2 All E.R. 1237 which was, however, reversed by the House of Lords, [1972] 3 All E.R. 101. For some of the pessimistic commentary that followed the Court of Appeal's decision *see* Hanna, *Two Ways to Salvage Union Law,* The Sunday Times (London) June 25, 1972, at 57; Elliott, *Industrial Relations After Two Big Tests in Court,* The Financial Times (London) June 14, 1972, at 16, col. 3.

24. *See* Routledge, *Employers Sign Deal With TUC for Independent Conciliation,* The Times (London), August 3, 1972, at 1, col. 1; Howell, *TUC and CBI Unveil Joint Peace Service,* The Financial Times (London), August 3, 1972, at 1, col. 6.

25. *See* LABOUR PARTY, STATEMENT ON INDUSTRIAL RELATIONS (1972). This has been said to set "the terms of the Labour Party's total surrender to the demands of its trade union paymasters." Wood, *Trade Union Rights, But No Duties,* The Times (London) July 31, 1972, at 13, col. 1. See also Rogers, *TUC and Labour Plans to Replace I.R. Act,* Financial Times (London) July 28, 1972, at 7, col. 4. For an account of recent trade union strategy against the Act, *see* pp. 1485-86 *infra.*

26. Midland Cole Storage Ltd. v. Turner and Others, The Times (London), July 22, 1972, at 31, col. 1. *See also* Jacobs, *Dockers Caught In The Act,* The Sunday Times (London), July 23, 1972, at 12, col. 1; Shuster, *Angry British Workers Testing New Labor Law,* N.Y. Times, July 24, 1972, at 3, col. 5; Shuster, *Heath, Unions Adamant as British Strikes*

may be just the beginning of a long struggle between a trade union movement, both obstinately resistant to the law and anxious for political combat with Prime Minister Heath and a Conservative Government determined to make good on election promises given in 1970 and before.[27]

This article does not purport to explain, or to apportion blame for, Britain's current industrial crisis. Compared to the peaceful acceptance by American unions of legal innovation in the labor-management field, the British crisis will afford intriguing parallels and contrasts in years to come for sociologists, political scientists, and historians. The task here, however, is a more modest one: to examine those provisions of the British Industrial Relations Act which resemble, in language or function, important provisions of the National Labor Relations Act in the United States. British critics and advocates of the Act all borrowed heavily,[28] though not always accurately,[29] from the American experience, and the Act can fairly be regarded as a highly selective transplant of American labor law. This article highlights the selections which were made and considers their wisdom in light of peculiar British traditions and problems.

The First Section gives the American reader a very brief, and necessarily incomplete, tour of British labor law and labor management practice prior to passage of the Industrial Relations Act. The Second Section introduces some of the novel institutions and concepts created by or used in the Industrial Relations Act. The Third, and main, Section discusses central issues raised by the Act upon which the American experience supplies provocative comment: (a) The Recognition of Union Bargaining Units and the Establishment of Collective Bargaining, (b) Union Security Arrangements, (c) The Enforcement of Collective Agreements and the Right to Strike, (d) The Secondary Boycott Problem, and (e) Emergency Dispute Procedures.

Spread, N.Y. Times, July 25, 1972, at 3, col. 1; Shuster, *Britain Facing Industrial Paralysis in Labor Dispute*, N.Y. Times, July 26, 1972, at 1, col. 5; Shuster, *Wide Strike Peril Eased in Britain*, N.Y. Times, July 27, 1972, at 1, col. 1. Apparently there was discussion in TUC quarters about not only a one day general strike against the dockers' jailing, but also a general strike against the Act. *See* Paterson, *1926 and All That*, NEW STATESMAN, Aug. 4, 1972, at 150.

27. *See, e.g.*, FAIR DEAL AT WORK: THE CONSERVATIVE APPROACH TO INDUSTRIAL RELATIONS (1968); Carr, *The Unions: What the Tories Would Put in Place of Strike*, The Sunday Times (London) June 22, 1969, at 12, col. 1; Clark, *Union Chiefs Challenged by Heath*, The Times (London) April 7, 1970, at 1, col. 2. For a discussion of the contending points of view on the eve of the 1970 election, *see* Gould, Book Review, 48 TEXAS L. REV. 987 (1970).

28. *See, e.g.*, P. LOWRY, THE GRASS IS GREENER (1970).

29. *See*, for instance, the comments of former Prime Minister Harold Wilson as reported in Lewis, *Commons Backs Plan to Reform Labor Relations*, N.Y. Times, Dec. 16, 1970, at 1, col. 1. *See also* 810 PARL. DEB. H.C. 839 (1971) (comments of Eric Heffer).

I. The Background and Setting

Until 1971, law played a remarkably small role in the British system of industrial relations. The state intervened, with some exceptions, only to provide a floor—in terms of wages, safety, health, etc.—below which employees could not be forced. The rules of the game between labor and management were written, and refereed, by the parties themselves. It was, as Professor Kahn-Freund has said, a system of *"collective laissez-faire."*[30]

At one time, however, the British interfered on a large scale with the employer-employee relationship in a manner which repressed workers and which favored the entrepreneurial class. These policies can be traced to the Black Death of the Fourteenth Century, when a badly shaken economy prompted adoption of the Statute of Laborers[31] to impose criminal and civil liability upon employees who, taking advantage of a shortage of labor, refused to accept "pre-plague prices." As Dean Landis has noted, the aim of such measures was to "strike at the individual bargaining power" of the workers involved.[32] Similarly, in placing the Combination Acts of 1799 and 1800[33] on the books, Parliament was not the least bit bashful (albeit sometimes quite unsuccessful[34]) about attempting to thwart the first stumbling efforts to establish something akin to what we now call the collective bargaining

30. To Professor Kahn-Freund,

   collective laissez-faire [means] . . . allowing free play to the collective forces of society, and limiting the intervention of the law to those marginal areas in which the disparity of these forces, that is, in our case, the force of organized labour and of organized management, is so great as to prevent the successful operation of what is characteristically called 'negotiating machinery.' It so happens that in this country, this principle of, if you like, 'collective laissez-faire' comes to be a preponderant characteristic of labor law of the first half of this century.

O. KAHN-FREUND, LABOUR LAW (reprint), p. 224. The system has, however, permitted more legal intervention than Professor Kahn-Freund's comments would lead one to believe. Prompted by the emergency of World War II, compulsory arbitration in the last resort existed between 1940 and 1951. *See generally* McCarthy, *Compulsory Arbitration in Britain: The Work of the Industrial Disputes Tribunal*, 31, RESEARCH PAPERS No. 8, ROYAL COMMISSION ON TRADE UNIONS AND EMPLOYERS ASSOCIATIONS (1968). McKelvey, *Compulsory Arbitration in Britain*, 37 CORNELL L.Q. 403 (1952). However, as Professor Kahn-Freund has said: "[I]n so far as it worked at all, it worked as a result of this understanding, and one government after another emphasized that it would be terminated if either side of industry desired this. Without this political background the system cannot be understood." O. KAHN-FREUND, LABOUR AND THE LAW 116-17 (1972).
   31. Statute of Labourers, 25 Edw. 3, Stat. 1 (1350) confirming the emergency Ordinance of Labourers, 23 Edw. 3 (1349).
   32. J. LANDIS AND M. MANOFF, CASES ON LABOR LAW 2-3 (2d ed. 1942).
   33. Combinations of Workmen Act, 39 & 40 Geo. 3, c.81 (1799); Combinations of Workmen Act, 39 & 40 Geo. 3, c.106 (1800).
   34. *See* S. WEBB & B. WEBB, THE HISTORY OF TRADE UNIONISM (2d ed. 1920). As one authority summarized: "The Act of 1800 was in reality the last prop of the already decayed wage-fixing system, and while it achieved its object of crushing workers' trade unions in some trades, it was ineffectual to prevent combinations, either of workmen or masters in other." M. HICKLING, CITRINE'S TRADE UNION LAW 6 (3rd ed. 1967).

process. These statutes were repealed in 1824 and 1825, thus making the mere combination of workers no longer illegal (although the right to strike was curtailed by the 1825 statute). But, in Britain, as in the United States,[35] the courts subsequently used the law of conspiracy to impose both tort and criminal liability upon workers bold enough to resort to economic pressures against employers with whom they could not resolve their differences.[36] Such liability was eliminated in Britain by the Conspiracy and Protection of Property Act of 1875,[37] the Trade Union Act of 1871[38] (which declared that a trade union was not an unlawful restraint of trade for criminal or civil purposes), and the Trades Disputes Act of 1906.[39]

Although narrowed by recent House of Lords rulings,[40] the 1906 statute became the cornerstone of trade union legislation in Britain. Not only did it make the civil law of conspiracy inapplicable to labor disputes,[41] but it also legalized peaceful picketing and the calling of strikes and supposedly conferred immunity from court actions on anyone who induced an individual to break his contract of employment in the context of a "trade dispute."[42]

---

35. For a review of this early use of the law of conspiracy see C. GREGORY, CASES AND MATERIALS ON LABOR LAW 3-79 (1941).
36. *Id.* For a brief and interesting discussion of this history see O. KAHN-FREUND, LABOUR AND THE LAW 167-72 (1972).
37. Conspiracy and Protection of Property Act, 38 & 39 Vict., c.86 (1875).
38. The Trade Union Act of 1871, 34 & 35 Vict., c.31.
39. Trades Disputes Act, 6 Edw. 7, c.47 (1906). The Act was prompted by Taff Vale Railway Co. v. Amalgamated Society of Railway Servants [1901] A.C. 426. Moreover, while the criminal law as a means to control the strike was discouraged by the 1875 statute, the judiciary then turned its attention to tort law. For the discriminatory attitude of the House of Lords, see Quinn v. Leathem, [1901] A.C. 495; Allen v. Flood, [1898] A.C. 1. An excellent treatment of the British legal tradition in this respect is contained in C. GRUNFELD, MODERN TRADE UNION LAW 386-404 (1966).
40. *See, e.g.,* Rookes v. Barnard, [1964] A.C. 1129; Stratford & Son, Ltd. v. Lindley, [1965] A.C. 269. *See also* Torquay Hotel Co. v. Cousins, [1969] 2 Ch. 106 (C.A.). Subsequent to the House of Lords' decision in *Rookes,* the newly elected Labour Government attempted to reverse some of its effects through the Trades Disputes Act of 1965, c.48 (repealed by Ind. Rela. Act 1971, sched. 9). Earlier judicial intervention of a different kind was countenanced by the House of Lords in Bonsor v. Musicians Union, [1956] A.C. 104. Meanwhile, comprehensive legislative proposals were developing. *See, e.g., A New Law for Trades Unions? Some Proposals for Reform,* Economist (London), Feb. 8, 1964, at 482, col. 1; *An Industrial Peace Board,* Economist (London), Oct. 6, 1962, at 21, col. 1.
41. Trades Disputes Act, 6 Edw. 7, c.47 (1906). *Cf.* Crofter Hand Woven Harris Tweed Co. v. Veitch, [1942] A.C. 435. *Compare* United Mine Workers v. Pennington, 381 U.S. 657 (1965); Local Union No. 189, Amalgamated Meat Cutters v. Jewel Tea Co., 381 U.S. 676 (1965); Allen Bradley Co. v. Local Union No. 3, IBEW, 325 U.S. 797 (1945); U.S. v. Hutcheson, 312 U.S. 219 (1940). *Allen Bradley* demarcates the line of self interest for unions under American labor law as does *Crofter* in British labor law. For further clarification of the British view see Huntley v. Thornton, [1957] 1 W.L.R. 321 (Q.B. 1956); Scala Ballroom Ltd. v. Ratcliffe, [1958] 1 W.L.R. 105.
42. The 1906 act protected picketing so long as the conduct was peaceful. Trades Disputes Act, 6 Edw. 7, c.47, § 2. The question of what constitutes peaceful picketing can be troublesome. *See* Tynan v. Palmer, [1967] Q.B. 91 (1966); Piddington v. Bates, [1961] 1 W.L.R. 162 (Q.B. 1960). Under both the 1906 and 1971 acts, producer picketing

The Trades Disputes Act of 1906 was the Magna Charta of the British labor movement. The American labor movement was still to go through the *Danbury Hatters*[43] experience of coping with anti-trust damages imposed for the use of secondary boycotts deemed to be in "restraint of trade."[44] Also, the American judicially enunciated doctrine of "unlawful objectives," whereby judge-made law permitted the assessment of damages in instances where economic pressure departed from what was philosophically acceptable to the courts, was yet to reach its zenith.[45] Not until 1932, with passage of the Norris-LaGuardia Act,[46] were the American unions successful in dismantling the federal judiciary's policy of indiscriminate and one-sided involvement in labor disputes.

In comparing the two countries, it is important to understand that by the 1930's American unions were unwilling and indeed unable to settle for the same live-and-let-live bargain which British unions struck in 1906 and adhered to for more than half a century. In Britain the unions had gained industrial power before they were able to assert their will in the political arena. Accordingly, they were fully content for the law to stay out of their affairs: They did not require parliamentary assistance at the bargaining table, and they feared that Parliament would not be an entirely friendly partner. For the emerging CIO unions, by contrast, legislative help was vital, and available. Fierce employer resistance, lack of solidarity amongst workers, rampant unemployment in the Great Depression, the struggle of the newly born unions to organize mass production industries from scratch—all these factors made affirmative legal protection seem imperative to the American labor movement. The result was the National Labor Relations Act, with its list of employer unfair labor practices and its obligation on management to bargain with an exclusive bargaining agent representing a majority of workers in an "appropriate unit."[47] The statutory scheme, of course, was at variance with the "hands off" policy

is not protected. *Compare* NLRB v. Local 760, Fruit and Vegetable Packers, 377 U.S. 58 (1964). Under the 1971 act, picketing at an individual's home is not immunized from suit. Ind. Rela. Act 1971, § 134(1)(b). Although Congress has seriously limited the right to picket in this country, NLRA § 8(b)(7), 29 U.S.C. § 158(b)(7) (1970), the First Amendment protects it to some extent. Teamsters Local 695 v. Vogt, Inc., 354 U.S. 284 (1957); Thornhill v. Alabama, 310 U.S. 88 (1940). Where a strike is unlawful, picketing to support it in this country is condemned. The question is somewhat unclear in Britain. *See* Hamilton, *Picketing Law to be Brought in Fine Focus by Court*, The Times (London), June 22, 1972, at 1, col. 3.

43. Loewe v. Lawlor, 208 U.S. 274 (1908).
44. *Id.* at 292-93.
45. *See, e.g.,* Duplex Printing Press Co. v. Deering, 254 U.S. 443 (1921).
46. Norris-LaGuardia Act of 1932, 47 Stat. 70 (1932), 29 U.S.C. §§ 101-64 (1970).
47. NLRA §§ 8, 9(a), 29 U.S.C. §§ 158, 159(a) (1970).

of the Norris-LaGuardia Act, and with the same bias in the British Trades Disputes Act of 1906.[48]

Owing their economic success to power rather than law, and relying safely on the pride and prejudice of British "class" distinctions,[49] British trade unions have, through the Trades Union Congress (the rough equivalent of the AFL-CIO in this country), continued to express unyielding hostility toward any legal restraint upon trade union activity. Enjoying relative success in organizing workers eligible for membership in existing unions,[50] the TUC has recognized little need for legislative aid. It is thus entirely unremarkable that the British labor movement has adopted a policy of "non-cooperation" with the Industrial Relations Act.[51]

But the TUC's adherence to "collective laissez-faire," a position once widely shared by the public, has placed it out of step politically[52] and has, arguably, injured the prospects of its ally, the British Labor Party. Public pressure for legal intervention in labor-management relations has been building for some time. A compulsory arbitration system was in force during World War II. Further, the Terms and Conditions of Employment Act of 1959[53] provided for the imposition upon a resisting management of the terms of a "relevant" bargaining agree-

48. More than a decade ago, Professor Kahn-Freund said of the British unions: "Does not their . . . unwillingness . . . to invoke the help of the law which, as is well known, the American unions found to be of the greatest assistance, demonstrate how much the aversion against State Intervention in industrial relations, how much in particular union preference for industrial rather than political or legislative action, dominate the impact of public opinion on the development of labour law in our time?" O. KAHN-FREUND, LABOUR LAW (reprint) 229.

49. *See generally* C. CROSLAND, THE FUTURE OF SOCIALISM (1956); Kessler, Britain's Docks and Henry Higgins, Wall St. J., Aug. 1, 1972, at 8, col. 3.

50. As of 1965, 28.5% of the non-agricultural employed labor force were union members in the U.S. while 38.7% were organized in England, D. BOK & J. DUNLOP, LABOR AND THE AMERICAN COMMUNITY, 49 (1970) (note caveat at 49 as to problems with statistical comparison of union membership among countries due to different standards of measurement); for a comprehensive study of the growth patterns of British trade unionism see G. Bain, *Trade Union Growth and Recognition*, RESEARCH PAPERS NO. 6, ROYAL COMMISSION ON TRADE UNIONS AND EMPLOYERS' ASSOCIATIONS (1967).

51. For representative accounts of the TUC's reaction, see Routledge, *TUC Letter Sets Union Style to Resist Registration*, The Times (London) Sept. 24, 1971, at 3, col. 1; Elliott, *TUC to Tell Unions Still on Register to Leave Congress*, The Financial Times (London), August 22, 1972, at 1, col. 3; Wigham, *Time Ripe for T.U.C. to Reconsider its Policy*, The Times (London) May 23, 1972, at 23, col. 1; Macbeath, *Politics of Resistance to the Unions Act*, The Times (London), Aug. 6, 1971, at 12, col. 1; Raskin, *Britain Goes Through Taft-Hartley Pains*, N.Y. Times, June 16, 1969, at 42, col. 3. The TUC has now stated that unions may appear before the Industrial Relations Court to defend themselves, *i.e.*, where an "offensive action" is being taken against a union. GENERAL COUNCIL, REPORT TO THE 104TH ANNUAL TRADES UNION CONGRESS 86-87 (1972); Murray, *Mr. Jack Jones is Shattered by Disloyalty to TUC Policy of Boycotting the Industrial Act*, The Times (London) May 1, 1972, at 2, col. 1; Hamilton, *Union's Appeal Over Dismissal First Before New Tribunal*, The Times (London) May 4, 1972, at 4, col. 1.

52. *See generally* Pickles, *Trade Unions in the Political Climate*, in INDUSTRIAL RELATIONS, CONTEMPORARY PROBLEMS AND PERSPECTIVES (B.C. Roberts ed. 1962).

53. Terms & Conditions of Employment Act, 7 & 8 Eliz. 2, c.26 (1959).

ment and for incorporation of those terms in each worker's individual contract of employment, the "relevant" agreement usually being read as the pattern of practice in the industry involved.[54] The 1959 Act was for the benefit of unions and employees,[55] and the TUC accepted it for that reason, but the Act represents a clear breach of the spirit of "collective laissez-faire" which the unions now invoke. Indeed, to have the substance of a collective agreement dictated by an outside body is so inconsistent with voluntarism that it would not generally be tolerated in the seemingly more legally regulated American system.[56]

In 1959, therefore, labor's resistance to state interference gave way to self-interest. This may partly explain why public opinion now shows little sympathy for the trade union position. At any rate, the public now appears convinced that the traditional, unregulated manner of resolving trade disputes produces wasteful strikes and inflationary wage settlements which Britain's foreign-trade-sensitive economy cannot safely tolerate. Whether, and by how much, Britain's peculiar labor-management procedures aggravate the inflation rate, retard the growth rate, and worsen the foreign payments imbalance are matters of dispute among economists.[57] But, beyond question, Britain's procedures are less organized, more acrimonious—at least in key export industries—and considerably more complicated than America's. In no other country is trade union structure as deeply plagued with the consequences of history. Without legislative rationalization, Britain's crazy-quilt multi-union structure has grown like Topsy, small craft unions formed in the mid-19th Century coexisting with large general unions arising from the New Unionism of the 1880's and cutting across industries as well as jobs.[58] All this contrasts sharply with the United States where

54. *Id.* § 8.

55. In addition, of course, employers who have entered into collective agreements through negotiations have an obvious self-interest in protecting themselves against "sweated" or substandard conditions.

56. NLRA § 8(d), 29 U.S.C.A. 158(d) (1970), while defining the obligation imposed on employers and employee representatives, specifically provides that "such obligation does not compel either party to agree to a proposal or require the making of a concession . . . ." *See* NLRB v. American National Insurance Co., 343 U.S. 395 (1952). *Cf.* General Electric Co., 150 N.L.R.B. No. 36 (1964), *enforced*, 418 F.2d 736 (2d Cir. 1969), *cert. denied*, 397 U.S. 965 (1970).

57. The relationship between union negotiated economic packages and inflation is a matter of considerable debate. *See, e.g.,* H.A. CLEGG, HOW TO RUN AN INCOMES POLICY AND WHY WE MADE SUCH A MESS OF THE LAST ONE (1971); F. W. PAISH, RISE AND FALL OF INCOME POLICY (1971); O.E.C.D. THE PROBLEM OF RISING PRICES (1961); Dale, *As Phase III Approaches: The Virtuous Circle or . . . The Vicious Circle,* N.Y. Times, August 27, 1972 (Magazine), at 12.

58. Britain's trade union structure is messy because there are a relatively large number of unions competing for members and because many unions are not organized along any definable industrial or skill lines, and thus represent different interest groups in different industries. *See* H. A. CLEGG, THE SYSTEM OF INDUSTRIAL RELATIONS IN GREAT BRITAIN 41-47 (1970); A. BRIGGS, *Social Background,* THE SYSTEM OF INDUSTRIAL RELATIONS

industrial unionism is well accepted, the CIO unions of the 1930's having grown within the mold of the National Labor Relations Act and according to its principles relating to representation.

In addition, Britain's post-World War II full employment economy substantially eroded the collective bargaining authority previously held by national trade union leaderships. As employers competed for scarce labor—particularly in southeast England and the Midlands, the areas of Britain's economic growth during this period—they began to yield to the demands of unorganized "work groups" and shop stewards. Power began to shift from the national leadership, which was short of staff and technical assistance, to the sub-plant level, where shop steward committees assumed de facto influence, although some had no responsibility to any of the unions which were theoretically authorized to bargain.[59] Bargaining predictably became fragmented: Management neglected to weigh the implications of the bargain for employees in other sections of the plant. Within the plant, employees represented by rival unions and/or work groups had every incentive to agitate for relative gains, regardless of productivity considerations.[60]

The result was that industry-wide negotiations, traditionally a major feature of the British industrial relations topography, became the forum at which only minimum conditions were set, the important

IN GREAT BRITAIN (A. Flanders & H. A. Clegg eds. 1954); O. KAHN-FREUND, *Legal Framework*, *id.*; Hughes, *Trade Union Structure and Government*, RESEARCH PAPERS No. 5, ROYAL COMMISSION ON TRADE UNIONS AND EMPLOYERS' ASSOCIATIONS (1967). This is attributable to the proliferation of small craft unions in the previous century, which were challenged but not entirely displaced by general and militant unions. *See* H. A. CLEGG, A. FOX, and A. F. THOMPSON, A HISTORY OF BRITISH TRADE UNIONS SINCE 1889 55-96 (1964); THE TRADE UNION SITUATION IN THE UNITED KINGDOM, REPORT OF A MISSION FROM THE INTERNATIONAL LABOR OFFICE 11-26 (1961). The contemporary weakness of national union organization also has historical antecedents. *See generally* L. ULMAN, THE RISE OF NATIONAL UNIONS (1960). The branch unions which evolved were less firmly knit to the center as are local structures in the United States. Hughes, *supra*. For the American situation, *see generally* L. SAYLES & G. STRAUSS, THE LOCAL UNION (rev. ed. 1967). This comparative weakness in formal union structure has provided British employers with more unilateral rule-making authority than is the case in the United States. *See* O. KAHN-FREUND, LABOUR AND THE LAW 128 (1972).

59. REPORT: OF A COURT OF INQUIRY INTO THE CAUSES AND CIRCUMSTANCES OF A DISPUTE BETWEEN THE FORD MOTOR COMPANY, LIMITED, DAGENHAM AND MEMBERS OF THE TRADE UNIONS REPRESENTED ON THE TRADE UNION SIDE OF THE FORD NATIONAL JOINT NEGOTIATING COMMITTEE, CMND. No. 1999 (1963); *see generally* H.A. CLEGG, A. KILLICK & R. ADAMS, TRADE UNION OFFICERS (1961); McCarthy, *The Role of Shop Stewards*, RESEARCH PAPERS No. 1, ROYAL COMMISSION ON TRADE UNIONS AND EMPLOYERS' ASSOCIATIONS (1967); McCarthy and Parker, *Shop Stewards and Workshop Relations*, RESEARCH PAPERS No. 10, ROYAL COMMISSION ON TRADE UNIONS AND EMPLOYERS' ASSOCIATIONS (1968). The automobile industry poses some of the most troublesome problems in this regard. See the treatment provided labor-management relations in this industry in H. TURNER, F. CLACK & G. ROBERTS, LABOUR RELATIONS IN THE MOTOR INDUSTRY (1967); Ensor, *Why Car-Plant Militancy is on the Increase*, The Financial Times (London), Sept. 5, 1972, at 16, col. 3.

60. *See* A. FLANDERS, INDUSTRIAL RELATIONS: WHAT IS WRONG WITH THE SYSTEM? AN ESSAY ON ITS THEORY AND FUTURE (1965); A. FLANDERS, COLLECTIVE BARGAINING: PRESCRIPTION FOR CHANGE (1967).

bargains being struck informally on the factory floor. This contrasts with the United States, where formalized plant-level bargaining is the rule and where, even in the case of industry or company-wide bargaining, specific supplemental agreements are often negotiated for a particular plant. The British pattern also fails to involve national union officials in local plant bargaining to the extent common in the United States or to require that negotiated contracts meet the approval of national headquarters, a practice common in the United States. This British "organizational gap," as Professor Stieber has called it,[61] encourages guerrilla type industrial strife, involving multiple stoppages of short duration.[62]

Also virtually unknown in the United Kingdom, though common in America, are detailed collective agreements relating not only to employment conditions and benefits but also to grievance machinery. Further, American agreements often provide for binding arbitration of grievances by an impartial third party;[63] this is almost never the case in Britain. While arbitration has by no means eliminated unauthorized stoppages or strikes in breach of contract in the United States, the fact that a dismissed or abused employee, and his co-workers, are aware of a process through which the claim can be equitably resolved (providing, where appropriate, reinstatement and back pay) obviously discourages resort to self-help in the form of walkouts or slowdowns. In Britain, by contrast, there is no sharp distinction between rights disputes over existing terms of contracts and interest disputes over new contract terms, and arbitration is used rarely in either instance.[64] In Britain, procedural agreements (the handling of grievances is known as the "procedural" part of the bargain in Britain) arrived at in industry-wide negotiations have been increasingly ignored by employees and plant-level worker organizations. Such procedures typically take too long and do not provide for a final and binding resolu-

---

61. J. Stieber, *Grievance Arbitration in the United States: An Analysis of its Functions and Effects*, RESEARCH PAPERS NO. 8, ROYAL COMMISSION ON TRADE UNIONS AND EMPLOYERS' ASSOCIATIONS (1967) at 27. *See also* LABOR RELATIONS AND THE LAW IN THE UNITED STATES 64-69 (Seyfarth, Shaw, Fairweather and Geraldson developers 1968); Gould, Book Review, 48 TEXAS L. REV. 987 (1970).

62. J. Stieber, *supra* note 61. *But see* J. KUHN, BARGAINING IN GRIEVANCE SETTLEMENT (1960); H. WELLINGTON, LABOR AND THE LEGAL PROCESS 96-125 (1970). *Cf.* Gould, Book Review, 16 WAYNE L. REV. 384 (1969); Shapiro, Book Review, 22 STAN. L. REV. 657 (1970). In the United States, national leaders keep a relatively close watch on most local disputes. *Cf.* DEP'T OF LABOR, ANALYSIS OF WORK STOPPAGES 1965, at 11 (1966), DEP'T OF LABOR, ANALYSIS OF WORK STOPPAGES 1961, at 9 (1962).

63. For a discussion of American arbitrators' remedies and functions, *see* F. ELKOURI & E. ELKOURI, HOW ARBITRATION WORKS (1960).

64. K. WEDDERBURN AND P. DAVIES, EMPLOYMENT GRIEVANCES AND DISPUTES PROCEDURES IN BRITAIN 66-74 (1969). Marsh & McCarthy, *Dispute Procedures in British Industry*, RESEARCH PAPERS NO. 2, ROYAL COMMISSION ON TRADE UNIONS AND EMPLOYERS' ASSOCIATIONS (Part I 1966, Part II 1968).

tion of the problem. Thus, economic pressure has been exerted at the plant level as a first rather than a last resort.

In 1965 public discontent with the inefficiencies plaguing labor-management relations prompted Prime Minister Harold Wilson to appoint a Royal Commission, chaired by Lord Donovan, to "[c]onsider relations between managements and employees and the role of the trade unions and employers' associations in promoting the interests of their members and in accelerating the social and economic advance of the nation, with particular reference to the Law affecting the activities of these bodies."[65] In its report,[66] three years later, the Donovan Commission recommended legislation to encourage formal plant-wide bargaining, which would result in detailed and precise collective agreements;[67] particular stress was laid on negotiating specific procedures to handle grievances.[68] The Commission recognized that lack of rational union organization and discipline was part of Britain's labor troubles: It found that ninety-five per cent of Britain's work stoppages were engaged in without trade union authorization.[69] But

65. Royal Warrant dated April 8, 1965, set out in ROYAL COMMISSION ON TRADE UNIONS AND EMPLOYERS' ASSOCIATIONS, REPORT, CMND. NO. 3623, at 1 (1968) [hereinafter cited as ROYAL COMM. ON TRADE UNIONS, REPORT].

66. ROYAL COMM. ON TRADE UNIONS, REPORT, supra note 65. A full treatment of all legal issues is contained in Grunfeld, Donovan—The Legal Aspects, 6 BRIT. J. INDUSTRIAL RELATIONS 316 (1969).

67. Donovan found that Britain had in effect two systems of industrial relations, one formal and the other informal: "[T]he formal system assumes Industry-wide organisations capable of imposing their decisions on their members. The informal system rests on the wide autonomy of managers of individual companies and factories and the power of industrial groups." ROYAL COMM. ON TRADE UNIONS, REPORT, supra note 65, at 36. Issues normally dealt with in American collective bargaining agreements—such as discipline, discharge, lay-offs, and work practices—were either ignored or handled inadequately in the industry-wide formal system, although some were dealt with informally at the local level. The Commission further noted that the gap between the actual pay packet in the plant and the rates set at industry-wide negotiations was continuing to grow. The main solution suggested by the Commission was the negotiation of formal and comprehensive collective agreements at the plant level. Id. at 50.

68. The Commission found a general failure of existing procedural agreements to "cope adequately" with disputes arising in factories. As a result, informal and "fragmented" bargaining was the means through which differences were resolved; many issues were left to "custom and practice." The Commission recommended that procedure agreements be comprehensive in scope so as to deal with disputes "whether they refer to the interpretation of existing, or the making of new, agreements . . . ." Id. at 50. Donovan further recommended establishment of a Commission on Industrial Relations to investigate and report on disputes concerning procedure agreements. As its central objective, the Commission was to guide the parties to collective agreements covering all employees in a company or factory under a single set of rules, a policy which Donovan argued was the best solution to all recognition disputes between labor groups. Id. at 51.

69. But see H. TURNER, IS BRITAIN REALLY STRIKE PRONE?: A REVIEW OF THE INCIDENCE, CHARACTER & COSTS OF INDUSTRIAL CONFLICT (University of Cambridge Department of Applied Economics, Occasional Papers No. 20, 1969). The trend now seems to have shifted so that it more nearly resembles the American pattern. See Thomas, Britain's Worst Year for Strikes since June 1926, The Times (London) Nov. 27, 1970, at 1, col. 1; Macbeath, The Changing Face of the British Strike, The Times (London) Dec. 16, 1971, at 23, col. 4.

the Commission rejected the notion that law could play an *activist* role in suppressing strike activity or enforcing collective agreements. The Commission reasoned that it would be futile to make agreements enforceable or to subject them to binding arbitration unless and until the agreements referred to plant-specific issues and became sufficiently comprehensive and detailed to bear impartial interpretation;[70] similarly, it would be futile to impose liability for breach of agreements on established unions or their officials, since the absence of orderly grievance machinery made strikes inevitable, and since most strikes were unofficial and were conducted by workers and stewards beyond conventional union discipline.[71] To sanction these unruly individuals, Donovan reasoned, would usually prolong and aggravate, not eliminate, wildcat strikes.[72]

Prior to the Commission's report, the Conservative Party issued its own document, *Fair Deal at Work*,[73] which envisioned a leading and dramatic role for law in restructuring labor-management relations. The collective agreement was to be a legally enforceable contract unless the parties "specifically agreed that the whole, or parts of it, should not be legally binding."[74] Damages against employers would normally consist of lost earnings or individual "entitlements," plus expenses incurred by the union. Against unions, damages would be specifically limited by statute. Responding to Donovan's conclusion that union liability would place sanctions on the wrong party, and would thus be futile, *Fair Deal at Work* suggested imposing liability on unions only if they had failed to do "all in their power to prevent" the particular breach of the collective agreement.[75] Such a rule, the Conservatives reasoned, would encourage negotiation of detailed

---

70. Royal Comm. on Trade Unions, Report, *supra* note 65, at 126.

71. *Id*. at 136.

72. This brief summary does not of course exhaust the Commission's important findings of major recommendations. Among other things, Donovan also opposed outlawing the closed shop, *id*. at 162-64, and the secondary boycott, *id*. at 234-37; expressed doubts that balloting procedures should be used to test union opinion or to determine inter-union jurisdictional issues, *id*. at 64-65; recommended that collective agreements be registered with the government, *id*. at 191-202 so that defects in the agreements could be studied; and suggested that Taft-Hartley's emergency strike provisions would have little utility for Britain's work stoppage problems, *id*. at 122-25. On this last point, the Commission reasoned that British strikes rarely threatened the national "health" or "safety" criteria which Taft-Hartley requires be met before invocation of emergency procedures. *Id*. at 113. This reasoning overlooked the peculiar vulnerability of Britain's foreign trade-dependent economy to strikes in key industries. For a thorough study of Britain's economic posture at the time of Donovan, *see generally* R. Caves, Britain's Economic Prospects (1968).

73. Conservative Political Center, Fair Deal at Work (1968).

74. *Id*. at 32.

75. *Id*. at 33.

agreements and would make the presence of national union leadership felt once more on the workshop floor.[76]

In 1969, the Labor Government entered the debate with its white paper, *In Place of Strife*.[77] Like Donovan, the government opposed making collective agreements enforceable. It recommended instead that agreements be required to contain provisions relating to settlement of grievance disputes and to set up arrangements for union-management consultation on matters not specifically negotiated. A Commission on Industrial Relations (CIR) was established by Royal Warrant,[78] in part to study and promote procedures for settling grievance disputes.[79] In its most controversial provision, *In Place of Strife* recommended that the government have discretionary reserve power to order a "conciliation pause" or "cooling off period" against strikes declared in breach of collectively negotiated procedures or in cases where no procedures were provided.[80]

The Wilson Government was compelled to withdraw its legislative proposals because of trade union pressure on the Parliamentary Labor Party.[81] Accordingly, after the Heath Government replaced it in June of 1970, the stage was set for the national debate on the Industrial Relations Bill. Although there was considerable doubt that the new government would adhere to *Fair Deal at Work* immediately in the wake of the election, the government showed that it was quite serious about making good on its campaign promises with the submission of its Consultative Document in October, 1970.[82]

---

76. FAIR DEAL AT WORK, *supra* note 73, made other points. It urged outlawing the closed shop, but recommended allowing the union shop to impose membership requirements on new employees and to require payment of equivalent of union dues into an agreed fund. *Id.* at 24-27. The document advocated outlawing the secondary boycott or "sympathy strike." *Id.* at 30. The Conservatives further proposed that a legal duty to bargain be imposed on an employer in the event that a majority of employees desired union membership. *Id.* at 44-45. Finally, the Conservatives recommended that the Minister of Employment and Productivity be empowered to impose a 60-day injunction during emergency strikes, with a ballot to be held, at the Minister's discretion, during the 60-day period on the employer's "last offer." *Id.* at 40-41.

77. IN PLACE OF STRIFE—A POLICY FOR INDUSTRIAL RELATIONS, CMND No. 3888 (1969).

78. *Id.* ¶ 33-38.

79. *Id.* ¶ 35.

80. IN PLACE OF STRIFE, *supra* note 77, made several other points. Like Donovan, it urged registration of collective agreements with the government. *Id.* at 14-15. It wished to obligate management to disclose certain sorts of information to unions which would facilitate collective bargaining. *Id.* at 16. The secondary boycott and the closed shop were to receive legal protection, *id.* at 30, 34, though conscientious objectors to union membership would be permitted to pay a contribution to charity rather than dues to the union. *Id.* at 34.

81. The best description of this episode is contained in P. JENKINS, THE BATTLE OF DOWNING STREET (1970).

82. DEPARTMENT OF EMPLOYMENT AND PRODUCTIVITY, INDUSTRIAL RELATIONS BILL: CONSULTATIVE DOCUMENT (1970), reproduced in K. WEDDERBURN, THE WORKER AND THE LAW 485-527 (2d ed. 1971).

What emerged, however, was an amalgam of Donovan, *Fair Deal at Work, In Place of Strife,* and more.[83]

II.   An Introduction to the Act

A.   *Institutions Created*

The National Industrial Relations Court (NIRC) created by the Act is given all the powers of Britain's High Court. It consists of both judges and lay members, the latter having special knowledge or expertise in industrial relations. Complaints of unfair industrial practices,[84] including disputes relating to the enforcement of collective agreements as well as violations of employer duties,[85] are to be adjudicated by the NIRC within six (6) months of the time of the event.[86] The Court is to make awards that it considers to be "just and equitable." The Court has the power to compel attendance and examination of witnesses as well as the production of documents and it has criminal contempt power to enforce its authority. Decisions of the NIRC on questions of fact are to be final. However, on questions of law, an appeal to the Court of Appeal is provided, as well as a further appeal procedure to the House of Lords.

The Court also has certain responsibilities with regard to union security arrangements, *i.e.,* where the right to refrain from union membership is concerned, and with regard to the enforceability of procedure agreements. Moreover, the Court has appellate jurisdiction over unfair dismissals, although the parties may devise their own procedures in this area. In considering an application by the parties to establish their own machinery in lieu of that of the Industrial Tribunals[87] (which have primary jurisdiction over unfair dismissals), the Court must determine whether the procedure agreement negotiated is as beneficial to the employee as are the provisions of the Act.[88]

The Court also has some responsibility with regard to a union application for exclusive bargaining representative rights. According to

---

83. *See* Howe, Address to Industrial Law Society in London, Nov. 21, 1970 (on file with author).
84. Ind. Rela. Act 1971, § 101.
85. *Id.* § 102.
86. *Id.* sched. 2, ¶ 25.
87. On Industrial Tribunals, *see* p. 1437 *infra.*
88. A "designating order" permitting the parties to utilize their own machinery may be granted and subsequently revoked if, in the opinion of the court, the agreement no longer meets the statutory requirements. Ind. Rela. Act 1971, § 32.

Section 45, an application may be made to the NIRC for reference to the Commission on Industrial Relations on the following issues: (1) whether a specified group of employees should be recognized or continue to be recognized as a bargaining unit; and (2) whether a "sole bargaining agent" or "joint negotiating panel" should be recognized and if so, what organization should be the bargaining agent or agents.[89]

The Court also has jurisdiction over so-called emergency strikes and has the authority to order the strike ballot in appropriate circumstances.[90]

The Commission on Industrial Relations (CIR), having been created initially by Royal Warrant in 1969, is given a permanent statutory base by the Act. The Commission has responsibility for the conduct of ballots in union security situations and in those involving exclusive bargaining representative questions. In union security matters as well as representation questions, it may hold the elections itself or designate another party to do so.

The jurisdiction of Industrial Tribunals, originally the result of previously enacted legislation,[91] is expanded by the Act. The Tribunals are authorized to hear complaints against employers concerning unfair dismissals or cases relating to the employees' right to join or refrain from union membership. Like the NIRC, they are authorized to fashion relief which is just and equitable.

Finally, the Industrial Court, created in 1919 to hear voluntary arbitrations, will continue its previous function as the Industrial Arbitration Board.

B. *Registration*

The system of registration is central to the statutory scheme. It has no real analogue in American labor law.[92] The Act creates a Chief Registrar of Trade Unions and Employers Associations and orders

89. The NIRC is not to entertain an application for representation unless notice of it is given to the Secretary of State (Minister of Employment and Productivity). Ind. Rela. Act 1971, § 45, ¶ 4.

90. *Id.* §§ 138-45.

91. Summarized *id.* § 100.

92. The only analogous provision among modern American statutes was the Taft-Hartley Act, 1947, ch. 120, Title I, § 101, 61 Stat. 146, adding § 9(h) to the National Labor Relations Act. This provision restricted investigation under NLRA § 9(c), 29 U.S.C. 159(c), and access to complaint procedures under NLRA § 10(b), to unions whose officers had filed non-Communist affidavits. This Section was, however, repealed in 1959 by the Landrum-Griffin Act, Pub. L. No. 86-257, § 201(d). Since then, the only vaguely similar restraint on US worker group activities has been the definition of a labor organization, to which a workers' group must conform before it has access to the Act's recognitional machinery. NLRA § 2(5), 29 U.S.C. 152(5) (1970).

him to register every organization which "immediately prior to the passing of this Act" was registered as a trade union under the Trade Unions Acts of 1871 to 1964.[93] The burden of de-registration is placed upon unions: Given the almost total opposition of the labor movement to the statute, it was thought that unions might not wish to register, but would nonetheless hesitate to seek de-registration because of the serious consequences for organizations which are not registered.[94]

The consequences of failing to register are enormous:[95] A worker is not protected against discrimination for trade union membership if the union is unregistered.[96] An unregistered union may not utilize the machinery through which a union may obtain recognition, agency shop or closed shop rights.[97] If an unregistered union violates a collective bargaining agreement, induces individuals to break their individual contract of employment, or engages in other activity condemned by the Act, the amount of damages that may be assessed against it is unlimited.[98] Unregistered unions thus lose the immunity,

93. Ind. Rela. Act 1971, § 78.
94. Ind. Rela. Act 1971, § 92.
The position of the government was expressed by the Solicitor General (Sir Geoffrey Howe): "Another effect is that non-registration which is clearly an important decision for organization to take if it is already registered, would involve a conscious decision." 814 PARL. DEB. H.C. (5th ser.) 257 (1971).
95. For summaries of the benefits of registration for unions, see I. MACBEATH, THE TIMES GUIDE TO THE INDUSTRIAL RELATIONS ACT 84-85 (1971); Elliott, Registration and the TUC, Financial Times, Industrial Relations Conference, London, May 17, 1972.
96. Ind. Rela. Act 1971, §§ 61(3), 5(1), 5(2)(a).
97. Ind. Rela. Act 1971, §§ 61(3), 45(2), 11, 17.
The policy considerations behind barring unregistered organizations from the processes referred to above emerge at 319 PARL. DEB. H.L. (5th ser.) 327-30 (1971).
98. This results from a combination of the effects of the repeal of the Trades Disputes Act of 1906, 6 Edw. 7, c.47 and of the Trade Disputes Act of 1965, c.48, sched. 9, §§ 96-98, 117. In effect, the Trades Disputes Acts, particularly § 3 of the 1906 Act, protected trade unions from liability for acts done in furtherance of trade disputes. These sections were repealed by the Industrial Relations Act. Their protections were replaced in part by §§ 96-98. But see § 132 as to tort actions. § 96 makes it an unfair industrial practice for any non-registered group to induce breach of contract. Collective bargaining agreements are excluded from the coverage of the term "contract" but employment contracts are included. § 97(2) makes certain steps, such as calling or organizing a strike, in furtherance of an unfair industrial practice also an unfair industrial practice. The limits on recovery in proceedings before the Industrial Court on complaints under the Act are only available to registered trade unions. Therefore, the practical effect may often be that stated by Mrs. Castle during the Committee stage of the bill in the House of Commons (albeit while discussing the Solicitor General's earlier acknowledgment that the principles of § 61 were expected to apply to unregistered groups): "The simple fact is that, if an unregistered union goes on strike, the protection of Section 3 of the 1906 Act is withdrawn. If an unregistered union goes on strike, it faces in specific terms under the Bill unlimited financial damages . . . . The Government themselves have to admit that it is almost impossible to have a strike without a breach of contract of employment. What they are doing is taking away something far more than just the protection of Section 3. The protection of Section 3, which gave to unions the present traditional immunity for action in furtherance of a trade dispute, does not apply under this Bill to unregistered unions. If such a union tries to operate such a strike, it faces actual unlimited damages." 811 PARL.

heretofore provided by the Trades Disputes Act of 1906, against tort liability for inducing breaches of individual employment contracts in a trade dispute.[99] This is of enormous significance: Most individual contracts require the worker to give proper notice to his employer before terminating work, and most strikes, and certainly most unofficial strikes (which arise spontaneously and often unpredictably), violate these proper notice clauses.[100] Moreover, unions which refuse to register relinquish tax rebates available to the registered unions with respect to interest on investments actually applied to the payment of non-strike or non-"industrial action" benefits (*e.g.,* sickness payments).[101] It has been estimated that non-registration will impose new tax liabilities of up to five million pounds a year on the unions.[102] For a trade union movement that is financially beleaguered, this is no small matter.[103] Further, while officials of registered unions acting within the scope of their authority are protected against personal liability, as are union officials in the United States, this is not the case with non-registered unions.[104]

DEB. H.C. (5th ser.) 636 (1971). Though the Labour Party protested the Act's removal of protection from unregistered unions, no complaint was made when the similar proposal was made by the Donovan Commission, ROYAL COMM. ON TRADE UNIONS, REPORT, *supra* note 65, at 215.

99. Under the 1971 Act the terminology is "industrial dispute" rather than "trade dispute." The two terms are defined in much the same manner. However, under the 1971 statute certain secondary, "sympathetic" and closed shop stoppages are not included. In the United States the reference is to a "labor dispute" under both the Norris-LaGuardia Act, 29 U.S.C. § 101 (1970) and the NLRA, 29 U.S.C. § 152(9) (1970). *See* Local 33, Bakery Sales Drivers v. Wagshal, 333 U.S. 437 (1948); Columbia River Packers Assn. v. Hinton, 315 U.S. 143 (1942); New Negro Alliance v. Sanitary Grocer Co., 303 U.S. 552 (1938). *Compare* New Negro Alliance *with* Scala Ballroom (Wolverhampton) Ltd. v. Ratcliffe, [1958] 1 W.L.R. 1057 (C.A.).

100. For an excellent discussion of British case law on the legal significance of the individual's failure to provide adequate notice in this context, see C. GRUNFELD, MODERN TRADE UNION LAW 319-22 (1966); Morgan v. Fry (1958), 2 Q.B. 710. A majority of the Donovan Commission took a position remarkably similar to the framers of the Industrial Relations Act on protection for unions inducing such breaches in either official or unofficial contexts, *i.e.,* the requirement of registration. ROYAL COMM. ON TRADE UNIONS, REPORT, *supra* note 65, at 235. However, the consequences of registration as recommended by the Commission were not the same as those under the Act.

101. Registered organizations of workers ("trade unions" according to the language of the Act) alone can recover income tax on funds applied to provident benefits, Income and Corporation Taxes Act, 1970, c.10, § 338. One important question will be whether unregistered groups may avoid this burden and obtain similar benefits by setting up a friendly society pursuant to the Friendly Societies Act, 1896, 59 & 60 Vict., c.25, to deal with provident funds. See also 322 PARL. DEB. H.L. (5th ser.) 58-74 (1971). *See also* Routledge, *Engineering Union Votes to Safeguard Funds,* The Times (London) Nov. 10, 1971, at 19, col. 1.

102. *See* Torode, *Unions Could Avoid Tax Under Act,* The Guardian, Aug. 12, 1971, at 7, col. 7.

103. *See* Harper, *TUC Challenges 'Concession' in Industrial Act,* The Guardian, Aug. 23, 1971, at 5, col. 4; Harper, *Brothers in a Cash Crisis,* The Guardian, Aug. 3, 1971, at 11, col. 1.

104. Ind. Rela. Act 1971, § 96(1)(b). That personal liability for extra-official actions (though not in tort) is contemplated was made apparent during the Second Reading debates in the House of Commons. 808

The Registrar has the authority to examine rules of the organization and, if they are not in accord with basic principles of the Act, the organization must revise them. If this is not done, the Registrar is to apply to the NIRC for registration to be cancelled. Although unregistered unions do not submit their rules to the scrutiny of the Registrar, the principles that the Registrar devises with regard to union rules are generally applicable to unregistered unions in legal proceedings before the Industrial Court, as well as to those which are registered.[105]

A complaint alleging unfair industrial practices or breaches of an organization's rules may be lodged with the Registrar. If he finds merit in the complaint, the Registrar may attempt to bring about a settlement. If no settlement is reached, the Registrar may present the case to the NIRC. (Challenges to the rules and internal practices are taken by an Industrial Tribunal where the union is unregistered.)

A significant purpose of the registration system is to determine who has responsibility for violations of collective agreements and for fulfilling various statutory obligations. The TUC and most of Britain's major unions have declared unequivocal opposition to submitting to registration.[106] Unregistered unions will also have ample incentive under the Act to revise their internal procedures and to regulate the times and manner in which shop stewards and other officials call stoppages: Strikes by an unregistered union will usually constitute a breach of the individual employment contracts of its members, and the union, no longer protected by the Trades Disputes Act of 1906,[107] will be subject to unlimited damages for inducement of this breach.[108] In case of registration, the Registrar facilitates internal reorganization of the union by requiring that officials responsible for industrial action be identified.[109]

PARL. DEB. H.C. (5th ser.) 981-82 (1970). *See also* 811 PARL. DEB. H.C. (5th ser.) 1705-09. As to protection from personal liability in the United States, see LMRA § 301(b), 29 U.S.C. § 185(b) (1970), and Atkinson v. Sinclair Refining Co., 370 U.S. 238 (1962). *See also* Atlantic Richfield Co. v. Oil, Chemical and Atomic Workers Union, 447 F.2d 945 (7th Cir. 1971). Whether individuals are subject to injunctions in American labor law remains a troubled question.

105. That this is the intended effect of § 61 was made apparent during the House of Commons committee stage. 814 PARL. DEB. H.C. (5th ser.) 274 (1971).

106. *See* note 51 *supra.*

107. 6 Edw. 7, c.47. The landmark case holding that there is tort liability for inducing breach of the contract of employment is Lumley v. Guy, [1853] 2 El. § Bl. 216, 118 Eng. Rep. 749.

108. *See* pp. 1462-63 *infra.*

109. Ind. Rela. Act 1971, sched. 4, ¶ 10. This identification provision is central to the Act's purposes. The Act requires unions to prevent and halt, through reasonably practicable steps, all actions contrary to the terms of an enforceable collective bargaining

C. *Policies*

The "general principles" of the Industrial Relations Act of 1971 are set forth in Part I of the statute.[110] The first principle supports the practice of collective bargaining "freely conducted on behalf of workers and employers and with due regard to the general interest of the community . . . ." The second, once again stated in the context of the general interest of the community, supports the "developing and maintaining of orderly procedures in industry for peaceful and expeditious settlement of disputes by negotiation, conciliation or arbitration." Third, the statute endorses the principle of "free association" of workers in "independent trade unions" and provides the same right to employers' associations. Finally, the Act states that the principle of "freedom and security" for workers is to be protected by the safeguards against unfair industrial practices whether engaged in by employers or unions.

In the United States, the National Labor Relations Act enunciates certain "policies" which are devised in light of "findings" set forth in § 1.[111] While both statutes pay specific heed to the self-organization rights of workers, as well as to the desirability of collective bargaining, the British statute makes specific reference to a "general interest of the community" which can presumably conflict with the objectives of both unions and employers. Moreover, the American statute, in its findings, contains statements which the British Parliament would have been reluctant to make in 1971. The central one is that an "inequality" of bargaining power between unions and employers, to the advantage of employers, is a cause of industrial strife. It is this factor which necessitated the right of self-organization, the promotion of collective bargaining and the encouragement to devise peaceful procedures to resolve differences in the United States. It is not at all clear that the same finding could have been made with regard to Brit-

---

agreement. *Id.* § 36(2). Individuals are liable for breach of this duty unless they are acting within the scope of union authority. *Id.* § 96. The identification provision is important in determining which individuals enjoy union authorization. If an individual acts under union authority, his breach of § 36(2) duties is imputed to the union as commission of an unfair industrial practice by the union.

110. Ind. Rela. Act 1971, § 1. The principles of § 1 are to guide the Secretary of State in preparing a draft Code of Practice. *Id.* § 2(1).

111. 29 U.S.C. § 51 (1970). The Act aims to eliminate the causes of certain "substantial obstructions to the free flow of commerce" by encouraging the "practice and procedure of collective bargaining" and by protecting the exercise by workers of self-organization rights and rights to designate representatives to negotiate the terms and conditions of employment or to provide other "mutual aid and protection." In particular 29 U.S.C. § 173(d) (1970) specifically promotes "final adjustment by a method agreed upon by the parties" as the best way to achieve a settlement of grievance disputes involving interpretation or application of the existing collective agreement.

ish unions. If inequality of bargaining power exists in Britain, the employer is arguably as likely as the union to be the weaker party.[112] Certainly that was the view of the Parliament which enacted the Industrial Relations Act of 1971.

D. *Code of Practice*

The purpose of the Code,[113] adopted by parliamentary resolution, is to provide practical guidance for the promotion of good relationships between unions and employers. It is an attempt to define the proper behavior of unions and employers in collective bargaining as well as to clarify the meaning of new statutory concepts, *e.g.*, the appropriate unit. While it binds no one and is without the force of law, the Code is to be "taken into account" by both the National Industrial Relations Court and Industrial Tribunals. Presumably, a violation of recommendations contained in the Code would be relevant in determining a remedy under the Act's "just and equitable" provisions. In a system where litigation has rarely been used to date, the effect of the Code upon the parties may be substantial. It may well be that, like the detailed collective agreement in the United States, the Code will soon become a critical element in the collective relationship. This could occur regardless of the Act's impact or failure in other respects.

III. An Analysis of the Act

A. *Recognition and the Establishment of Collective Bargaining*

The 1971 Act represents Parliament's first attempt to outlaw antiunion discrimination by employers and thus to shield the right to organize from employer pressures. The Act establishes procedures under which employers may be obligated to bargain with unions and under which recognition rights as a sole bargaining agent may be granted and withdrawn. After the Industrial Court promulgates an order obligating an employer to recognize the union as a sole bargaining agent, it is an unfair industrial practice for the employer to carry on bargaining in that unit with any other organization of workers.[114] Moreover, it is an unfair practice for a union to engage

---

112. *Cf.* O. KAHN-FREUND, LABOR LAW: OLD TRADITIONS AND NEW DEVELOPMENTS (1968).
113. DEPARTMENT OF EMPLOYMENT, THE CENTRAL OFFICE OF INFORMATION, INDUSTRIAL RELATION CODE OF PRACTICE (1972) [hereinafter cited as CODE OF PRACTICE].
114. Ind. Rela. Act 1971, § 55(1)(a).

in a strike aimed at compelling negotiations with another union, or for an employer to engage in a lock-out which is an attempt to induce a party to withdraw an application for recognition under the Act.[115] The Act requires employers to bargain collectively with unions where they have been properly recognized (although no corresponding duty is imposed on unions),[116] and employers must disclose to unions information which is necessary for the "carrying on [of] collective bargaining" and information the disclosure of which is "in accordance with good industrial relations practice."[117]

The Act in Section 5 authorizes every worker to join a trade union "as he may choose" and, subject to the statute's union security provisions, to be a member of no union or "other organization of workers."[118] The statute makes it an unfair industrial practice for an employer to "prevent or deter" the exercise of these rights or to "dismiss, penalize, or otherwise discriminate" [against] a worker for the exercise of these rights.[119] As in the United States, the closed shop is prohibited in most circumstances,[120] although the agency shop, in

115. *Id.* §§ 55(3), (7), and (8). Even if there is no Court order subsequent to a ballot, but rather a CIR report to the Court, industrial action by unions and employers is precluded to the same extent.

116. Ind. Rela. Act 1971, § 55(1)(b).

117. A general duty to disclose, applicable only to registered trade unions (see 319 PARL. DEB. H.L. (5th ser.) 415-22 (1971), is imposed by § 56. Under § 158, however, certain information need not be disclosed if it would be "against the interests of national security," "seriously prejudicial to the interests of the employer's undertaking for reasons other than its effect on collective bargaining," etc. In addition § 57 provides that a company employing more than 350 non-excepted persons must issue a yearly financial statement to its employees (an obligation which is subject to such exemptions as are allowed under regulations issued by the Secretary of State).

It should be noted that this obligation on the part of employers was introduced by the government. See 808 PARL. DEB. H.C. (5th ser.) 975-76 (1970). Some attempts to increase the burden were made in the House of Lords. See 319 PARL. DEB. H.L. (5th ser.) 402-31 (1971); 321 PARL. DEB. H.L. (5th ser.) 1058-80 (1971); 322 PARL. DEB. H.L. (5th ser.) 899-902 (1971). However, relatively little commotion arose over the imposition of this obligation. By contrast, fierce battles have been waged in the United States both before and after the obligation was imposed by the Supreme Court in NLRB v. Truitt Mfg. Co., 351 U.S. 149 (1956), upholding an NLRB decision that an employer breached its obligation to bargain in good faith by not disclosing information to support its claimed inability to pay increased wages.

118. Ind. Rela. Act 1971, § 5(1)(a) and (b). The union security provisions specifically referred to in this section are found in § 6 (the agency shop) and § 17 (the approved closed shop). The government's policy motivations in conferring a right not to join a union may be found in 810 PARL. DEB. H.C. (5th ser.) 667-68, 671-73 (1971).

119. Ind. Rela. Act 1971, § 5(2)(a) and (b).

120. Approved post-entry closed shop agreements are allowed under § 17 of the Act. However, a worker with a conscientious objection to joining a trade union can be "specially exempted," in which case he must make "appropriate contributions" to charity. The procedures for obtaining such an exemption and for determining the amount of such contribution are set out in Part IV of Schedule 1 of the Act. Provision is made therein for reference to an Industrial Tribunal of disputes concerning genuineness of a worker's objection to membership. See 813 PARL. DEB. H.C. (5th ser.) 850-84 (general threat to certain unions, particularly entertainment, if closed shops were not allowed), 689-96 (threat to seafaring unions) (1971).

which the equivalent of union dues and initiation fees must be paid by the worker, is permitted.[121]

Difficult problems of legal theory and practice are raised by this injection of statutory rules into the heretofore informal procedures by which unions won the membership of workers and the recognition of employers. Here three of the major problems are considered: How, if at all, will the formal rules and traditional TUC procedures co-exist? Does the statutory language sufficiently protect an employee's right to join, to refrain from joining, or to resign from a union? Is the machinery whereby unions gain recognition for bargaining realistic and workable?

1. *Bridlington and Croydon: Internal TUC Procedures.*

In establishing legal recognition machinery, and in creating the right to join and resign from unions, the Act is in potential conflict with the Trades Union Congress Bridlington Principles and Procedures[122] and with the 1969 Croydon Congress,[123] under which the TUC has authority to settle both membership disputes and differences about which unions should be recognized. To the extent that the TUC designates a particular union as representative, and insofar as this requires other unions to discourage their members from recruiting and to desist from further organizational efforts, Bridlington and Croydon both interfere with employee free choice as prescribed by the Act. Apparently, however, the statute's provisions concerning recognition and right to join and resign will be interpreted with due deference to the established TUC practice. The Code of Industrial Relations Practice, which controls interpretation of the statute's guiding principles in cases arising under the Act, states that "responsibility for avoiding disputes between trade unions about recognition lies principally with the unions themselves and, in the case of affiliated unions, with the Trades Union Congress," and unions are to make full use of the available procedures.[124] Evident here is one of the main themes of the Act, *i.e.*, the encouragement of voluntary machinery or efforts to re-

---

121. Ind. Rela. Act 1971, § 5(1)(b), § 6.

122. On major disputes, the TUC Disputes Committee adjudicates, with the only sanction being disaffiliation. I. MACBEATH, THE TIMES GUIDE TO THE INDUSTRIAL RELATIONS ACT 102 (1971).

123. Croydon simply applies the principles of Bridlington, under which recognitional disputes are heard by TUC, to jurisdictional stoppages. Croydon was the product of the 1969 Labour Party-TUC accord. *See* Wood, *Anti-Strike Bill Abandoned by Wilson: Agreement Heals Breach in the Labour Movement*, The Times (London) June 19, 1969, at 1, col. 1.

124. CODE OF PRACTICE, *supra* note 113, at ¶ 85.

solve disputes. The Code refers to "recognition" disputes, which are the subject of Bridlington, and not to "membership" or jurisdictional disputes, which are the subject of Croydon. Presumably, however, since it is often difficult to differentiate between the two in a given situation,[125] TUC procedures will be of relevance in interpreting the Act in both contexts. The Act further buttresses the position taken in the Code by precluding unions from denying application for membership only if the denial is arbitrary.[126] Thus, though an employee has a statutory right to resign from a union to which he has been assigned by TUC procedures,[127] he does not have an absolute right to join another union, and the Bridlington procedures will apparently be taken into consideration by authorities weighing whether a particular union's refusal to admit a new member is arbitrary within the meaning of the Act.[128]

2. Restraining Employer and Union Pressure on Employee Rights

Developing in the courts, case by case, the American law on employer discrimination against union activity has acquired a certain flexibility. In attempting to accomplish this task with a single, though concededly detailed, statute, the British may have missed important subtleties. For example, Section 5(4) of the Industrial Relations Act states that where an employer offers a benefit of "any kind" to a worker as an inducement to refrain from the exercise of Section 5 rights, the employer violates the Act if the employer has (a) conferred the benefit on workers who agree to refrain from exercising Section 5 rights and (b) withheld the benefit from one or more who did not agree to refrain. The narrow, technical terms in which these criteria are framed may defeat achievement of a praiseworthy objective. In the United States the Board and the Supreme Court have prohibited more broadly the promising and granting of benefits during organizational campaigns. In a leading case,[129] Mr. Justice Har-

---

125. See Carey v. Westinghouse Electric Corp., 375 U.S. 261 (1964).

126. Ind. Rela. Act 1971, §§ 65(1), (2). Enforcement is via unfair industrial practice sanction under § 66.

127. Resignation is specifically allowed under § 65(3).

128. That this was the thinking of the government emerges from the lengthy debate at 319 Parl. Deb. H.L. (5th ser.) 610-25 (1971). For some of the problems in American labor law, see Atleson, Union Fines and Picket Lines: The NLRA and Union Disciplinary Power, 17 U.C.L.A. L. Rev. 681 (1970); Gould, Some Limitations Upon Union Discipline: The Radiation of Allis Chalmers, 1970 Duke L.J. 1067. See NLRB v. Local 1029, Textile Workers, 446 F.2d 369 (1st Cir. 1971), cert. granted, 405 U.S. 987 (1972); Boeing Co., 185 N.L.R.B. No. 23 (1970) modified, 459 F.2d 1143 (D.C. Cir. 1972); General Gravure Co., 186 N.L.R.B. No. 69 (1970).

129. NLRB v. Exchange Parts Co., 375 U.S. 405 (1964).

lan stated that the granting of such benefits during organizational campaigns could be regarded by the Board as an unlawful and improper interference with the rights of self-organization. The Court's reasoning was that employees will recognize that an employer which has the authority to grant such benefits can also take them away. Fearing a "get tough" policy by the employer after the campaign, if the union should win, employees might be deterred from showing an interest in union organizational activity. Of course this theory is not without difficulties. As commentators have pointed out,[130] employees could use the benefits as a floor for future bargaining once the union representative is on the scene. Alternatively, the employees might not have had any interest in the union to begin with and might be using the representation petition simply to extract the benefits granted. Nevertheless, a law dealing with employer campaign strategies should be broad and flexible enough to cover a wide variety of coercive employer techniques. The Act is surely too rigid in assuming that employers are so unsophisticated as to confer benefits for refusal to exercise rights and simultaneously withhold them from those engaged in union activity.

Rigidity may also plague Section 5(1)(c), which states that employees have the right as trade union members to participate politically "at an appropriate time." Section 5(5) defines an appropriate time as one "outside" working hours or as a "time within his [the employee's] working hours at which, in accordance with the arrangements agreed with, or consent given by or on behalf of his employer, it is permissible for him to take part in those activities." Conceivably, the language of Section 5 may mean that union organizational activity and political participation in union matters may never take place on company property, and never during working time, absent management consent.[131] One may hope, however, that the meaning is otherwise, because such a blanket prohibition would surely be draconian.

In an apparent divergence from American law,[132] the Industrial Relations Act, in Section 5(3), specifically permits an employer to "encourage" workers to become union members subsequent to the time that the union has achieved recognition and bargaining status. Accordingly, it might be said that Section 5 is less neutral, and more

---

130. See Bok, *The Regulation of Campaign Tactics in Representation Elections Under the National Labor Relations Act*, 78 HARV. L. REV. 112 (1964).

131. Debates on two amendments dealing with the section suggest that the government's purpose was to moderately expand workers' inplant union rights somewhat, without in any way limiting extant rights. See 318 PARL. DEB. H.L. (5th ser.) 301-12 (1971).

132. 29 U.S.C. § 158(a)(3) (1970).

solicitous of the right to join, than is the case in the United States. For two reasons, however, this conclusion would be erroneous. First, the American statute, while neutral in the sense of protecting the right to refrain, nevertheless has as a basic policy the promotion of free collective bargaining. Second, employer encouragement of union activity has its obvious analogue in the National Labor Relations Act's legitimization of check-off provisions[133] and of employer arrangements for unions to meet on company property and for union officials to use company facilities.[134] Further, unlike the British Act, Taft-Hartley specifically provides employers with a right of free speech,[135] which effectively permits management to express a view in favor of unionization. Finally, like the NLRA, which opposes company dominated or assisted unions,[136] the Act provides that Section 5 rights, and the statute's support of the principles of collective bargaining, pertain only to "independent" trade unions.[137] Thus, despite superficial appearances, the statutes adopt similar policy toward employer encouragement of union activity.

Unlike the NLRA,[138] the British Act does not specifically prohibit unions from interferring with an individual's right to refrain from joining a union. Unions are, however, effectively barred from pressuring employers to discriminate against non-members, for Section 5 prohibits employer discrimination against an employee who refrains from membership, and an employer charged with a statutory violation may claim that a third party, *i.e.*, the union, is primarily or jointly liable, and damages may, as in the United States, be assessed against the union.[139]

133.   LMRA § 302, 29 U.S.C. § 462 (1970).
134.   NLRA § 8(a)(2), 29 U.S.C. § 158(a)(2) (1970).
135.   NLRA § 8(c), 29 U.S.C. § 158(c) (1970).
136.   NLRA § 8(a)(2), 29 U.S.C. § 158(a)(2) (1970).
137.   Section 5 rights exist in a registered union only if it "is an independent organization of workers," §67(1)(a). Under the interpretation provision § 167, except as the context otherwise requires, "independent," in relation to a trade union or other organization, means "not under the domination or control of an employer or of a group of employers or of one or more organizations of employers."
    Similarly, labor applications to the Industrial Court for recognition as a sole bargaining agent under § 45 may be made only by "trade unions," a term of art which, according to § 61, covers only those organizations of workers which are registered. See 813 PARL. DEB. H.C. (5th ser.) 1541-86 (1971) and 321 PARL. DEB. H.L. (5th ser.) 932-42 (1971). Regarding the issue of independence, it has been alleged that unions are being permitted to register although only a small percentage of their activities are devoted to bargaining, and with no inquiry into the "union's" financial viability rules or accounts. *But see Acid Test of Registration*, The Times (London), Sept. 12, 1972, at 17, col. 1, which indicates that the Registrar is now removing a number of "staff associations" from the register.
138.   29 U.S.C. §§ 158(b)(1)(A), (2) (1970).
139.   Ind. Rela. Act 1971, § 5(2). For American labor law on joint liability, see NLRA § 10(c), 29 U.S.C. § 160(c) (1970). *See also* Acme Mattress Co., 91 N.L.R.B. 1010 (1950).

Section 65 prohibits unions from excluding individuals from membership unreasonably or arbitrarily,[140] and from imposing unreasonable or unfair disciplinary action.[141] A union must give reasonable notice to terminate a member.[142] As in the United States, however, the scope of an individual's right to resign from a union is somewhat clouded. Developing American case law indicates that employees generally have the right to renounce union membership at the time that they resign,[143] but it appears that unions may qualify this right in their constitutions or by-laws.[144] In Britain, under the Act, an employee may resign his membership by giving reasonable notice and complying with reasonable conditions.[145] Since this provision reads in the conjunctive, union rules may apparently impose additional rules for retirement than the mere giving of reasonable notice.

Generally, the Act's Section 65, and its registration provisions, indicate that statutory agencies in Britain will be much concerned with internal union affairs. In the United States, by contrast, Section 8(b)-(1) (A) creates a presumption against interference in internal union affairs.[146]

140. See note 126 *supra*. It should also be noted that unsuccessful attempts were made to enlarge reasonableness to include exclusion of members who previously resigned pursuant to the exercise of § 5 rights, 319 Parl. Deb. H.L. (5th ser.) 633-40 (1971), and to include exclusion of publicly anti-union individuals, 319 Parl. Deb. H.L. (5th ser.) 641-48 (1971).

141. The Labour Party voiced no opposition to the principle of limiting unfair or unreasonable disciplinary action by unions. An amendment to delete § 65(7) (the section that prohibits unfair or unreasonable disciplinary action) was introduced in the professed hope of getting clarification of the Registrar's probable view of rules possibly inconsistent with § 65(7) when exercising his responsibility to review the rules of trade unions as to their consistency with the Act. See 319 Parl. Deb. H.L. (5th ser.) 674-75 (1971).

In addition, an unsuccessful attempt was made to give unions the power to discipline employees for non-participation in industrial action without violating the provision of subsec. 7, 319 Parl. Deb. H.L. (5th ser.) 675-86 (1971).

142. Ind. Rela. Act 1971, § 65(9).

143. *Cf.* Gould, *Some Limitations Upon Discipline Under the National Labor Relations Act: the Radiations of Allis Chalmers*, 1970 Duke L.J. 1067, 1096-1107 (1970) and cases cited therein.

144. *Id.* However, even in the absence of constitutional limitations, one court has held—in a case now before the Supreme Court—that union members may temporarily waive their resignation rights by voting to strike. NLRB v. Local 1029, Textile Workers, 446 F.2d 369 (1st Cir. 1971), *cert. granted*, 405 U.S. 987 (1972).

145. The government's motive for including this right was apparently to make explicit a right implicit in the larger right not to be a union member. That this right is to be exercisable only within reasonable limits is apparent from the Lord Chancellor's reply to an amendment (which was defeated) to delete § 65(3), the resignation section. 319 Parl. Deb. H.L. (5th ser.) 649-50 (1971); 321 Parl. Deb. H.L. (5th ser.) 1155-58 (1971). (Debate on requiring payment of dues before union membership could be terminated where the government representative, Lord Belstead, again voiced the expectation that any reasonable restrictions in union rules would be acceptable but contended it would be inappropriate to spell out what rules would be reasonable in the Act).

146. 29 U.S.C. § 158b(1)(A) (1970). Of course, the Landrum-Griffin Act of 1959, 29 U.S.C. §§ 153, 158-60 *et seq.* (1970) cuts quite deeply into internal union rules. *See* Summers, *American Legislation for Union Democracy*, 25 Modern L. Rev. 278 (1962).

3. *The Recognition Machinery*

Under the National Labor Relations Act labor organizations, employers, employees or groups of employees may file representation petitions with the Board.[147] If the Board finds that there is a question of representation, it may hold a hearing on this and other issues. The Board has the obligation to determine the appropriate unit within which the election shall take place and, assuming that a majority of employees designate a union representative, within which bargaining shall take place.[148] The Board has devised numerous criteria for the purpose of determining which unit is appropriate. Employees who have a "community of interest" with one another are generally regarded as part of one appropriate unit.[149] In making this determination the Board looks to whether employees work geographically proximate to one another, are under the same common supervision, interchange positions with one another, have similar wages, hours and fringe benefits and other employment conditions. The employer's administrative structure is also studied, to determine whether the employees are on the same payroll or under the same accounting system.[150] The Board may not lump professionals with non-professionals in one unit,[151] unless the professionals vote for inclusion in such a unit, nor may the Board determine that a craft unit is inappropriate simply because a different unit was previously established by the Board.[152] And the Board may not include building guards in a unit which contains other employees.[153] Once a valid election has been held, no election is to be held within the next twelve months.[154] If a union wins the election and is certified, the employer cannot challenge the union's majority status during the first certification year absent unusual circumstances. Even subsequent to the first certifica-

---

Compare the discussion in O. KAHN-FREUND, LABOUR AND THE LAW 210-22 (1972). Moreover, the Civil Rights Act of 1964 prohibits denial of union membership on grounds of race, color, sex, nationality or religion. 42 U.S.C. § 2000(e)(2) (1970).

147. NLRA § 9(c), 29 U.S.C. § 159(c) (1970).

148. NLRA § 9(b), 29 U.S.C. § 159(b) (1970).

149. Continental Baking Co., 99 N.L.R.B. No. 123 (1952) and cases cited therein. *See generally* THE DEVELOPING LABOR LAW 217-22 (C. Morris ed. 1971). In order to encourage plant bargaining, the Industrial Relations Act of 1971 indicates that an appropriate unit will not normally consist of a national bargaining arrangement. Such arrangements are referred to as "more extensive bargaining arrangements" and are distinguished from a "bargaining unit." *Id*. § 44.

150. However, employer administrative structures alone do not determine the appropriate unit. *Cf*. Swift & Co., 101 N.L.R.B. No. 2 (1952).

151. NLRA § 9(b)(1), 29 U.S.C. § 159(b)(1) (1970). *See also* Leedom v. Kyne, 358 U.S. 184 (1958).

152. NLRA § 9(b)(2), 29 U.S.C. § 159(b)(2) (1970).

153. NLRA § 9(b)(3), 29 U.S.C. § 159(b)(3) (1970).

154. NLRA § 9(c)(3), 29 U.S.C. § 159(c)(3) (1970).

tion year, a negotiated collective bargaining agreement operates as a bar for up to three years against an intervening representation petition, and an employer challenging a union's majority status must overcome a presumption that the union retains that status.[155]

In Britain the machinery is more complicated, in large measure because an attempt has been made to encourage the parties to rely upon their own devices.

Applications for recognition and sole bargaining agent status may be made to the NIRC by trade unions and employers which are registered under the Act, and by the Secretary of State as well.[156] The Court is not to entertain an application under Section 45 unless notice has been given to the Secretary of State and the Secretary has first provided advice and assistance to the parties giving the notice that the Secretary believes to be appropriate.[157] This provision aims to promote agreement between the parties concerning matters referred to in the application. While the NLRA also encourages voluntary settlement, once a petition is filed with the Board, negotiations look toward a consent election through which employee free choice will manifest itself at the ballot box. This is clearly not the case with the Industrial Relations Act. Even if settlement is not achieved, a recommendation of the Commission on Industrial Relations on recognition can be accepted by the parties without further proceedings before the Court—proceedings which would lead to a ballot and order.[158] If the

---

155. The bar on representation petitions is referred to as the "contract bar" rule. Its term was extended to 3 years in 1962 by the Board in General Cable Corp., 139 N.L.R.B. 1123 (1962).

The continuing majority status presumption was recently reiterated by the Board in Terrell Machine Co., 173 N.L.R.B. 1480 (1969), *citing* Celanese Corporation of America, 95 N.L.R.B. 664, 671-72 (1951).

156. Ind. Rela. Act (1971), § 45. Clause 3 of section 45 requires the Secretary of State, before making an application with respect to a group of employees, to consult the employer(s) and "any organization of workers or joint negotiating panel appearing to him to be directly concerned in the matters to which the proposed application would relate." One of the reasons for such consultation is that the parties in respect of whom he was making the application "should not . . . be taken by a reference to the court in that way." 813 PARL. DEB. H.C. (5th ser.) 1546 (1971). Thus, a non-registered trade union could be consulted; for that matter, a company union could be consulted.

157. Subsection 4 of § 45 was originally introduced and accepted as an amendment to the replaced cl. 42, and was included in the later introduced section. See 811 PARL. DEB. H.C. (5th ser.) 427-28 (1971), and 813 PARL. DEB. H.C. (5th ser.) 1547-50 (1971).

158. The Act is structured so that, even though the Commission has recommended that a particular organization of workers or joint negotiating panel should be recognized as sole bargaining agent for a bargaining unit, application must be made to the Industrial Court for an order making the recommendation binding. Ind. Rela. Act 1971, §§ 49, 50. Only after such an application has been made is a ballot taken to ascertain employee sentiment (sentiment, that is, on the question of whether the Commission's recommendation should be made binding). *Id.* § 49(3). Thus, employee sentiment is not canvassed via ballot until the very last stage of the recognition procedure, prior to which time the question of who will represent employees can be set-

Court is satisfied that the parties have endeavored to settle the issues concerning the scope of the bargaining unit as well as the identity of the bargaining agent, the Court may refer the questions to the Commission so that a "lasting settlement" may be promoted. Here the Court must not only examine the extent to which the parties have exerted themselves, but also satisfy itself that the parties have made adequate use of conciliation facilities made available by the Department of Employment. If settlement cannot be achieved, the Commission is to report to the Court on the outstanding issues.

In determining the appropriate bargaining unit, the Commission is specifically directed to consider the "nature of the work" performed by the employees as well as their "training, experience and professional and other qualifications."[159] (The Code of Practice provides more detailed criteria.)[160] Since the unit may not extend to employees other than those "of an employer or two or more as-

tled by employer-union agreement. The chances for mistake via this procedure are minimized, however, by the admonition to the Commission in § 48(4) that:

> A report of the Commission under this section shall not recommend the recognition of an organization of workers or joint negotiating panel as sole bargaining agent for a bargaining unit unless it appears to the Commission . . . .
> . . . .
> (b) that its recognition as sole bargaining agent for that bargaining unit would be in accordance with the general wishes of the employees comprised in that bargaining unit, and would promote a satisfactory and lasting settlement of the question in issue in the reference.

Should mistakes occur, there is the potential for rectification via decertification of the sole bargaining agent. *Id.* at 51-53.

159. Ind. Rela. Act 1971, § 48(3). The inclusion of the word "professional" in the list of considerations resulted from a desire by both the Labour and Conservative Parties to protect the interests of true professionals. Though finally included as the result of a government proposed amendment in the House of Lords, the same amendment was offered earlier by the opposition, 319 Parl. Deb. H.L. (5th cer.) 343-48 (1971). The earlier amendment was withdrawn pending government consideration of the best way to define professional so that every skilled group could not make a claim of professionalism. Unable to do that adequately without being over-inclusive or, worse, leaving out some clearly recognizable professionals, the government stayed with the single word description "professional," leaving further refinement to the Commission on Industrial Relations, 321 Parl. Deb. H.L. (5th ser.) 346-47 (1971). Debate on the initial amendment offered by the opposition centered mostly on the problem of imposing dual loyalties on professionals, *i.e.*, to professional standards and associations and to unions. Both Labour and the Conservatives, however, seemed favorably disposed to the distinction between professional and non-professionals. However, the Opposition in the House of Commons was more recalcitrant. Their hesitancy stemmed from fears that such a distinction would impede the progress of middle-class and professional organization by unions. The government countered by arguing that professionals must be free to develop their own organizations for representation and that many professionals fear being swallowed up, and having their interests ignored, by non-professional unions. In fact, this rationale for the distinction strongly suggests that the term was included not because of limited concerns about possible conflicts of interest, but rather because of a broader fear of inadequate representation. 822 Parl. Deb. H.C. (5th ser.) 1621-34 (1971). It should be noted that professional organizations can be entered on a special register under §§ 84-86, giving them a standing similar to that of a registered trade union.

160. Code of Practice, *supra* note 113, ¶¶ 74-81.

sociated employers," industry-wide bargaining units are ruled out. The provision comports with the Donovan Commission's promotion of company and plant agreements, but the Act does not intend to eliminate industry-wide or company bargaining on matters not covered by plant bargaining. The Commission may recommend recognition of an organization of workers if it appears to the Commission that the organization is "independent" and that its recognition would be in "accordance with the general wishes of the employees comprised in that bargaining unit." The Commission, in this connection, is also to consider whether recognition would provide a "satisfactory and lasting settlement" of the issues involved. More particularly, the Commission is to determine whether the organization in question possesses the support of a "substantial proportion" of the employees in the appropriate unit and whether the organization has the resources requisite to effective representation of the employees in question. Presumably, the Commission will conduct the same kind of soundings undertaken by that agency before the Act's existence. While an unregistered union may not apply for recognition under Section 45, the CIR may recommend that such a union should be the sole bargaining agent. Moreover, an unregistered union may achieve sole bargaining status through voluntary agreements with the employer.[161] In neither instance, however, may such a relationship be protected by an NIRC order.

Subsequent to the Commission's recommendations, the employer or the union may make an application to the Court and, if the Court is satisfied that the recommendations of the Commission were unconditional or that any conditions have been "sufficiently complied with," the Court is to request the Commission to establish a ballot of the employees in the unit to determine whether the recommendations of the Commission should be binding. The Commission or some other "body" may conduct the ballot but it must be kept "secret." If a "majority of the employees voting on the ballot are in favor" of making the Commission recommendation a binding one, the Court is to issue an order defining both the bargaining unit and the parties who are obligated to bargain. In Great Britain, one bargaining agent or joint panel recommended by the Commission is to be considered by the workers in an Industrial Court-ordered election, rather than any number of unions being on the ballot as in an NLRB-ordered election.

161. *See* 319 PARL. DEB. H.L. (5th ser.) 353-55 (1971).

Where there is no order by the Court—and this includes unregistered union relationships—a decertification petition or application may be entertained by the Court if it is "satisfied that not less than one-fifth of the employees for the time being comprised in the bargaining unit have signified in writing their concurrence in the application."[162] This may be done at any time. Accordingly, where settlement has been achieved or where no ballot has been applied for subsequent to a Commission recommendation, the relationship between union and employer is relatively unsheltered. Where there is an order by the Court in effect, such an application cannot be heard if it is filed within two years of the time that the initial recognition order was issued by the Court. Moreover, where there is an order by the Court the requisite number of employees supporting the petition is two-fifths rather than one-fifth. In the United States, of course, there are no such distinctions. In all cases a petition can be triggered by thirty per cent of the workers in an appropriate unit—the same number requisite to the filing of a representation petition.[163]

Finally, where an application with the Court has been filed pursuant to Section 45, and where questions have been referred to the Commission or are to be referred, neither the employer nor union may engage in lockouts, strikes or "irregular industrial action" or threaten to do so concerning the issues in dispute, while the matter is pending.[164] Further, where the Court has issued an order, it is an unfair industrial practice for the employer to bargain with an organization other than that referred to in the order or to refuse to bargain collectively with the appropriate party. Similarly, it is an unfair industrial practice for any party to engage in or threaten a strike or other irregular industrial action which would induce or attempt to induce the employer to engage in the above-mentioned violations. Accordingly, if a party moves quickly to utilize the Act's recognition

---

162. Ind. Rela. Act 1971, § 51(2).

163. The thirty per cent requirement for decertification petitions is contained in the National Labor Relations Act, 29 U.S.C. § 195(e) (1970). However, the thirty per cent requirement for the filing of a representation petition is an administrative regulation of the NLRB, promulgated pursuant to the Board's investigatory power under § 159. The regulation reflects the Board's administrative experience that in the absence of special factors the conduct of an election serves no purpose under the statute unless the petitioner has been designated by at least thirty per cent of the employees. 29 C.F.R. § 101.18 (1972).

164. See note 115 supra. Such activities are declared to be unfair industrial practices by § 54 of the Act. The purpose of the section is relatively clear on its face. The section does contain two rather wooly definitions of what questions qualify to create the potential for an unfair industrial practice and of when such questions are pending. See 319 Parl. Deb. H.L. (5th ser.) 397-400 (1971).

machinery under appropriate circumstances,[165] economic pressure that would otherwise be lawful becomes unlawful. However, although there is no American-type requirement that the union have made a demand for recognition as a prerequisite to the issuance of an injunction,[166] the Industrial Relations Court has already held that a recognition dispute must exist for an unfair industrial practice to be made out.[167]

The most glaring problem with the British recognition machinery is its apparent inability to function expeditiously. Section 45 sets into motion a very lengthy and complicated procedure. The involvement of two separate agencies would appear to compound such difficulties. The American experience is that speed is of special importance in the representation arena. Procedures have been devised to make the Board's representation process move more quickly[168] because employers are otherwise able to undermine union representation claims by delaying the workers' right of free choice. Consequently, although British employers may not prove as litigious or as likely to play for time in which to mount an effective anti-union campaign as their American counterparts, one should not be surprised if unions complain about the effectiveness of the procedures. However, if CIR investigation of a representation claim indicated that the employer were attempting to undermine the union during a delay, the Commission could report such a finding to NIRC. There is no indication that the Court will brook interference with the administration of the Act and, where the Court's own processes are at stake, the contempt power promises to catch short employers as well as unions. The American statutory scheme provides an unfavorable contrast by encouraging delay without providing judicial powers to a specialized labor court able to end the delay.

165. United States employers' attempts to frustrate union organization campaigns by initiating § 9(c) representation petitions before the union is ready to face a representation election are barred by an NLRB Regulation that if
a petition is filed by an employer, the petitioner must supply, within 48 hours after filing, proof of demand for recognition by the labor organization named in the petition and, in the event the labor organization named is the incumbent representative of the unit involved, a statement of the objective considerations demonstrating reasonable grounds for believing that the labor organization has lost its majority status.
29 C.F.R. § 101.17 (1972).
166. See, e.g., International Hod Carriers Building & Common Laborers, 135 N.L.R.B. 1153 (1962).
167. Car Collection Co., Ltd. v. Transport and General Workers Union, [1972] 2 All E.R. 97.
168. Effective May 15, 1961, the NLRB delegated to its regional directors "its power under § 9 to determine the unit appropriate for the purpose of collective bargaining, to investigate and provide for hearings, and determine whether a question of representation exists, and to direct an election or take a secret ballot under subsection (c) or (e) of section 9 and certify the results thereof." 26 Fed. Reg. 3911 (1961).

Of course, the recognition procedures have been established with a view towards reaching settlements without the recommendations of the Commission and the orders of the Court. Although in the United States the NLRA does not so explicitly promote the parties' own arrangements, many employers and unions do enter into recognition agreements without a secret ballot and, indeed, some are compelled to do so on the basis of authorization cards by the Board.[169] It would appear, therefore, that private settlements may be encouraged by statutory machinery less unwieldy and delay-prone than that in the Act. Moreover, the statutory provisions which provide more protection to union-employer relationships established through court order than to those voluntarily negotiated contradict the spirit of voluntarism. Unions and employers which settle or accede to CIR recommendations without the ballot are more exposed to another union's raids than they would be otherwise. The principal reason for this is that a union which files for recognition must be both registered and independent, and it would detract from the importance of registration and independence to allow unions which lack these characteristics the same protection as those which have them.

So far as the recognition issue is concerned, the most difficult, and important, of the unanswered questions relate to the principle of exclusivity. It is quite clear that the Act obligates an employer confronted with an NIRC order to negotiate with none other than the "sole" or exclusive bargaining agent. Although joint panels of bargaining agents are contemplated by the statute, the indirect effect here may be to rationalize the untidiness of British trade union structure and to squeeze out the weaker or smaller unions and groups of shop stewards who now negotiate on behalf of a relatively small group of employees. Further, it seems likely that factory or plant comprehensive agreements can be more effectively negotiated where management is dealing with a sole bargaining agent. But union jurisdictional conflicts are typically bitter and, to the extent that the recognition machinery is used by unions and employers, the first years of Section 45 will be difficult ones indeed.

To some degree, however, the impact of the Act's provisions on recognition will be more gently felt if the parties devise their own solutions, as the framers of the statute hoped. Moreover, just as the Act provides for bargaining by a joint negotiating panel of trade unions, The Code of Industrial Relations Practice encourages co-

169. NLRB v. Gissel Packing Co., Inc., 395 U.S. 575 (1969); United Mine Workers of America v. Arkansas Oak Flooring Co., 351 U.S. 62 (1956).

operation between the stewards of different unions bargaining with one employer.[170] Therefore, unions which negotiate alongside other organizations, where relationships cut across the lines of an appropriate unit, need not fight to determine which party will be obliterated. The joint panel arrangement allows unions to come together in a process short of amalgamation.

The exclusivity issue will be troublesome for another reason as well. The individual contract of employment, which has little weight in the United States, is an important element in British labor laws.[171] No change in this tradition is attempted by the Act. Yet, the Act does not clarify the rights and responsibilities of unions with regard to non-union employees who are included in the bargaining unit. In the U.S., exclusivity means that a union bargains for all within the unit regardless of union membership and that a union owes each worker a duty of fair representation.[172] But, contrary to United States law, the individual contract of employment is retained in Britain even where the collective relationship between labor and management exists. Indeed, some of the Act's provisions relating to strike liability are framed around the inducement to breach an individual contract of employment.[173] The unions will apparently bargain only for those in the unit who desire to have them do so.[174]

Several provisions of the Act seem to look toward American-style exclusivity, but appearances here are deceptive. First, the Act amends the Contracts of Employment Act of 1963[175] so as to obligate the

---

170. Code of Practice, *supra* note 113, ¶¶ 112-15.

171. *See generally* C. Grunfeld, Modern Trade Union Law (1966); K. Wedderburn, The Worker and the Law 51-94 (2d ed. 1971); O. Kahn-Freund, *Legal Framework*, in The System of Industrial Relations in Great Britain 45-52 (A. Flanders & H. Clegg eds. 1954).

172. Vaca v. Sipes, 386 U.S. 171 (1967); Ford Motor Co. v. Huffman, 345 U.S. 330 (1953); Steele v. Louisville & Nashville R.R., 323 U.S. 192 (1944).

173. Ind. Rela. Act 1971, § 96. Liability premised on inducement of such breaches provides a sizeable deterrent to non-registered trade unions' organization of industrial action simply because of the omnipresence and nature of individual contracts of employment. *See generally* R. Hepple & R. O'Higgins, Individual Employment Law (1971).

174. The individual contract issue aside, the British wished to avoid involvement in the complicated, frustrating, and largely ineffectual duty of fair representation doctrine so prominent in United States law. *See* Herring, *The "Fair Representation" Doctrine: An Effective Weapon Against Racial Discrimination?*, 24 Md. L. Rev. 113 (1964). This duty comes fully into play only when the union speaks for all individuals in the bargaining unit. Whether the British can avoid the problems raised by the duty through mere avoidance of legal doctrine is questionable. Even more puzzling is the encouragement provided to individual bargaining in legislation designed to promote union responsibility.

175. Contracts of Employment Act 1963, c.49, *amended by* Ind. Rela. Act 1971, §§ 19, 20, 21 (amplified by Sched. 2). For a discussion of the purposes of such notification and past experience under the 1963 Act see 318 Parl. Deb. H.L. (5th ser.) 1352-71 (1971). The amendment of the 1963 Act by § 20 of the Industrial Relations Act was

employer to notify the employee of the grievance procedure which he may utilize. This obligation might reasonably imply that all workers have access to the procedure negotiated and that the union be held responsible for processing the grievances of non-unionists. However, it is possible that the Act's framers contemplated the existence of non-negotiated procedures for non-unionists in an otherwise unionized work place. Professor Selwyn, in one of the early writings on the Act,[176] said that a union has no responsibility to process grievances for non-unionists. If this is true, it will be necessary, where designating orders are obtained, to provide a parallel procedure for non-union employees. Secondly, the statutory provision for the agency shop[177] might reasonably imply adoption of American-style exclusivity. In an agency shop, the individual's freedom of choice regarding membership is preserved, but no premium is placed upon being a non-union member, *i.e.*, a "free rider," as would be the case if all payments could be avoided. The "free rider" problem, and thus the chief rationale for the agency shop, derives from a union's ability to negotiate for *all* within the union and its obligation to represent all fairly.[178] However, the framers of the Act did not articulate the "free rider" argument, which attracted Senator Taft during the 1947 debate in this country,[179] and we must assume that the agency shop was allowed for other reasons. Thus, without statutory or contractual instruction to the contrary, representation of non-unionists clearly overstates what the British intended in the Industrial Relations Act of 1971.

B. *Union Security Arrangements*

Under the Act, a worker covered by an agency shop agreement may refuse to become a member of a trade union if he agrees to pay "ap-

not all to the liking of the Opposition, however. Notification must be made of employees' § 5 rights, which include the right not to belong to a trade union. See 822 PARL. DEB. H.C. (5th ser.) 1161-76 (1971).

176. N. SELWYN, GUIDE TO THE INDUSTRIAL RELATIONS ACT, 1971 (1971).

177. The agency shop provisions are in Ind. Rela. Act 1971, §§ 11-16. Post-entry closed shop agreements can be made if approved by the Industrial Court but are intended to apply only in very limited situations, *i.e.*, when a closed shop is necessary to maintenance of union benefits. Examples offered during debate concerning where closed shops would be allowed were the entertainment and shipping industries. See 813 PARL. DEB. H.C. (5th ser.) 926-28 (1971), and debate there following. See The Times (London), May 6, 1972, at 4, col. 1.

178. *See* S. REP. No. 105, 80th Cong., 1st Sess., 6 (1947) *cited in* 1 LEGISLATIVE HISTORY OF THE LABOR MANAGEMENT RELATIONS ACT 1947, at 409, 412-13 (1948). *Cf.* NLRB v. General Motors Corp., 373 U.S. 734 (1963); Radio Officers Union v. NLRB, 347 U.S. 17 (1954).

179. For a discussion of legislative history see Union Starch & Ref. Co., 87 N.L.R.B. 779 (1949), *enforced*, 186 F.2d 1008 (7th Cir.), *cert. denied*, 342 U.S. 815 (1951).

propriate contributions to the trade union in lieu of membership in it."[180] Unions and employers may enter into collective agreements containing agency shop clauses. If the employer is unwilling to do so, and the union is unregistered, there will be no agency shop. A registered union may, however, apply to the Industrial Court, and thus trigger a balloting procedure. Preliminarily, the Court must determine whether the petitioning union has "negotiating" rights with the employer. If the union has such rights, the Court requests the CIR to take charge of the matter "with a view to the taking of a ballot on the question of whether an agency shop agreement should be made between the parties."[181] The Commission determines what group of workers should be covered by the ballot and reports to the Court on this matter. If a majority of the workers "eligible to vote" or not less than two-thirds of those who actually voted are in favor of an agency shop, the employer must enter into such a contract.[182] If a majority of those eligible to vote or two-thirds of those voting do not vote in favor of the agency shop, the Court shall make an order directing that no agency shop agreement involving the workers in question shall be negotiated for two years beginning with the date upon which the result of the election was reported by the Commission to the Court. Any such agreement made during that period shall be "void."[183]

This is to be contrasted with the procedures relating to the recognition of trade unions both in the United States and Great Britain, where a majority of those voting is required.[184] Moreover, this provision compares unfavorably with the now repealed portions of Taft-Hartley which provided for union shop elections in which, once again, a mere majority of those voting resulted in the creation of that form of union security. Employers will of course often negotiate the agency shop voluntarily but, where they do not, the voting is likely to prove a waste of the taxpayers' money, just as have union shop elections in the United States: Workers overwhelmingly vote for such clauses.[185] One would assume that voting will seem even more superfluous in Britain, where union security concepts are more

180. Ind. Rela. Act 1971, § 11; appropriate contributions are defined in § 8.
181. *Id.* § 11.
182. *Id.* § 13.
183. *Id.* § 13(3)(b). Where an agency shop has been instituted by a negotiation or an election, an application to rescind the agreement may be made by one-fifth of the workers covered by it. The Court will rescind the agreement unless a majority of those eligible to vote or those voting are in favor of the provision's continuance. *Id.* §§ 14, 15.
184. New York Handkerchief Mfg. Co. v. NLRB, 114 F.2d 144 (7th Cir. 1940), *cert. denied,* 311 U.S. 704 (1941).
185. *See* H.R. REP. No. 1082, 82d Cong., 1st Sess., 2-3 (1951).

firmly established[186]—albeit on a more informal basis. Accordingly, this aspect of the Act seems to be wasted motion, and the "two-thirds" provision, violating the concept of majority rule, can only cause acrimony and hard feelings.

In contrast to American law,[187] an employee who objects on "the grounds of conscience both to being a member of a trade union and paying contributions to a trade union" may, in lieu of membership, agree to make equivalent contributions to a charity to be determined by agreement between him and the union.[188] Whether conscience includes non-religious moral convictions is not clear at this time.[189] In the United States employees who have had religious objections to joining a union have been permitted to pay dues and initiation fees in lieu thereof.[190]

In the United States, Taft-Hartley specifically prohibits the closed shop, although some of the provisions make it possible for such an arrangement to survive in the construction industry.[191] In Great Britain the Act makes the pre-entry closed shop void,[192] even though its existence in that country on both the formal and informal basis is widespread. A worker who is refused employment because of a closed shop provision may apply to the Industrial Court and, if the Court finds that the clause in question is in "substantial derogation" of Section 5 rights, the Court declares the provision void. As in the United States, this legislation will strike down formal contract provisions, but may have little impact upon informal arrangements,

---

186. For instance, "the 'closed shop' affected in 1964 about three and three-quarters million workers in Britain, about one in six of the total work force but about two in five of trade union members." K. WEDDERBURN, THE WORKER AND THE LAW 461 (2d ed. 1971). *See also* W. McCARTHY, THE CLOSED SHOP (1964).

187. No exceptions are contained in NLRA § 8(a)(3), 29 U.S.C. § 185(a)(3) (1970), which allows union shop agreements under which membership in the union is required after thirty days employment. Membership, in fact, means payment of initiation and dues. See NLRB v. General Motors Corp., 373 U.S. 734 (1963).

188. Ind. Rela. Act 1971, § 9(b).

189. For a typical discussion of the moral vs. conscientious objector controversy, see 318 PARL. DEB. H.L. (5th ser.) 655-86 (1971).

190. Union Starch & Refining Co., 87 N.L.R.B. 779 (1949), *enforced,* 186 F.2d 1008 (7th Cir. 1951), *cert. denied,* 342 U.S. 815 (1951). Indeed the Supreme Court has made it clear that the strongest mandatory form of union security is the agency shop. This is quite contrary to a very general impression held by both lawyers and workers, *i.e.,* that membership and the union shop can be required. *See* Note, *Judicial Enforcement of Union Disciplinary Fines,* 76 YALE L.J. 563 (1967).

191. NLRA § 8(f), 29 U.S.C. 158(f) (1970) encourages the de facto closed shop in the construction industry, because it both permits pre-hire collective agreements, which allow the union to be recognized prior to a demonstration of majority support, and provides a seven day grace period for the union shop. NLRA § 8(f), along with Local 357, Teamsters v. NLRB, 365 U.S. 667 (1961), legitimize the hiring hall, which perpetuates the closed shop on a de facto basis.

192. Ind. Rela. Act 1971, § 7.

i.e., on the de facto closed shop. These arrangements are common and well-established in British industry. Thus, the Act encourages acrimony over an issue important to many unions without any real prospect of changing the conditions which triggered the individual employee's complaint.

Britain will permit "approved closed shop agreements." These are so-called post-entry closed shops, equivalent to our union shop (membership being required after employment). Here too a worker to whom the agreement applies may pay appropriate contributions to a charity in lieu of membership or the payment of monies to the union. But the parties cannot make a post-entry closed shop agreement themselves. Application must be made to NIRC by both parties jointly. If there has been no ballot rejecting the closed shop within the past two years, the Court will send the matter to the Commission for examination. The Commission must satisfy itself that certain criteria are met. The Commission may sanction an agreement where it is necessary to enable employees to be organized or to continue to be organized, to maintain reasonable terms and conditions of employment as well as reasonable prospects of continued employment, to promote or maintain stable arrangements for collective bargaining relating to such workers, or to prevent collective bargaining agreements from being frustrated.[193] If the Commission finds that *all* factors warrant a closed shop, and the purposes involved could not be achieved through the agency shop, the Court orders a ballot to be taken, if such has been applied for, or simply approves the closed shop. The voting requirements for approved closed shops are identical to those for agency shops—either a majority of those eligible to vote or two-thirds of those voting must support this form of union security. It should be noted that the amendment to the Act which established the "approved closed shop" was aimed at the peculiar problems of two or three industries,[194] and such shops will probably be approved in very few cases.

Taken as a whole, the union security provisions generate much wasted motion, since the closed shop prohibitions will be nearly impossible to enforce, the approved closed shop criteria are difficult to

193. Ind. Rela. Act 1971, Sched. I. pt. I, ¶ 5(1). For a discussion of the effect of these criteria on the scope of the closed shop exception see 813 PARL. DEB. H.C. (5th ser.) 1011-34 (1971).
194. The central two being the entertainment and shipping industries, *see* note 120 *supra*. *See also* debate following quoted material at 813 PARL. DEB. H.C. (5th ser.) 929-1082 (1971); 822 PARL. DEB. H.C. (5th ser.) 941-42 (1971). It should be remembered however that attempts to retain pre-entry closed shops in these industries were successfully resisted. See 318 PARL. DEB. H.L. (5th ser.) 919-27, 950-1024 (1971).

satisfy, and the agency shop elections will be mere formalities. The various procedures and prohibitions also undermine somewhat the Act's larger goal of promoting union responsibility and eliminating fragmented bargaining. These defects may be tempered, however, by management's statutory right to "encourage" union membership through non-coercive advice.[195] One must assume that, for the sake of amicable relations, many British employers will make good use of this right.

C. Enforcement of Collective Bargaining Agreements and the Right to Strike

The malaise of British industrial relations consists of both fragmented bargaining and the unconstitutional (in breach of agreed upon procedures) or unofficial (unauthorized) work stoppage. To some extent, statutory procedures concerning recognition and the appropriate bargaining unit cope with the former problem. But just as the alleged contractual irresponsibility of trade unions prompted Congress to pass the Taft-Hartley amendment, making labor contracts enforceable, so also has Britain's labor unrest led Parliament to embrace enforceability: The Industrial Relations Act creates a "conclusive presumption" that a collective bargaining agreement is a "legally enforceable contract"[196] and allows the parties to escape this presumption only by expressly specifying non-enforceability in the agreement.[197] In both countries legislative concern focussed on the disruption of orderly negotiation or grievance procedures by "wildcat" or unofficial strike action.[198] But the solutions devised differ markedly.

1. The Role of the Collective Bargaining Agreement

It is important to understand that, under the Industrial Relations Act, the employer's right to discharge an employee for any reason,[199] including the exercise of the strike weapon,[200] and the employee's

---

195. Ind. Rela. Act 1971, § 5(3).
196. Ind. Rela. Act 1971, § 34(1).
197. Id. § 34(2).
198. For the United States, see S. REP. No. 105, Pt. I, 80th Cong., 1st Sess., 15-18 (1947).
199. As summarized in dicta by Lord Reid in Ridge v. Baldwin, [1964] A.C. 40, 65: The law regarding master and servant is not in doubt. There cannot be specific performance of a contract of service, and the master can terminate the contract with his servant at any time and for any reason or for none. But if he does so in a manner not warranted by the contract, he must pay damages for breach of contract.
200. Dismissal for striking was possible without the incurrence by the employer of breach of contract responsibility because a strike was itself considered a breach. K. WEDDERBURN, THE WORKER AND THE LAW 109 (2d ed. 1971).

right to strike or engage in slowdowns, are governed almost exclusively by an individual's contract of employment and by the unfair dismissal provisions of the Act.[201] By contrast, under the principles of exclusivity in American labor law, these matters are typically governed by the collective bargaining agreement, which almost completely submerges any individual contract of employment.[202] Of necessity, given their central importance, American collective bargaining agreements are typically comprehensive and precise in their terms. This presents a stark contrast to Britain, and to most other industrially advanced countries, where the formal collective agreement, quite often an industry-wide document, speaks merely in terms of minimum wages and conditions of employment.[203]

The Industrial Relations Act accords a central role to the individual contract of employment. Under the Act, it is an unfair industrial practice for "any person, in contemplation or furtherance of an industrial dispute, knowingly to induce or threaten to induce another person to break a contract to which that other person is a party" unless the party so inducing or threatening is a registered trade union within the meaning of the Act, or is an individual acting "within the scope of his authority on behalf of a [registered] trade union."[204] The new provision, carrying with it the potential for unlimited judgments for unlawful stoppages, is the Act's most formidable weapon against strikes by unregistered unions. The burden imposed upon the union in many instances may be substantial, because the notice provisions of contracts of employment of individual employees may vary considerably. It is quite possible that the union will be obligated to refrain from striking or engaging in other forms of

201. Ind. Rela. Act 1971, § 22.
202. This has been definitively established ever since the Supreme Court's landmark decision in J.I. Case Co. v. NLRB, 321 U.S. 332 (1944). Because American labor law seeks affirmatively to promote unionization and employee solidarity, the statutory scheme, as interpreted by *J.I. Case*, seeks to discourage individual advantages which will lead to divisiveness.
203. See Bok, *Reflections on the Distinctive Character of American Labor Laws*, 84 HARV. L. REV. 1394, 1436 (1971).
204. Ind. Rela. Act 1971, § 96(1). Until 1971, inducing an individual breach of an employment contract was immunized from liability by the Trades Disputes Act of 1906, 6 Edw. 7, c.47, §§ 1, 3. But that Act did not immunize the secondary boycott. Under the new Act, it must be remembered, the liability imposed is not tort liability or liability for civil or criminal conspiracy. Rather, if an individual acts without the authority of a registered union to persuade others to strike in breach of their individual contracts, whether the strike is primary or secondary, he commits an *unfair industrial practice*. Action against him can only be taken in the NIRC. Thus the secondary boycott exception to the immunity provided by the Trades Disputes Act of 1906 is eliminated. The Solicitor General referred to § 96(1) as a "narrow modest" proposal. 811 PARL. DEB. H.C. (5th ser.) 1762 (1971). But the Opposition characterized it as not only "intolerable" but "vicious." 811 PARL. DEB. H.C. (5th ser.) 1703 (1971).

economic pressure until the workers or the union have given the employer notice of termination for each individual contract and the time required in each contract between notice and actual termination has elapsed. Moreover, unregistered unions cannot trigger industrial action where the procedural agreement which sets forth the manner for dispute resolution has been breached, even though the parties do not intend the agreement to be enforceable in court. On the other hand, registered unions may strike or engage in other kinds of economic pressure even though due notice for the individual contract of employment has not been provided or the procedure agreement has not been followed by the union.[205]

Similarly, the Act directly addresses the issue of unfair dismissals of employees, rather than leaving the problem to negotiation and to the collective-agreement. Section 22 of the Act protects employees[206] against an unfair dismissal and makes such employer conduct an unfair industrial practice.[207] American law does, of course, bar unfair discharges if they represent discrimination against union membership, or are in retaliation for other concerted activities but the closer American analogue to Section 22 is the "just cause" provision, typically found in collective agreements, which imposes a burden on the employer to evidence a substantial reason for the discharge.[208] A key advantage of Britain's statutory approach is that all employees are protected against unfair dismissals, while in America collective agreements protect only a minority of the labor force. The British Act also innovates by providing "conciliation officers" to administer the unfair dismissal rule, a feature conducive to the voluntary settlement of disputes which has no counterpart either in privately negotiated American grievance-arbitration machinery or in the unfair labor practice provisions of the NLRA.

---

205. See the thorough treatment of notice and the right to strike in N. SELWYN, GUIDE TO THE INDUSTRIAL RELATIONS ACT 1971, at 138-43 (1971).

206. It should be noted that the section protects "employees," not the broader class, "workers." An employee is "an individual who has entered into or works under (or, where the employment has ceased, worked under) a contract of employment." Ind. Rela. Act 1971, § 167.

That a conscious choice was made between the two terms is apparent from the dialogue at 318 PARL. DEB. H.L. (5th ser.) 1399-1402 (1971).

207. That the intent of the Government here was to create a third right in addition to the right to redundancy payments or to the right to sue in contract if a breach had occurred is apparent from 318 PARL. DEB. H.L. (5th ser.) 1388-92 (1971). For a discussion of law and proposals prior to the Act see G. CLARK, REMEDIES FOR UNJUST DISMISSAL: PROPOSALS FOR LEGISLATION (1970); Levy, The Role of Law in the United States and England in Protecting the Worker From Discharge and Discrimination, 18 INT'L AND COMP. L.Q. 558 (1969).

208. F. ELKOURI & E. ELKOURI, supra note 63, at 410-13.

But, compared with American practice, the British approach is not without flaws. First, the Act apparently places the burden of proving a dismissal is unfair upon the worker once the employer has provided his reason for the discharge.[209] Accordingly, the Act may provide less substantial protection than American "just cause" clauses in collective agreements. Second, the Act appears to allow an employer to dismiss any worker for engaging in any kind of strike. The appearance, however, may be deceptive. The Industrial Court may hold that Section 22's prohibition on unfair dismissals precludes discharge of employees for engaging in strike activity for registered unions, just as American arbitrators often hold that dismissal for union activity is inconsistent with a "just cause" provision in the collective agreement. Section 5 of the Act, which protects involvement in union activity, supports this view. At any rate, British management will not have much flexibility: An employee dismissed for strike activity must be reinstated if other striking employees of that employer have been reinstated[210] or were never similarly dismissed.[211] Though an American employer cannot discharge a worker for engaging in a walkout,[212] he can permanently replace the worker, even if other workers are not replaced.[213]

Finally, the British scheme may be crippled by a substantial reluctance in Britain to compel reinstatement as a remedy for unfair dismissal because of the common law view that the courts cannot compel the performance of personal services.[214] This view is reflected

---

209. See Hanna, *You're Fired*, The Sunday Times (London), July 23, 1972, at 53, col. 1.

210. Ind. Rela. Act 1971, § 26(2)(b).

211. Ind. Rela. Act 1971, § 26(2)(a). It should be noted that once again registration is important since the third clause of § 26 is applicable only to situations where dismissal or refusal to reinstate was premised on the exercise of § 5(1) rights, which are enjoyed only by members of registered trade unions. 318 PARL. DEB. H.L. (5th ser.) 1941-42 (1971). For a general description of the section's intent, see 318 PARL. DEB. H.L. (5th ser.) 1483-84 (1971). A proviso which would have limited the protection of the section only to pre-strike activities was eliminated in the House of Lords, 321 PARL. DEB. H.L. (5th ser.) 753-60 (1971). This elimination was upheld in the House of Commons, 822 PARL. DEB. H.C. (5th ser.) 1345-48 (1971) apparently because the proviso conflicted with recommendation of the 1970 ILO Conference.

212. NLRA § 7, 29 U.S.C. § 157 (1970); NLRA § 13, 29 U.S.C. § 163 (1970). *See generally* Getman, *The Protection of Economic Pressure by Section 7 of the National Labor Relations Act*, 115 UNIV. OF PA. L. REV. 1195 (1967); Gould, *The Status of Unauthorized and "Wildcat" Strikes Under the National Labor Relations Act*, 52 CORNELL L.Q. 672 (1967).

213. See NLRB v. Mackay Radio & Telegraph Co., 304 U.S. 333 (1938). See also NLRB v. Erie Resistor Corp., 373 U.S. 221 (1963).

214. Kahn-Freund, *Legal Framework*, in THE SYSTEM OF INDUSTRIAL RELATIONS IN GREAT BRITAIN (A. Flanders & H. Clegg eds. 1954).

For a somewhat critical discussion of the absence of reinstatement as a remedy, *see* K. WEDDERBURN, THE WORKER AND THE LAW 81-85, 137-51 (2d ed. 1971). The other

in the Act. The NIRC or Industrial Tribunals may assess damages, but cannot impose reinstatement or re-engagement as a remedy.[215] However, re-engagement may be recommended by a Tribunal, and the threat of damages may, of course, be used to encourage reinstatement. In the United States, reinstatement is a well-accepted remedy in cases arising under the National Labor Relations Act.[216] Arbitrators appointed under collective bargaining agreements are more prone to reinstate workers than to award back-pay. The absence of similar authority in Britain could contribute to industrial strife rather than reduce it. Trade unions retain the right to strike to compel reinstatement when it is not forthcoming or where resort has not been made to the appropriate machinery.[217] In America, workers generally abjure self-help measures in discharge cases, since the remedy of reinstatement is available through arbitration. Although the prospect of damages may promote settlement providing for re-engagement, the process could be bitter and lengthy in Britain if the parties have not provided their own machinery of settlement.

Thus, although the Act affords the collective agreement a lesser role than it enjoys in the United States, the Act's success may turn on its ability to encourage labor and management to compose agreements of greater scope and precision than is customary in Britain. Several features of the Act provide such encouragement.

On the subject of unfair dismissals, the parties may obtain "designating orders" which permit them to devise their own machinery, so long as it provides benefits equal or superior to those contained in the statute.[218] Although other problems may provide a more substantial impetus to the arbitral process, this provision could con-

section of the Act dealing with specific performance, § 128, proscribes enforced specific performance of employment contracts and seems to be in harmony with the historical position concerning employee protection.

215. Ind. Rela. Act 1971, § 106.

216. Reinstatement is specifically provided as an affirmative remedy under NLRA § 10(c), 29 U.S.C. 160(c) (1970). *Cf.* Phelps Dodge Corp. v. NLRB, 313 U.S. 177 (1941). As to the effectiveness of this remedy *see* Comment, *N.L.R.B. Power to Award Damages in Unfair Labor Practice Cases*, 84 HARV. L. REV. 1670, 1674-75 (1971).

217. This right is retained since "it is not specifically made an unfair industrial practice to take industrial action to secure the reinstatement of a dismissed employee, even if a complaint is currently before a tribunal or the tribunal has found the dismissal to be fair." Rideout, *Statutes: The Industrial Relations Act 1971*, 34 MOD. L. REV. 655, 657 (1971).

218. Ind. Rela. Act 1971, § 31. Section 31(2)(a) was designed to prevent collusion between a company and a company dominated union to secure a procedure agreement setting up a dismissal procedure under company control. *See* 318 PARL. DEB. H.L. (5th ser.) 1508-10 (1971); 822 PARL. DEB. H.C. (5th ser.) 1355-58 (1971). The Government definitely hoped that § 31 would lead to the extensive development of consensual dismissal procedures. Section 31(2)(e) was amended to remove any foreseeable bars in the statute itself to this development. *See* 318 PARL. DEB. H.L. (5th ser.) 1510-13 (1971).

stitute the beginning of a system of arbitration similar to that in the United States. Because of the large number of these cases, Section 22 could be one of the most important provisions of the Act. However, one important factor stands in the path of this development—and that is the attitude of the unions. Part of their policy of "non-co-operation" is a refusal by TUC-affiliated unions to apply for designating orders. While this position preserves consistency with overall trade union policy toward the Act, it ironically prevents workers from escaping the clutches of the Act's institutions and rules.

Like Taft-Hartley, the Act imposes an obligation to bargain collectively upon the employer, and this may encourage the negotiation of comprehensive agreements. This is particularly likely since the remedy for failure to bargain collectively is the imposition on the employer of contract terms by the government.[219] While contrary to the freedom of contract principles found in American labor law, and once adhered to in Britain, this solution should avoid the frustrations this country has faced in fashioning remedies for breach of the duty to bargain. The imposition of terms may also help some of the more obstreperous unions to accept the notion of comprehensive agreements.

It must be anticipated, however, that a good number of parties in Britain—usually at union insistence—will choose to make their agreements non-enforceable under Section 34(2). In Britain provision for this possibility was appropriate since, as the Donovan Commission noted, many collective agreements are not in a state to be enforced.[220] Looking to the long term, the Act, through the Code of Practice, attempts to improve agreements by inducing in the parties a sense of responsibility about bargaining.[221] If problems develop because of the ineffectiveness or absence of grievance procedures, the Act establishes a means of coping with this problem which is entirely foreign to the American experience. The Secretary of State or parties may apply to the Industrial Court claiming that existing procedure agreements are unsuitable to settle "disputes or grievances properly and fairly" or that a strike or irregular industrial action short of a strike is occurring contrary to the "terms or intentions" of the agreement that has been negotiated.[222] The Court may then, in

219. Ind. Rela. Act 1971, §§ 56, 126, 127.
220. ROYAL COMM. ON TRADE UNIONS, REPORT, *supra* note 65, at 126.
221. Paragraphs 1-23 enumerate the responsibilities of management, trade unions, employers' associations and the individual employee, portraying an ideal scheme based on awareness of a community of interests. CODE OF PRACTICE, *supra* note 113.
222. Ind. Rela. Act 1971, § 37(a).

some circumstances, impose grievance machinery upon the parties, a remedy once again antithetical to the collective bargaining philosophy incorporated in § 8(d) of the National Labor Relations Act.[223]

Unlike the Act, American law does not provide stop-gap solutions where the parties have made their agreement non-enforceable. Although the possibility was discussed at the time of Taft-Hartley's enactment,[224] the non-enforceable agreement has been a rare phenomenon in the United States. It raises, however, difficult legal questions—sufficiently difficult to make understandable the British desire to avoid them through detailed statutory mechanisms.

First, suppose that an American employer acquiesces to a union demand that the contract not contain a no-strike pledge[225] or that it contain an express employer waiver of the right to sue for breach of the contract. Since § 301 of the L.M.R.A. creates substantive law predicated on contract,[226] the courts would presumably respect such provisions. A second, and more difficult question, is whether a union would violate its duty to bargain in good faith by insisting on such forms of non-enforceability. Because that duty presumably requires the parties to have a good faith intention to reach an agreement,[227] the union could not simply insist on having no collective agreement. If, however, the union's demand were only to exclude the no-strike clause or to include the right-to-sue waiver, the matter would be less clear. Arguably, the manner in which disputes are to be resolved (*e.g.*, strikes, arbitration, court suits, etc.) is a condition of employment and a mandatory subject of bargaining, and, if so, insistence upon a particular view to the point of impasse would not violate the duty to bargain in good faith.[228] While there is authority that a particular remedy for contract breach, *i.e.*, the requirement of a performance bond, is not a mandatory item of bargain-

---

223. 29 U.S.C. 158(d) (1970). However, voluntary settlement is still the British goal. *See* 810 PARL. DEB. H.C. (5th ser.) 1520-26, 1557-66 (1971); 319 PARL. DEB. H.L. (5th ser.) 220-25 (1971).
Conciliation was emphasized by a Government amendment which required any applicant to Industrial Court to notify the Secretary of State, who would then offer his services in the cause of promoting agreement. 810 PARL. DEB. H.C. (5th ser.) 1577-1600 (1971). The opposition, however, still feared the effects of introducing law into the shop via imposition. 810 PARL. DEB. H.C. (5th ser.) 1541-43, 1546-52 (1971).
224. S. REP. No. 105, 80th Cong., 1st Sess., Pt. I, 15-18 (1947).
225. The most prominent example of a union attempt to exclude a no-strike clause was made by the United Mine Workers, who insisted that their no-strike pledge be operative only if the workers were "able and willing" to work. *See* S. ALINSKY, JOHN L. LEWIS: AN UNAUTHORIZED BIOGRAPHY 337 (1970).
226. Textile Workers Union v. Lincoln Mills, 353 U.S. 448 (1957).
227. *See* United Electrical, Radio and Machine Workers v. NLRB, 409 F. 2d 150 (D.C. Cir. 1969). *But see* NLRB v. American National Insurance Co., 343 U.S. 395 (1952).
228. Lloyd A. Fry Roofing Co., 123 N.L.R.B. 647 (1959).

ing,[229] the Supreme Court in *Boys Markets* stated that the employer's remedy for union breach of a no-strike pledge was critical to the very existence of the employer's contract right to be free of strikes during the term of the agreement.[230] This argues for construing the question of remedy as a mandatory subject of bargaining.

As a practical matter, however, the no-strike pledge and the employer's right to sue often constitute the vital *quid pro quo* for the employer's acceptance of arbitration. If, as the *Steelworkers Trilogy*[231] teaches, arbitration is essential to industrial peace, and if, as *Boys Markets* teaches, an enforceable no-strike pledge may sometimes be essential to maintaining the integrity and attractiveness of arbitration, we might expect the Court to find a breach of the duty to bargain when a union insists to the point of impasse on excluding the no-strike pledge or on securing a waiver-of-suit from the employer. It does appear, however, that a union can more modestly insist that the employer seek his remedy for breach of the no-strike pledge in the forum of arbitration, rather than in a court; in *Drake Bakeries*,[232] the Court stayed judicial proceedings where the employer had a contractual right to grieve and arbitrate union violation of the no-strike pledge.

2. *Regulation of Industrial Warfare*

Section 36(1)(a) makes it an unfair industrial practice for any party to a collective agreement to break it where the contract is enforceable. The primary question here is whether the parties will utilize the provision. The Labor Government, in its proposed anti-strike legislation which provided for a "conciliation pause," placed responsibility for bringing actions to the judiciary in the hands of the Minister of Employment and Productivity. In vain, employers sought the same statutory scheme from the Conservative Government in 1970 and 1971.

To critics of the Act, this employer lobbying confirmed that man-

229. NLRB v. American Compress Warehouse, Div. of Frost-United Co., 350 F.2d 365 (5th Cir. 1965), *cert. denied*, 383 U.S. 982 (1966).
230. Boys Market, Inc. v. Local 770, Retail Clerks, 398 U.S. 235, 249 (1970). On the closely related question of whether no-strike injunctions are a procedural or substantive remedy, see Lesnick, *State-Court Injunctions and the Federal Common Law of Labor Contracts: Beyond Norris-LaGuardia*, 79 HARV. L. REV. 757 (1966).
231. United Steelworkers of America v. American Mfg. Co., 363 U.S. 564 (1960); United Steelworkers v. Warrior & Gulf Nav. Co., 363 U.S. 574 (1960); United Steelworkers of America v. Enterprise Wheel & Car Corp., 363 U.S. 593 (1960).
232. Drake Bakeries, Inc. v. Local 50, American Bakery Workers, 370 U.S. 254 (1962). *Cf.* Local 721, Packing House Workers v. Needham Packing Co., 376 U.S. 247 (1964).

agement would not take legal action in any event, and that Section 36 was at best an irrelevance. This view was bolstered by the accurate (but nevertheless incomplete) reporting on the American system which indicated that employers in the United States rarely sue.[233] It was also pointed out that damage actions in the courts based upon no-strike violations are often withdrawn as part of the settlement reached after termination of the stoppage.[234] Withdrawal of the action is often the price of ending the strike. What was pushed into the background in this discussion, however, was evidence that the legal right to sue serves as a deterrent against the use of the strike weapon and that the withdrawal of the suit is often a *necessary quid pro quo* for the withdrawal of the strike. Doubters could focus upon the reluctance of British employers to sue individual workers for breach of employment contract, a remedy which was available prior to the passage of the Act.[235] But large union treasuries, albeit protected by statutory limitations upon the amount of damages that may be collected from registered unions,[236] may present a more inviting target than suits which might be entertained against individual employees. Section 36(2) obliges a party to the agreement to take all such steps that are "reasonably practicable" to prevent breach, language devised specifically for unofficial strike situations where individual employees, work groups, and shop steward committees, rather than unions, are normally the offending parties.[237] Since the effective date of the Act, all indications are that British management will not be bashful about relying upon litigation where there is no practicable alternative; indeed, the main criticism now seems to be that employers are too trigger-happy in filing actions with the Industrial Court.[238]

Nevertheless, while the Government may have exhibited wisdom in refusing to involve itself in enforcing breaches of contracts, and

233. P. Lowry, *supra* note 28.
234. *See* Gould, *On Labor Injunctions, Unions, and the Judges: The Boys Market Case,* 1970 Supreme Ct. Rev. 230-31 (1970).
235. Nat'l Coal Bd. v. Galey, [1958] All E.R. 91; Camden v. Lynott, [1966] 1 Q.B. 555.
236. Ind. Rela. Act 1971, § 117. Trade unions of less than 5,000 membership may be assessed a maximum of £5,000; those with 5,000 to 25,000 members, a maximum of £25,000; 25,000 to 100,000 a maximum of £50,000; 100,000 or more members, a maximum of £100,000. In addition a formula recovery limit of up to 104 weeks or £4,160, whichever is less, is imposed by § 118 on recoveries involving irregular treatment of members by trade unions or employee associations, employer violations of the basic rights section or unfair dismissal section, or breach by employers or workers organizations of the basic principles set out in the Act or their own rules.
237. Royal Comm. on Trade Unions, Report, *supra* note 65, at 128-40.
238. *See generally* The Sunday Times (London), July 30, 1972, for background on last summer's dock strike, which was aggravated by employer readiness to invoke the Act's remedies.

while this stance preserves the spirit of voluntarism, government involvement does carry with it the trappings of impartiality. The National Labor Relations Board, while it is not primarily concerned with breach of contract actions,[239] has responsibility for enforcing secondary boycotts, jurisdictional stoppages and organizational and recognitional picketing prohibitions contained in Taft-Hartley.[240] Although private parties may bring suits in the first two areas,[241] the Board has carried most of the burden. That unions have reconciled themselves to these prohibitions is undoubtedly attributable in part to the fact that the Board and not employers is the litigant.[242]

The Conservatives did not wish government to impinge unduly upon the parties' autonomous relationships and feared the political undertones of government-initiated litigation.[243]

But, ironically, the case for a government role seems stronger now that private litigation arising out of the dock strike has polarized TUC and the Government. If the Commission on Industrial Relations, for instance, occupied a position similar to that of the National Labor Relations Board, and could exercise discretion in the matters that could be heard by the Court, the statute would possess more flexibility. The CIR or some other agency could screen out those cases not suited to the judicial forum with its contempt powers. Perhaps the 1972 dock strike would have been less bitter if the CIR had been able to break it off before it reached the Court. It would also help if the CIR could require or encourage the parties to submit to arbitration. In the United States, the Board has held in the *Collyer Insulated Wire* case[244] that grievance-machinery is appropriate for deferral purposes where unfair labor practice charges are filed. Once arbitration begins to flourish in England, an amendment to the Act looking in this direction should be considered.

239. *See* NLRB v. C. & C. Plywood Corp., 385 U.S. 421 (1967).
240. NLRA § 8(b), 29 U.S.C. § 158(b)(4), and (7) (1970).
241. *Id.*
242. *Cf.* Cox, *The Role of Law in Labor Disputes,* 39 CORNELL L.Q. 592 (1954). However, charges must be filed by private parties and, under § 303, employers may file suits for § 8(b)(4) violations.
243. These were entirely reasonable fears given the militant and politically charged opposition of the trade union movement to both the Act and the Conservative Government responsible for it. *See* Jacobs, *Million May Strike on December 8,* The Sunday Times (London), Nov. 29, 1970, at 3, col. 1; Lewis, *Heath Government Taking A Firm Line Against Growing Turmoil of Walkouts,* N.Y. Times, Dec. 9, 1970, at 3, col. 4; Lee, *Unions Protest as Tories Press Bill to Regulate Labor Relations,* N.Y. Times, Dec. 4, 1970, at 13, col. 1; Weinraub, *British Workers March In Protest,* N.Y. Times, Feb. 22, 1971, at 7, col. 1.
244. 192 N.L.R.B. No. 150 (1971).

3. Trade Union Reorganization: The Role of Law

Although Professor Turner has contended that making collective agreements enforceable will simply create friction *inside* the union and, if anything, produce industrial warfare on a grander scale,[245] the Conservative Party's prophecies are equally plausible. The Government's view is that Section 36 will induce the unions to take a more active interest in employment conditions at the plant level.[246] This, of course, means more staff and technical assistance as well as involvement in both the negotiation and administration of the contract, changes which would move Britain toward the American model insofar as industrial unions are concerned.

But the unions, particularly the Transport and General Workers Union, have rationalized the absence of central union authority as "grass roots democracy." They fear that cumbersome procedures for calling strikes and instituting policy will diminish both the spontaneity and the effectiveness of the workers' representatives. Also, it may be that the unions' organizational structure is too weak to support legal regulation. Even though the impact of law in this context is concededly long run, the short run may see shop stewards, work groups and other local officials driven *away* from the national unions, which bargain minimum rates, and into the arms of small rival or "breakaway" unions.[247] This would, of course, be antithetical to the objectives of the Act's framers, and it would most certainly be disruptive. The dynamics of industrial relations in both the United States and Great Britain make local union acceptance of orders from Washington, D.C. or London a very chancy business. The risk is that local leaders have more to gain from defiance than acquiescence. Quite clearly, Parliament is relying upon what it hopes to be the law-abiding character of British workers. After this summer's events, that reliance seems somewhat questionable.

In the United States, union responsibility for membership actions exists by virtue of the collective agreement and is governed generally by Taft-Hartley common law agency principles.[248] A mem-

---

245. Turner, *Is Britain Really Strike Prone?: A Review of Incidence, Character, and Costs of Industrial Conflict* (1969).

246. Of course rationalization of trade union structures is also the aim of the Act's recognition and registration provisions.

247. *See generally* S. Lerner, Breakaway Unions and the Small Trade Unions (1961).

248. Contractual responsibility in federal and state courts exists by virtue of LMRA § 301(b), 29 U.S.C. § 185(b) (1970). *Cf.* United Construction Workers v. Haslip Bakery Co., 223 F.2d 872 (4th Cir. 1955), *cert. denied*, 350 U.S. 847 (1955). The rule of agency for the NLRA is contained in 29 U.S.C. § 152 (1970). *See* Sunset Line & Twine Co.,

ber's acts are not imputed to the union, generally speaking,[249] but officers, including unpaid stewards, can make unions responsible for their behavior.[250] Remaining somewhat cloudy is the extent of the union's obligation in a contempt action, particularly in a Section 301 proceeding where the agreement normally sets forth the steps to be taken by the union in urging its members back to work. The sanctions for contempt, as John L. Lewis and the United Mine Workers learned to their dismay, bite into the union's treasury.[251]

The British Act requires unions to use their best endeavors to prevent breaches of the collective agreement. Such endeavors include bona fide urgings and, when that cannot achieve the back-to-work objective, disciplinary action in the form of fines or expulsion. As stated by Solicitor General Geoffrey Howe:

> Section 36 does not necessarily require a union, for example, to discipline those of its members who do no more than *participate* in an unconstitutional strike. But it does require (and this is surely reasonable) a union which has itself agreed not to call, support or finance a strike in given circumstances to take active steps to discourage and prevent its members or officials from playing any part in promoting just such a strike. And this is the main purpose behind Section 36.[252]

In the recent landmark case, *Heaton's Transport, Ltd. v. Transport and General Workers Union*,[253] the House of Lords upheld an

79 N.L.R.B. 1487, 1508 (1948). Congress was against extending to the NLRA the very narrow rule of agency contained in the Norris-LaGuardia Act. *See* Ramsey v. United Mine Workers, 401 U.S. 302, 309-11 (1971). *Cf.* United Brotherhood of Carpenters & Joiners v. United States, 330 U.S. 395 (1947).

249. *See* 93 CONG. REC. 4022 (1947) (Remarks of Senator Taft). *But see* United States v. United Mine Workers, 77 F. Supp. 563 (D.D.C. 1948), aff'd, 177 F.2d 29 (D.C. Cir. 1949); United States v. Bhd. of Railroad Trainmen, 95 F. Supp. 1019 (D.D.C. 1951).

250. *See, e.g.,* NLRB v. Local 135, Teamsters, 267 F.2d 870 (7th Cir. 1959), *cert. denied*, 361 U.S. 914. *But see* NLRB v. P. R. Mallory & Co., 237 F.2d 437 (7th Cir. 1956).

251. United States v. United Mine Workers, 330 U.S. 258 (1947). *Cf.* Walker v. Birmingham, 388 U.S. 307 (1967). The British Industrial Court is in a much better position to impose contempt than is the NLRB. *See* Bartosic and Lanoff, *Escalating the Struggle Against Taft-Hartley Contemnors*, 39 CHI. L. REV. 255 (1972).

252. Howe, *The Industrial Relations Act and Its Impact on Collective Agreements and Bargaining Structure*, IND. RELA. REV. & REPORT 8 (reprint, undated).

253. [1972] 3 All E.R. 101. For British reaction to this decision see Elliott, *What the Lords' Decision Means for the Union Leadership*, Financial Times (London), July 28, 1972, at 14, col. 3; Hanna, *New Decisions on Strike Law May Add to the Chaos*, The Sunday Times (London), July 30, 1972, at 47, col. 1; Wigham, *Ruling the Unions Are Unable to Enforce*, The Times (London), Aug. 1, 1972, at 21, col. 1. Mr. Wigham, a member of the Donovan Commission, states that the principal roadblock to union enforcement of discipline is the open shop which permits non-unionists to escape the union's wrath. "The Act attempts to do virtually contradictory things—to force the unions to exercise greater central authority and to prevent them from doing so by giving workers the right to leave their unions whenever they wish without suffering any adverse consequences." *Id.* While the charge that workers have the right to leave *whenever they wish* is erroneous, nevertheless the criticism is valid and argues persuasively for repeal of the closed shop provisions of the Act. It is interesting to note

Industrial Court ruling, which the Court of Appeals had reversed,[254] that shop stewards may be regarded as officers and agents of the unions who must be disciplined by national officers if the union is to purge itself of contempt. The House found that the union's stewards were acting as agents because (1) the union rule book did not preclude shop steward industrial action, (2) custom and practice implied the grant of the requisite authority for stewards, (3) shop stewards were instructed by the union to represent their union and its members, and (4) the circumstances indicated that the stewards here were enforcing the national union's policy.[255] With regard to disciplinary actions which should have been taken by the union against stewards, the Industrial Court had noted simply that no union rules or policy had been issued to stewards concerning unfair industrial practices.[256]

But how will the unions be induced to take whatever steps are necessary? While injunctions can be issued against unions, no orders can be issued compelling individuals to work.[257] While the officials of unregistered unions are exposed to personal liability,[258] and the Court has the traditional contempt sanctions to be employed against union officials and strike leaders, in the final analysis the use of such procedures merely creates instant martyrdom. The principal remedies are apparently damages against a union treasury, not to be recovered against individuals even if they are union officials, and the deterrent of contempt. Unions threatened with sequestration of their property (as occurred in *Heaton*) will think again about their course of conduct. This, according to the House of Lords in *Heaton*, is the "primary method contemplated by the Act" to implement the contempt power.[259] For unregistered unions the amount of compensation that may be assessed is unlimited.[260]

---

that Professor Cox made this criticism of Taft-Hartley. *See* Cox, *Some Aspects of the Labor Management Relations Act, 1947*, 61 HARV. L. REV. 274, 298-99 (1948). For other British views on this subject prior to the Act see Roberts, *The Unions Must Pay for Unofficial Strikes*, The Sunday Times (London), June 1, 1969, at 12, col. 1; Jacobs, *Unions: Can Mr. Wilson Check the Wildcats?*, The Sunday Times (London), Oct. 22, 1967, at 12, col. 1.

254. The NLRC opinion is at [1972] 2 All E.R. 1214; the reversal by the Court of Appeals is at [1972] 2 All E.R. 1237.

255. [1972] 3 All E.R. 101.

256. [1972] 2 All E.R. 1214, 1232.

257. Ind. Rela. Act 1971, § 128.

258. Ind. Rela. Act 1971, §§ 101, 153.

259. [1972] 3 All E.R. 101, 108.

260. This is because no limit is placed on compensation against unregistered workers' organizations under § 117 and because § 96 makes all persons liable, with a special reservation for trade union officials operating within the scope of their authority. In addition, trade union officials alone are exempted from compensation awards by § 101 while the personal property of union trustees is protected by § 153.

In the U.S., under Section 301, the Court has held that union officials are not individually liable.[261] The contrary rule prevailing at the time of the *Danbury Hatters* case, where organized labor literally had to pass the hat to pay off damages assessed against the union, left an extremely bad taste in the mouths of unionized workers. Congress did not wish to reintroduce that bitterness under Section 301. Insofar as the Act permits British employers to sue entities other than the union itself, it risks serious discord. Insofar as the statute *encourages* employers to sue the unions rather than individuals, it seems to be soundly conceived.

Finally, and unfortunately, Section 36 apparently requires a union to take reasonably practicable steps to suppress a work stoppage even if the stoppage was precipitated by the improper, or indeed unlawful, conduct of the employer.[262] One is reminded of the sorry failure of the courts and the NLRB in this country to protect the rights of those who incidentally break collective agreement provisions when striking or picketing to protest employer and union discrimination against minority group workers.[263] As this example shows, the American system's greatest deficiency is its refusal to permit considerations of public policy to override strict legal doctrine. In Britain, fortunately, the NIRC has remarkably broad discretion to weigh the equities in assessing damages or in issuing other decrees.[264] Certainly, in any action against a union, the Court should consider whether the employer has himself adhered to the standards established in the Code of Practice.

261. Atkinson v. Sinclair Refining Co., 370 U.S. 238 (1962), and cases discussed therein.

262. This is because no exceptions are provided in § 36 for action taken in light of mitigating circumstances. *But see* discussions at 321 PARL. DEB. H.L. (5th ser.) 864-70 (1971) over an amendment which would have conditioned the obligation of trade unionists on the "reasonable justification" for a strike. The issue in point during that "presence or absence" discussion was the analogous one of strikes over unsafe working conditions. The Lord Chancellor replied that the protection afforded by the "just and equitable standard," to be applied to remedies, gave far more protection than would the amendatory language. Debate on § 36 generally focused on the inequity of forcing union officials to act as policemen and on the ambiguity of the phrase "reasonably practical steps." *See generally* 810 PARL. DEB. H.C. (5th ser.) 1397-1419, 1466-1504 (1971); 822 PARL. DEB. H.C. (5th ser.) 1493-1505 (1971).

263. *See* Gould, Judicial Review of Employment Discrimination Arbitration, Paper Delivered to 25th Annual Meeting of the National Academy of Arbitrators, Boston, Mass. April 7, 1972; Gould, *Black Power in the Unions: The Impact Upon Collective Bargaining Relationships*, 79 YALE L.J. 46 (1969); *see, e.g.*, NLRB v. Tanner Motor Livery Ltd., 419 F.2d 216 (9th Cir. 1969); The Emporium, 192 N.L.R.B. No. 19 (1971).

264. Thus § 101 provides that the NIRC if it finds an unfair industrial practice, may grant compensation or prohibitory injunctions "if it considers that it would be just and equitable to do so." In addition § 116 introduces the just and equitable concept into the determination of the amount of such compensation. *See* 319 PARL. DEB. H.L. (5th ser.) 1358-74 (1971). *Compare*, in the United States, Mastro Plastic Corp. v. NLRB, 350 U.S. 270 (1956); Arlan's Department Store, 133 N.L.R.B. 802 (1961); Nat'l Tea Co., 198 N.L.R.B. No. 62 (1972).

4. *Adjudication of the Act*

The Act places exclusive jurisdiction for the interpretation of collective agreements in the hands of the Industrial Relations Court which is composed of both lawyers and lay people knowledgeable about industrial relations. While Parliament did not provide any grant of authority to the Court to fashion a law of contract for collective agreements similar to what Mr. Justice Douglas was able to extrapolate from Section 301 in *Lincoln Mills*,[265] it is obvious that the composition of the Court, and its charge to conduct itself in an informal manner, means that special rules of law were anticipated. By contrast, Section 301 places authority and confidence in courts which are not specialized and not nearly so well equipped. Of course, in reality, both before and after the *Steelworkers Trilogy*,[266] most collective agreement interpretation went to arbitration. In Britain the framers of the Act contemplate a similar trend. Indeed, the Act gives a boost to arbitration by encouraging the parties to devise their own procedures on dismissals.[267] This year's pact between the Trades Union Congress and the Confederation of British Industry providing for conciliation and arbitration, may also be a step in the right direction, although it is difficult at this point to say what role arbitration will play in the mix. There is no corps of arbitrators ready to be pressed into action, as was the case in the United States after World War II, when War Labor Board personnel—both knowledgeable and familiar to the parties—moved into private arbitration. When the unions decide to participate with employers in making joint applications for "designating orders" permitting them to establish their own unfair dismissal settlement machinery, arbitrators may begin to appear on the British industrial relations scene.

How broadly the NIRC will construe the concept of collective agreement is not clear. Written minutes which reflect agreements, as well as documents which set forth "side" agreements or amendments to existing contracts, will probably be included. A more difficult problem relates to oral contracts. On the one hand, one might assume that the rules established by the *Ford*[268] decision would argue

265. 355 U.S. 448 (1957).
266. *See* note 231 *supra*.
267. Ind. Rela. Act 1971, § 31. In neither country, however, is arbitration mandated by statute. Such a mandate is given in the Railway Labor Act in the United States, 45 U.S.C. §§ 151 *et seq.* (1970). *See* Brotherhood of Railroad Trainmen v. Chicago R. & I. Railroad Co., 353 U.S. 30 (1957). Note also that arbitration is specifically encouraged in the United States by LMRA § 203(d), 29 U.S.C. § 173(d) (1970).
268. Ford Motor Co. v. A.U.E.F.W., [1969] 2 Q.B. 303, which held collective agreements not enforceable in a court of law. For the contrary view, argued persuasively, see Selwyn, *Collective Agreements and the Law*, 32 Mod. L. Rev. 377 (1969). Selwyn

against legal enforceability for such contracts. On the other hand, it would appear that Parliament assumed that there might be a new legal status for agreements not specifically covered by Section 34. (That Section excludes from its coverage both oral contracts and pre-1971 contracts.) After all, the Act repealed prospectively Section 4 of the Trade Union Act of 1871,[269] which had previously precluded the enforcement of agreements negotiated between unions and employer associations. The Industrial Relations Act does not state that agreements must be in writing or must be made subsequent to the effective date of the Act to be enforceable. Accordingly, it is arguable that Parliament viewed such agreements as enforceable in the courts.

5. Reminder on the American Experience

It is obviously difficult to predict whether, and to what degree, the Act, and in particular its enforceability provisions, will lead to comprehensive collective bargaining agreements, to acceptance of arbitration as an institution, and to more centralized and responsible national unions. To expect an immediate replication of American practices would, however, be clearly naive. Americans often forget, and the British fail to understand, that the law did not shape the institutions which are at the heart of the industrial relations system in this country. To be sure, the duty to bargain established by statute in 1935 forced employers to come to the bargaining table where many of them would not have done so without the law, and to some extent the obligation to negotiate to the point of impasse over particular subjects influences what items go into the contract.[270] But grievance-arbitration machinery in collective agreements, with some form of no-strike pledge[271] by the unions, was well on its way before the Taft-Hartley amendments with Section 301 came on the scene. Indeed, six years before the enactment of Section 301, the Supreme Court held that the obligation to bargain in good faith includes the requirement that both parties must reduce their agreement to writing

has since maintained that the NIRC will enforce agreements entered into prior to passage of the Industrial Relations Act of 1971. N. SELWYN, GUIDE TO THE INDUSTRIAL RELATIONS ACT, 1971, at 83-84 (1971). Compare the American law, as described in Summers, *Collective Agreements and the Law of Contracts*, 78 YALE L.J. 529 (1969).

269. Ind. Rela. Act 1971, sched. 9.

270. *See* NLRB v. Borg-Warner Corp., 356 U.S. 342 (1958); H. WELLINGTON, LABOR AND THE LEGAL PROCESS 49-125 (1968).

271. *See generally* BUREAU OF NATIONAL AFFAIRS, BASIC PATTERNS IN UNION CONTRACTS (1971).

once they have reached accord.[272] This legal doctrine facilitated the negotiation of comprehensive and detailed contracts in writing. Moreover, the War Labor Board during World War II set the stage for the more activist role which Congress, the Court, and arbitrators were later to play.[273] The Board encouraged and sometimes ordered the use of grievance and no-strike clauses in contracts and familiarized the parties with impartial arbitrators upon whom they might rely for the interpretation of such documents. Accordingly, Section 301 as well as the Court's holdings in *Lincoln Mills, Steelworkers Trilogy* and *Boys Markets* essentially reflect what the private parties, albeit operating within a legal framework which did not hesitate to nudge them, had done for themselves already. While the Court and Congress have since become more activist, through the enactment of and interpretation given to Taft-Hartley, and while it would appear that the rules of law have thus had some impact on the parties' behavior, this impact has never been measured with any exactitude.[274] The promotion of arbitration and of informal, non-legal procedures makes actual judicial intervention infrequent.[275] The American experience thus teaches that law is most useful in ratifying prior trends, and that legal rights contribute to industrial peace—but only when invoked as a last resort.

D.   *Secondary Boycotts*

Section 98 of the Act makes it an unfair industrial practice to threaten or engage in strikes or "irregular industrial action" against a third per-

---

272.   H.J. Heinz Co. v. NLRB, 311 U.S. 514 (1914). The rule articulated in *Heinz* was enacted in 1947, LMRA § 101, 29 U.S.C. § 158(d) (1970). Moreover, the NLRB has held that a contract must be in writing to act as a contract bar to a rival union's representation petition. Appalachian Shale Co., 121 N.L.R.B. 1160 (1958). The contract must not only be written but also "comprehensive."

273.   Frank and Edna Elkouri appraised the War Labor Board's effect in this way: A great impetus in the use of arbitration was given by the National War Labor Board during World War II. The work of the Board constitutes an extensive experience in the use of arbitration. It was created by executive order in 1942 and was given statutory authority by the War Labor Disputes Act in 1943. Most of the 20,000 labor dispute cases determined by the Board during the war emergency were disputes over the terms of collective agreements. Of special importance was the Board's policy of requiring the use of clauses providing for arbitration of future disputes over the interpretation or application of the agreement. This policy of the Board laid the foundation for the popular practice today of terminating the contract grievance procedure with the final step of arbitration.
F. ELKOURI & E. ELKOURI, HOW ARBITRATION WORKS 10 (1960). *See also* Freiden & Ulman, *Arbitration and the War Labor Board*, 58 HARV. L. REV. 309 (1945).

274.   *Cf.* H. WELLINGTON, LABOR AND THE LEGAL PROCESS 96-125 (1968).

275.   Mr. Justice Brennan, speaking for the Court in *Boys Market*, where it was held that injunctions could be issued by the courts in cases of strikes over arbitrable grievances, reasoned that if the courts could enjoin stoppages and order arbitration of the underlying dispute, employers might be less tempted to sue for damages. Boys Market, Inc. v. Local 770, Retail Clerks, 398 U.S. 235, 248 (1970).

son who has entered into a contract with the primary employer, where the purpose is to induce a breach of the contract or to prevent the third person from performing it. Though phrased more specifically than its American counterpart in Section 8(b)(4) of the NLRA, Section 98 presents the same concepts.[276]

The British secondary boycott provisions are defective in prohibiting a union only from threatening or engaging in economic pressure to break the commercial contract between the primary and secondary. As American unions were quick to realize in 1947, there are more subtle means available to bring pressure on a secondary, and the statute was amended in 1959 to reach such methods.[277] The Industrial Relations Act is more narrowly drawn than the 1959 amendments, and this may encourage union appeals to management which have the unlawful object but which contain no threat of economic sanctions by the union.

Section 98(1)(c) states that the party whose commercial contract is interfered with must be "extraneous" to the dispute. This seems a formulation of the "ally" doctrine, a product of case law in the United States.[278] It is no easy task to determine when a secondary is an ally of the primary and thereby without immunity from trade union action. The ally doctrine permits unions to picket and encourage strikes where the primary employer has farmed out or subcontracted work that would have been performed, but for the strike, by primary employees. If unions could not take action against the secondary under such circumstances, primary strikes could be broken easily. But what is struck work? How substantial must be the benefit to the primary from the subcontract to permit union action? To use the British statutory language, how "material" must the support of the secondary be? Does it matter when the subcontract was made—or whether or not the subcontract can be justified on an economic basis unconnected with

276. In the United States, the Supreme Court has held that union pressure for an unlawful object, *i.e.*, to require a third party to cease doing business with a primary employer, is found even where the pressure simply has the effect of disrupting the business relationship. NLRB v. Local 825, Operating Engineers, 400 U.S. 297 (1971).

277. *See* note 3 *supra*. Under the 1947 amendments, the NLRA did not "speak generally of secondary boycotts. It describes and condemns specific union conduct directed to specific objectives. It forbids a union to strike against or to refuse to handle goods . . . . Employees must be induced; they must be induced to engage in a strike or concerted refusal. . . . A boycott voluntarily engaged in by a secondary employer for his own business reasons is not covered by the statute." Mr. Justice Frankfurter for the Court in Local 1976, United Brotherhood of Carpenters & Joiners v. NLRB, 357 U.S. 93, 98-99 (1958). This situation was altered by the 1959 amendments. *See* NLRB v. Servette, Inc., 376 U.S. 46 (1964).

278. *See* NLRB v. Business Machine & Office Appliance Mechanics Local 459, 228 F.2d 553 (2d Cir. 1955), *cert. denied*, 352 U.S. 962 (1956); Douds v. Architects, Engineers, Chemists & Technicians Local 231, 75 F. Supp. 672 (S.D.N.Y. 1948).

the strike? These are but some of the questions left open, both in America and in Great Britain.[279]

A union breaks the British Act, only by "knowingly" inducing the secondary employer to break its contract with the primary or, in the absence of a full breach, by knowingly preventing performance of the contract. But the Act does not state whether the secondary employer must also knowingly enter into the commercial contract, in the sense of knowing about the industrial dispute between the union and the primary. In the United States an employer can be viewed as an ally of the primary by "unknowingly" performing strike work, if the secondary might have reasonably ascertained that a labor dispute was in progress.[280] The Board has stated that the employer has the "burden of determining whether he is engaged in neutral or ally type work."[281]

These problems aside, it seems unlikely that Britain will go through the same painful twists and turns which have characterized American labor law in the secondary boycott arena. In the first place, even in this country, secondary boycott litigation is concentrated in the construction and trucking industries—and, generally speaking, in areas of work where the International Brotherhood of Teamsters represents workers. Major industrial unions, like the United Auto Workers, rarely, if ever, use the boycott. Second, as Bok has pointed out,[282] secondary boycotts are less prevalent in a country like Britain where bargaining is industry-wide and thus where replacements can rarely be brought in to keep the primary enterprise operating. Nevertheless, whatever the forum of bargaining, British *strikes* often occur on a plant basis. But given British working class solidarity, workers thrown out of work by a stoppage in another plant are not likely to break ranks and move to replace their striking "brothers." In the United States, where unions are less well organized in some industries, one cannot always make the same confident estimate of worker loyalty.

Section 98(3) does attempt to answer some questions which are frequently litigated in the United States. That subsection states; for instance, that a party is not to be regarded as an ally "only" because it is an employer who is "associated" with the primary or because it is "a

279. *See generally* Lesnick, *Job Security and Secondary Boycotts: The Reach of N.L.R.A. §§ 8(b)(4) and 8(e),* 113 U. PA. L. REV. 1000 (1965); Lesnick, *The Graveman of the Secondary Boycott,* 62 COLUM. L. REV. 1363 (1962).
280. Fox Valley Material Supplies Ass'n, 176 N.L.R.B. No. 51 (1969).
281. *Id.*
282. Bok, *Reflections on the Distinctive Character of American Labor Laws,* 84 HARV. L. REV. 1394, 1442-43 (1971).

member of an organization of employers of which a party to the industrial dispute is also a member."[283] Similarly, the fact that a party has contributed to a fund established to defray losses in connection with the labor dispute will not automatically establish the employer as an ally. Where the contract between the secondary employer and the primary was established prior to the time when the "industrial dispute began," the secondary is not regarded as an ally. Presumably, however, the way is open for the Industrial Court to inquire carefully into the circumstances surrounding the negotiations of the commercial agreement so as to determine whether the secondary had notice or should have had notice of the impending industrial dispute. The mere fact that the contract was entered into prior to the dispute ought not to be conclusive, and it appears that Section 98(3)(d) of the British law, like its American counterpart, intends no such result.

E. *Emergency Dispute Procedures*

Applications may be made by the Secretary of State to the Industrial Court where industrial action has caused or would cause an interruption in services "likely" to be "gravely injurious to the national economy, to imperil national security or to create a serious risk of public disorder . . . ."[284] An application may also be made where

283. For the American analogue on interference with the commercial contracts of secondary employees and their employers, see NLRB v. Internat'l Rice Milling Co., 341 U.S. 665 (1951). The opposition in Britain not only expressed fears that this provision of the statute would be a backdoor approach to curtailing all legitimate striking but also argued that the clause as drawn was fundamentally unfair. This argument was founded in part upon the fact that "associated employer" is defined in § 167(8) as a company under the control of another company, either directly or indirectly, or under the control of the same third person as another company. The argument was that such companies were not innocent and that combinations of employers for mutual support were being allowed while combinations of workmen for mutual support were not. *See generally* 811 PARL. DEB. H.C. (5th ser.) 1923-2005 (1971). *Compare, e.g.*, J. G. Roy & Sons Co. v. NLRB, 251 F.2d 771 (1st Cir. 1958); Local 46, Miami Newspaper Pressmen v. NLRB, 322 F.2d 405 (D.C. Cir. 1963).

284. Ind. Rela. Act 1971, § 138(2)(c). Section 138 of the Act speaks of "irregular industrial action short of a strike" as a triggering mechanism for the emergency strike procedures. In Secretary of State for Employment v. Aslef and Others, reported in The Times (London), May 20, 1972, at 5, col. 3, the Court of Appeals held that a "working to rule"—a sophisticated British version of the slowdown in which the employee strictly adheres to rules not normally followed—constitutes irregular industrial action within the meaning of the Act. (The NIRC decision is at [1972] 2 All E.R. 853.) This decision will trouble British authorities like Professor Kahn-Freund who regard work to rule as an "insoluble problem" for lawyers. *See* O. KAHN-FREUND, LABOUR AND THE LAW 266-67 (1972). The decision in *Aslef* is significant because all of the anti-strike provisions of the Act attempt to catch "irregular industrial action" and because "work to rule" is a favorite tactic of British unions. Much of the debate surrounding this whole section of the Act centered on the relative success or lack of success of the American Taft-Hartley procedure. *See generally* 812 PARL. DEB. H.C. (5th ser.) 665-732 (1971). Concern was also expressed over removing control of such issues from Parliament and

the dispute endangers the lives of a substantial number of individuals or exposes many people to serious risk of disease or personal injury.[285] Although Section 138 differs superficially from Taft-Hartley in scope, the latter statute covering only disputes which affect the national "health and safety," the American cases interpreting the NLRA have not yet established whether strikes injurious to the national economy, and of massive dimension, may be enjoined as contrary to the national health and safety. Mr. Justice Douglas, dissenting in the one national emergency dispute to reach the Court, stated that the majority applied a "material" well-being test to Taft-Hartley.[286] Facially, however, the British statute is broader. The justification for this is that the British economy is more open to, and dependent on, foreign trade; strikes in export industries are thus more likely to affect directly the nation's well-being than is the case in the United States.

The Industrial Court may, subsequent to receiving an application, order the discontinuance of a strike or other form of industrial action for a period not to exceed sixty days.[287] This sixty-day "injunction" parallels American law which, subsequent to the petition by the Attorney General to a federal district court, allows the issuance of an injunction for a period of eighty days if the dispute affects the nation's health and safety.

The most controversial portion of the emergency procedures, Section 141, provides for a ballot by the workers where "there are reasons for doubting whether the workers who are taking part or expect to take part in the strike or other industrial action are or would be taking part in accordance with their wishes, and whether they have

giving it to the courts. 322 PARL. DEB. H.L. (5th ser.) 386-98 (1971). As for § 83(2) concern was expressed that the standard "injurious to the national economy . . . etc." was too vague and hence prone to abuse. See, e.g., 812 PARL. DEB. H.C. (5th ser.) 689-700; 721-24; 322 PARL. DEB. H.L. (5th ser.) 399-408 (1971). This argument was answered by the Solicitor General, at 812 PARL. DEB. H.C. (5th ser.) 708-12 (1971).

285. Ind. Rela. Act 1971, § 138(2)(b). British emergency strike powers, such as they were prior to the 1971 Act, were contained in the Emergency Powers Act of 1920. However, that statute was more narrowly geared to essential services and provided for the requisitioning of troops, goods and property and the control of prices rather than for strike injunctions.

286. United Steelworkers v. United States, 361 U.S. at 62-77. Some of the recent American cases indicate that the meaning of "health and safety" is not defined with clarity as of this time. See, e.g., United States v. Local 418, ILA, 78 L.R.R.M. 2801 (7th Cir. 1971); United States v. Longshoremen, 79 L.R.R.M. 3043 (S.D. Ga. 1971).

287. Ind. Rela. Act 1971, § 139(1)(c). The relative success of the Taft-Hartley cooling-off procedure was cited by the government as support for instituting such a plan in Britain. However, the government opted for a plan with no mandatory "best offer" vote because of an evaluation that this element of the American Taft-Hartley procedure was more conducive to heightened tensions than to settlement. See 812 PARL. DEB. H.C. (5th ser.) 687-88 (1971).

had an opportunity to indicate their wishes in this respect . . . ."[288] The Court of Appeal has already held that the Minister himself is only required to have the doubts and the burden is upon the opposing party to show that a reasonable man could not have doubts on this question.[289] Unlike Taft-Hartley which provides for a ballot fifteen days prior to the expiration of the eighty-day injunction on the employer's last offer, the Industrial Relations Act permits the Secretary of State to order a ballot at his discretion. That there is nothing automatic about the process is fortunate, for American experience indicates that ballot procedures weaken emergency dispute legislation.

The American legislation was predicated upon the notion that the rank-and-file in many instances are more reasonable than their leaders. In fact, however, the rank-and-file are typically *more* militant than the leadership, and despite the fact that the British Ford workers undercut union leaders in a ballot procedure in 1970,[290] all indications are that British workers will also put pressure upon, rather than tamely follow, their leaders. In the 1972 railway strike the Government sought a ballot and achieved the same result as do the American authorities, *i.e.*, rejection of the offer.[291] In the United States, the ballot procedure has made the emergency pause a time for heating up rather than cooling off. Union leaders and the rank and file see the ballot as a vote of confidence for union leadership. The bargaining position of the parties becomes frozen as they posture for advantage.

Another major weakness of emergency strike provisions is that the parties come to rely upon them to "save the day." This stultifies col-

288. Ind. Rela. Act 1971, § 141(c). Section 143 prohibits economic pressure from the time the ballot is ordered by the Industrial Court until the result is reported to the court. The Secretary of State can apply for such a ballot if he has the doubt referred to in the text, and if in addition it appears to him there are or will be risks to the national economy or security, public order, or people's lives, or risks to the livelihood of a substantial number of workers in the industry involved. *Id.* § 141(2). The first of these tests derives from the emergency cooling-off order section. The second is unique to the ballot section and was seriously questioned in the debates. In addition, concern was expressed that such a ballot procedure would be more conducive to heightened tensions than to resolution of disputes. On the standard for the test regarding effect on livelihood see 322 Parl. Deb. H.L. (5th ser.) 413-16 (1971). On the absence of court review of the secretary's doubts, and possible CIR involvement in the ballot order procedure, see 320 Parl. Deb. H.L. (5th ser.) 315-19 (1971), dealing with § 142, which is the section providing for ballot orders pursuant to a 141 application. *See also* 322 Parl. Deb. H.L. (5th ser.) 421-26 (1971). Though there is a sixty day limit on cooling-off periods under § 139, the Industrial Court determines the period within which ballot results are to be reported to the court, and concern was expressed that this extends the cooling-off periods, given that no limit is placed on the ballot period. *See* 320 Parl. Deb. H.L. (5th ser.) 328-34 (1971).
289. Secretary of State for Employment v. Aslef and Others, *supra* note 284. Both American and British law place primary interpretive authority in the hands of the executive branch of government.
290. *See* Routledge, *Ford Strike Rejected in Mass Vote*, The Times (London), Feb. 16, 1970, at 1, col. 2.
291. The Times (London), June 1, 1972, at 15, col. 1.

lective bargaining. Moreover, the remedy, *i.e.*, injunction, is one-sided relief, inequitable from the union's point of view, even where the status quo is preserved. These factors have prompted scholars to propose a "choice of procedures" approach which would provide the government with more flexibility and a wide variety of weapons to be used in different situations.[292] Under this approach, the parties would be uncertain what would happen in the event government intervened, an uncertainty which might encourage them to resolve their problems on their own. Under the related "final offer" approach, both parties would make a final offer representing their true and uncompromisable positions and, after mediation of remaining issues, an arbitrator would be compelled to pick between the two offers.[293] The arbitrator would have to select one of the two *in toto*, thus encouraging the parties to make reasonable offers or to settle voluntarily.[294]

On balance, however, the Taft-Hartley procedures have been successful.[295] Before the two longshore strikes of 1971, the provision had been invoked only twenty-nine times since 1947.[296] Strikes had actually taken place in twenty-four instances. Of these twenty-four, sixteen have been settled without resort to another stoppage, thirteen during the eighty-day cooling-off period. The statistics show that Taft-Hartley works reasonably well; its provisions are accepted by trade unionists today and proposed by them as an acceptable alternative to an unqualified right to strike in public employment disputes. While the British labor unions are just as upset today with the sixty-day cooling-

292. Wirtz, *The "Choice of Procedures" Approach to National Emergency Disputes*, in EMERGENCY DISPUTES AND NATIONAL POLICY 159 (I. Bernstein, H. Enarson & R. Fleming eds. 1955); A. COX, LAW AND THE NATIONAL LABOR POLICY 48-63 (1960).

293. This approach was embodied in R. NIXON, RECOMMENDATIONS AND PROPOSALS TO DEAL WITH NATIONAL EMERGENCY LABOR DISPUTES, DOC. No. 91-266, 91st Cong., 2d Sess., March 2, 1970 [hereinafter cited as RECOMMENDATIONS]. However, a recent version of the proposal has been withdrawn. Bernstein, *Nixon Switch on Anti-Strike Bill Seen as Bid for Labor Support*, Los Angeles Times, July 21, 1972, at 1, col. 1.

294. "[W]hen the final offer selection is the ultimate recourse, the disputants will compete to make the most reasonable and realistic final offer, one which will have the best chance to win the panel's endorsement." RECOMMENDATIONS, *supra* note 293, at p. 4. *See also* Silberman, *National Emergency Disputes—The Considerations Behind a Legislative Proposal*, 4 GEORGIA L. REV. 673 (1970). The final offer procedure has, however, several possible defects: (1) The union may be less able to compromise once its offer is made public, and this may encourage employers to offer less than they otherwise might. (2) The parties may hold back compromises until the final offer, in which case final offers will diverge by large margins. (3) It may be very difficult for a side to put together a reasonable final offer without knowledge of the other party's position on all the unresolved issues. (4) The "win or lose" nature of the procedure would not seem conducive to good relations between the parties during the term of the agreement.

295. On the success of Taft-Hartley generally, see pp. 1421-23 *supra*.

296. U.S. BUREAU OF LABOR STATISTICS, DEP'T OF LABOR, BULL. No. 1633, NATIONAL EMERGENCY DISPUTES, LABOR-MANAGEMENT RELATIONS (TAFT-HARTLEY) ACT 1947-68.

off provisions contained in the Industrial Relations Act as were their American counterparts twenty-five years ago, their fears may well be as unfounded.

Conclusion

In selectively borrowing from American law, the drafters of the Industrial Relations Act have made some advantageous choices, and a few unfortunate ones. In determining appropriate bargaining units, the British have supplied detailed criteria in the Act and in the Code of Practice, while the American statute leaves details to the NLRB, but the concepts are similar, and should prove workable. Like the NLRA, the British Act sensibly permits the parties to establish voluntary machinery for settlements. The Act's dismissal provisions, for instance, specifically encourage the parties to fashion their own procedures, and further—if inadvertent—encouragement is supplied by the Act's crusty refusal to impose reinstatement as a statutory remedy for wrongful dismissal. By permitting the parties to have unenforceable agreements, and by relying on a "best endeavors" theory of union liability when the agreement is enforceable, the Act allows the parties to adapt their relationships to change in a gradual and orderly manner. As a last resort, the Commission on Industrial Relations is usefully empowered to impose grievance machinery on the parties. The Act also promises to rationalize trade union structures and practices. The recognition machinery should bring the unions and their stewards together in one bargaining panel. The duty to bargain, the presumption of enforceability, and the system of registration, which requires unions to identify their responsible officers, should bring the leadership into the workplace and should thus foster negotiation of comprehensive collective agreements.

On the other hand, the union security provisions are either irrelevant or inimical to the Act's larger purposes. Prohibiting the closed shop will hardly help unions to discipline and control their members and stewards, as *Heaton* requires. There is no justification for the stringent vote procedures necessary to obtain an agency shop. In America, union security elections have proved largely a waste of time. In Britain, where the tradition of union security is more deeply rooted, the voting procedures may cause unnecessary bitterness in the Act's early years.

Two other major flaws in the Act contributed directly to last summer's turmoil. The controversial provision for contempt sanctions against individuals was used to jail the shop stewards in the *Heaton* case after the Court of Appeals held that the national union was not responsible for their actions and could not thus be sanctioned by sequestration of union property. As soon as the House of Lords reversed the Court of Appeals in *Heaton*, the Industrial Court quite properly released the stewards, since future contempt could be dealt with by sanctions against the union itself. But the stewards had by then been martyred, and the labor movement's resistance to the Act had hardened, perhaps irreversibly. Second, the Government foolishly relied on the emergency strike ballot procedure during the acrimonious railway dispute. Predictably, the rank-and-file rallied to the leadership, and negotiations made no progress during the emergency pause. The Government had wasted the one asset possessed in the Act's emergency provisions and not contained in Taft-Hartley, *i.e.*, the discretion *not* to hold a strike ballot.

Amendment of the Act seems certain. No legislation so comprehensive and detailed can escape change.[297] The Government has announced its intention to consider amendments sometime within the next year.[298] The Labor Party insists on complete repeal. The TUC, encouraged by the Government's tactical blunders, believes that Prime Minister Heath can be forced to back down on the whole subject of labor legislation, just as the Wilson Government was successfully pressured in June of 1969.[299] While thus far rejecting left wing exhortations to refuse to appear defensively before the NIRC,[300] the TUC remains ready to expel unions which comply with the Act's registration provisions.[301] The TUC's position may be strong, in part because the Government needs union cooperation on wage restraint

---

297. The history of American labor legislation has, for instance, been one of substantial amendment.

298. Bourne, *Offer to Unions of Deal Over I.R.A. Act May Be Considered*, The Financial Times (London), August 7, 1972, at 1, col. 3.

299. *See* Routledge, *TUC To Fight for Drastic Change in the Industrial Relations Act*, The Times (London), September 4, 1972, at 1, col. 1; *see* Elliott, *The TUC Takes Stock of its Labour Law Campaign*, The Financial Times (London), September 4, 1972, at 10, col. 3; The Times (London), August 3, 1972, at 17, col. 1.

300. Elliott, *TUC "Left" Unite in All-Out Opposition to the IR Act*, The Financial Times (London) September 4, 1972, at 1, col. 2.

301. The Seamen's Union seems prepared to litigate the question of whether the T.U.C. may lawfully suspend or expel unions because they seek access to the Act's institutions, *i.e.*, because they seek to register with the Registrar. Routledge, *Seamen's Union May Sue General Council*, The Times (London), Sept. 5. 1972, at 1, col. 1. For the American position on this subject, *see* NLRB v. Marine & Shipbuilding Workers of America, 391 U.S. 418 (1968). *But see* Local 4028, United Steelworkers, 154 N.L.R.B. 692 (1965), *enforced*, 373 F.2d 443 (9th Cir. 1967), *cert. denied*, 392 U.S. 904 (1968), which indicates that the general rule protecting employees against expulsion for filing unfair labor practice complaints is not applicable where the filing of decertification petitions prompts the discipline. Query to what extent this is analogous to the British case where unions may compete more effectively with other TUC affiliates by utilizing the Act's recognition and union security machinery.

if the current inflation is to be halted. At the same time, that strength may be eroded if enough unions resist the TUC's edict against registration. The prospect of a rival labor federation of registered unions is not entirely beyond the realm of possibility at this time.[302] If such a federation develops, one can anticipate extensive attempts by each to "raid" or "poach" the members of the other.[303]

In the end, whatever amendments are adopted, the Act will not succeed without the consent and cooperation of the governed. Employers must learn to rely on the Act's machinery only as a last resort; a continued absence of effective voluntary institutions and procedures to settle disputes will undermine the Act as certainly as would a continued labor boycott. For their part, union leaders might review the American experience. In the years after Taft-Hartley's enactment, American unions forecast a flood of anti-union contract litigation, sponsored by employers colluding with misbehaving union members and non-unionists, whom the union would be powerless to discharge. The unions resolved to avoid enforceable contracts and to refrain from no-strike obligations. Nothing came of all this, largely because arbitration supplanted the judiciary as the principal forum to hear disputes arising during the term of the agreement. Arbitration is both a form of adjudication and an extension of the collective bargaining process. Its widespread adoption in Britain would reduce reliance on the NIRC. The transplanting of no other American institution or technique offers greater promise of effectuating the ultimate purposes of the British Act.

The experience of America is that law cannot coerce where resistance is unyielding, but that it can shape attitudes and, ultimately, conduct. *Brown v. Board of Education*,[304] despite all the difficulties of its implementation, has altered opinions about integration, and some practices are changing in consequence. There may be more "summers of '72" in Britain's future. But that country still enjoys a better reputation for respecting law than does America, and the Industrial Relations Act—if sensibly amended—therefore retains a decent chance to achieve some of its central objectives.

302. *See* Elliott, *E.P.T.U. in Big Row at the TUC*, The Financial Times (London), Sept. 7, 1972, at 1, col. 3; Routledge, *Electricians' Union May Quit the Congress*, The Times (London), Sept. 7, 1972, at 1, col. 7.
303. *See* Torode, *T.U.C. Cuts Off 32 Rebel Unions*, The Manchester Guardian Weekly, Sept. 9, 1972, at 10, col. 1, where it is reported that the protection from raiding afforded by the Bridlington Agreement would be withdrawn from suspended unions. *See also* Elliott, *TUC Suspends 32 Rebel Unions*, The Financial Times (London), Sept. 5, 1972, at 1, col. 3. The prospect is that a rival union federation would use the Act's machinery to fight back against T.U.C. affiliates.
304. 347 U.S. 483 (1954).

Bibliographic Essay on Taft-Hartley Comes to Great Britain

The Conservative Government, led by Prime Minister Edward Heath, was defeated by the Labor Party in February, 1974. Although the principal issue in that election which brought Labor to power was a nationwide strike in the coal mines, it was not essentially related to the provisions of the Industrial Relations Act of 1971. True to its pledge while in opposition, however, the Labor Government repealed the Industrial Relations Act and enacted the Trade Union and Labor Relations Act of 1974. This Act provided for immunities which the Industrial Relations Act had eliminated. Section 13 of the Act restored to individuals immunity from liability for (1) civil conspiracy, (2) inducement to breach of contract of employment, and (3) interference with business, trade, or employment. This took the law back to the Trades Disputes Act of 1906.

Out of all of this emerged a conventional wisdom which had no basis in fact, i.e., that the defeat of the conservative government and the repeal of the Industrial Relations Act was proof that the law could play no role in industrial relations.[1] In fact, the Heath government had been willing to amend the statute in certain respects prior to the 1974 election—particularly insofar as the registration scheme was concerned, as this had proved to be the most basic mistake made by the framers of the law. And had the Tories not met such misfortune at the hands of the coal miners, and consequently the electorate, the trade union movement would have undoubtedly had to accept some kind of accommodation or compromise in this area, confronted, as they would have been, with five more years of Conservative Government rule.

In some respects, the 1974 Act broadened union and individual employee protection that had existed prior to 1971—particularly with reference to immunity to induce breach of any contract. The Government, because it did not have a majority in the House of Commons, was not able to get approval of this provision in 1974, but obtained it by virtue of the Trade Union and Labor Relations (Amendment) Act of 1976.

The Employment Protection Act of 1975, amended in 1978, (and again by the Conservatives in 1980) also provided for affirmative protection for unions and employees. Thus this trilogy of statutes ushered in an era of a new conventional wisdom that the law had no role in industrial relations—that is, only that law which sought to impose restraints upon unions as opposed to employers. The new legislation enacted by the Labor Governments of 1974–79 thus broke from the past and the philosophy of collective *laissez faire* articulated by the late Professor Otto Kahn-Freund.

An outbreak of strikes, particularly in the public sector, produced the so-called "winter of discontent" in January 1979, which led to the election of the Thatcher government in May 1979. Soon thereafter, new labor legislation was introduced by that government which contradicted the view that the law had no role in industrial relations.

The Employment Act of 1980 restricted the immunity conferred upon union activity by the Trade Union and Labor Relations Acts of 1974 and 1976. Section 16 provides that immunity does not apply to an act done in the course of picketing, unless the picketing is engaged in the picketer's own place of work. Section 17 provides that secondary economic pressure is not to be immunized unless the action is undertaken by employees of the customers or suppliers of the employer who is in the dispute (the primary employer) and the principal purpose is to interfere with the supply of goods between the secondary and the primary employer. And finally, Section 18 provides that immunity does not apply where an employee induces another employee to breach his contract of employment in order to compel workers to join a particular union, unless the breach occurs in connection with a dispute involving workers at the same facility.

The 1980 Act also provided for limited government subsidies for postal ballots and union elections and ballots on decisions relating to union economic pressure. An affirmative vote of 80 percent was required in order for a closed shop to be enacted, and a dismissal without such a vote was an unfair dismissal under the law. Employers could seek to have all or part of the liability for violations of these provisions shifted to the union.

The Employment Act of 1982 broadened the closed shop provisions so that employees dismissed under closed shops between the 1974 and 1980 Acts who were employees of their employer before the closed shop agreement took effect, or who objected to union membership on grounds of conscience or deeply held personal conviction, could not be dismissed. Where a closed shop took effect prior to April 15, 1980 and had not in the five years preceding been supported by a secret ballot of 80 percent of the employees covered or 85 percent of the employees voting, the dismissal had to be regarded as invalid.

Employees who were, in the view of an industrial tribunal, unreasonably excluded or expelled from a union, also could not be dismissed for such reasons. The principal effect of the 1982 statute, insofar as legal immunity for trade union activity, is that trade unions may not be held liable for unlawful acts that had been previously declared unlawful by the 1980 statute.

Finally, the Trade Union Act of 1984 removed legal immunity for unions which did not provide for ballots for members for union leadership position and in connection with "industrial action." Ballots were also required for union political funds.

Thus, in essence, the Conservative Government has challenged the assumptions behind the repeal of the Industrial Relations Act. But it has not created a specialized National Industrial Relations Court, as did the framers of the Industrial Relations Act, so as to avoid an institution which could be the object of controversy and dispute. Moreover, the Government has thus far avoided direct involvement in labor disputes and encouraged public and private employers to proceed cautiously in utilizing the provisions of the statute—the concern with the Industrial Relations Act of 1971 being that it had been used indiscriminately by employers in many instances.

NOTES

1. The literature on the other side of the Atlantic is too voluminous to cite, let alone describe. But it is reflected well in Wedderburn, Lewis, and Clark, eds., *Labour Law and Industrial Relations: Building on Kahn Freund* (Oxford University Press, New York, 1983). *See* also "Sandison a Rejected Transplant: The British Industrial Relations Act (1971-1974)," 3 Indus. Relations L. J. 247 (1979). An objective description of the events which have transpired since the early 1970s is contained in Roberts, "Recent Trends in Collective Bargaining in the United Kingdom," 123 International Labour Review 287 (1984).

11

Solidarity Forever—or Hardly Ever: Union Discipline, Taft-Hartley, and the Right of Union Members to Resign

American labor law embraces an abiding tension between maintaining workers' collective interests in solidarity through labor unions and protecting the worker's ability to dissent from the majoritarian decisions of unions that affect significant individual rights.[1] These competing interests are at the core of the historical debate concerning union security arrangements negotiated in collective bargaining agreements that compel membership in a union as a condition of employment.[2] More recently, these interests have been the focal point of another labor policy debate—the union's authority to discipline members whose conduct compromises the solidarity interests of other members.

Litigation in this area has expanded geometrically in the past twenty years,[3] producing concern and consternation among many militant, progressive, and other liberal trade unionists. These individuals, along with other union, civic, and political leaders, view

---

[1] See generally L. BRANDEIS, S. PERLMAN, P. TAFT & J. COMMONS, HISTORY OF LABOR IN THE UNITED STATES (1966); H. MILLIS & R. MONTGOMERY, ORGANIZED LABOR (1945); S. WEBB & B. WEBB, INDUSTRIAL DEMOCRACY (1965); S. WEBB & B. WEBB, THE HISTORY OF TRADE UNIONISM (rev. ed. 1973).

[2] See generally W. OBERER, K. HANSLOWE & J. ANDERSEN, CASES AND MATERIALS ON LABOR LAW 42-50, 167-68, 808-14, 838-53 (2d ed. 1979). See also K. HANSLOWE, D. DUNN & J. ERSTLING, UNION SECURITY IN PUBLIC EMPLOYMENT: OF FREE RIDING AND FREE ASSOCIATION (Inst. Pub. Employment Monograph No. 8-1978).

[3] See note 27 infra.

with alarm a perceived decline in the American labor movement brought about by the threat to the voluntary support of rank and file workers who form the heart and strength of trade unions.[4] This Article analyzes the tension between a union's right to discipline its members and the member's concomitant right to avoid discipline by resigning from the union. The Supreme Court has not adequately addressed this issue, leaving the lower courts and the National Labor Relations Board (NLRB) to forge ahead relatively unguided in these troublesome waters.

A trade union should lawfully be able to restrict a member's right to resign.[5]   Many union constitutions and bylaws, however, fail to accommodate the union's interest in restricting the right to resign with the union member's legitimate interest in refraining from collective activity. This Article suggests that these interests could be balanced by union constitutions that freely allow members to resign until ten or fifteen days after contract negotiations begin. Unions should not be allowed to discipline members for their post-resignation conduct unless those unions provide mid-strike democratic ballot box procedures for challenging union decisions. In addition, many of the problems caused by member resignations and post-resignation discipline could be avoided if unions fully informed their members that union membership is never required under any collective bargaining contract if the worker satisfies the same financial obligations that regular union members must meet. If the unions shirk this responsibility, the Board should establish an educational program to fill this gap.

---

[4] See generally S. BARKIN, THE DECLINE OF THE LABOR MOVEMENT (1961); Raskin, The Big Squeeze on Labor Unions, ATLANTIC MONTHLY, Oct. 1979, at 41; Raskin, The Squeeze on the Unions, ATLANTIC MONTHLY, June 1961, at 55.

Many trade unionists strongly oppose fining members and are embarrassed by the notion that union officers should be compelled to impose monetary sanctions on members who must support themselves and their families.

[5] In an article published several years after NLRB v. Allis-Chalmers Mfg. Co., 388 U.S. 175 (1967), I asserted that the Board should strictly scrutinize union discipline: "[T]he Board [should] not . . . abdicate its responsibility to limit discipline which is offensive to public policy where penalties are involved." Gould, Some Limitations Upon Union Discipline Under the National Labor Relations Act: The Radiations of Allis-Chalmers, 1970 DUKE L.J. 1067, 1137. Subsequent events and a re-analysis of the union's interest in restricting member resignations in certain circumstances have instigated a moderate retraction of my earlier opinions.

I

ALLIS-CHALMERS AND SECTION 8(b)(1)(A) OF THE NATIONAL LABOR RELATIONS ACT

A. *Section 8(b)(1)(A): A Limit on Union Autonomy*

In the United States, a labor organization[6] acts as the exclusive bargaining representative[7] empowered to negotiate an employment contract covering all workers, union and nonunion,[8] within an appropriate bargaining unit.[9] Congress purposefully designed the National Labor Relations Act (NLRA) to promote union autonomy[10] by creating this exclusive status and by pro-

---

[6] The term "labor organization" means any organization of any kind, or any agency or employee representation committee or plan, in which employees participate and which exists for the purpose, in whole or in part, of dealing with employers concerning grievances, labor disputes, wages, rates of pay, hours of employment, or conditions of work.
National Labor Relations Act of 1935, § 2(5), 29 U.S.C § 152(5) (1976).

[7] Section 9(a) of the National Labor Relations Act of 1935, 29 U.S.C. § 159(a) (1976), provides:

Representatives designated or selected for the purposes of collective bargaining by the majority of the employees in a unit appropriate for such purposes, shall be the exclusive representatives of all the employees in such unit for the purposes of collective bargaining in respect to rates of pay, wages, hours of employment, or other conditions of employment: *Provided,* That any individual employee or a group of employees shall have the right at any time to present grievances to their employer and to have such grievances adjusted, without the intervention of the bargaining representative.

[8] *See* Radio Officers Union v. NLRB, 347 U.S. 17, 47 (1954).

[9] The employer may be obligated to bargain on a plant, company, or multi-employer basis. "The Board shall decide in each case whether, in order to assure to employees the fullest freedom in exercising the rights guaranteed by this Act, the unit appropriate for the purposes of collective bargaining shall be the employer unit, craft unit, plant unit, or subdivision thereof." National Labor Relations Act of 1935, § 9(b), 29 U.S.C. § 159(b) (1976).

[10] Industrial strife which interferes with the normal flow of commerce and with the full production of articles and commodities for commerce, can be avoided or substantially minimized if employers, employees, and labor organizations each recognize under law one another's legitimate rights in their relations with each other, and above all recognize under law that neither party has any right in its relations with any other to engage in acts or practices which jeopardize the public health, safety, or interest.

It is the purpose and policy of this chapter, in order to promote the full flow of commerce, to prescribe the legitimate rights of both employees and employers in their relations affecting commerce, to provide orderly and peaceful procedures for preventing the interference by either with the legitimate rights of the other, to protect the rights of individual employees in their relations with labor organizations whose activities affect commerce, to define and proscribe practices on the part of labor and management which affect commerce and are inimical to the general welfare, and to protect the rights of the public in connection with labor disputes affecting commerce.
National Labor Relations Act of 1935, § 1(b), 29 U.S.C. § 141(b) (1976).

hibiting employers from "interfer[ing], restrain[ing], or coerc[ing]" employees in the exercise of their right to form and join, or refrain from forming and joining, labor unions.[11] This well-established principle of exclusivity imposes an obligation on the union to represent all workers within the unit fairly and to deal with them in good faith.[12] Congress and the courts have imposed several other significant limits on union autonomy that reflect the inherent conflict between the rights of an individual and the interests of the union.

The 1947 Taft-Hartley amendments to the NLRA proscribed the closed shop by prohibiting collective bargaining contracts that require all job applicants to belong to a union as a prerequisite for employment eligibility.[13] These amendments did not, however, ban "union shop" contracts, which require new employees to become union members thirty days or more after they accept employment.[14] In addition, state "right to work" laws, which prohibit union security clauses requiring union membership as a condition of employment,[15] are not preempted by the NLRA.[16] The Supreme Court's decision in *NLRB v. General Motors Corp.*,[17] which held that under the Taft-Hartley amendments an employee was a "member" of a union if he paid union dues and initiation

---

[11] National Labor Relations Act of 1935, § 8(a)(1), 29 U.S.C. § 158(a)(1) (1976). This provision is more restrictive than the comparable statute governing union conduct.

[12] Vaca v. Sipes, 386 U.S. 171 (1967). *See also* Steele v. Louisville & Nashville R.R., 323 U.S. 192 (1944) (duty of fair representation imposed under Railway Labor Act).

[13] *See* National Labor Relations Act of 1935, § 8(a)(3), 29 U.S.C. § 158(a)(3) (1976); *cf.* Algoma Plywood & Veneer Co. v. Wisconsin Employment Relations Bd., 336 U.S. 301 (1949) (state may prohibit maintenance-of-membership clause that requires employee to remain union member once he voluntarily joins union).

[14] *See* 29 U.S.C. § 158(a)(3) (1976).

[15] Section 8(a)(3) of the National Labor Relations Act of 1935, 29 U.S.C. § 158(a)(3) (1976), provides in part:

> [N]othing in this subchapter, or in any other statute of the United States, shall preclude an employer from making an agreement with a labor organization (not established, maintained, or assisted by any action defined in [section 8(a) of the Act] as an unfair labor practice) to require as a condition of employment membership therein on or after the thirtieth day following the beginning of such employment or the effective date of such agreement, whichever is the later.

[16] Section 14(b) of the National Labor Relations Act of 1935, added by the Labor Management Relations (Taft-Hartley) Act of 1947, authorizes states to enact right to work laws that prohibit collective bargaining agreements from "requiring membership in a labor organization as a condition of employment in any State." 29 U.S.C. § 164(b) (1976).

[17] 373 U.S. 734 (1963).

fees, further restricted union autonomy.[18]   The NLRA does not require actual membership in the union.[19]   Thus, contracts requiring union shops today effectively require only "agency shops,"[20] a phrase from the labor lexicon used to refer to contract clauses that explicitly require the employee to meet only the financial responsibilities, but not the membership obligations, of union membership.

Section 8(b)(1)(A) of the NLRA, added to the Act by the Taft-Hartley amendments, is another major limitation on union authority.[21]   By prohibiting unions from "restrain[ing] or coerc[ing] . . . employees in the exercise of the rights guaranteed in section [7 of the NLRA],"[22] section 8(b)(1)(A) mandates that unions—as well as employers—must respect the individual worker's right to join or refrain from joining labor unions. Congress partially preserved internal union autonomy, however, with a proviso to section 8(b)(1)(A) exempting union "rules with respect

---

[18] *Id.* at 741-44.

[19] [N]o employer shall justify any discrimination against an employee for non-membership in a labor organization . . . if he has reasonable grounds for believing that membership was denied or terminated for reasons other than the failure of the employee to tender the periodic dues and the initiation fees uniformly required as a condition of acquiring or retaining membership.
29 U.S.C. § 158(a)(3)(B) (1976).

[20] *See* R. Gorman, Basic Text on Labor Law 644-45 (1976).

[21] National Labor Relations Act of 1935, § 8(b)(1)(A), 29 U.S.C. § 158(b)(1)(A) (1976).

[22] *Id.* Section 7 of the National Labor Relations Act of 1935, 29 U.S.C. § 157 (1976), provides:

> Employees shall have the right to self-organization, to form, join, or assist labor organizations, to bargain collectively through representatives of their own choosing, and to engage in other concerted activities for the purpose of collective bargaining or other mutual aid or protection, and shall also have the right to refrain from any or all of such activities except to the extent that such right may be affected by an agreement requiring membership in a labor organization as a condition of employment as authorized in section 158(a)(3) of this title.

The Supreme Court explained the purpose for this provision as follows:

> Section 7 affirmatively guarantees employees the most basic rights of industrial self-determination, "the right to self-organization, to form, join, or assist labor organizations, to bargain collectively through representatives of their own choosing, and to engage in other concerted activities for the purpose of collective bargaining or other mutual aid or protection," as well as the right to refrain from these activities. These are, for the most part, collective rights, rights to act in concert with one's fellow employees: they are protected not for their own sake but as an instrument of the national labor policy of minimizing industrial strife "by encouraging the practice and procedure of collective bargaining."

Emporium Capwell Co. v. Western Addition Community Org., 420 U.S. 50, 61-62 (1975) (quoting 29 U.S.C. § 151 (1970)). *See generally* Cox, *The Right to Engage in Concerted Activities,* 26 Ind. L.J. 319 (1951).

to the acquisition or retention of membership" from the restriction against union restraint and coercion of employees.[23]   Until 1967, courts and the Board interpreted this proviso to allow any internal union discipline that did not affect a worker's employment status;[24] external sanctions imposed by employers because of an employee's union or nonunion activities, on the other hand, were outlawed by this proviso. The Supreme Court modified this relatively simple dichotomy in 1967 when it recognized that fines, expulsion, or other sanctions imposed by a union may affect the worker's pay envelope more than discipline imposed by the employer.[25]   In so doing, it created a new standard from which the fallout has not yet settled.[26]

B. *NLRB v. Allis-Chalmers Manufacturing Co.*

In *NLRB v. Allis-Chalmers Manufacturing Co.*,[27] two UAW locals initiated internal proceedings against union members who had crossed picket lines during a valid economic strike.[28] Local

---

[23] The proviso states: "[T]his paragraph [section 8(b)(1)] shall not impair the right of a labor organization to prescribe its own rules with respect to the acquisition or retention of membership therein...." 29 U.S.C. § 158(b)(1)(A) (1976).

[24] *See, e.g.,* Local 248, UAW (Allis-Chalmers Mfg. Co.), 149 N.L.R.B. 67, 70, 57 L.R.R.M. 1242 (1964), *rev'd,* 358 F.2d 656 (7th Cir. 1965), *aff'd,* 388 U.S. 175 (1967); Minneapolis Star & Tribune Co., 109 N.L.R.B. 727, 728-29, 34 L.R.R.M. 1431, 1432 (1954).

[25] *See* text accompanying notes 137-40 *infra.*

[26] The literature on this subject is voluminous. *See, e.g.,* Atleson, *Union Fines and Picket Lines: The NLRA and Union Disciplinary Power,* 17 U.C.L.A. L. Rev. 681 (1970); Cox, *Some Aspects of the Labor Management Relations Act, 1947,* 61 Harv. L. Rev. 1 (1947); Craver, *The Boeing Decision: A Blow to Federalism, Individual Rights and Stare Decisis,* 122 U. Pa. L. Rev. 556 (1974); Gould, *Some Limitations Upon Union Discipline Under the National Labor Relations Act: The Radiations of Allis-Chalmers,* 1970 Duke L.J. 1067; Silard, *Labor Board Regulation of Union Discipline After Allis-Chalmers, Marine Works and Scofield,* 38 Geo. Wash. L. Rev. 187 (1969); Note, *Restrictions on the Right to Resign: Can a Member's Freedom to "Escape the Union Rule" Be Overcome by Union Boilerplate?,* 42 Geo. Wash. L. Rev. 397 (1974); Note, *Union Power to Discipline Members Who Resign,* 86 Harv. L. Rev. 1536 (1973); Comment, *The Inherent Conflict Between Sections 7 and 8(b)(1)(A) of the National Labor Relations Act — Union Attempts to Discipline Resigning Strikebreakers,* 1978 Wis. L. Rev. 859.

[27] 388 U.S. 175 (1967).

[28] An economic strike is a protected activity under the NLRA. Although economic strikers may not be dismissed or disciplined by an employer, they may be permanently replaced. 29 U.S.C. § 163 (1976); *see* NLRB v. Mackay Radio & Tel. Co., 304 U.S. 333 (1938); Gould, *The Status of Unauthorized and "Wildcat" Strikes Under the National Labor Relations Act,* 52 Cornell L. Rev. 672, 675-80 (1967).

trial committees found the members guilty of "conduct unbecoming a Union member,"[29] and assessed fines against them. After one of the union locals obtained a state court judgment against a member who had refused to pay a fine,[30] the company filed an unfair labor practice charge with the Board alleging that the local unions' disciplinary actions violated section 8(b)(1)(A) of the Act. The Board dismissed the charge on the ground that the proviso to section 8(b)(1)(A) exempted all internal union discipline from unfair labor practice liability.[31] The Seventh Circuit reversed the Board, holding that in spite of the proviso, section 8(b)(1)(A) unambiguously prohibits union discipline that restrains or coerces employees who exercise their right to refrain from union activities.[32]

A closely divided Supreme Court reversed.[33] The majority concluded it was "highly unrealistic" that the statutory language "precisely" proscribed this union discipline.[34] The majority examined the proviso's legislative history, finding that the

> [n]ational labor policy has been built on the premise that by pooling their economic strength and acting through a labor organization freely chosen by the majority, the employees of an appropriate unit have the most effective means of bargaining for improvements in wages, hours, and working conditions. . . .
>
>   . . . .
>
> Integral to this federal labor policy has been the power in the chosen union to protect against erosion its status under that policy through reasonable discipline of members who violate

---

[29] 388 U.S. at 177.

[30] *Id.* The Wisconsin Supreme Court's decision affirming the trial court's finding that it was not unlawful for the union to collect these fines by suits in state courts is reported in Local 248, UAW v. Natzke, 36 Wis. 2d 237, 153 N.W.2d 602 (1967).

[31] Local 248, UAW (Allis-Chalmers Mfg. Co.), 149 N.L.R.B. 67, 57 L.R.R.M. 1242 (1964).

[32] Allis-Chalmers Mfg. Co. v. NLRB, 358 F.2d 656 (1966), *rev'd,* 388 U.S. 175 (1967).

[33] Justice White filed a concurring opinion expressing his "doubt . . . about the implications of some of [the] generalized statements" in the majority opinion. 388 U.S. at 199. He reasoned that logic compelled the Court to uphold the discipline because the Court had previously upheld more severe discipline (*i.e.,* expulsion from the union) imposed on other strikebreakers. Moreover, he qualified the majority opinion:
> I do not mean to indicate, and I do not read the majority opinion otherwise, that every conceivable internal union rule which impinges upon the § 7 rights of union members is valid and enforceable by expulsion and court action. There may well be some internal union rules which on their face are wholly invalid and unenforceable.
388 U.S. at 198.

[34] *Id.* at 179.

rules and regulations governing membership. That power is particularly vital when the members engage in strikes. The economic strike against the employer is the ultimate weapon in labor's arsenal for achieving agreement upon its terms. . . . Provisions in union constitutions and bylaws for fines and expulsion of recalcitrants, including strikebreakers, are therefore commonplace and were commonplace at the time of the Taft-Hartley amendments.[35]

The Court advanced two important arguments to support its conclusion that the unions' sanctions did not violate section 8(b)(1)(A). First, the Court reasoned that the failure to acknowledge a union's right to fine its members under the NLRA would encourage unions to expel or exclude workers from the union as alternative forms of discipline. Because the expulsion remedy could be utilized by only strong unions that can afford to lose members, this approach would penalize weak unions.[36]   Second, the Court observed that the union security clause in the collective bargaining agreement between the company and the two local unions did not compel full union membership; an employee was required to become a member only "to the extent of paying his monthly dues."[37]   Consequently, because the employees had become full union members voluntarily, they knowingly assumed all membership obligations—including subjection to union discipline. The Court argued that

the relevant inquiry here is not what motivated a member's full membership but whether the Taft-Hartley amendments prohibited disciplinary measures against a full member who crossed his union's picket line. . . . Whether those prohibitions would apply if the locals had imposed fines on members whose membership was in fact limited to the obligation of paying monthly dues is a question not before us. . . .[38]

---

[35] *Id.* at 180, 181-82 (footnotes omitted).

[36] *Id.* at 183.

[37] *Id.* at 196.

[38] *Id.* at 196-97. The Court also relied on two other arguments to support its holding that the union discipline did not violate § 8(b)(1)(A). First, the Court noted that a contrary interpretation of § 8(b)(1)(A), stripping unions of their ability to fine members for strikebreaking, would imply that the Labor-Management Reporting and Disclosure (Landrum-Griffin) Act of 1959, 29 U.S.C. §§ 401-531 (1976), which had apparently established the first explicit set of procedural and substantive protections for union members vis-a-vis their unions, was actually preceded by an even more comprehensive, albeit implicit, code regulating internal union affairs. 388 U.S. at 181, 183. Second, the Court referred to the legislative history of § 8(b)(1)(A) and noted that Congress specifically disavowed any intent

Although the *Allis-Chalmers* decision appeared to strengthen the union's right to discipline its members, under section 8(b)(1)(A)'s proviso, it also raised many questions concerning union discipline imposed upon employees who are not members. The remaining sections of this Article examine the ramifications of *Allis-Chalmers* upon discipline of nonmembers and former union members.

II

CLARIFYING THE RELATIONSHIP BETWEEN UNION DISCIPLINE AND UNION MEMBERSHIP

The *Allis-Chalmers* Court indicated that it may regard the degree of union membership significant in determining the extent of a union's disciplinary authority. Although the Court did not explicitly address this question,[39] it implied that a worker whose union "membership" was limited to paying dues and initiation fees should be less vulnerable to sanctions than a "full" union member.[40] The issues that arise more frequently, however, con-

---

to interfere with the internal affairs of trade unions. *Id.* at 184-85. Section 8(b)(1)(A) was designed by Congress solely to protect workers from union threats and reprisals during organizational campaigns. *Id.* at 185-91. This conclusion was consistent with the " 'contract theory' of the union-member relationship that prevailed at [the] time" Congress enacted the National Labor Relations Act. *Id.* at 192. Although fines and sanctions were sanctioned by § 8(b)(1)(A)'s proviso, the Court noted that judicially enforceable fines existed only under the contract between the union and the member as embodied in the union's constitution and bylaws. *Id.* at 192-95.

Justice Black, joined by Justices Douglas, Harlan and Stewart, wrote a lengthy dissent, arguing that the union discipline in this case was clearly designed to coerce workers in violation of § 8(b)(1)(A). *Id.* at 199, 202-08.

[39] *Id.* at 196.

[40] Under an agency shop provision, a worker is required only to pay union dues and initiation fees. A union shop provision, on the other hand, requires the worker to join the union and become a full member as well as pay dues and initiation fees. *See* text accompanying notes 142-49 *infra*.

The relatively few cases concerning union discipline of limited members supports the proposition that limited members—those paying dues only under an agency shop provision—can be disciplined only for nonpayment of dues. *See* Local Union No. 167, Progressive Mine Workers v. NLRB, 422 F.2d 538 (7th Cir.), *cert. denied*, 399 U.S. 905 (1970) (union cannot deny nonmembers access to welfare plan provided they pay equivalent of union dues); UAW Local 1756 (Am. Hoechst Corp.), 240 N.L.R.B. No. 13, 100 L.R.R.M. 1208 (1979) (union cannot assess readmission fee and threaten employee with dismissal after employee resigned from union but continued paying equivalent of union dues); Bricklayers' Union No. 11 (Rochester Floors, Inc.), 221 N.L.R.B. 133, 90 L.R.R.M. 1621 (1975) (nonunion employees who tender dues and initiation fees not required to pay new initiation fees after union negotiates new security clause); Laborers' Local 573 (Mengel Constr. Co.), 196 N.L.R.B. 440 (1972), *enforced*, 83 L.R.R.M. 2988 (7th Cir. 1973) (union cannot terminate from hiring hall nonmembers who tender dues).

cern the validity of post-resignation union discipline and union restrictions on the right to resign.

A. *Discipline of Former Union Members*

The clearest case for invalidating union sanctions would arise when a worker resigns his union membership before violating a union rule. In *Scofield v. NLRB*,[41] the Supreme Court held that union fines imposed on members who had exceeded production quotas in violation of a legitimate union rule were valid under the proviso to section 8(b)(1)(A).[42]   Justice White, writing for the majority, observed:

> [Section] 8(b)(1) leaves a union free to enforce a properly adopted rule which reflects a legitimate union interest, impairs no policy Congress has imbedded in the labor laws, and is reasonably enforced against union members *who are free to leave the union and escape the rule.*[43]

The Court squarely addressed the question of whether the ability to resign union membership was a precondition for valid union discipline in *NLRB v. Granite State Joint Board, Textile Workers*.[44]   An eight member majority held in *Granite State* that a union had violated section 8(b)(1)(A) by fining workers for returning to work during a lawful strike after they had resigned from the union.[45]   The union membership had voted to strike shortly after the expiration of the collective bargaining agreement if their demands were not met. After the strike began, the membership ratified a proposal to levy fines on any member who aided the employer during the strike.[46]   Notwithstanding this warning, a number of workers resigned from the union and returned to work during the strike.[47]   The union fined the strike-breaking former members and sued in state court to collect the fines.

The Court distinguished *Allis-Chalmers* on the ground that the workers disciplined in *Allis-Chalmers* "enjoyed full union membership" whereas the workers in *Granite State* had lawfully re-

---

[41]   394 U.S. 423 (1969).
[42]   *Id.* at 428-30.
[43]   *Id.* at 430 (emphasis added).
[44]   409 U.S. 213 (1972).
[45]   *Id.* at 215-18.
[46]   NLRB v. Granite State Joint Bd., Textile Workers, Local 1029, 446 F.2d 369, 370 (1st Cir. 1971). Only one member dissented when the strike vote was taken. *Id.*
[47]   409 U.S. at 214.

signed from the union.[48]   Noting that section 7 of the NLRA gives the worker the " 'right to refrain from any or all ' concerted activities relat[ed] to collective bargaining,"[49] the Court concluded:

> [T]he power of the union over the member is certainly no greater than the union-member contract. Where a member lawfully resigns from a union and thereafter engages in conduct which the union rule proscribes, the union commits an unfair labor practice when it seeks enforcement of fines for that conduct. That is to say, when there is a lawful dissolution of a union-member relation, the union has no more control over the former member than it has over the man in the street.[50]

The Court rejected the argument that the workers were properly disciplined because they had participated in the votes approving the strike and the strike-breaking penalties.[51]   Thus, the Court confirmed in *Scofield* and *Granite State* what it had hinted in *Allis-Chalmers*—that union membership is a prerequisite for valid discipline under section 8(b)(1)(A).

B. *Protecting the Right to Resign*

In *Granite State*, the Court did not rule on the validity of "a union's constitution or bylaws [that] defin[ed] or limit[ed] the circumstances under which a member may resign from the union";[52] it held that the workers had lawfully resigned from the union before violating the union rules. The opportunity to consider this question soon arose, however. In *Booster Lodge No. 405, Machinists v. NLRB*,[53] a group of workers who had crossed picket lines during a lawful strike was fined by the union under a constitutional provision that prohibited "members" from strikebreaking.[54]   Although the union's constitution did not expressly prohibit or permit members to resign, some of the fined members sent letters of resignation to the union before returning to work and the others sent similar letters shortly after they returned to work.[55]

---

[48] *Id.* at 215.

[49] *Id.* at 216 (quoting National Labor Relations Act of 1935, § 7, 29 U.S.C. § 157 (1976)).

[50] *Id.* at 217. *See* Justice Blackmun's dissenting opinion, 409 U.S. at 218, 220-21.

[51] *Id.* at 217-18.

[52] 409 U.S. at 216.

[53] 412 U.S. 84 (1973) (per curiam).

[54] *Id.* at 87.

[55] *Id.* at 85.

In a per curiam opinion, the Court held that the union committed an unfair labor practice by seeking judicial enforcement of fines that stemmed from post-resignation activities.[56]   Although the Court left "open the question of the extent to which contractual restriction[s could be placed] on a member's right to resign,"[57]—as it had done in *Granite State*[58]—it concluded that the fine was illegal because the union presented "no evidence that the employees here either knew of or had consented to any limitation on their right to resign."[59]   Rejecting the union's argument that the strikebreaking penalty could be enforced against a former member as part of a contract entered into before termination of membership, the Court noted:

> Nothing in the record indicates that Union members were informed, prior to the bringing of the charges that were the basis of this action, that the provision was interpreted as imposing any obligation on a resignee. Thus, in order to sustain the Union's position, we would first have to find . . . that the Union constitution by implication extended its sanctions to nonmembers, and then further conclude that such sanctions were consistent with the Act. But we are no more disposed to find an implied post-resignation commitment from the strikebreaking proscription in the Union's constitution here than we were to find it from the employees' participation in the strike vote and ratification of penalties in *Textile Workers* [*Granite State*].[60]

Thus, the Court appears to have established a new statutory "right to resign," grounded in section 8(b)(1)(A) and recognized in *Scofield, Granite State,* and *Booster Lodge.* Yet it has left undefined the scope of that right. The *Granite State* Court noted in dicta that members should be free to resign from the union at any time— even during a strike—in order to avoid discipline.[61]   The employees' valid resignations in both cases effectively nullified otherwise lawful union discipline. The issue raised by these decisions, then, is the extent to which a union may restrict its members' right to resign. The Board has addressed this issue in several

---

[56] *Id.* at 88.

[57] *Id.*

[58] "We do not now decide to what extent the contractual relationship between union and member may curtail the freedom to resign." 409 U.S. 212, 217 (1972).

[59] 412 U.S. at 88.

[60] *Id.* at 89-90 (footnote omitted).

[61] 409 U.S. at 217. *See* text accompanying notes 91-93 *infra*.

cases, but it has yet to find that any union's constitutional provision restricting member resignations falls within the protective ambit of the proviso to section 8(b)(1)(A).[62] The Ninth Circuit, on the other hand, recently upheld a provision of the International Association of Machinists' (Machinists) constitution restricting the right to resign.[63] After reconsidering its decision on a motion for rehearing, the court issued a second opinion remanding the case to "give the Board, the expert body in the field of labor relations, an opportunity to consider and decide" whether the restriction was valid under section 8(b)(1)(A).[64]

Three types of union constitutional restrictions on a member's right to resign have been challenged. The Court in *Booster Lodge* invalidated one potential restriction, implied from a union constitution's silence on member resignation, when it held that a member was free to resign from the union at any time if the constitution did not explicitly prohibit or limit resignations. The following subsections discuss two other types of restrictions: absolute prohibitions on resignations and partial restrictions allowing resignations during limited escape periods.

1. *Absolute Prohibitions*

Constitutional provisions that effectively place an absolute prohibition on resignation present the clearest case for invalida-

---

[62] *See, e.g.,* Oil Workers Local 6-578 (Gordy's, Inc.), 238 N.L.R.B. No. 172, 99 L.R.R.M. 1639 (1978), *enforced,* 103 L.R.R.M. 2895 (8th Cir. Mar. 13, 1980); Machinists Local 1327 (Dalmo Victor), 231 N.L.R.B. 719, 719, 96 L.R.R.M. 1160 (1977), *enforcement denied and remanded,* 608 F.2d 1219 (9th Cir. 1979); Local 1384 UAW (Ex-Cell-O Corp.), 227 N.L.R.B. 1045, 1050-51, 94 L.R.R.M. 1145 (1975); UAW Local 647 (General Electric Co.), 197 N.L.R.B. 608, 80 L.R.R.M. 1411 (1972); Aeronautical Indus. Dist. Lodge 751 (Boeing Co.), 173 N.L.R.B. 450, 69 L.R.R.M. 1363 (1968); *cf.* Meat Cutters Local 81 (Empire Enterprises), 241 N.L.R.B. No. 125, 100 L.R.R.M. 1607 (1979) (union did not violate § 8(b)(1)(A) by adopting rule banning resignations when strike is imminent because no evidence union enforced rule). *See also* Anheuser-Busch, Inc. v. Teamsters Local 822, 584 F.2d 41 (4th Cir. 1978) (union restriction on revocation of dues checkoff authorization invalid).

[63] NLRB v. Machinists Local 1327, 101 L.R.R.M. 3096 (9th Cir. 1979). *See* text accompanying notes 122-35 *infra.*

[64] NLRB v. Machinists Local 1327, 608 F.2d 1219, 1222 (9th Cir. 1979), *denying enforcement and remanding* 231 N.L.R.B. 719, 96 L.R.R.M. 1160 (1977).

At this time, the Board has yet to rule on the *Dalmo Victor* case after remand from the Ninth Circuit. The Board has consolidated with *Dalmo Victor* an appeal from the administrative law judge's (ALJ) decision in Pattern Makers' League (Rockford-Beloit Pattern Jobbers Ass'n), No. 33-CB-1132 (NLRB, Div. Judges, San Francisco, filed Nov. 28, 1978) (on file at the *Cornell Law Review*). In that case, the ALJ invalidated the Pattern Makers' League Law 13 and ruled that it must be "expunged" from the union's league laws because it 'unequivocally prohibits resignations during the course of a strike or when a strike appears to be imminent." *Id.,* slip op. at 10.

tion. These provisions, which typically allow a member to resign only if he leaves the trade or industry,[65] subject a worker to the Hobson's choice of relinquishing his livelihood or accepting union discipline. The Board has held that this method of restricting member resignations offends public policy and constitutes unlawful restraint and coercion under section 8(b)(1)(A).[66] Absolute prohibitions on member resignations also conflict with the Board's interpretation of the NLRA that an employee's lack of union membership cannot affect his employment status under a union shop provision unless he fails to tender periodic dues and initiation fees.[67]

2. Resignation Limited to "Escape Periods"

Union constitutions and bylaws that limit a member's ability to resign to a fixed time period present more complex issues. The Board has considered numerous challenges to the United Auto Workers' (UAW) constitution, which permits members to resign only if they send a signed, written communication by registered or certified mail to the financial secretary of the local union within ten days of the end of the union's fiscal year.[68]

---

[65] In Paperworkers Local 725 (Boise S. Co.), 220 N.L.R.B. 812, 90 L.R.R.M. 1358 (1975), the Board characterized the UNITED PAPERWORKERS INT'L UNION CONST. art. XI, § 7 (1972), as follows: "We note that this provision only deals with withdrawal from the union when a member is leaving the International's jurisdiction. . . . [W]e conclude that [under this provision, the member is] able to resign at will. . . ." 220 N.L.R.B. at 813-14, 90 L.R.R.M. at 1359.

[66] See, e.g., Sales Workers Local 80 (Capitol-Husting Co.), 235 N.L.R.B. 1264, 98 L.R.R.M. 1123 (1978); Paperworkers Local 725 (Boise S. Co.), 220 N.L.R.B. 812, 90 L.R.R.M. 1358 (1975); Local 205, Lithographers Union (General Gravure Serv. Co.), 186 N.L.R.B. 454, 75 L.R.R.M. 1356 (1970); cf. NLRB v. Machinists Lodge 1871, 575 F.2d 54 (2d Cir. 1978) (union cannot fine members for resigning during strike when constitution did not explicitly restrict such resignations). See also Local 357, Teamsters v. NLRB, 365 U.S. 667 (1961) (hiring halls valid under NLRA); Radio Officers' Union v. NLRB, 347 U.S. 17 (1954) (union unlawfully caused employer not to rehire employee by refusing employee member in good standing status).

[67] See John J. Roche & Co., 231 N.L.R.B. 1082, 1083-84, 96 L.R.R.M. 1281, 1284 (1977); Communications Workers Local 6135 (Southwestern Bell Tel. Co.), 188 N.L.R.B. 971, 971, 76 L.R.R.M. 1635, 1636 (1971); Chemical Workers Local 143 (Lederle Laboratories), 188 N.L.R.B. 705, 707-08, 76 L.R.R.M. 1385, 1387 (1971).

[68] A member may resign or terminate his membership only if he is in good standing, is not in arrears or delinquent in the payment of any dues or other financial obligation to the International Union or to his Local Union and there are no charges filed and pending against him. Such resignation or termination shall be effective only if by written communication, signed by the member, and sent by registered or certified mail, return receipt requested, to the Financial Secretary of the Local Union within the ten (10) day period prior to the end of the fiscal year of the Local Union as fixed by this Constitution, whereupon it shall become effective sixty (60) days after the end of such fiscal year; pro-

The resignation will become effective sixty days after the close of the fiscal year. The constitution also provides that a resignation from an employee who has executed a dues check-off authorization becomes effective either upon the termination of this authorization or sixty days after the end of the fiscal year, whichever is later.[69]

In *UAW Local 647 (General Electric Co.)*,[70] the Board first ruled on the validity of a union's discipline imposed on members who failed to resign in accordance with these provisions of the UAW constitution. After the union fined two employees for crossing a picket line during a valid strike, the employees and the company filed unfair labor practice charges with the Board, claiming that the fines violated section 8(b)(1)(A). The union argued that the discipline was valid because the employees had not resigned within ten days of the end of the union's fiscal year,[71] as required by the constitution. The Board rejected the union's ar-

---

vided, that if the employer of such member has been authorized either by such member individually or by the Collective Bargaining Agreement between the employer and the Union to check off the membership dues of such member, then such resignation shall become effective upon the effective termination of such authorization, or upon the expiration of such sixty (60) day period, whichever is later.

UNITED AUTO WORKERS UNION CONST. art. 6, § 17 (1977).

[69] *Id.* Unions have employed a variety of methods and procedural hurdles for employees seeking to tender an effective resignation. The Board has often invalidated the most complicated and unnecessary restrictions on tendering a valid resignation. *See, e.g.,* Meat Cutters Local 81 (Empire Enterprises), 241 N.L.R.B. No. 125 (1979) (slip op.) (union ban of resignations when strike imminent invalid); Sheet Metal Workers Local 170 (Able Sheet Metal Prods., Inc.), 225 N.L.R.B. 1178, 93 L.R.R.M. 1071 (1976) (union cannot prohibit oral resignations that are clear and unequivocal expression of intent to resign); Bookbinders' Local 60 (Interstate Book Mfg., Inc.), 203 N.L.R.B. 732; 83 L.R.R.M. 1518 (1973) (resignations submitted orally or by registered mail valid); Communications Workers Local 6135 (Southwestern Bell Tel. Co.), 188 N.L.R.B. 971, 76 L.R.R.M. 1635 (1971) (resignations effective when union received surrendered membership cards if constitution is silent on resignation question); Electrical Workers Local 1522 (Western Elec. Co.), 180 N.L.R.B. 131, 73 L.R.R.M. 1091 (1969) (resignation effective when worker sent dues check-off deauthorization form to company and union demonstrating intent to resign); Aeronautical Indus. Dist. Lodge 751, Machinists (Boeing Co.), 173 N.L.R.B. 450, 69 L.R.R.M. 1363 (1968) (member may resign by notifying union in writing during interim period between expired and new collective bargaining contracts); Local 621, Rubber Workers (Atlantic Research Corp.), 167 N.L.R.B. 610, 66 L.R.R.M. 1109 (1967) (oral resignation effective); Oil Workers Union (United Nuclear Corp.), 148 N.L.R.B. 629, 57 L.R.R.M. 1061 (1964) (resignation effective in face of silent constitution when made either orally or by telegram prior to effective date of contract). *See generally* Wellington, *Union Fines and Workers' Rights,* 84 YALE L.J. 1022 (1976).

[70] 197 N.L.R.B. 608, 80 L.R.R.M. 1411 (1972).

[71] *Cf.* NLRB v. UAW, 320 F.2d 12 (1st Cir. 1963) (union did not violate § 8(b)(1) by requesting employer discharge employees whose resignations did not comply with union constitution).

gument, analogizing the provision to an absolute prohibition on
the right to resign:

> [T]he provision imposes such narrow restrictions as to amount,
> in effect, to a denial to members of a voluntary method of sev-
> ering their relationship with the Union. In short, the present
> provision does not make it possible for a member to avail him-
> self of the "strategy" of leaving the Union. . . .
>   We cannot view union members as being "free to leave the
> union" when their right to leave is as narrowly restricted as it is
> here. We need not pass upon the broader question of whether
> *any* provision in the union's constitution or bylaws which pur-
> ports to regulate the means or timing of resignations would
> have to yield to the members' freedom to leave the union. . . . It
> is sufficient in this case to hold that the very limited escape
> route contained in [the UAW's] constitution is inade-
> quate. . . .[72]

The Board reconsidered the UAW constitution three years
later. In *Local 1384, United Auto Workers (Ex-Cell-O Corp.)*,[73] the
union sought not to fine employees, but to secure their discharge
from employment under a maintenance of membership clause
contained in a collective bargaining agreement.[74] Before May 1,
the effective date of the maintenance of membership clause, a
group of employees who had previously signed membership cards
sent resignation letters to the union. The union argued that because the members had not resigned during the ten day escape
period at the end of the fiscal year, their subsequent failure to
tender dues required the employer to discharge them under the
collective bargaining agreement.[75] The Board affirmed the administrative law judge's finding that the UAW's constitutional
impediment to resignation was impermissibly broad and violated
section 8(b)(1)(A).[76] After considering the union's petition for re-

---

[72] 197 N.L.R.B. at 609, 80 L.R.R.M. at 1412.

[73] 219 N.L.R.B. 729, 90 L.R.R.M. 1152 (1975).

[74] A maintenance of membership clause in a collective bargaining agreement requires
that once a worker voluntarily joins the union, he must remain a union member during the
life of the agreement. *See* R. GORMAN, *supra* note 20, at 642-43. An escape period is usually
provided either at the expiration of the old contract or prior to the effective date of the
new contract. *See* Aeronautical Indus. Dist. Lodge 751, Machinists (Boeing Co.), 173
N.L.R.B. 450, 69 L.R.R.M. 1363 (1968) (employees validly resigned membership before
maintenance of membership clause became effective); *cf.* NLRB v. Allied Prod. Workers
Local 444, 427 F.2d 883 (1st Cir. 1970) (union may not prohibit resignations during interim period between old and new contract when new contract does not contain security
clause).

[75] 219 N.L.R.B. at 732-33, 90 L.R.R.M. at 1154.

[76] *Id.* at 729-30, 90 L.R.R.M. at 1153-54.

view and the Board's cross-application for enforcement, the Seventh Circuit remanded the case to the Board for reconsideration of whether the union's restriction on the right to resign was a reasonable union rule falling within the proviso to section 8(b)(1)(A).[77]

On remand, the Board considered the union's "justifications for curtail[ing the] employees' statutory rights."[78] The union conceded that the provision did, in effect, require workers to remain union members for an entire year, but claimed the limited resignation period was necessary to stabilize relations between the union and its members.[79] Because they provided the union with greater control over its members, the restrictions helped the union prevent wildcat strikes and internal union schisms.[80] This limited resignation period was also necessary, the union argued, to promote solidarity during strikes and to protect it from raiding by rival labor organizations.[81] The Board rejected these arguments, concluding that the union had failed to demonstrate adequately the need for a one year waiting period before a resignation became effective.[82] Although it recognized the union's interest in maintaining solidarity during strikes, the Board concluded the union's "limitations upon the member are broader than those which are necessary to serve the union interest because resignations are barred during nonstrike periods as well [as during strike periods]."[83] In addition, the Board concluded that the resignations were valid because the union had not informed the workers that their resignations were ineffective nor even that the constitution placed any limit on their right to resign.[84]

The Board found support for its conclusion in dicta from the *Granite State* opinion:

> Not only does the rule lack precise tailoring to the Union's needs, but also gives no regard to the important considerations

---

[77] Local 1384, UAW v. NLRB, No. 75-1910 (7th Cir. 1976). Part of the Court's unpublished order is reproduced in Local 1384, UAW (Ex-Cell-O Corp.), 227 N.L.R.B. 1045, 1045, 94 L.R.R.M. 1145, 1145 (1977), *supplementing and affirming* 219 N.L.R.B. 729, 90 L.R.R.M. 1152 (1975).

[78] 227 N.L.R.B. 1045, 1050, 94 L.R.R.M. 1145, 1151 (1977).

[79] *Id.*

[80] *Id.* For an example of internal union schisms caused by a lack of solidarity, see Hershey Chocolate Corp., 121 N.L.R.B. 901, 42 L.R.R.M. 1460 (1958).

[81] 227 N.L.R.B. at 1050, 94 L.R.R.M. at 1151.

[82] *Id.* at 1051, 94 L.R.R.M. at 1151-52.

[83] *Id.*

[84] *Id.* at 1049, 94 L.R.R.M. at 1149.

that the Supreme Court has explained may necessitate an employee's resignation during a strike:

> Events occurring after the calling of a strike may have un-settling effects, leading a member who voted to strike to change his mind. The likely duration of the strike may increase the specter of hardship to his family; the ease with which the employer replaces the strikers may make the strike seem less provident.[85]

Unless a strike arose during the ten day period at the end of the fiscal year, a dissenting employee would never be able to resign under the UAW constitution.[86]   Thus, the Board held that the provision did not fall within the proviso to section 8(b)(1)(A) because it was not "tailored" to "reasonabl[y] accommodat[e] between the Union's and the employees' conflicting interests."[87] Subsequent decisions have invalidated other constitutional provisions requiring sixty days notice before a resignation became effective.[88]

The *Granite State* dicta is troublesome. The Court implied that a union can *never* restrict the right to resign, even during a strike. It is unclear whether the Board will give the dicta this expansive reading. The Board has, however, declined to state specifically how a union may validly restrict the time or manner of resignation. The Supreme Court has thus left two questions unanswered: the extent to which a union may restrict the right to resign and the extent to which unions may regulate post-resignation conduct.

III

DEVELOPING AN APPROPRIATE UNION PROCEDURE
FOR LIMITING THE RIGHT TO RESIGN

Allis-Chalmers and its progeny clearly demonstrate the relationship now required between valid discipline and the union

---

[85] *Id.* at 1051, 94 L.R.R.M. at 1151-52 (quoting *Granite State*, 409 U.S. at 217).

[86] *Id.* If the employee was a union member who had authorized the checkoff of union dues, he could resign only when his checkoff revocation became effective, or 60 days after notifying the union of his wish to resign, whichever occurred later. *See* note 68 *supra.*

[87] 227 N.L.R.B. at 1051, 94 L.R.R.M. at 1152.

[88] *See, e.g.,* Local 444, Electrical Workers (Sperry Rand Corp.), 235 N.L.R.B 98, 98 L.R.R.M. 1526 (1978); UAW Local 469 (Master Lock Co.), 221 N.L.R.B. 748, 90 L.R.R.M. 1563 (1975); *cf.* TKB Int'l Corp., 240 N.L.R.B. No. 114, 100 L.R.R.M. 1426 (1979) (local union bylaw requiring statement of reasons for resignation held invalid).

member's right to resign from the union. On the other hand, the Court also stressed in *Allis-Chalmers* that federal labor policy must protect the union's ability to maintain solidarity by permitting reasonable discipline of members who violate rules and regulations governing membership.[89] Protecting this solidarity interest is particularly vital when the union exercises its ultimate economic weapon: the strike. Although the Court has separately acknowledged both interests—the individual's right to resign and the union's need for solidarity—it has not attempted to accommodate these interests, thus leaving the Board relatively unguided in its own balancing efforts. Moreover, a principled balancing is difficult because the dicta in *Granite State* recognizing a right to resign during strikes obviously undermines the solidarity interest of *Allis-Chalmers.*

Nonetheless, the Board struck an appropriate balance between these two interests in holding that the UAW constitution inappropriately restricted the individual employee's right to resign. Foremost among the UAW constitution's deficiencies was its extremely abbreviated time period at the end of the union's fiscal year for resignations and the substantial delay for the effective date of the resignations. Because strikes involving UAW members employed in the auto industry often occur in the autumn and not at the end of the union's fiscal year,[90] the UAW rule completely failed to accommodate the worker's interest in resigning from the union prior to the strike. This rationale, however, does not justify extending the right to resign to periods during the strike. As the Court recognized in *Granite State,* the potential unsettling effects of a strike may induce the worker to change his mind about the union.[91] This *Granite State* dicta is extremely misguided and inconsistent with the Court's explicit sanction of union discipline

---

[89] 388 U.S. at 181.

[90] Gould, *supra* note 26, at 1105-07.

[91] Events occurring after the calling of a strike may have unsettling effects, leading a member who voted to strike to change his mind. The likely duration of the strike may increase the specter of hardship to his family; the ease with which the employer replaces the strikers may make the strike seem less provident. We do not now decide to what extent the contractual relationship between union and member may curtail the freedom to resign. But where, as here, there are no restraints on the resignation of members, we conclude that the vitality of § 7 requires that the member be free to refrain in November from the actions he endorsed in May and that his § 7 rights are not lost by a union's plea for solidarity or by its pressures for conformity and submission to its regime.
409 U.S. at 217-18 (footnote omitted).

during a valid strike in *Allis-Chalmers*.[92]   Interpreting *Granite State* to prohibit unions from guarding against "fair weather" members who leave the fold during a strike would unfairly circumscribe union authority over members.[93]   The Board now applies the *Granite State* standard, as it must, and as a result has invalidated most union restrictions on the right to resign.

The Court should overrule its decision in *Granite State*.[94]   The disciplinary authority approved in *Allis-Chalmers* is most important when union members participating in a strike are likely to become strikebreakers. Although workers know that a strike may cause hardships, they generally expect to surmount these difficulties. Indeed, labor is almost always the winner in short strikes.[95]   Thus, workers may eagerly support work stoppages that they believe will be brief. Long strikes, on the other hand, are more likely to cause "unsettling effects" that induce the worker to leave the fold.[96] This fact alone, however, does not justify allowing members to resign during the strike, even if they later become dissatisfied; majority rule is the cornerstone of labor solidarity. Notwithstanding *Granite State*, a member should generally be compelled to follow a union's decision. Justice Blackmun persuasively argued in his dissenting opinion in *Granite State* that the majority

> seems to . . . exalt the formality of resignation over the substance of the various interests and national labor policies that are at stake here. Union activity, by its very nature, is group activity, and is grounded on the notion that strength can be garnered from unity, solidarity, and mutual commitment. This concept is of particular force during a strike, where the individual members of the union draw strength from the commitments of fellow members, and where the activities carried on by

---

[92] *See* text accompanying notes 33-38 *supra*.

[93] The need to use discipline is greatest when the union instigates a strike. *See* Gould, *supra* note 5, at 1106-07.

[94] *See* Boys Market, Inc. v. Retail Clerks Union, 398 U.S. 235, 240-41 (1970) (" '[S]tare decisis is . . . not a mechanical formula of adherence' " (quoting Helvering v. Hallock, 309 U.S. 106, 119 (1940)); *id.* at 255 (Stewart, J., concurring).

[95] *See* Gould, *The Supreme Court and Labor Law: The October 1978 Term*, 21 ARIZ. L. REV. 621, 625-30 (1979); Livernash, *The Relation of Power to the Structure and Process of Collective Bargaining*, 6 J.L. ECON. 10 (1963).

[96] The strike in *Granite State* was in effect for about six weeks before the workers resigned their membership and crossed the picket lines. 409 U.S. 213, 214 (1972). The workers in *Dalmo Victor* resigned from the union and crossed the picket lines approximately nine months after the strike began. NLRB v. Machinists Local 1327, 608 F.2d 1219, 1221 (9th Cir. 1979).

the union rest fundamentally on the mutual reliance that in-
heres in the "pact." [97]

A. *Creating Democratic Procedures for Mid-Strike*
Challenges to Union Decisions

As long as *Granite State* remains the law, unions desiring to
prohibit resignations both before and during strikes [98] must establish procedures that not only ensure employees free choice when
the strike decision is made but also accommodate *Granite State's*
concern for post-strike reassessment of the strike decision. One
way to achieve this balance would be by utilizing secret ballot box
procedures both before and during the strike. Giving employees
the opportunity to express their views about the desirability of a
strike without fear of censure would allow all members to address
those potential unsettling effects of a strike, [99] and would justify
binding the member to the group decision. The secret ballot box
would also accommodate the union's solidarity interests recognized by the Court in *Allis-Chalmers*. [100]

---

[97] 409 U.S. at 221.
 Although he concurred in Justice Douglas' majority opinion, Chief Justice Burger expressed a similar concern in his concurring opinion:
> I join the Court's opinion because for me the institutional needs of the Union
> important though they are, do not outweigh the rights and needs of the individual
> The balance is close and difficult; unions have need for solidarity, and at no
> time is that need more pressing than under the stress of economic conflict.
Id. at 218.
[98] *See, e.g.,* AMALGAMATED CLOTHING & TEXTILE WORKERS UNION CONST. art. IX, § 11
(1976) (prohibiting any resignation during strikes); INTERNATIONAL ASS'N OF MACHINISTS
CONST. art. L, § 3 (1977) (prohibiting member who resigns after fourteenth day preceding
strike from working at struck establishment).
[99] Several union constitutions provide for a membership vote on continuing or terminating a strike. *See, e.g.,* UNITED AUTO WORKERS UNION CONST. art. 50, § 5 (1977) (either
International Executive Board or majority vote by local union membership may terminate
strike); INTERNATIONAL ASS'N OF MACHINISTS UNIONS CONST. art. XVIII, § 4 (1977) (either
Executive Council or vote by local lodge membership may terminate strike); COMMUNICA-
TIONS WORKERS OF AMER. UNION CONST. art. XVIII, § 8(a)-(b) (1979) (either local union
in accordance with local bylaws or Executive Board or Convention may terminate strike);
ALUMINUM WORKERS INT'L UNION CONST. art. IX, § 2 (1975) (Although local union membership may terminate strike by majority vote, local's executive board may override decision to terminate); INTERNATIONAL BHD. OF TEAMSTERS UNION CONST. art. XII, § 1(b)
(1976) (majority vote of local members may terminate strike); UNITED ASS'N OF PLUMBERS
AND PIPEFITTERS UNION CONST. § 188(b) (1976) (majority vote by either Metal Trades
Branch or Building and Construction Trades Branch of local union may terminate strike).
[100] This approach would also comport with other provisions of the NLRA permitting
employee free choice. For example, 29 U.S.C. § 159(c)(1) (1976) provides that the Board
"shall [direct an election by] secret ballot . . . and certify the results thereof" when a petition for election of a bargaining unit representative has been filed. *But cf.* Rocket Freight

Testing employee sentiment by secret ballot is infinitely preferable to forcing the union member who wishes either to challenge the strike decision on behalf of all workers or to plead for a hardship exemption allowing him to cross union picket lines during a strike to appear before an internal union tribunal that will weigh loss of employee income against the union's solidarity interest.[101] Employees who might disagree with a strike or the penalties for strikebreaking may be unwilling to risk the wrath of their more militant brethren by advertising their dissidence at a union-controlled hearing. Even if it is fairly staffed, the tribunal will not be particularly hospitable towards members wishing to resign.[102]

This solution would not create insurmountable practical problems for initiating a vote on the appropriateness of the strike or the strikebreaking penalties. A union rule providing that 10% to 20% of the workers may petition for a secret ballot would not be inconsistent with *Granite State*. Certainly, the percentage should be considerably below the 30% showing of interest now required for employees to request a secret ballot election to rescind the authority of their bargaining representative.[103]

The primary difficulty with this proposal is that the voting procedure would, without any specific statutory authorization, modify, and sometimes contravene, internal union policy.[104]   Na-

---

Lines v. NLRB, 427 F.2d 202, 204-05 (10th Cir.), *cert. denied*, 400 U.S. 942 (1970) (even though majority of local union members approved contract offer, international validly fined them for crossing picket lines when international rejected this offer).

[101] *See* Comment, *supra* note 26, at 879-80.

[102] Several unions, including the UAW, have experimented with "public review boards" consisting of nonunion members appointed by the union hierarchy. *See* Brooks, *Impartial Public Review of Internal Union Disputes: Experiment in Democratic Self-Discipline*, 22 Ohio St. L.J. 64 (1961); Klein, *UAW Public Review Board Report*, 18 Rutgers L. Rev. 304 (1964); Oberer, *Voluntary Impartial Review of Labor: Some Reflections*, 58 Mich. L. Rev. 55 (1959); Stieber, *The UAW Public Review Board: An Examination and Evaluation* (1960-61) (monograph no. 35, Mich. St. Univ. Indus. Rel. Ctr.).

[103] *See* 29 U.S.C. § 159(c)(1) (1976).

A procedure that will effectively limit the individual employee's right to refrain must not create an insurmountable barrier to the exercise of that right. Requiring a majority vote against the previous union decision as a precondition for a mid-strike reconsideration would be unduly restrictive.

[104] The labor "bill of rights" established by the Landrum-Griffin Act, 29 U.S.C. § 411(a)(1)-(5) (1976), guarantees union members the right of free speech in internal union affairs. *See, e.g.*, Soto v. Masters, Mates and Pilots Union, 100 L.R.R.M. 3125, 3129 (S.D.N.Y. 1979) (right of free speech for opposing contract bargained by union not abridged by union rules of order); Lacy v. Teamsters Local 667, 99 L.R.R.M. 2403, 2405 (W.D. Tenn. 1978) (union cannot punish member who invokes right of free speech). This right of free speech, however, does not guarantee a member the right to vote for approving a contract unless the union's restrictions on voting rights are unreasonable. *See, e.g.*,

tional and international unions often exercise significant control over strikes at the local union level. For example, one union constitution provides that "[w]henever the International Executive Board decides that it is unwise to longer continue an existing strike, it will order the members of the local unions who have ceased to work in connection therewith to resume work and thereupon . . . all assistance from this International Union shall cease."[105] The UAW's Constitution contains a similar provision:

> Before a strike shall be called off, a special meeting of the Local Union shall be called for that purpose, and it shall require a majority vote by secret ballot of all members present to decide the question either way. Wherever the International Executive Board decides that it is unwise to longer continue an existing strike, it will order all members of Local Unions who have ceased work in connection therewith to resume work and thereupon and thereafter all assistance from the International Union shall cease.[106]

The Board and courts should validate discipline imposed by unions with constitutional provisions that either create democratic internal union procedures for convening special union meetings to vote on the continuation of a strike or require a majority vote on strike decisions and strike sanctions. Unfortunately, these democratic ballot box guarantees are often effectively nullified by provisions that allow union executive bodies to exercise complete control over the continuation of a strike. Although a provision such as the UAW's gives members a right to limit the continuation of a strike, it empowers the international union to override the decision at the local union level. Limiting the ability to continue a strike with effective mid-strike democratic procedures complies only in part with *Granite State*'s dicta; placing plenary veto power in international tribunals, on the other hand, is not consistent with *Granite State*'s fear of the unsettling effects of strikes.[107] Similarly, an administrative mechanism must be established for implementing these democratic ballot box proposals; current union procedures often provide that a certain number of union members in

---

Williams v. Typographical Union, 423 F.2d 1295, 1298 (10th Cir. 1970), *cert. denied*, 400 U.S. 824 (1970) (union may reasonably restrict members' right to vote on wage scales); *cf.* Trail v. Teamsters, 542 F.2d 961 (6th Cir. 1976) (member stated cause of action against union that did not submit local rider governing wages to local membership vote).

[105] INTERNATIONAL UNION, UNITED PLANT GUARD WORKERS CONST. art. XXXVII, § 5 (1975).

[106] UNITED AUTO WORKERS UNION CONST. art. 50, § 5 (1977).

[107] *See* note 91 *supra*.

the executive board may initiate these special meetings rather than allowing a relatively small percentage of members to petition for a meeting.[108]   These procedures, however, clash with both the international union's veto power and with the requirement under *Granite State* for effective mid-strike democratic procedures because the spectre of unfavorable union control might intimidate potential dissidents. Accommodating *Granite State* by utilizing the secret ballot box, therefore, will disrupt the normal course of American industrial relations.

B. *An Alternative Proposal: Allowing Unions to Restrict the Right to Resign Shortly After Negotiations Commence*

At the heart of the problem of creating valid union restrictions on the right to resign is the competition between the interest in labor solidarity, necessary for promoting effective collective bargaining, and the individual's interest in refraining from union activity.[109]   A framework for analyzing this conflict can be developed by examining the nature of the union-employee relationship. The *Allis-Chalmers* opinion characterizes this relationship as contractual.[110]   This is not, however, an entirely accurate characterization; the contract, if any, resembles a contract of adhesion.[111]   The union constitution or contract is only the starting point for this analysis. The union's solidarity interest and the employee's right to refrain are based not on this union-employee contract but rather on the federal labor statutes. Recognizing the fundamental source of these competing interests is crucial to resolve the right to resign issue. Once the interests are recognized, they can be properly balanced. Justice Blackmun's dissent in *Granite State* is the proper starting point for this balancing. Any prohibition on the right to resign should become effective only when

---

[108] *See* text accompanying notes 105-06 *supra*.

[109] *See generally* Local 444, Electrical Workers (Sperry Rand Corp.), 235 N.L.R.B. 98, 98 L.R.R.M. 1526 (1978); Machinists Lodge 1871 (General Dynamics Corp.), 231 N.L.R.B. 727 (1977), *enforced*, 98 L.R.R.M. 2170 (2d Cir. 1978); Broadcast Employees Local 531 (Skateboard Prod., Inc.), 245 N.L.R.B. No. 77, 102 L.R.R.M. 1250 (1979).

[110] 388 U.S. at 196. Thus, the Board will not enforce individual contracts between the employer and worker that will usurp either the collective bargaining agreement or the union member's relation to the union. *See* Sheet Metal Workers Local 29 (Metal-Fab, Inc.), 222 N.L.R.B. 1156, 91 L.R.R.M. 1390 (1976).

[111] *See* 6A A. CORBIN, CONTRACTS § 1420, at 349 & n.74 (2d ed. 1962). *See generally* Gould, *supra* note 26, at 1101 n.134.

the worker can make an intelligent and knowledgeable decision on whether to refrain from concerted activities.

Unions could adequately balance these interests by prohibiting resignations during the strike, but allowing members to resign before the strike becomes effective. The group decision would prevail after a cutoff date for resignations, and thereafter the member would be bound by, and subject to discipline for violating, the strike decision. Admittedly, this approach does not fully comport with *Granite State*'s dicta, which seemingly requires the opportunity to modify the group decision during the course of the strike. Failure to fully accommodate this dicta, however, is not fatal because this dicta conflicts with the union's solidarity interests protected under federal labor policy.[112]   The legitimate interest recognized in *Granite State* would be partially served by this approach; it protects the individual's right to refrain, which was promoted in *Granite State*, because employees would be free to resign up to the point when the union's solidarity interest peaks. This approach also ensures that the worker will have the opportunity to assess both sides of the controversy before making a decision about refraining from concerted union action. The question that remains to be answered, however, is at what point may the union lawfully restrict the right to resign.

Although many union constitutions fail to address the strikebreaking and resignation issues, those that do have prohibited dissident conduct, including the right to resign, not only during the strike but also for a short period of time preceding the strike.[113]   The Board is currently considering such a provision in *Machinists Local 1327 (Dalmo Victor)*.[114]   In most respects, these limitations successfully accommodate the union's solidarity interest with the worker's right to refrain. The union constitution crosses the border line into "coercion and restraint" only when the effective date limiting the right to resign substantially precedes a scheduled strike vote. Workers will not have the information needed to make a knowledgeable decision about resigning union membership at such an early stage in the negotiations. On the

---

[112] *See* note 91 and accompanying text *supra*.

[113] Union constitutions do not typically allow dissidents to leave the union immediately before or during a strike. *See* note 98 *supra*.

[114] *See* notes 123-37 and accompanying text *supra*.

other hand, unions should not be allowed to fix an inflexible across-the-board date for limiting the right to resign. For example, a union might prohibit resignations fifteen days before a strike becomes effective or ten or fifteen days after a strike vote is taken. Depending upon the union involved and its pattern of negotiation, a variety of dates might insure that members can make a knowledgeable decision about their continued union affiliation and the need to place economic pressure on the employer. The difficulty of establishing a fixed date in advance of a strike is undiminished by the "no contract, no work" approach of many unions.[115] Unions that ostensibly rely on this philosophy may postpone the strike indefinitely, thereby confusing employees about the resignation cut-off date. Unions should not formulate this date far in advance of a strike, and thereby miscalculate the point at which the employee can make a reasoned decision that will bind him. The Board and courts should not allow such arbitrary dates to fall within the proviso to section 8(b)(1)(A).

Adding to the difficulty of pinpointing a date when members can make knowledgeable decisions about exercising their right to refrain is that union leaders may be tempted to publicize unreliable rhetoric that will push the bargaining parties into rigid and unworkable positions that promote industrial strife. A potential solution to this dilemma would be to allow union constitutions to prohibit resignations for a short period of time before a strike unless the worker can show that he could not knowledgeably participate in the strike decision prior to the cut-off date. Providing this "affirmative defense" to a subsequent union allegation of either improper resignation or strikebreaking would accommodate the individual interests recognized in *Granite State* while creating a presumption of union legitimacy.

Guaranteeing employees the ability to freely resign until shortly before the strike, on the other hand, may overcompromise the union's interest in solidarity. In addition to his attitude toward the union, the employee bases his decision to resign on such factors as the union's bargaining stance, the union's willingness to strike (or the likelihood of an employer lockout), and the potential benefits or hardships that may accompany a strike, particularly a long one. Escape routes will be most utilized when there is a strong prospect of a strike, thus jeopardizing the union's solidarity

---

[115] Some unions automatically strike when their contracts expire if negotiations have not produced an acceptable tentative agreement at that time. Collective bargaining agreements often suspend the no-strike obligation when negotiations have not produced any acceptable settlement. *See* [1979-80] Coll. Barg. Negotiations & Contracts (BNA) 36:61-65, 36:301-304, 77:101-103.

interest recognized in *Allis-Chalmers*. The group interest is more easily protected, irresponsible bargaining avoided, and the rank and file encouraged to challenge stale union leadership if the resignation prohibition is imposed at an early or intermediate juncture in the negotiations.

Although most contract negotiations do not produce strikes, bargaining in the private sector is induced by the union's credible threat to use its economic weaponry.[116] Management and labor tend to negotiate seriously only after labor manifests its solidarity by demonstrating its ability to utilize economic pressure. Allowing members to resign on the eve of the contract expiration date will deprive the union of its credibility. Thus, the last date for effective resignations must be set early enough for the union to ascertain the potential effectiveness of its strike weapon but late enough to ensure that the worker can make a knowledgeable resignation decision. The Board and courts should uphold union constitutions that prohibit resignations ten to fifteen days after negotiations have commenced if those negotiations are initiated approximately sixty days before the contract expires.[117] This approach not only satisfies the worker's need to know the last possible date for exercising the resignation option[118] but also avoids problems that arise if the resignation date is tied to a strike date that the union leadership may postpone indefinitely. Moreover, a solution focusing on the start of the negotiation process recognizes the noncontractual nature of the union-employee relationship by setting the last date for resignations when the union's solidarity interest exceeds the individual's interest in refraining from union activity. This solidarity interest is at the heart of the federal labor statutes and federal labor policy[119]—it cannot be ignored.

IV

Union Prohibitions on Post-Resignation Conduct

Even if reasonable escape periods that restrict the right to resign fifteen days after contract negotiations commence are es-

---

[116] NLRB v. Insurance Agents' Int'l Union, 361 U.S. 477, 489 (1960); *cf.* American Ship Bldg. Co. v. NLRB, 380 U.S. 300, 308-13 (1965) (employer lockout after bargaining impasse held valid application of economic pressure).

[117] There is some experience under the NLRA with contract expiration dates. Section 8(d)(1) of the NLRA, 29 U.S.C. § 158(d)(1) (1976), provides that a party may not modify or terminate an agreement unless that party "serves a written notice upon the other party to the contract of the proposed termination or modification sixty days prior to the expiration date thereof."

[118] *See* Booster Lodge 405, Machinists v. NLRB, 412 U.S. 84, 89 (1973).

[119] *See* note 10 *supra*.

tablished, some unions may attempt to restrict resignations indirectly by threatening to discipline former members for their post-resignation conduct. A worker's post-resignation activities, however, should not be subject to union control unless it provides a method for members to challenge the union's collective decisions about the strike and strikebreaking penalties during the strike. The *Granite State* Court did not settle whether union control over an employee's post-resignation conduct constitutes an implicit restriction on the right to resign, even though the Court held that the post-resignation discipline at issue was unlawful.[120] The Court subsequently held in *Booster Lodge* that the union violated section 8(b)(1)(A) by fining employees for strikebreaking after they had resigned from the union.[121] The Machinists' constitution in that case, however, had no provision governing resignation rights. After the Court's decision, the Machinists union amended its constitution by adding a provision that explicitly prohibited members from strikebreaking or crossing picket lines *after* they resigned from the union:

> Accepting employment in any capacity in an establishment where a strike or lockout exists as recognized under this Constitution, without permission [shall constitute improper conduct by a member]. Resignation shall not relieve a member of his obligation to refrain from accepting employment at the establishment for the duration of the strike or lockout or within 14 days preceding its commencement. Where observance of a primary picket line is required, resignation shall not relieve a member of his obligation to observe the primary picket line for its duration if the resignation occurs during the period that the picket line is maintained or within 14 days preceding its establishment.[122]

In *Machinists Local 1327 (Dalmo Victor)*,[123] the Board held that fines imposed under this provision violated section 8(b)(1)(A).[124] The union fined three workers who had apparently validly resigned from the union and returned to work during a lawful economic strike; the fines equalled the total amount of strike ben-

---

[120] 409 U.S. at 217.

[121] *See* text accompanying note 56 *supra*.

[122] INTERNATIONAL ASS'N OF MACHINISTS CONST. art. L, § 3 (1977). *See* Machinists Local 1327 (Dalmo Victor), 231 N.L.R.B. 719, 719, 96 L.R.R.M. 1160, 1160 (1977), *enforcement denied and remanded*, 608 F.2d 1219 (9th Cir. 1979); Local 1994, Machinists (O.K. Tool Co.), 215 N.L.R.B. 651, 88 L.R.R.M. 1120 (1974).

[123] 231 N.L.R.B. 719, 96 L.R.R.M. 1160 (1977).

[124] *Id.* at 720-21, 96 L.R.R.M. at 1161-62.

efits received by the former members.[125] The Board noted that
the question left unanswered in *Granite State*—the extent to which
a union could restrict the right to resign—was not before it. In
the majority's view, the Machinists' constitution "place[d] no clear
restriction, no subtle restriction, no restriction by implication, and,
in sum, no restriction whatsoever upon the employee's right to
resign."[126] The Board's majority also rejected the dissenters' argument that the proscription against post-resignation strikebreaking was actually a valid restriction on the right to resign under the
proviso to section 8(b)(1)(A).[127] The majority only considered
whether the union could control the post-resignation conduct of
former members in the absence of a contractual relation.[128] The
Board concluded that this question had been clearly settled by the
Court in *Granite State* and *Scofield*—union discipline of former
members violated section 8(b)(1)(A).[129]

A three-judge panel from the Ninth Circuit reversed the
Board's order.[130] The majority rejected as a "hypertechnical
reading of the Union's constitution"[131] the Board's argument that
the provision did not restrict the right to resign:

> [The constitutional provision] plainly tells its members that res-
> ignation "shall not relieve a member from his obligation to re-
> frain from accepting employment" at the struck establishment,
> or from his "obligation to observe the primary picket line" dur-

---

[125] *Id.* at 720.

[126] *Id.*

[127] *Id.*

[128] *Id.* at 721.

[129] In a previous case involving the same provision in the Machinists' constitution, the
Board noted that the employees fined in *Allis-Chalmers*

> enjoyed full union membership . . . . Not only do full members reap the benefits
> of their continuing union membership, but they also have a continuing voice in
> the union's course of action, a factor the Court relied on in *Allis-Chalmers* . . . .

> Balancing an individual's right under Section 7 to refrain from concerted
> activity following resignation from a union against that of a union to maintain
> solidarity during a strike, we conclude that the latter must give way. Conformity
> may be none too high a price for the benefits of union membership. But the
> choice, at least in the absence of reasonable restrictions on resignation, is the
> individual's to make, not the union's. Should he choose to resign and forgo [*sic*]
> the benefits of union membership, the union may not nonetheless seek to exact
> conformity without regard to the individual's Section 7 rights.

Local 1994, Machinists (O.K. Tool Co.), 215 N.L.R.B. 651, 653, 88 L.R.R.M. 1120, 1122
(1974). In *Dalmo Victor*, the Board expressed a similar theme, noting that a worker surrenders his right to participate in union affairs when he resigns. 231 N.L.R.B. at 721, 96
L.R.R.M. at 1162.

[130] NLRB v. Machinists Local 1327, 101 L.R.R.M. 3096 (9th Cir. 1979).

[131] *Id.* at 3098.

ing the strike or the picketing, if the resignation occurs during that time or 14 days before. Surely that is "a restriction on a member's right to resign," Booster Lodge, supra, a "defining or limiting [of] the circumstances under which a member may resign," Granite State, supra. Apparently the Board majority would confine these phrases to provisions that expressly prohibit resignation at certain times or under certain circumstances. Such a provision would be a more drastic limitation on the member's right to resign, and thus less likely to be upheld, than the provision that is before us. In short, we conclude that this case presents the question reserved by the Court in Granite State and Booster Lodge.[132]

The majority agreed with the Board's dissenters that this provision was a "reasonable regulation" falling within the proviso to section 8(b)(1)(A) protecting union rules regarding "the acquisition or retention of membership."[133]

In a second opinion issued after a rehearing,[134] the majority abandoned its holding that this constitutional provision was valid under the proviso.[135] The court remanded the case to the Board so that it could first consider whether the provision was a protected union rule under section 8(b)(1)(A).[136]

---

[132] Id.

[133] Id. The court quoted the Fifth Circuit's decision in Local 1255, Machinists v. NLRB, 456 F.2d 1214 (1972) to support its conclusion:

"The proviso [to section 8(b)(1)(A)] makes no distinction between acts done while [someone is] a member and those done while [someone is] not a member." It is true that in [Local 1255, Machinists] the only penalty for not paying a fine for strikebreaking was expulsion, a fact upon which the court relied. But that is not a particularly effective sanction against one who has resigned. That is why we think that the sanction of a fine . . . is also permissible . . . in this case.

101 L.R.R.M. at 3098 (quoting Local 1255, Machinists v. NLRB, 456 F.2d 1214, 1217 (5th Cir. 1972)). See also NLRB v. District Lodge 99, Machinists, 489 F.2d 769 (1st Cir. 1974) (discipline for post-resignation strikebreaking, not unfair labor practice).

Judge Kennedy dissented from the panel's decision. He argued that union authority is limited by the "concept of membership." 101 L.R.R.M. at 3099. Since the members had validly resigned, the degree of membership required by Allis-Chalmers as a prerequisite for union discipline was lacking; thus, he concluded that the discipline in this case was improper; "[t]he Union's right to enforce the fines it imposes on its members is a corollary of the member's rights not only to reap the benefits of continuing union membership, but also to maintain a continuing voice in the union's courts of action." Id. at 3099-3100.

[134] NLRB v. Machinists Local 1327, No. 77-3723 (9th Cir., petition for rehearing granted Oct. 9, 1979).

[135] NLRB v. Machinists Local 1327, 608 F.2d 1219 (9th Cir. 1979).

[136] Id. at 1222.

The majority's original view of the Board's "hypertechnical" refusal to characterize the Machinists' provision as an implicit resignation restriction was appropriate. If a member contemplating both strikebreaking and resignation is threatened with union sanctions after he resigns, it is unlikely he will utilize the resignation escape route contemplated by *Granite State*. This is, at the bare minimum, a "subtle restriction" on the right to resign.

Although this provision, which ostensibly controls the post-resignation conduct of workers, is a restriction on the right to resign, the question remains: is the restriction protected by the proviso to section 8(b)(1)(A)? The Ninth Circuit originally held, and the two dissenting Board members argued, that it was so protected. This conclusion, which creates a labor law minefield by approving post-resignation discipline that is tantamount to an absolute restriction on the right to resign, is the product of the Ninth Circuit's overly generalized interpretations of the proviso to section 8(b)(1)(A). The *Granite State* dicta, which adopts an opposite view, *i.e.* that a union can never control the "man on the street," also hinders a cogent analysis of this issue. The apparent superficial illogic of precluding unions from controlling nonmembers, implicit in these conclusions, is inconsistent with reality. Unions commonly exercise control over both members and nonmembers. Union membership is prerequisite for access to joint union-employer apprenticeship programs and to union administered hiring halls that operate as de facto closed shops.[137] Congress enacted the proviso to allow unions to deny membership to those individuals the union deemed undesirable, *e.g.*, Negro workers,[138] thus enabling the union to control access to many employment opportunities not available to nonmembers. Without union membership, a worker may be unable to participate in

---

[137] *See* NLRB v. Local 2, Plumbers & Pipefitters, 360 F.2d 428 (2d Cir. 1966), *enforcing* 152 N.L.R.B. 1093, 59 L.R.R.M. 1234 (1965); W. GOULD, BLACK WORKERS IN WHITE UNIONS 281-315 (1977).

[138] *See* 93 CONG. REC. 2955 (1947) (remarks of Rep. Smith); *id.* at 4272 (remarks of Rep. Cole). *See also* Oliphant v. Brotherhood of Locom. Firemen & Enginemen, 262 F.2d 359 (6th Cir. 1958), *cert. denied*, 359 U.S. 935 (1959) (Railway Labor Act does not prohibit union from denying membership to employee).

The Civil Rights Act of 1964, Pub. L. No. 88-352, tit. VI, §§ 703(c)-(d), 78 Stat. 253, *as amended by* the Equal Employment Opportunity Act of 1972, Pub. L. No. 92-261, 86 Stat. 103 (codified at 42 U.S.C. §§ 2000e(c)-(d) (1976)), now prohibits unions from discriminating against members on the basis of sex, race, religion and national origin. When it enacted the proviso to § 8(b)(1)(A), Congress emphasized that unions could continue to exclude blacks from membership pursuant to the authority retained under the proviso. *See* 93 CONG. REC. 4193 (1947) (remarks of Rep. Taft). *See generally* Sovern, *The National Labor Relations Acts and Racial Discrimination*, 62 COLUM. L. REV. 563, 583-84 (1962).

strike and contract ratification voting.[139]   Moreover, the union may initiate an action to recover delinquent dues against a worker even after he resigns from the union.[140]   In sum, the relationship between the union and the worker is neither as simple as it was characterized in *Granite State* nor as contractual as viewed in *Allis-Chalmers.* The superficial illogic of precluding unions from controlling nonmembers is indeed erroneous.

The Board and courts should require a reasonable accommodation of the various competing interests that make up the union-employee relationship before they uphold post-resignation union discipline. The Machinists' constitution partially accommodates the union's interest in solidarity during strikes recognized in *Allis-Chalmers,* but fails to account for the individual worker's interests in refraining from concerted activity. The worker who resigns from the union and is fined for post-resignation strikebreaking bears the burdens of union membership without any of its benefits. There is no ballot procedure available for such a worker after the strike decision is made. *Granite State* seems to require some form of a *post-strike* decision ballot procedure allowing the worker to change his mind about either the strike or the strikebreaking penalties as a prerequisite to valid post-resignation discipline. Thus, the effect of the Machinists' constitution is to extend union control and influence over former members in a manner not contemplated by Congress when it enacted the proviso.

Because the provision of the Machinists' constitution authorizing post-resignation discipline is overinclusive, it seriously impinges on a worker's right to refrain in another way. A worker who starts working fourteen days before a strike cannot participate in the strike decision. The presumed rationale for this fourteen day requirement is that workers should be bound by the strike decision only after they have participated in the delibera-

---

[139] *See* General Motors Corp., 133 N.L.R.B. 451, 456-57 n.12, 48 L.R.R.M. 1659, 1661 (1961), *enforcement denied,* 303 F.2d 428 (6th Cir. 1962), *rev'd and remanded,* 373 U.S. 734 (1963); Gould, *supra* note 5, at 1094 n.118.

A corresponding duty is imposed on unions to refrain from utilizing the dues paid by nonmembers for purposes other than collective bargaining. *See* Abood v. Detroit Bd. of Educ., 431 U.S. 209 (1977); Reid v. UAW, 479 F.2d 517 (10th Cir.), *cert. denied,* 414 U.S. 1076 (1973); Detroit Mailers Union No. 40 (Detroit Newspaper Publishers Ass'n), 192 N.L.R.B. 951, 78 L.R.R.M. 1053 (1971). Limited members whose "membership" has been impaired by union discipline may refuse to pay dues. Local 1101, Communications Workers (New York Tel. Co.), 211 N.L.R.B. 114, 87 L.R.R.M. 1253 (1974), *enforced,* 520 F.2d 411 (2d Cir. 1975), *cert. denied,* 423 U.S. 1051 (1976).

[140] *See* Summers, *Legal Limitations on Union Discipline,* 64 HARV. L. REV. 1049 (1951); note 30 *supra.*

tions and decision. Job applicants hired shortly before the strike who are also union members do not have the freedom to refrain from any strike decision because they are bound by a decision made before they were hired.

The Machinists' constitutional provision should not be validated under the proviso to section 8(b)(1)(A). Notwithstanding the union's strong interest in unfettered control over the strike weapon, the post-resignation activities of a worker should not be subject to union control unless the union provides a method for members to challenge the strike decision during the strike. Of course, such ballot procedures may not be popular with unions because they may encroach upon the union's solidarity interest.[141]   The best approach for unions is to explicitly restrict the right to resign fifteen days after negotiations begin, rather than indirectly restrict resignations by the threat of post-resignation discipline.

V

THE RELATIONSHIP BETWEEN UNION
DISCIPLINE AND UNION SECURITY

No area of labor law has created more confusion for unions, management and individual workers than the relationship between valid union discipline and union security.[142]   In *Allis-Chalmers*, the court emphasized the nonmandatory nature of union membership under the agency shop provision of the collective bargaining agreement involved in that case.[143]   The Court did not, however, consider the workers' motivation for becoming full-fledged union members. Most collective bargaining agreements contain union security clauses that require union membership as a condition of employment, *i.e.,* union shop clauses. Few of these clauses explicitly refer to the Supreme Court's interpretation of the term "membership"—that membership obligations are fully satisfied if periodic dues and initiation fees are paid to the union; actual membership is not required.[144]   Many of the prob-

---

[141] *See* text accompanying notes 116-19 *supra.*

[142] Union security clauses in collective bargaining contracts, such as an agency or union shop clause, establish the status of the union in the plant. *See* text accompanying notes 145-49 *infra.*

[143] 388 U.S. at 196.

[144] *See* Haggard, *A Clarification of the Types of Union Security Agreements Affirmatively Permitted by Federal Statutes,* 5 RUT.-CAM. L.J. 418, 425-32 (1974).

lems caused by union discipline and restrictions on the right to resign would be avoided if workers were accurately informed that they can never be forced to join a union even though the collectively bargained union security clause ostensibly requires a worker to "join" the union within thirty days of his hiring. Although the union has a fiduciary obligation to inform workers of their real membership obligations, they will probably shirk this responsibility. The Board should step in to fill this educational gap to reduce the potential for future discipline and resignations.

Many union security clauses establish union shops that require each worker to join the union within thirty days after accepting the job.[145] In *NLRB v. General Motors Corp.*, the Court clarified the meaning of the term "membership" by holding that a worker satisfies all membership obligations by paying dues and initiation fees to the union that is the bargaining representative of all workers within the unit.[146] Although the union security clauses in some collective bargaining agreements explicitly state that union membership status is satisfied by meeting these union financial obligations, the individual worker, along with union and management representatives, is often unaware that he is not required to become a union member if he fulfills his financial obligations. This problem was compounded by the Court's statement in *Booster Lodge* that "[s]ince the collective-bargaining agreement expired prior to the times of the resignations, the maintenance-of-membership clause therein was no impediment to resigning."[147] Although dicta, this statement suggests that actual union membership could be required under a union security clause in a collective bargaining agreement. The Court indicated that members could resign in that case without forfeiting their jobs because of nonmembership only when either the contract did not require it or when the agreement had expired. If this interpretation is correct, then *Allis-Chalmers* can no longer be interpreted to require union membership as a prerequisite for imposing union discipline because union membership would no longer be voluntary. The *Allis-Chalmers* Court based its decision upholding discipline of union members on the assumption that union membership was voluntary under the agency shop clause.[148] The Court in *General Motors* went even further when it held that membership was not

---

[145] *See* note 13 *supra.*
[146] 373 U.S. 734, 741-44 (1963).
[147] 412 U.S. at 88.
[148] 388 U.S. at 196.

required even under a union shop clause. The significance of these cases is that workers who become union members must do so with the understanding that they are bound by the union's rules. *Booster Lodge's* dicta, however, would overrule this important assumption. Subsequent court and Board decisions fortunately have not followed this path,[149] and the Court's interpretation of the meaning of membership obligations in *General Motors* is still the accepted law.

Notwithstanding *General Motors'* apparent disposition of this question, workers, union officers and personnel directors often equate the union shop with the agency shop.[150] It is highly unlikely that the workers in *Allis-Chalmers* or *Dalmo Victor* knew that the membership obligations they assumed were not required either by statute or by contract.[151] The Board and courts should require, as a prerequisite for validating union discipline under the NLRA, that the union inform the worker when he begins work about the potential discipline that accompanies full-fledged union membership and the opportunity—or lack of it—to resign union membership. Unions should also be required to advise workers through the contract and the union constitution, as well as by personal communication, that their responsibility to the union encompasses nothing more than meeting the financial obligations of regular union membership. Typically, the worker knows very little about either his right to refrain or the obligations of union membership when he accepts employment in a plant covered by a union security clause. The union has a fiduciary obligation to

---

[149] *See, e.g.,* Electrical Workers v. NLRB, 487 F.2d 1143, 1167-68 n.26 (D.C. Cir.), *cert. denied,* 418 U.S. 904 (1973); Local 749, Boilermakers v. NLRB, 466 F.2d 343, 344-45 (D.C. Cir.), *cert. denied,* 410 U.S. 926 (1972); Leeds & Northrup Co. v. NLRB, 357 F.2d 527, 536 (3d Cir. 1966); American Fed. Tel. Radio Artists (William F. Buckley, Jr.), 222 N.L.R.B. 197, 199, 91 L.R.R.M. 1094, 1096 (1976).

[150] *See generally* Haggard, *supra* note 144.

[151] Shortly after CTI and Dalmo Victor merged, the work force expanded to well over 400 employees all of whom had to join the union. We were never told by either the Machinists union or the company that we did not have to become full members of the union. Quite the contrary, we were told to join the union or lose our jobs.

Throughout my employment at Dalmo Victor, I was never informed that I did not have to be a full union member in order to retain my job but instead could simply pay the equivalent of dues and fees required of members. I would never have formally joined the union had I been informed of all my rights.

Affidavit of Hilda Hall in Support of Motion to Reopen Record at 2-3, Machinists Local 1327 (Dalmo Victor), No. 20-CB-3491 (NLRB, Dec. 18, 1979) (on file at the *Cornell Law Review*).

provide this information to the workers that it represents.[152]   The
Court implicitly recognized this obligation in *Booster Lodge,* finding
that without such information, employees lacked the knowledge,
consent and notice necessary for valid union discipline.[153]

Unions should recognize that workers will often receive information about resigning their membership in either garbled or
anti-union form.[154]   Unions would promote their interest in preserving solidarity by informing dissidents who are unwilling to
support the union when the strike weapon is utilized of the adverse consequences of union discipline before they join the union.
If the union fails to provide this information, the workers may
turn to the employer. Some employers are only too pleased to
volunteer this information—not only during union organizing
campaigns but also during a strike or other labor dispute. Although it is unlikely that employers with established, sophisticated
trade union relationships in industries such as steel, auto and
rubber will utilize these tactics, other employers may rely on this
type of propaganda when confronted with a long economic strike.
The employer's ability in certain circumstances to pay the fines
levied on dissident union members exacerbates this danger.[155]

---

[152] *Cf.* Local 315, Teamsters (Rhodes & Jamieson, Ltd.), 217 N.L.R.B. 616, 617-18, 89
L.R.R.M. 1049, 1051 (1974), *enforced,* 545 F.2d 1173 (9th Cir. 1976) (emphasizing duty of
fair representation's fiduciary nature).

[153] 412 U.S. at 89.

[154] The Board set aside union representation elections in Hollywood Ceramics Co., 140
N.L.R.B. 221, 51 L.R.R.M. 1600 (1962), *overruled,* Shopping Kart Food Market, Inc., 228
N.L.R.B. 1311, 94 L.R.R.M. 1705 (1977), *reinstated,* General Knit of Calif., Inc., 239
N.L.R.B. 619, 99 L.R.R.M. 1687 (1978), because the employer had misrepresented the
consequences of unionization or union membership to employees. *See, e.g.,* TRW-United
Greenfield Div., 245 N.L.R.B. No. 147, 102 L.R.R.M. 1520 (1979) (election set aside be-
cause employer falsely asserted that union was responsible for two plant closings); Robbins
& Myers, Inc., 241 N.L.R.B. No. 11, 100 L.R.R.M. 1523 (1979) (election set aside because
of cumulative effect of employer's misleading statements).

An issue raised in many cases concerns the employer's confidential communications
with his employees. Professor Wellington notes that if William F. Buckley, Jr., was misled
about his rights as a union member, *see* Evans v. American Fed. Tel. Radio Artists, 354 F.
Supp. 823 (S.D.N.Y. 1973), *rev'd and remanded sub nom.* Buckley v. American Fed. Tel.
Radio Artists, 496 F.2d 305 (2d Cir.), *cert. denied,* 419 U.S. 1093 (1974), it is likely that the
average union member will be confused. Wellington, *supra* note 69, at 1051-52. If the
average worker, or even a sophisticated one such as Buckley, is bewildered about his rights
as a union member, he also may be very susceptible to employer misstatements. *See* Gould,
supra note 5, at 1108. Professor Wellington believes, however, that the employer is unlikely
to "[risk] the wrath of a firmly entrenched union by advising prospective members" that
full membership is not required. Wellington, *supra* note 69, at 1052 n.156.

[155] *See* Electrical Workers v. Illinois Bell Tel. Co., 496 F.2d 1, 2 (7th Cir.), *cert. denied,*
419 U.S. 879 (1974); Cox v. Northwest Airlines, Inc., 319 F. Supp. 92, 101 (D. Minn.
1970); Standard Plumbing & Heating Co., 185 N.L.R.B. 444, 75 L.R.R.M. 1065 (1970);

Knowing that he can pay the fine, the employer may advise or subtly encourage the worker to resign.[156] Employers will exploit the dissent created by the union's nondisclosure. This result is undesirable under a statute designed to encourage collective bargaining.

How should unions advise prospective members about the relationship between membership status and disciplinary sanctions? Even after the Court's decision in *Granite State,* most workers probably assume that they are bound by the group decision in a strike vote. Justice Blackmun argued in his dissenting opinion in *Granite State* that "it seems likely that the three factors of a member's strike vote, his ratification of strikebreaking penalties, and his actual participation in the strike, would be far more reliable indicia of his obligation to the union and its members than the presence of boilerplate provisions in a union's constitution."[157] The majority held, however, that workers are immune to disciplinary sanctions for strikebreaking if they resign from the union before crossing picket lines.[158]

Even if Justice Blackmun's characterization of typical employee behavior is only partially correct, it is unlikely that a boilerplate union constitutional provision can adequately inform a union member about membership obligations and strikebreaking. By emphasizing that the contract failed to place any limits on the right to resign,[159] the Court in *Granite State* may have boosted the importance of such provisions.[160] The Board, on the other hand, has concluded that a boilerplate constitutional provision is inadequate to put union members on notice of strikebreaking penalties.[161] Similarly, the Board has also regarded a worker's failure

---

Barney Wilkerson Constr. Co., 145 N.L.R.B. 704, 55 L.R.R.M. 1030 (1963); *cf.* Leeds & Northrup Co., 155 N.L.R.B. 1292, 60 L.R.R.M. 1482 (1965) (employer providing legal counsel). *See also* UAW v. Right to Work Found., 590 F.2d 1139 (D.C. Cir. 1978).

[156] *See* Gould, *supra* note 5, at 1126-27. *But see* Wellington, *supra* note 69, at 1052 n.156.

[157] 409 U.S. at 220.

[158] *Id.* at 215-16.

[159] *Id.* at 214.

[160] Such provisions would comport with the contract approach to the union-member relationship. *See* NLRB v. Allis-Chalmers Mfg. Co., 388 U.S. 174, 192 (1967); Machinists v. Gonzales, 356 U.S. 617, 618 (1958).

[161] *See, e.g.,* Broadcast Employees and Technicians Local 531 (Skateboard Prod., Inc.), 245 N.L.R.B. No. 77, 102 L.R.R.M. 1250 (1979); Machinists, Lodge 1871 (General Dynamic Corp.), 231 N.L.R.B. 727, 96 L.R.R.M. 1158 (1977), *enforced,* 575 F.2d 54 (2d Cir. 1978); Local 1384, UAW (Ex-Cell-O Corp.), 227 N.L.R.B. 1045, 94 L.R.R.M. 1145 (1977); *accord* Booster Lodge 405, Machinists v. NLRB, 412 U.S. 84, 90-91 (Blackmun, J., concurring).

to receive a copy of the union constitution and the failure of union pledge cards to spell out constitutional provisions governing membership ties and the right to resign as significant in determining whether the worker was aware of his resignation rights.[162]

Putting the union member on notice of a constitutional provision that clearly defines membership obligations is only half of the battle—the other half is drafting the provision so that the typical worker understands it. The likely result, however, is confusion. If the Ninth Circuit and the Board cannot agree on an interpretation of the provision in the Machinists' constitution in *Dalmo Victor*, how can workers understand a similar union provision defining union membership obligations? The Second Circuit recently emphasized the importance of clear notice and understanding of the union constitution in its analysis of the same Machinists' provision litigated in *Dalmo Victor*:

> The Union argues that any reasonable union member would know that the act of resigning during a strike would injure the Union and would call for sanctions. However . . . nothing in the Union's constitution unmistakably gave employees notice that mid-strike resignation could result in fines. If anything, the Union constitution implicitly recognized the right to resign without sanction by specifically referring to a member's obligation *after resigning* not to return to work during a strike. Other provisions of the constitution, e.g., sanctions for "other conduct unbecoming a member" of the Union, were too vague to limit the right to resign.[163]

To avoid these practical difficulties unions, as part of their fiduciary obligation, should explain orally the legal interpretation of union security clauses requiring union membership, the relationship between union membership and union discipline, and the clear meaning of constitutional provisions governing discipline and circumstances where a member may resign. If unions are not capable of explaining the rules embodied in its own constitution and bylaws, either the leadership or the rules, or both, ought to be discarded.

This approach, however, does have its drawbacks. Even high-priced labor counsel may have difficulty articulating the shifting currents of law. Every union local should certainly not be

---

[162] Local 1384, UAW (Ex-Cell-O Corp.), 227 N.L.R.B. 1045, 1048, 94 L.R.R.M. 1145, 1149 (1977).

[163] NLRB v. Machinists Lodge 1871, 575 F.2d 54, 55 (2d Cir. 1978) (per curiam).

required to retain counsel for this purpose. A substantial policing effort may be required to ensure that the union fulfills its fiduciary duty. Policing may be difficult, moreover, because unions are often uninterested in providing information about any of these subjects,[164] even though many employees will prefer the benefits of full union membership, *e.g.*, participation in strike and contract ratification voting, notwithstanding the union's desire to counter employer propaganda and misrepresentations on union membership in discipline. The Board is already overburdened with other administrative responsibilities to fully ensure compliance.[165] In addition, employers working with established unions under a traditional union security clause may not be willing to risk the disruption that could result when employees are fully informed of their membership obligations.[166] The crucial point is that unions should undertake this responsibility even though it may be contrary to their short run interests in expanding membership because union solidarity in the long run will be improved if dissidents are able to refuse union membership when they are hired. The Board and courts may be able to judicially enforce this obligation by making notice and knowledge of membership rights a prerequisite for valid union discipline. Workers in union discipline cases are often represented by their employers rather than by their own counsel. This not only signifies that the dispute between the union and the worker is actually part of the

---

[164] Professor Wellington's solution to the union discipline problem rests on the assumption that unions can be forced to comply with their fiduciary duty to inform workers of their right to abstain from full union membership. Wellington, *supra* note 69, at 1055-59. Although he recognizes that it is unlikely that "fellow workers or union officials" will fully inform workers of the true meaning of a union security clause, *id.* at 1058, he concludes that the Board can enforce this duty by sanctioning union discipline as a violation of § 8(b)(1)(A) when the union fails to inform the disciplined members of their right to limited membership. *Id.* at 1057-58. Historical evidence fails to demonstrate, however, that unfair labor practice sanctions will force unions to alter their primary conduct. *Cf.* Smith, *Landrum-Griffin After Twenty-One Years: Mature Legislation or Childish Fantasy?*, 31 LAB. L.J. 273, 277-79 (1980) (worker "bill of rights" has not prevented undemocratic union conduct).

[165]   For the nineteenth consecutive year, the National Labor Relations Board in fiscal 1979 was called upon to process a record number of unfair labor practice and representation election cases arising under the National Labor Relations Act.

The total was 54,907 cases of all types filed by employees, labor organizations, and business firms with the independent agency which administers the basic U.S. labor relations law. . . .

The case intake was up 3.1 percent from the preceding fiscal year.

NLRB, FORTY-FOURTH ANNUAL REPORT OF THE NATIONAL LABOR RELATIONS BOARD 1 (1979).

[166] Wellington, *supra* note 69, at 1052 n.156.

power struggle between labor and management but also explains why the voluntarism issue, *i.e.*, the worker's knowledge of the relationship between full union membership and union discipline, is seldom raised. The voluntarism issue was raised in *Dalmo Victor* only after the Ninth Circuit remanded the case to the Board and the workers then obtained their own counsel.[167]

Unions may more likely comply with this fiduciary obligation if the Court, through a limited reversal of *Allis-Chalmers*, ignored the distinction between limited and full members for the purpose of imposing union discipline. As an alternative, Congress could authorize union discipline imposed upon all workers who pay union dues or their equivalent under a union security clause that compels union membership when the union is involved in negotiations which may culminate in the use of economic pressure. Such congressional authorization is consistent with *Allis-Chalmers'* approval of union discipline of union members during strikes. The *quid pro quo* for this union authority should be legislation allowing employees with both religious and nonreligious conscientious objections to pay the equivalent of union dues to another nonunion organization.[168] Thus, if unions impose disciplinary sanctions upon limited members who have been compelled to join the union under a union security clause, nonreligious conscientious objectors should be able to opt out in the same manner as religious objectors. If unions do not desire this authority, the workers' ability to opt out can be more circumscribed. This approach not only strikes an appropriate balance between union solidarity and individual rights but also simplifies the rules regarding union discipline by eliminating both the differences between full and limited members and the need for relying on full disclosure by the unions of membership obligations.

---

[167] *See* note 151 *supra.*

[168] Even before the Court's decision in *General Motors,* religious objectors could decline full union membership. Union Starch & Refining Co. v. NLRB, 186 F.2d 1008 (7th Cir.), *cert. denied,* 342 U.S. 815 (1951). The House recently approved legislation to provide a religious exemption under the NLRA. The religious accommodation provision of the Civil Rights Act of 1964, tit. VII, § 701(j), 42 U.S.C. § 2000e(j) (1976), may have prompted this legislation. *See* McDaniel v. Essex Int'l, Inc., 571 F.2d 338 (6th Cir. 1978); Cooper v. General Dynamics, 533 F.2d 163 (5th Cir. 1976); Ross, *Caesar and God: A Statutory Balance — Union Security and Religious Discrimination under the Title VII Requirement of Reasonable Accommodation,* 3 IND. REL. L.J. 321 (1979). A bill is currently pending in Congress that would amend the National Labor Relations Act and the Railway Labor Act to require employers and unions to accommodate an employee's religious beliefs. S. 101, 96th Cong., 1st Sess. (1980).

Notwithstanding the union's fiduciary obligation to supply this information, the Board should also begin its own educational campaign because unions may be unable or unwilling to satisfy this need. The Board could begin by posting election notices and distributing books or pamphlets prepared for the layman that describe these rights. This approach would be consistent with the method currently utilized by the Board for providing information on other subjects.[169] Many workers do not understand the subtle intricacies governing union discipline and union membership; the assistance provided by unions and management is fraught with conflicts and is subject to abuse by propagandization. This problem is exacerbated by the legal counsel available to workers in union discipline cases; workers are often represented by employers and their lawyers rather than by the workers' own counsel. The Board has contributed to the confusion[170]—it should not shy away from attempting to rectify that result.

CONCLUSION

In *Allis-Chalmers,* a narrowly divided Court attempted to strike an appropriate balance between the union's interest in labor solidarity and the worker's right to refrain from concerted activity. That balance was subsequently upset when unions began restricting the right to resign union membership and disciplining former members for post-resignation strikebreaking. The Supreme Court failed to realign these interests in its post-*Allis-Chalmers* decisions; in fact, its *Granite State* opinion heavily tips the scale in favor of the individual worker's rights, especially during a strike. Federal labor policy, however, requires that unions be able to invoke disciplinary sanctions during strikes. Thus, unions should be allowed to prohibit resignations ten to fifteen days after full-fledged contract negotiations begin. Post-resignation discipline should not be validated unless the union establishes procedures for its members to challenge the strike decision during the course of a strike. As a prerequisite for any valid union discipline, unions

---

[169] *See* NLRB, A GUIDE TO BASIC LAW AND PROCEDURES UNDER THE NATIONAL LABOR RELATIONS ACT 2-7 (1976) [hereinafter cited as GUIDE].

[170] The GUIDE fails to address the relationship between union membership and discipline. It simply states that a valid union security clause may require workers to "join" a union. *Id.* at 2-3. Although it notes that a union commits an unfair labor practice by fining a worker for post-resignation conduct, *id.* at 31, the GUIDE does not advise the worker of his right to resign in spite of a union security agreement that ostensibly compels membership.

must fully inform their members about membership obligations, particularly that union membership is not required—even under a union shop clause—if the worker pays regular union dues and initiation fees. Congress enacted the federal labor statutes to protect the rights of individual workers. The vitality of those rights rests on both knowledge and solidarity. It is ironic that laws designed to protect them are now being used to exploit them. If unions are not allowed to prohibit resignations during a strike, and choose to promote solidarity by punishing members for post-resignation activities, they must establish democratic, albeit disruptive, procedures that permit workers to change their minds and return to work during a strike.

Bibliographic Essay on
Solidarity Forever

The remand to the National Labor Relations Board in *Dalmo Victor II*[1] produced a split inside the Board and the first in a series of decisions at both the Board and circuit court level, which have not yet come to grips with the delicate accommodation between competing statutory interests that are at stake. Members Fanning and Zimmerman, in a "majority opinion," concluded that a union " . . . is entitled to reasonable notice of the effective date of resignations which occur immediately before or during a strike."[2] Accordingly, this opinion deemed a thirty-day period to be a reasonable one and thus invalidated the fourteen-day period provided for in the Machinists' constitution. But the opinion provided no convincing support for thirty days as the appropriate period.

Chairman Van de Water and Member Hunter correctly concluded that the thirty-day rule promulgated by Members Fanning and Zimmerman was "an arbitrary exercise" of the Board's authority and inconsistent with the statutory right to refrain afforded individual employees. But they refused to address the accommodation issue. Member Jenkins, in dissent, took the position that the union constitutional prohibition was appropriate.

The Court of Appeals for the Ninth Circuit, the second time around, in an opinion authored by Judge Pregerson, refused to enforce the Board's order to the effect that the rule was invalid because of its failure to adhere to a thirty-day requirement. The court held that the Machinists' rule did not impair any congressional labor policy and met the tests contained in the Supreme Court's *Scofield* decision. The court concluded that post-resignation strike-breaking was a "serious threat to a union's viability . . . [because it] can set off a chain reaction capable of destroying the collective bargaining environment."[3] Secondly, stated the court, members who participate in a strike vote and then fail to honor the result of it are breaching a promise to their colleagues. The court concluded that a union could impose a duty to refrain from strike-breaking upon individuals through the sanctions employed here.

Meanwhile, the Reagan Board reversed itself in *Neufeld Porche-Audi, Inc.*[4] and concluded that a union may not impose any kind of restriction upon the right to resign inasmuch as it interferes with the worker's right to refrain protected under Section 7. One difficulty with this line of reasoning, as Member Zimmerman pointed out in dissent, is that the *Allis-Chalmers* decision itself imposes a limitation upon the right to refrain by permitting union fines to be imposed. Suffice it to say that these opinions do not attempt to strike the balance that is needed.[5] Articles have not yet been written that discuss this issue in light of these new decisions. The Supreme Court has agreed to review this issue at some point during 1985.

NOTES

1. 263 NLRB No. 141 (1982).
2. Dalmo Victor II, p. 11.
3. *Machinists' Local 1327 v. NLRB,* 725 F. 2d 1212, 1217 (9th Cir., 1984).
4. 270 NLRB No. 209 (1984).
5. E.g., *Patternmakers League v. NLRB*, 724 F. 2d 57 (7th Cir., 1983); cert. granted—U.S., 165 S. Ct. 79 (Oct. 1, 1984).

Index

Alexander v. Gardner-Denver Co., 13
*Allis-Chalmers Manufacturing Co.,
NLRB v.*, 272-75, 284-93, 299-308.
See also Union Discipline
*Amcar Division, ACF Industries v.
NLRB*, 190-91
American Arbitration Association
(AAA), 7, 8, 14
Arbitration: chilling effect of, 37-39, 40;
expedited arbitration, 16-17; final
offer arbitration, 40; nature of
hearing, 8-9; NLRB and deferral, 16;
in public sector, 15, 21, 33-35, 39-40;
rights arbitration, 5-6, 11, 33; and
Title VII, 13, 14-15; and wrongful dis-
charge, 17. *See also* No-Strike
Clause; Public Sector
Arlan's Department Store, NLRB ruling,
177-83
Armour-Dial, Inc., NLRB v., 192-94
Atkinson v. Sinclair Refining Co., 125
Avco Corp. v. Aero Lodge No. 735,
88, 92

*Booster Lodge No. 405, Machinists v.
NLRB*, 277-84, 300-302. *See also*
Union Discipline

*Boys Markets, Inc. v. Retail Clerks
Union*, 78-127. *See also*
No-Strike Clauses
*Brotherhood of Locomotive Engineers
v. Missouri-Kansas-Texas Railroad
Co.,* 104-108, 112-13
Buffalo Forge Co. v. United Steelmakers,
129-58, 171-73. *See also* No-Strike
Clauses

Carbon Fuel v. UMW of America, 165-
67
*Chicago River & Indiana Railroad Co.,
Brotherhood of Railroad Trainmen
v.*, 101-103
*Coca Cola Bottling v. Teamsters Local
326,* 186-90
Collyer Insulated Wire, NLRB ruling, 16
Complete Auto Transit, Inc. v. Reis,
163-69. *See also* No-Strike Clauses
Condon-Wadlin law, 19-21, 23

Dalmo Victor (Machinists Local 1327),
NLRB ruling, 291-92, 294-99, 301,
304, 309. *See also* Union Discipline
Danbury Hatters ruling, 163, 204, 250
Dow Chemical Co. v. NLRB, 175-84.

See also No-Strike Clauses
Draper Corp., NLRB v., 51, 57, 68, 71, 75
Duplex Printing Press Co. v. Deering, 99

East Chicago Rehabilitation Center v. NLRB, 76
Employment Act of 1980, 264
Employment Act of 1982, 264
Employment Protection Act of 1975, 264
Emporium Capwell v. NLRB, 75-78
Energy Coal Income Partnership 1981, NLRB ruling, 75

Federal Mediation and Councilator Service (FMCS), 7, 30
Fact-Finding, 31-33, 41

Gardner-Denver Co., Alexander v., 13
Gateway Coal Co. v. UMW, 135-38, 141-42
General American Transportation Co., 16
General Motors Corp., NLRB v., 300-301
Granite State Joint Board, Textile Workers, NLRB v., 276-81, 284-99, 303, 307
Great Britain: arbitration 5, 6; labor legislation, 11, 197-266. *See also* Industrial Relations Act of 1971
Greyhound Lines, Inc. (Greyhound II), Transit Union Division 1384 v., 152-57

Howlett, Robert, 31-32
Haislip Baking Co., United Construction Workers v., 159-61
Hoh v. Pepsico, Inc., 151-52

Industrial Arbitration Board, 9
Industrial Relations Act of 1971, 11, 197-265; Code of Practice, 218; collective bargaining under, 218-25; emergency dispute procedures, 256-60; enforcement of collective bargaining agreement; 237-44; history, 202-12; National Industrial Relations Court, 212-13; policies under, 217-18; recog-

nition machinery, 225-33; registration under, 213-17; right to strike, 244-47; secondary boycotts, 253-56; subsequent legislation, 263-65; trade union reorganization, 247-51; union security arrangements, 233-37
Injunctions. *See* No-Strike Clauses

Jacksonville Bulk Terminals, Inc. v. International Longshoremen's Association, 171-72
Johnson, Lyndon Baynes, 19-20

Labor-Court, 34; in Great Britain, 212-13. *See also* Industrial Relations Act of 1971
Landram-Griffin Act, 47
Lincoln Mills, Textile Workers Union v., 81-84, 95, 100, 109-11, 132-34
Lucas Flour Co., Local 174 International Brotherhood of Teamsters v., 135-38

Marathon Electric, NLRB ruling, 177, 181, 183-84
Mastro Plastics Corp. v. NLRB, 63-64
Mediation: "med-arb," 41-42; in public sector, 30, 41
Metropolitan Edison Co. v. NLRB, 195
Missouri-Kansas-Texas Railroad Co., Brotherhood of Locomotive Engineers v., (M-K-T), 104-108, 112-13

National Academy of Arbitrators (NAA), 7
National Labor Relations Act. *See under specific issues,* (e.g., Union Discipline)
National Packing Co., NLRB Ruling, 67
Neufeld Porsche-Audi, NLRB ruling, 310
New Orleans Steamship Association v. General Longshore Workers, 108-14
NLRB v.: Allis-Chalmers Manufacturing Co., 272-75, 284-93, 299-308; *Armour-Dial, Inc.,* 192-94; *Draper Corp.,* 51, 57, 68, 71, 75; *General*

Motors Corp., 300-301; *Gould, Inc.*, 189-90; *Granite State Joint Board, Textile Workers*, 276-81, 284-99, 303, 307; *R.C. Can Co.*, 55-56, 58-60, 61-62, 68, 75; *Shop Rite Foods, Inc.*, 75; *Tanner Motor Livery, Ltd.*, 75; *Washington Aluminum Co.*, 48, 56, 70
Norris-LaGuardia Act, 83-89, 95-103, 130-38, 144-46, 204

Olin Corp. 16

Pacemaker Yacht Co., NLRB ruling, 184-90
Philadelphia Marine Trade Association v. ILA Local 1219, 120
Pittsburgh Steel Co. v. Steelworkers, 191-92
Public Sector: arbitration in, 15, 21, 33-35, 39-40; emergency strikes, 19-21; right to strike 24-25, 28-35. *See also* Arbitration; Strikes

Railway Labor Act: emergency strike provisions, 25-26
R.C. Can Co., NLRB v., 55-56, 58-60, 61-62, 68, 75

Scofield v. NLRB, 276-84, 309. *See also* Union Discipline
Simmons, Inc. v. NLRB, 67-68
Sinclair Refining Co. v. Atkinson, 85-97, 102, 109, 133-34
Spielberg Manufacturing, 16
Steelworkers Trilogy, 81-103, 109-11, 114-19, 132-38
Strikes: in Great Britain, 244-47; national emergency strikes, 19-21, 31; in public sector, 24-25, 28-35. *See also* No-Strike Clauses; Wildcat Strikes
Sunbeam Lighting Co., 53-54, 58-60, 68 70, 72

Taylor Law, 23-24, 29-33
Taylor Report, 31
Textile Workers Union v. Lincoln Mills, 81-84, 95, 100, 109-11, 132-34
Trade Union Act of 1984, 265
Trade Union and Labor Relations Act of 1974, 263-64
Transit Union Division 1384 v. Greyhound Lines, Inc., 152-57

Union Discipline, 267-310; of former union members; for post-resignation conduct, 293-99; right to resign, 277-93; and union security, 299-307. *See also* Wildcat Strikes
United Construction Workers v. Haislip Baking Co., 159-61
United Federation of Postal Workers v. Blount, 24
United Postal Service (N.Y.), Inc. v. Local 804 International Brotherhood of Teamsters, 173
United Technologies Corp., 16
Usery, William J., 10

Wagner Act, 6
War Labor Board, 6
Washington Aluminum Co., NLRB v., 48, 56, 70
Western Contracting Corp. v. NLRB, 64-65, 71, 72
Wildcat Strikes 8, 45-73; employer responses to, 69-73; during contract negotiations, 53; during life of collective bargaining agreement, 63-65; and rival unions, 65-69; and union internal procedures, 61-63; and union liability, 163-69. *See also* No-Strike Clauses; Union Discipline
Wirtz, W. Willard, 46
Wrongful discharge: and arbitration, 17

About the Author

WILLIAM B. GOULD IV is Charles A. Beardsley Professor of Law at Stanford University Law School. Prior to teaching, he was Assistant General Counsel for the United Auto Workers, Attorney for the National Labor Relations Board, and a Consultant to the Equal Employment Opportunity Commission. Professor Gould was a Guggenheim Fellow in 1978 and is a member of the National Academy of Arbitrators. His previous books include *A Primer on American Labor Law*, *Black Workers in White Unions: Job Discrimination in the United States*, and *Japan's Reshaping of American Labor Law*.